# A
# History of
# American
# Life

PAUL LAUNE

# A HISTORY OF AMERICAN LIFE

### IN

### TWELVE VOLUMES

## ARTHUR M. SCHLESINGER
## DIXON RYAN FOX

*Editors*

ASHLEY H. THORNDIKE · CARL BECKER

*Consulting Editors*

*The Lure of the City*

A HISTORY OF AMERICAN LIFE
Volume X

# THE RISE OF THE CITY

## 1878-1898

BY

ARTHUR MEIER SCHLESINGER

PROFESSOR OF HISTORY, HARVARD UNIVERSITY

THE MACMILLAN COMPANY

PRINTED IN THE UNITED STATES OF AMERICA

*We are now a nation of cities.*

> W. H. TOLMAN, *Municipal Reform Move-*
> *ment in the United States* (N. Y., 1895), 35.

*What shall we do with our great cities? What will*
*our great cities do with us? These are the two prob-*
*lems which confront every thoughtful American.*
*For the question involved in these two questions does*
*not concern the city alone. The whole country is*
*affected, if indeed its character and history are not*
*determined, by the condition of its great cities. . . .*
*The city is not all bad nor all good. It is humanity*
*compressed, the best and the worst combined, in a*
*strangely composite community.*

> LYMAN ABBOTT, "Introduction," HELEN
> CAMPBELL AND OTHERS, *Darkness and*
> *Daylight* (Hartford, 1891), 40, 42.

# CONTENTS

# ILLUSTRATIONS

### (By the Editors)

From the frontispiece of Will Carleton, *City Ballads* (N. Y., 1885), a book of poems designed "to reproduce some of the effects of city scenes and character upon the intellect of two people from the country," page v. The drawing is by the Anglo-American artist Harry Fenn (1838-1911), though by no means one of his best.

(a) Electioneering in upland Georgia. This unsigned drawing in *Harper's Weekly*, XXXII, 696 (Sept. 15, 1888), 9 x 7 inches, illustrates the new importance of the mountaineer's vote as the old hierarchies were being vanquished. Note the boy outside off to shoot a meal.

(b) The Highland Gingham Mills, near Charlotte, N. C. This plant with 500 gingham looms cost $150,000 and was paid for within two years at a rate of $1.00 per week per share. From D. A. Tompkins, *Cotton Mill, Commercial Features* (Charlotte, N. C., 1899).

(a) Pueblo, Colorado. From a full page of drawings by Charles Graham in *Harper's Weekly*, XXXII, 332 (May 12, 1888). Founded in 1858 and at first slow in development, Pueblo had 20,000 population in 1888 and, with its extensive steel works, was already known as the "Pittsburgh of the West." The highest tower is on the high school and the long building somewhat to the left is the insane asylum.

(b) Using Graham's borders we have substituted a figure from a drawing by Frederic Remington, entitled "Dragging a Bull's Hide over a Prairie Fire," in the same periodical, XXXII, Oct. 27, 1888, supplement. After studying art Remington (1861-1909) went west for actual experience as a cowboy and became the most famous delineator of life on the ranches and of the western Indian wars.

A map of the United States "corrected" to show the importance of states with respect to population rather than area, prepared for this volume by Margaret Hilferty and Jane Worcester of the statistical staff of the School of Public Health, Harvard University. Locating where the Mississippi River would be, note the comparative importance of

# EDITORS' FOREWORD

American civilization in the 1880's and 1890's offers a study in contrasts. Different in many respects from anything that had preceded it, different too from what would follow, it was itself marked by diversities and contradictions which give distinctive color and tone to the era. The South, emerging from the deep shadows of Reconstruction, was troubled by strange new stirrings, by a pressing sense that it must modernize its economic order, by a growing apprehension that it must treat as full-fledged human beings both the Negroes and the mass of white commoners. The Great West had its own variety and interest, but it too was undergoing rapid change as the old glamour of mystery and bold adventure gave way before the myriad husbandmen, brought in by the railroads, with their women and children and their prosaic round of unremitting toil. Even in the older agricultural districts to the eastward, contrasts abounded, the emaciated farmer on his bleak New England hillside forming a curious foil for the sturdy yeoman of the Mid-Western prairies. This varied rural scene the author paints with broad strokes clearly limning the main masses of the changing picture, while with reflected lights he indicates relationships in different parts and animates the whole with vivid instance. It is, indeed, replete with incident and illustration, for he is, above all, concerned with the human consequences of what are oftentimes depicted as large impersonal movements.

But Professor Schlesinger's purpose is not merely to make live again a phase of American life that has half faded from memory. His account is strongly charged with meaning. The United States in the eighties and nineties was trembling between two worlds, one rural and agricultural, the other urban and industrial. In this span of years the fateful decision was made. Traditional America gave way to a new America, one more akin to Western Europe than to its own former self, yet retaining an authentic New World quality. The author recognizes that Americans formed a part of the larger human family and had behind them the general history of mankind; their achievements, therefore, are measured by world standards—a procedure rare among American historians. Such writers, too, gazing eastward toward the Atlantic Seaboard, have been accustomed to emphasize the long-time influence of the frontier upon American civilization and the disastrous effects of the passing of free fertile lands. The present volume is devoted, rather, to describing and appraising the new social force which waxed and throve while driving the pioneer culture before it: the city.

In the ever widening reach of its influence the author finds the key to an understanding of the most multifarious developments. The city, in Josiah Strong's phrase, was "the mighty heart of the body politic, sending its streams of life pulsating to the very finger-tips of the whole land." Aside from the part played by urban leadership in building a new structure of industry and trade—a theme treated in a companion volume—the city is envisaged as the dominant force of all those impulses and movements which made for a finer, more humane civilization. Education, literature, science, invention, the fine arts, social reform, public hygiene, the use of leisure, the "good life"—all these were given lift and direction by those who lived in urban centers. As rumor of the city's fascination and its opportunity reached the far-flung countryside, a townward trek set in, which in magnitude recalls the hosts who once had sought a larger life in the unpeopled wilderness. The author investigates the rich cultural record of these years, the so-called "buried renaissance," and makes clear its contributions toward the achievements of the twentieth century.

But the city was also a center of evil as well as of good; the children of darkness as well as of light congregated there. Crime, vice and graft, deeply rooted in the slum and the saloon, offered problems which this generation solved as best it could. Dense populations also presented new difficulties of transit, lighting, sewerage, fire protection and sanitation. American childhood rapidly lost its rural heritage of outdoor life, necessitating a larger measure of social concern for the welfare of the growing generation. The status of women was vitally affected, not always for the better, while the presence of hordes of immigrants, sharply different in their cultural types from those who had made America throughout the previous three hundred years, raised grave questions as to the effective working of the "melting pot." Religion itself was confronted with the need for adapting its teaching and methods to an urban rather than to a rural constituency.

There is incident, as in the rush into Oklahoma, and color, as in the magnificent World's Fair; interesting individuals appear, like Burbank, Tillman, Gladden, Riis, Howells, Saint-Gaudens, Pulitzer, Booker T. Washington, each with his aspirations and accomplishments. We learn, too, what such observant foreigners as Kipling, Bryce and Robert Louis Stevenson thought of the changing American scene. But all these come not for their own sake. Significance is emphasized and the large averages of life are accounted of greater consequence than the unusual and the picturesque. There is high respect throughout for definite, concrete facts, but these, with a logic too rare in social history, build forward to support a major thesis, that suggested in the title. It is this which integrates the book. Modern America had emerged by 1878, as Professor Nevins has pointed out in another volume, but the rise of the city, together with the nationalizing of the economic order, brought it very much nearer to the America we know today.

These chapters deal with times not yet the stock of many general histories. The sources indicated as their basis, so various and abundant, suggest innumerable inquiries useful and rewarding. At least, it may be hoped that a reading of this book will help win for these two decades an appreciation of their rightful place in the history of American life.

D. R. F.

# THE RISE
# OF THE CITY
## 1878-1898

# THE RISE OF THE CITY

## CHAPTER I

### THE NEW SOUTH

AMERICAN civilization in 1878 was, in one essential respect, like that of earlier times: it rested upon the farms and country towns of the nation. An American Sully of that day might truly have remarked, "Tillage and pasture are the two breasts of the state." His observation would have applied no less to the sources of material prosperity than to those subtler currents of thought and aspiration which from the beginning had given tone and color to American life. The generation destined to dominate the scene during the next twenty years was to be responsible for turning the needle of national interest from the country to the city, but as the period opened there was little to show that so momentous a change impended. Of the fifty million people counted in the census of 1880, three fourths, or nearly forty million, lived on the open land or in villages of less than four thousand inhabitants.

The term, "rural," was a cloak covering all types of country life from the meager existence eked out on the tiny breakneck farms of northern New England to the far-flung activities of the great bonanza farms of the West. Without leaving the national borders the student of social development could have discovered ample contemporary evidence of the historic evolution of agriculture from the use of primitive soil-scratching implements, as in the Kentucky hill country, to the puffing, snorting black monsters that threshed the grain of the

1

prairie farmers. Had he wished, he could have unrolled
the scroll further and have found great patches of country in which mankind had not yet passed beyond the
hunting or the pastoral stage. One traveler in 1878
found men in a secluded valley of southwestern Virginia
hunting squirrels and rabbits with the English short
bow, the arrows hefted in the ancient manner.[1]

Only in a few Atlantic states—Massachusetts, Rhode
Island, Connecticut, New York and New Jersey—were
the rural inhabitants outnumbered by the urban in
1878, though throughout the region north of the Potomac and the Ohio the city was unmistakably gaining
at the expense of the country. The stamp of ruralism
lay heaviest upon the remaining sections of the nation—
on the South, stretching in a broad belt along the Atlantic and the Gulf from the Potomac to the Rio Grande,
and the Great West, spreading its imperial expanse over
plain and mountain from Minnesota and the Missouri
River to the rim of the Pacific. One was a region, long
occupied and much tilled, still in process of readjust-
ment to the profound changes wrought by the Civil War
and its aftermath. The other was a section so recently
taken over by the whites that in 1878 its chief characteristic continued to be unsettlement rather than settlement.

As of old, the vast majority of Southerners were
farmers and the typical farmer was addicted to the
staple-crop system.[2] If he lived in the Lower South he
cultivated cotton, or perhaps rice or sugar cane. If he
lived in the Upper South he was apt to make tobacco

[1] N. S. Shaler, "The Transplantation of a Race," *Pop. Sci. Mo.*, LVI
(1899-1900), 519.

[2] R. H. Edmonds, *Facts about the South* (Balt., 1902), 14-33, gives
a good summary of Southern economic progress, 1880-1900. See also
P. A. Bruce, *The Rise of the New South* (G. C. Lee and F. N. Thorpe,
eds., *The History of North America*, Phila., 1903-1907, XVII), 17-306,
and J. A. C. Chandler and others, *The South in the Building of the
Nation* (Richmond, 1909), VI, *passim*.

his main reliance. Yet every year showed that the people were learning the unwisdom of pivoting their prosperity on one or two staple crops. Corn, hay, wheat, potatoes and other products began to count in the Southern agricultural list during the 1880's. The demand of the swiftly growing urban centers of the North for a greater abundance and variety of fruits and vegetables led to the rapid spread of orcharding and trucking in the lands along the Atlantic from Maryland to the Gulf. The Albemarle pippin of the Virginia piedmont and the peanut of the tidewater, the Scuppernong wine grape of North Carolina, the luscious watermelon of Georgia, soon commanded a nation-wide patronage. Stimulated by the example of California, Florida awoke to the golden possibilities of developing her subtropical fruits; and her oranges, lemons and pineapples began to vie on Northern fruit stands with those of the Coast and far-off Sicily.[1] These years demonstrated the ability of the South to raise almost any crop that could be grown in the United States.

Equally striking was the continuance of the postwar trend toward smaller units of cultivation. The attempt to resume agriculture on a large-scale basis had generally broken down after the war because of the heavy taxes, lack of operating capital and the irresponsible character of the Negro workers.[2] The impoverished aristocrat eagerly seized the opportunity to sell or lease "parcels" or "cuts" of ground to Negroes or landless whites. Already in 1880 there were one and a half million farms of all kinds in the South, more than double the number when the war broke out. By 1890 three hundred thousand additional ones had come into existence and the

[1] A. K. McClure, *The South: Its Industrial, Financial, and Political Condition* (Phila., 1886), 149-162.
[2] See Allan Nevins, *The Emergence of Modern America* (*A History of American Life*, VIII), 20-21, 24-25.

process was far from halted.[1] Some of the new holdings
resulted from clearing the forest from land that had
never known hoe and plow, or had known them so
long since that a new growth of pine or hickory had
replenished the worn-out soil. But most of them represented further subdivision of the great plantations. A
marked decline in average acreage resulted. The Georgia
farmer who in 1880 tilled 188 acres held but 147 ten
years later. In Mississippi in the same decade the typical
holding shrank from 156 to 122 acres, and in Tennessee
and Kentucky from 127 to about 118.

The effects of this democratizing process were far-
reaching both economically and socially. In increasing
number the patrician families which had traditionally
dominated Southern life and politics fled the countryside for the towns. Cut off from the expansive life on
their great estates, the members of the younger generation gave their attention to the professions or, in continuance of an old tradition, to politics. The pursuit of
agriculture, once a badge of social distinction, suffered
a serious loss of prestige.

On the other hand, the partition of land offered a
new footing to the unprivileged folk, not only to the
former slaves but also to the mass of white people. A
minority of the latter consisted of a sturdy yeomanry
who for generations had tilled their small farms in the
fertile backcountry valleys, usually without the help of
slaves and always without the social and political rewards that accrued to the large planters. In sharp contrast to them stood the poor whites of the black belt,
a numerous folk who had always formed the very dregs

[1] From 1880 to 1900 over a million new farms were added. See *U. S.
Twelfth Census* (1900), V, 688-689, 692-693, for these and later
statistics. The census definition of farm refers to operation, not ownership; thus a tract of a thousand acres divided among a dozen tenants
is reported as twelve farms.

of Southern white society. Lacking both capital and ambition, they had in early times allowed themselves to be crowded off into waste lands, like the pine barrens of south-central Georgia and the sand hills of northern Alabama and eastern Mississippi. There, rearing great litters of children, they had fallen into a squalid, ignorant, shiftless way of living hardly superior to that of the swine that ran half wild about their rude cabins.[1]

They seemed to be of a debased, if not vicious, strain, the local contempt for them being reflected in the names by which they were best known—"crackers" and "clay eaters" in Georgia, "hill billies" in Mississippi and "po' white trash" everywhere. Yet their stock had originally been as sound as any; and their customs, speech and ballads, like those of the isolated mountain folk of the South, preserved much of the Elizabethan flavor that their ancestors had brought with them to America. That they labored under a very special handicap was not revealed until a later day when it was discovered that a tiny intestinal parasite, the hookworm, had for generations been sapping the vital energies of many of them and thus thwarting every impulse to enterprise.[2]

The plight of the former planter class gave all who would a chance to share in a new partition of the kingdom. While the yeoman farmers, able to outbid their poorer rivals, succeeded in securing the choicest cuts, in the long run the poor whites were the chief beneficiaries. For the first time since their forebears ventured into the

---

[1] S. A. Hamilton, "The New Race Question in the South," *Arena*, XXVII (1902), 352-358, is one of few articles on the poor whites of the Lower South.

[2] The morbid appetites of the clay eaters were, it is believed, due to the hookworm infection. On this whole subject, see C. W. Stiles, *Report upon the Prevalence and Geographic Distribution of the Hookworm Disease in the United States* (U. S. Treas. Dept., Hygienic Lab., *Bull.*, no. 10, 1903), and H. U. Faulkner, *The Quest for Social Justice* (*A History of American Life*, XI), 233-234.

section they were able to escape their piney-woods
solitudes and take a self-respecting part in the life of
the countryside. Normal social relations became theirs;
schools began to touch the lives of their children; glass
panes in the windows and carpets on the floors evidenced
an increasing sense of pride and taste.

The road to economic independence, however, was a
steep and rocky one, conditions in the eighties showing
little improvement over those which had prevailed in
Reconstruction days.[1] The aspiring but poverty-stricken
husbandman must first become a "cropper" or share
tenant, obtaining tools, seed and draft animals from the
landlord and usually giving him half of the crop grown.
To safeguard his interests the landlord often retained a
measure of centralized control. Sometimes, as on the
D. C. Barrow plantation near Oglethorpe in central
Georgia, the oversight was loose and general;[2] but more
typical was the arrangement whereby the landlord or
his manager planned and directed the work, kept the
implements and mules at a central barn and controlled
the marketing of the crop.[3] This system, while lending
itself to many abuses, had the advantage of providing a
period of apprenticeship for the unskilled and protecting
them from destitution in times of low prices or crop
failure. It also preserved the benefits, enjoyed under
slavery, of large-scale operation. The plan was more
characteristic of the Lower South than of other parts
and more workable with the ex-slaves than with the
white toilers.

[1] See Nevins, *Emergence of Modern America*, 18-20.
[2] Anon., "A Georgia Plantation," *Scribner's Mo.*, XXI (1880-1881),
830-836.
[3] L. C. Gray and others, "Farm Ownership and Tenancy," U. S.
Dept. of Agr., *Yearbook for 1923*, esp. 529-532; Bureau of the Census,
*Plantation Farming in the United States (Special Rep.*, 1916), 7, 13;
R. P. Brooks, *The Agrarian Revolution in Georgia, 1865-1912* (Univ.
of Wis., *Bull.*, no. 639), 48-49. 65-68.

Given favorable conditions and the exercise of thrift, the cropper might advance to the position of renter or cash tenant and, in time perhaps, to full ownership. The chief obstacle in his path was the vicious credit system which constantly tempted him to borrow from the local merchant or banker at excessive rates of interest in anticipation of his harvest. This "lazy 'descent into hell,' " as Ben Tillman called it, plunged him into a bog of debt-peonage from which extrication was heartbreakingly difficult.[1] It was also an important deterrent to the rapid development of mixed farming, for the money lender insisted upon the one-crop routine—cotton or tobacco—with which he had always been familiar. Perhaps eighty or ninety per cent of the cotton growers— tenants and proprietors, whites and blacks—were normally enmeshed in the crop-lien system.[2] Despite all discouragements, however, the number of farmers who graduated from share tenancy to cash renting, as well as those who became freeholders, grew steadily through these years.[3]

The credit system also added to the difficulties of farmers of yeoman strain. Of this class Ben Tillman was typical in many respects. He had at first been able to make money on his upcountry farm in South Carolina, enlarging his holdings from time to time and buying more mules. In 1881, according to his own account, "I ran thirty plows, bought guano, rations, etc., as usual,

[1] G. K. Holmes, "The Peons of the South," Am. Acad. of Polit. and Social Sci., *Annals*, IV (1893-1894), 265-274; C. H. Otken, *The Ills of the South* (N. Y., 1894); M. B. Hammond, *The Cotton Industry* (Am. Econ. Assoc., *Publs.*, n.s., no. 1), chap. v; B. B. Kendrick, "Agrarian Discontent in the South, 1880-1900," Am. Hist. Assoc., *Rep. for 1920*, 270-272.

[2] A. M. Arnett, *The Populist Movement in Georgia* (Columbia Univ., *Studies*, CIV, no. 1), 57-58. Cf. Hammond, *Cotton Industry*, 155.

[3] The figures for the years 1880-1900 are given in *U. S. Twelfth Census*, V, 688-689; the two races are not separated. See also Brooks, *Agrarian Revolution*, chap. iv.

and the devil tempted me to buy a steam engine and other machinery, amounting to two thousand dollars, all on credit." Quickly the situation changed. Drought and crop failures, the usurious exactions of his creditors, extortionate prices paid to country storekeepers, forced him to sell much of his land.[1] Others found themselves in a similar dilemma. Not all were as ready as the fiery South Carolinian to "do something about it," but they shared his resentment that, with the mass of the people engaged in agriculture, the Southern state governments seemed so indifferent to their welfare.

This indifference was due in some quarters to a conviction that the South might more profitably devote its chief energies to the development of factory industry. The idea appealed to a variety of motives. How better to retaliate on the late enemy than to fight the devil with fire? "If we have lost the victory on the field of fight," declared the *Columbia Register* in 1881, "we can win it back in the work shop, in the factory, in an improved agriculture and horticulture, in our mines and in our schoolhouses."[2] More important, however, was the belief that economic salvation rested upon the exploitation of the raw materials, water power and cheap white labor which lay immediately at hand. The South, relieved of the incubus of slavery, had at last a chance to take its place in modern industrial society. Efforts in that direction were urged forward by the doubling of the Southern railway net in the twelve years after 1878. But many were not ready for the change; much inertia had to be overcome. The enemies of progress, asserted the *Register* in the same editorial, "are the prejudices of

[1] F. B. Simkins, *The Tillman Movement in South Carolina* (Duke Univ., *Publs.*; Durham, 1926), esp. 51-52.

[2] Quoted in the *Charleston News and Courier*, March 18, 1881, and cited by Broadus Mitchell, *The Rise of Cotton Mills in the South* (Johns Hopkins Univ., *Studies*, XXXIX, no. 2), 90.

the past, the instincts of isolation, the brutal indifference and harmful social infidelity which stands up in
our day with the old slave arguments . . . on its lips,
'I object' and 'You can't do it.' "

As a matter of fact, the South, even during slavery
times, had engaged in a considerable amount of manufacturing activity. Most of this effort, however, centered
in the mechanical trades which every well-equipped
plantation maintained, production being only for local
use. One of the natural, though unanticipated, effects
of subdivision of the great estates was the dispersion or
destruction of these local industries. Though a few of
the largest plantations continued to support a carpenter,
a blacksmith, a saddler, a shoemaker and a weaver, such
workmen generally were obliged to move to the nearest
crossroads where their little establishments served a whole
circle of small farms. Spinning and weaving vanished
as household occupations, and the people learned to de-
pend increasingly upon the cheap fabrics bought at the
country stores, goods supplied from the manufacturing
districts of the North.

While this unobtrusive economic revolution was
going on, nascent industrialists were cheered by the success which greeted tobacco manufacturing in the Upper
South. From humble beginnings shortly after the war
the industry had already by 1878 reached a position of
importance. The new decade brought fresh enterprise,
more economical production, improved methods of
marketing.[1] Through skillful advertising, brands like
Bull Durham and Duke's Mixture, made at Durham,
North Carolina, became known throughout the world.
Across the Atlantic Tennyson was a devotee of Bull

---

[1] W. K. Boyd, *The Story of Durham* (Duke Univ., *Publs.*; Durham,
1925), chaps. iv-v; Meyer Jacobstein, *The Tobacco Industry in the
United States* (Columbia Univ., *Studies*, XXVI, no. 3), pt. ii, chap. iii.

Durham, to which he had been introduced by James Russell Lowell. Thomas Carlyle likewise found its pungent aroma congenial to his taste. For a time misguided zeal even caused the taurine lineaments of its trademark to decorate the pyramids of Egypt. The Dukes' business was based upon the making of smoking tobacco, snuff, chewing tobacco and cigars, but they saw interesting possibilities also in the cigarette, which prior to 1867 had been produced exclusively in Europe. Early in the 1880's, when they effected a satisfactory means of making the white tubes by machinery and invented a sliding pasteboard box for their sale to smokers, the cigarette trade began to add materially to their revenues. In the three states of North Carolina, Virginia and Kentucky the value of tobacco manufactures rose from about twenty-one million dollars in 1880 to nearly thirty-one million in 1890.[1]

The enthusiasm for manufacturing was even more strikingly shown in the so-called cotton-mill campaign of the eighties. Only a feeble start had been made at cotton manufacturing before 1878. Now something akin to a religious fervor swept over the seaboard states, directed toward the establishment of local factories for utilizing the basic Southern crop. Newspapers, large and small, helped propagate the new gospel, none more effectively than the *Charleston News and Courier* under the editorship of the brilliant Anglo-American F. W. Dawson.[2] Soon the rallying cry, "Bring the mills to the cotton!" was echoed from village to village and from hamlet to hamlet. Money for launching the enter-

---

[1] If Maryland and Missouri be included as part of the Upper South the totals would be $30,765,441 and $54,372,568. Florida also became important in tobacco manufacturing, producing over eight million dollars' worth of cigars and cigarettes by 1890. *U. S. Tenth Census* (1880), II, 78, 79; *U. S. Twelfth Census*, IX, 647, 649, 661.

[2] Mitchell, *Rise of Cotton Mills*, 112-115.

prises was not to be had from the North where, for
example, such a man as Edward Atkinson, biased perhaps
by his Massachusetts mill connections, publicly counseled
his Southern friends against the new departure.[1] Capital
had to be raised from the people of the neighborhood
out of their meager savings. While a few upcountry mills
such as Piedmont, Pacolet, Clifton and Pelzer were
financed in part by Charleston investors, this was the
exception rather than the rule.[2] The zeal often outran
prudent business considerations, but everywhere it evidenced a heartening spirit of enterprise and a resolve to
rescue the community from the slough of agricultural
distress.

If a town could not set up a large factory, it set up
a small one; if not a sheeting, then a spinning mill.
Merchants, doctors, bankers, preachers, teachers—men
outstanding in their neighbors' eyes—were at the forefront of such efforts. Thus Charles Estes, well known
to his fellow townsmen because of his success in the
drygoods and grocery businesses, was made president of
a mill in Augusta, Georgia, at the urging of a local
judge who backed his opinion by taking one hundred
thousand dollars' worth of stock. At Salisbury, a down-
at-the-heels North Carolina town, a gaunt, fiery-eyed
Tennessee evangelist conducted a month's revival in
1887, driving home with such force the thought that
the wickedness and misery of the poor came from idle-
ness that three local ministers promptly joined with other
citizens in organizing a highly successful factory.[3] In
general, the great natural advantages of locating along
the fall line of the rivers in the Carolinas and Georgia

[1] Edward Atkinson, *Address Given in Atlanta* (Boston, 1881).

[2] Mitchell, *Rise of Cotton Mills*, chap. iv; Holland Thompson, *From
the Cotton Field to the Cotton Mill* (N. Y., 1906), 59 ff., 81; Edmonds, *Facts about the South*, 25.

[3] Mitchell, *Rise of Cotton Mills*, 108, 135-136.

appealed strongly to the mill promoters and there, with the aid of cheap water power, the most flourishing factories were apt to be found.

While a few men like Daniel A. Tompkins of Charlotte had the proper technical training for cotton manufacturing, many more succeeded because their native shrewdness carried them through a period when close figuring was not necessary.[1] Others were plain incompetents, chosen for social reasons, and the enterprises they headed quickly languished. The success of the cotton-mill campaign is attested by the fact that from 1880 to 1890 the number of spindles and looms nearly trebled. Before the close of another decade the production of coarse cottons would be virtually monopolized by the South. Even the cottonseed, generally neglected before 1878 as valueless, was discovered to have commercial possibilities in its various uses as fertilizer, cattle food, salad oil, etc. The forty-five cottonseed mills of 1880 grew into one hundred and fourteen in 1890 with a capital of twelve million dollars.[2]

Less spectacular in its development than the cotton industry, the manufacture of iron made almost as notable an advance.[3] Not only were new beds discovered, but they were found in close proximity to deposits of coal and limestone, as if nature had designedly associated the necessary ingredients for reducing the ore. Between 1880 and 1890 fifty new blast furnaces were erected in the three states of Alabama, Tennessee and Virginia,

[1] Tompkins's chief services were as a builder and distributor of mill machinery and supplies, as adviser to other manufacturers, as a promoter of industrial and technical education and, in general, as an apostle of Southern industrialization. G. T. Winston, *A Builder of the New South* (Garden City, 1920), chaps. vii-xii.

[2] Bruce, *Rise of New South*, 206-209.

[3] Bruce, *Rise of New South*, 112-113, 210-217; R. H. Edmonds, *The South's Redemption* (Balt., 1890), 12-24; Ethel Armes, *The Story of Coal and Iron in Alabama* (Birmingham, 1910), chaps. xvii-xix, xxi-xxv.

the sites so well chosen that most of them continued in operation well into the twentieth century. Though other manufactures made less progress, yet many a local community did what it could in its straitened circumstances to utilize such raw materials as lay within reach. A Northern visitor to Southern cities in the eighties reported the section "wide awake to business, excited and even astonished at the development of its own immense resources in metals, marbles, coal, timber, fertilizers . . . ." [1] He hardly needed to add that "the nonsense that it is beneath the dignity of any man or woman to work for a living is pretty much eliminated from the Southern mind." [2]

Leading cities like New Orleans and Louisville were the natural centers of the new industrial development. Other places such as Atlanta, Memphis and Chattanooga forged rapidly ahead in population and manufacturing importance, though without attaining a size that would have been considered large according to Northern standards.[3] No champion of Southern industry failed to take pride in the meteoric rise of Birmingham. Without existence until 1871, its location in the heart of the Alabama iron and coal district had by 1890 caused it to become a bustling town of twenty-six thousand, the center of rolling mills, foundries, iron furnaces and machine shops.

Generally speaking, however, Southern manufactur-

[1] C. D. Warner, *Studies in the South and West* (N. Y., 1889), 111.
[2] Warner, *Studies*, 112-113. See also W. P. Trent, "Dominant Forces in Southern Life," *Atlantic Mo.*, LXXIX (1897), 49-50. Compare F. L. Olmsted's prewar comment: "To work industriously . . . is, in the Southern tongue, to 'work like a nigger.' " *The Cotton Kingdom* (N. Y., 1861), I, 22.
[3] The population of the principal cities in 1890 was: New Orleans, 242,039; Louisville, 161,129; Richmond, 81,388; Atlanta, 65,533; and Memphis, 64,495. Chattanooga, like Birmingham an iron center, grew from 12,892 in 1880 to 29,100 in 1890. *U. S. Twelfth Census*, I, 430-433.

ing was conducted on too small a scale to breed important urban communities. Even Durham had less than six thousand residents as late as 1890. The typical mill village possessed but a few hundred people, mostly laborers and their families gathered for the purpose of working in a particular factory and living in unpainted shanties along a single street ankle-deep with dust. The entire South in 1880 contained only ten cities of twenty-five thousand or more inhabitants and this number had grown to but nineteen in 1890. Historic old cities like Charleston and Mobile showed little sign of new life, resting tranquilly in the autumnal glory of their past renown.

In emulating the industrial course of the North, the South had never been more truly Southern. Unlike New England or Great Britain she depended for her basic supplies entirely upon the tobacco produced in her own fields, the cotton grown on her own lands, the coal and iron mined in her own hills, the timber cut in her own forests. Not a dollar's worth of raw materials did she need to buy from outside her own borders. Moreover, apart from the railways, the new undertakings were nourished largely by her own capital, usually in the form of an aggregation of petty savings. It was only after the path had been blazed and the certainty of profits demonstrated that Northern investors began to show an active interest. The turning point perhaps came in the mid-eighties when the important Thomas Iron Company of Pennsylvania constructed a million-dollar branch plant in Alabama, one of the finest in America.[1] In 1889 a large party of Northern capitalists and bankers, including Andrew Carnegie and the two leading partners of Cooper, Hewitt & Company, toured the South and brought back glowing reports. Soon an in-

[1] Edmonds, *South's Redemption*, 5-6, 14.

creasing stream of Northern capital began to flow southward.

What was true of financial support was even truer of
the human energies devoted to the new developments.
Northern promotion played a negligible part. The editor
of the *Manufacturers' Record* could well say in 1890:
"Southern energy and enterprise mainly are entitled to
the credit for what has been accomplished." [1] In the
South itself the drive toward industrialization came
chiefly from the former nonslaveholding class, for, as
we have seen, the members of the old landed gentry
turned to the professions rather than to manufacturing.
The typical *entrepreneur*, as he may be generalized from
a few hundred random instances, was the son of a
country merchant.[2] Beginning as a clerk with perhaps a
common-school education, he rose in time to store-
keeper and petty money lender, laid by his profits and,
with his savings, aided in starting a local factory or mine
which he headed as president. When it is recalled how
much of the leadership and financial strength of the
prewar South was monopolized by the slavocracy, this
change may be regarded as little short of revolutionary.

Similarly the manual labor was supplied by the South.
This was not wholly a matter of choice, for ever since
the close of the war an active campaign had been waged
to make the section attractive to foreign immigrants.
Most of the states had passed laws to encourage their

[1] R. H. Edmonds in issue of Dec. 21, 1889, and in his *South's Redemption*, 47. See also F. W. Moore, "The Condition of the Southern
Farmer," *Yale Rev.*, III (1894-1895), 63.

[2] This generalization is based on a manuscript study of the background of three hundred postwar industrialists of Virginia, North and
South Carolina, Georgia, Alabama and Tennessee, made in 1928 by
G. W. Adams of the Harvard Graduate School. Of a total of two
hundred and fifty-four, about eighty per cent came of nonslaveholding
parentage; of the entire three hundred, only thirteen per cent were
born in the North, about half of them having gone South before the
war.

coming, boom literature was circulated under official
auspices, and recruiting agents were dispatched to
European countries, Virginia, it is said, sending several
hundred to Great Britain and Germany in 1870.[1] Not
discouraged by the negligible results, renewed efforts
were made in the eighties as the industrial possibilities of
the section were disclosed. State immigration bureaus
were reëstablished or given enlarged powers; and official
endeavors were supplemented by the activities of popular
conventions, land companies, boards of trade and, most
important of all, the new railways eager to build up their
satellite territories. In 1883 a Southern Immigration
Association was formed for the purpose of redoubling
such exertions and to press for the opening of direct
steam communication between Southern ports and
Europe.[2]

Immigrant wage-earners, however, continued to prefer
the North and the West where their countrymen had
long been accustomed to go and where they need fear
no competition from cheap native labor. Thus Southern
manufacturing development had to rest on the brawn of
the poor whites. By the same token it opened a fresh
road of escape for this submerged element. The new
industrialism did for the unprivileged commoners of

[1] *American Annual Cyclopedia*, X (1870), 749. Of course, the South
sought farmers as well as factory hands. See 61 Cong., 3 sess., *Senate
Docs.*, XXI, *passim*, for abstracts of Southern laws relating to immigration. Coolie labor was envisaged as a solution of the Southern economic problem in A. P. Merrill, "Southern Labor," *De Bow's Rev.*,
VI (1869), 586-592; in refutation, see W. M. Burwell, "Science and
the Mechanic Arts against Coolies," same issue, 557-571. An English
visitor reported having seen six or seven hundred Chinese digging ditches
alongside Negroes on the Alabama & Chattanooga Railway in 1870; but
this was exceptional. Robert Somers, *The Southern States since the
War* (London, 1871), 163-164, 225.

[2] Southern Immigration Association, *Proceedings* (Nashville, 1884).
See also W. M. Barrows, *The New South* (N. Y., 1884), 4-5, and
U. S. Industrial Commission, *Reports* (Wash., 1900-1902), XV, 550-
575.

the upland South what the break-up of the great plantations was doing for those of the lowland districts. As fast as factories were set up, labor was drawn from the foothill and mountain country to operate them. Employers, somewhat to their surprise, discovered that as workers they were industrious, self-improving and reliable, thus giving color to the belief that the highlanders were not degenerate but simply unstarted.[1] Machine shops, the cotton industry and furniture factories were wholly dependent upon their labor. Only in the sawmills, tobacco factories and a few other less skilled employments did they find it necessary to compete with Negroes for jobs. With every factory owner a law unto himself, the workday was long, wages were low, conditions wretched. Yet, even so, the new job in the busy mill village, with its opportunities for human fellowship, held more attraction than the bleak life in a distant mountain cove.

Since the whole family had worked together on the farm, it seemed natural to comply with the wishes of the mill proprietor to have the family as the working unit in the factory. So arose the evil of child labor—not the healthful outdoor choring of the farm, but the steady, benumbing toil of the ill-ventilated, ill-lighted mill—and its concomitant evil, the idle father living off the working child. By 1890 twenty-three thousand children were employed in industry in the thirteen states.[2] A distinct "factory people" was in process of

[1] D. A. Tompkins, "The Mountain Whites as an Industrial Labor Factor," Chandler and others, *South in Building of Nation*, VI, 58-61; W. G. Frost, "Our Contemporary Ancestors in the Southern Mountains," *Atlantic Mo.*, LXXXIII (1899), 311-319. For a discussion of the various mountaineer groups, see S. T. Wilson, *The Southern Mountaineers* (N. Y., 1906), chaps. ii, iv-vi.

[2] The census definition of child laborer is a boy of sixteen or under and a girl of fifteen or under. E. G. Murphy, *Problems of the Present South* (N. Y., 1904), 96-125; *U. S. Eleventh Census* (1890), IV, 89.

creation—a folk whose life was shaped by a common origin and a social experience not reaching beyond the sound of the factory whistle. When all was said and done, however, the mill hand was a part of the pulsing world; he had gained a real foothold in the struggle for existence. A few became superintendents of the new instrumentalities that had called them from their long sleep. Even the most wretched of them were unwilling to return to their mountain solitudes.

Though far fewer in numbers than the tenant farmers of the lowlands, the mill workers were like them in constituting a new economic and social class in Southern life. Together, these two sections of the poor-white population formed a Third Estate of which the earlier South offered no counterpart. The mill people were too new to their situation and too scattered to be alert to their grievances—the "damn factory class," Tillman impatiently called them—but each year marked increasing restiveness among the small-farmer contingent.[1] Politically untrained, they had, since the overthrow of the Carpetbaggers, accepted the leadership of the old gentry. This leadership, however, little heeded the critical conditions which beset the rural majority, such as the nefarious credit system, "landlordism," high transportation costs and low crop prices.

The decade after 1878 saw a rapid spread of farmers' clubs and societies where the ills and needs of agriculture were hotly debated and new men fresh from the people trained for leadership. Enough pressure was exerted upon the ruling class in various states to secure the establishment of departments of agriculture, state agricultural

---

[1] A. D. Mayo, "The Third Estate of the South," *Journ. of Social Sci.*, XXVII (1890), xx-xlii; Simkins, *Tillman Movement*, 176-177. See also a speech by E. A. Alderman before the National Congress of Education, Oct. 25, 1895. U. S. Commissioner of Education, *Report for 1894-95*, II, 1748.

*Politics sought the votes of the poor whites*

*of the South and manufacturing their labor.*

The New South

experiment stations and agricultural and mechanical colleges. But the more acute grievances remained unsolved, and the farmers themselves came to doubt whether measures which looked to increased production were what the situation called for.

Throughout the lean hard years of the eighties, in state after state, discontent with the rule of the well-born flickered and flared. The pretext for the Readjuster movement, which captured the Virginia legislature in 1879, was the resolve to scale down the prewar state debt, but the real animus was supplied by "men of the people" determined to cast off the leadership of the upper classes and the towns.[1] In South Carolina the "wool-hat boys" had a tribune of great promise in Martin Gary, demagogic foe of the "aristocratic oligarchy," but his premature death, in 1881, occurred before he had had time to mobilize the forces he had helped to rouse.[2] What he failed to accomplish Tillman, one of his lieutenants, eventually succeeded in bringing about, being swept into the governorship in 1890 by a popular demand for reform.[3] The same year an agrarian upheaval in Texas catapulted into the executive mansion "Jim" Hogg, a man of crude force, whose very name endeared him to the horny-handed sons of the soil.[4] In other states like forces were pushing from below. Everywhere the new leaders made political capital out of arraying the rural white masses against the railways, business

[1] C. C. Pearson, *The Readjuster Movement in Virginia* (*Yale Hist. Publs. Miscellany,* IV), esp. chap. ix.

[2] Simkins, *Tillman Movement,* 20-22, 49.

[3] Though the factory vote had played little part in his success, Governor Tillman secured the passage in 1893 of a law limiting the hours of labor to sixty-six a week. Simkins, *Tillman Movement,* 103-134, 164, 176-177.

[4] Herbert Gambrell, "James Stephen Hogg: Statesman or Demagogue?," *Southwest Rev.,* XIII (1928), 338-366. For similar movements in other states, see J. D. Hicks, *The Populist Revolt* (Minneapolis, 1931), 170-179.

men, bankers and aristocrats of the towns. Everywhere, too, their opponents sought to checkmate them with warnings of the danger of black supremacy if they pushed their insurgency to the point of splitting the ranks of the "white man's party."

A time of economic distress and political upheaval, the decade of the eighties was pivotal in the history of the postwar South. While the brave attempts at factory industry foreshadowed the future, the section retained its predominantly rural character. Agriculture passed through a period of storm and stress which aroused the agrarian masses to organized activity and eventually to political triumph. For better or for worse the Third Estate mounted the saddle. Southern politics was no longer to be merely government of the people and for the people but also by the people.[1] But it was equally clear that the people must be white people, for, as we shall see, legal disfranchisement of the Negro was one of the first fruits of the new dispensation.[2] Though the farmers' difficulties were largely of local origin, they were similar in kind to those of the other great agricultural region of the nation, the Great West. Thus, as the decade ended, the Southern agrarian leaders were ripe for coöperation with their Western brethren in demands upon the federal government for remedial action.

If the changes which the section underwent during this critical decade made its way of life more nearly like that of the remainder of the United States, the responsibility rested squarely upon the South itself. The homogeneity which characterized the white population in slavery times continued unaltered. The dominant race in the thirteen states advanced in the ten years from nine

---

[1] J. W. Johnston, *The Emancipation of the Southern Whites and Its Effects on Both Races* (Balt., 1887), argued that the whites had derived greater benefit from emancipation than the blacks.

[2] See later, 383-384.

and a half million to nearly twelve.[1] The number of Americans born outside the section who lived in the South in 1880 was four hundred and fifty thousand and the total had increased to probably not more than six hundred thousand in 1890. As for foreign infusions, at no time during the decade did aliens number more than one in fifty of the entire population. In 1890 fully seven eighths of the white inhabitants were of Southern nativity. On the other hand, the section contributed to the upbuilding of other parts of the nation a wealth of human material that it could ill afford to lose. The Negroes, while increasing at a slower rate than the former master class, advanced from five and a half million to six and a half.

In view of the frantic efforts made to attract immigrants an incident at the close of the decade caused many Southerners to question the wisdom of such endeavors and rejoice at their lack of success. Sometime during the 1880's a compact colony of Sicilians settled in New Orleans where they worked mainly as longshoremen, forming a turbulent and lawless element. The bloody clashes of their secret oath-bound societies led finally to the assassination of the Irish chief of police. When a trial of three of those accused of the crime resulted in their acquittal, a mob of citizens formed on the morning of March 14, 1891, and strung up all eleven.[2] The affair precipitated an international crisis, caused the withdrawal of the Italian minister and even-

[1] For population data, see *U. S. Eleventh Census*, I, xcviii, 560-563; *U. S. Tenth Census*, I, 480-483; *U. S. Twelfth Census*, I, 485.

[2] None of the mob was ever indicted or brought to trial. *U. S. Foreign Relations for 1891*, 665-667, 671-672, 674-686, 712-713; J. B. Moore, *A Digest of International Law* (Wash., 1906), VI, 837-841. Later mob outbreaks occurred against the Italians elsewhere in Louisiana: at Hahnville in 1896 when three held on a charge of homicide met violent death; and at Tallulah in 1899 when five others were taken from jail and lynched. Moore, *Digest*, VI, 843-845.

tually brought the payment of an indemnity by the Washington government. Though the Southern people might in many ways have benefited from a more varied racial make-up, they were at least saved the possibility of adding to their own inherited race problem one which they had no experience to meet.

Within the section itself there was considerable shifting of population during the decade, notably toward the rich farming country of the Gulf region and particularly into the half-developed state of Texas.[1] Railroads were penetrating the Texan interior; the great ranches in the western section were slowly crumbling before the farmer advance; cotton was asserting its primacy among agricultural crops. As heavy beef cattle and dairy cows crowded out the longhorns, so Merinos and Shropshires replaced the old Mexican sheep, and stocky, quickly grown hogs the lean and voracious razorbacks. Despite the great drought of 1886, which lasted twenty-three months and affected thirty-seven western counties, the total number of people in Texas increased by three quarters of a million, reaching two and a quarter million in 1890 drawn from many parts of the country as well as other portions of the world. What had been a thinly inhabited region ten years before had become well populated and the edge of settlement had reached the escarpment of the Staked Plains. This phenomenal growth, however, betrayed the essential kinship of Texas with the Great West rather than with the South.

[1] W. B. Bizzell, *Rural Texas* (L. H. Bailey, ed., *Rural State and Province Series;* N. Y., 1924), 123-136, 155-232; W. C. Holden, "West Texas Drouths," *Southwestern Hist. Quar.,* XXXII, 103-123.

# CHAPTER II

## THE GREAT WEST

MOST of the Great West in 1878 lay as yet beyond the pale of statehood.[1] Five states had indeed been formed as a result of mining rushes, partisan exigency at Washington or other fortuitous circumstance. The bulk of this vast region, however, consisted of eight great territories—Dakota, Montana, Idaho, Wyoming, Washington, Utah, New Mexico and Arizona—and of a special reserve, Indian Territory, set aside for the red men. These eight territories embraced nearly a third of the total national area and already contained six hundred thousand white inhabitants—the vanguard of the restless, dusty army of civilization moving westward. As the 1880's began, the main body came into view, their advent hastened by the taming of the wild Indians and the completion of the transcontinental railways. Over twice as many settlers scattered through this region in the years from 1880 to 1890 as in the two picturesque decades preceding. Wealth, adventure, health, *Wanderlust*, the desire for an easier living, all played their part in swelling the tide of migrants.

The results as recorded by the census delighted the heart of the Westerner with his love of bigness and quick results, while furnishing some excuse for the saying of skeptical Easterners that it was impossible to tell the truth about the West without lying. By 1890 the popu-

[1] By the Great West is meant that section of the country lying between the Pacific and the first tier of states west of the Mississippi River, exclusive of Texas.

23

lation of Utah had grown nearly one half beyond that
of 1880, Idaho held two and a half times as many
people, Wyoming almost three times as many. Aided
by silver and copper discoveries near Butte, Montana
more than tripled its population by 1890, while in
Dakota, where farming was the chief lodestone, the
numbers grew quite as rapidly notwithstanding the
shortage of rainfall toward the close of the decade.[1] The
progress of Washington was even more remarkable.
There the farmer could count not only on a fertile soil
but on ample rainfall, and the rush of settlement enlarged the population nearly fivefold. The number of
whites in the eight territories exceeded one and a half
million in 1890.[2]

The states of the Great West did nearly as well as
the territories in their rate of growth and achieved an
even greater increment of population.[3] Though thousands of families were forced by the drought late in
the eighties to abandon their farms, Nebraska doubled
her population by 1890, passing the million mark and
reducing her unoccupied domain to a third of what it
had been in 1880, while Kansas, adding a half-million
people to the million she possessed at the outset, had
settlers strewn through her entire area. In Colorado and
California the decline of the mining fever might have
had disastrous results but for the growth of their agricultural districts and towns. The former state numbered
four hundred thousand inhabitants in 1890, a gain of
one hundred per cent, and California grew from eight

[1] H. E. Briggs, "The Great Dakota Boom, 1879-1886," *N. D. Hist.
Quar.*, IV, 78-108.

[2] *U. S. Twelfth Census* (1900), I, xxii-xxv. These figures should
be read in the light of a gloomy prediction recorded in the *Washington*
(D. C.) *Star,* June 14, 1877, that the Great West could never develop
into populous and prosperous communities.

[3] *U. S. Compendium of Eleventh Census* (1890), I, xlvii; *U. S.
Statistical Atlas* (U. S. Twelfth Census), plates 11 and 12.

hundred thousand to one million two hundred thousand. Nevada alone could not recover from the blow and in the ten-year period lost a third of her citizens.

Except in early colonial times Western growth had always been a drain on the older American communities from which the migrants came. The familiar story was repeated once more, and for the last time, as the trans-Missouri country passed under the hand of the settler. Broadly speaking, the Middle West was the motherland of the newer states and territories. Her children fared forth to face the hardships and hazards of life in strange parts with the same dauntless spirit that their fathers and mothers had once set forth from the still older lands to the east. To their ranks were added many from those counties of New York and Pennsylvania bordering on the Ohio Valley. It is significant that these colonizing areas were also the parts of the North where the white population was breeding its largest families and which, according to the standards dictated by a simple rural economy, were threatened with overpopulation.[1]

The restless Middle Westerners were at home in all parts of the region.[2] They flocked into Kansas in such numbers that by 1890 one fifth of the inhabitants consisted of natives of Illinois and Ohio. Farther to the west, the major strains in the population of Colorado and California derived from Iowa, Missouri, Illinois, Ohio, New York and Pennsylvania; and a similar situation prevailed elsewhere. From Illinois alone a third of a million persons settled in the newer commonwealths. This was a "wandering of the nations" that was none the less notable because confined within the boundaries of a single country. It involved a transplantation, not

[1] U. S. Eleventh Census (1890), I, 914.

[2] For the data in this paragraph, see U. S. Eleventh Census, I, cxii-cxv, cxxiv.

only of men and material possessions but also of
ideas and institutions, which, in spite of different conditions of geography and climate, were, after the initial
shock of adjustment, to shape the lives of Westerners
along traditional American lines.

In making the journey westward the "prairie
schooner" was rapidly giving way to swifter means of
travel. Many, however, clung to the time-tried mode.
But the old-fashioned ox team had now been supplanted
by horses or mules, the necessity for carrying large stores
of food no longer existed, and few or no cattle were
driven along. Mr. and Mrs. C. D. Ide and a large party
from Mondovi, Wisconsin, made such a journey in the
spring of 1878, reaching their destination at Dayton in
Washington territory four and a half months later.
Despite the better trails and other ameliorations of travel
Mrs. Ide's diary shows that hardship and excitement
remained a-plenty.[1]

The number who went in this way, however, steadily
diminished. Railways advertised their advantages, offered
special rates and sometimes, as in the case of the Northern
Pacific Railroad, temporarily gave free transportation
to persons intending to settle upon railway land.[2] "Without the railroad," declared a prominent Dakotan in
1884, "it would have required a century to accomplish
what has been done in five years under its powerful
influence." [3] The Ide party made such a strange appearance while moving through southern Minnesota as to

[1] Mrs. Lucy A. Ide's diary of this journey has been edited by J. O.
Oliphant under the title, "In a Prairie Schooner, 1878," *Wash. Hist.
Quar.*, XVIII, 122-131, 191-198, 277-288.

[2] J. B. Hedges, "The Colonization Work of the Northern Pacific
Railroad," *Miss. Valley Hist. Rev.*, XIII, 320-321, 327, 332-333;
same author, "Promotion of Immigration to the Pacific Northwest by
the Railroads," same mag., XV, 183-203; G. D. Bradley, *The Story
of the Santa Fé* (Boston, 1920), chap. v. The emigrant guidebooks of
the 1880's ignored the possibility of traveling by wagon.

[3] Briggs, "Great Dakota Boom," 80.

cause people in a passing train to mistake them for a circus. The space-conquering locomotive inevitably rang the death knell of the covered wagon.[1]

The spell of the Great West was felt not only within the national borders but across the seas as well. Though a majority of the alien newcomers to America stopped in the industrial centers to the east, others sought the farming life with which they were familiar in their home lands, and special immigrant trains distributed them by the thousands through the remote trans-Missouri country. In a single week in the spring of 1882, according to the *Chicago Tribune*, nine thousand foreigners arrived in Chicago, most of them destined for Dakota.[2] Robert Louis Stevenson, short of funds and in search of health and a bride, boarded a transcontinental immigrant train in 1879, carrying with him a minimum of luggage and Bancroft's *History of the United States*.[3] The trip was marked by greater discomfort than the passage by immigrant ship from the Clyde to New York.[4] After many stops and transfers he and his bewildered polyglot companions reached the Pacific Transfer Station, near Council Bluffs, where they exchanged to the Union and Central Pacific railways for their ten days' trip to the Coast.

Every passenger was sold a board and three straw cushions; when darkness fell, the seats were rearranged

[1] But travelers must complain however they ride! See Helen Hunt Jackson's amusing account of her trip by Pullman from Chicago to San Francisco in 1878 in H. H. (*pseud.*), *Bits of Travel at Home* (Boston, 1878), 3-40.

[2] Briggs, "Great Dakota Boom," 86.

[3] R. L. Stevenson, *Across the Plains* (N. Y., 1892), esp. 26-39. See also Rosaline Masson, *The Life of Robert Louis Stevenson* (N. Y., 1923), 147-153, 168-169, 178-181.

[4] Described in R. L. Stevenson, *The Amateur Emigrant* (Chicago, 1895). For a detailed account of a steerage passage made by a Swedish immigrant in 1891, see A. G. Carlson, *En Emigrants Resa* (Chicago, 1894).

and the distance between each pair bridged with the boards, thus forming a perilous couch for two sleepers in a cramped position. For food and comforts the travelers relied chiefly upon the newsboys who noisily peddled fruit, canned beans and bacon, coffee, soap and tin basins. A single flat-topped stove at the end of the car provided cooking facilities. Stevenson good-naturedly took part in the rough camaraderie of the train. He even succeeded in attaining the democratic distinction of a nickname, no less a one than "Shakespeare," bestowed perhaps because of his accent and the erudition implied by the six volumes of Bancroft. None too robust when he began the adventure, Stevenson reached his destination "feverish and sick," looking "like a man at death's door."

The business of transporting immigrants was eagerly sought by the railroads, not so much because of the immediate returns of the passenger traffic as because of their desire to hasten settlement, develop a shipping business and enhance the value of their land holdings. After a period of relative quiet during the five hard years following the Panic of 1873 the railway immigration departments in the Atlantic ports and Europe resumed their activities with redoubled energy.[1] In 1883, for instance, the Northern Pacific had one hundred and twenty-four agents stationed on the Continent and eight hundred and thirty-one in the British Isles. Over half a million copies of its publications, printed in five languages, issued from its Liverpool office within the year.

By 1890 one in every five persons in the Great West was foreign-born. The total number of immigrant settlers had increased three quarters of a million in ten

---

[1] For accounts of such activities, see Hedges, "Northern Pacific Railroad," 315-319, 322-325, 329-330, and Bradley, *Santa Fé,* 113 ff. The state governments also carried on similar work. See, for example, Briggs, "Great Dakota Boom," 105-108.

years. In particular places, as in Dakota, Montana or
Nevada, every third or fourth person might be of alien
birth.[1] No other section of the country contained so
high a percentage except the North Atlantic states where
the proportion was about the same. To an Eastern
student of Western conditions it seemed that "No such
experiment in the blending of the different races of men
into one homogeneous nation, has ever been attempted,
on a scale so grand and extensive." [2] Yet, despite the
strong foreign admixture, the West impressed Bryce as
"the most distinctively American part of America." [3]
He, of course, was thinking not of racial origins but of
qualities of character, conduct and ideals. In all these
respects, though it is often forgotten, the immigrant on
the frontier had, from earliest times, contributed signi-
ficantly to a genuine Americanism.

As in the nation at large, the Germans were the most
numerous of any alien strain.[4] Nearly two hundred and
seventy thousand of them had spread over the Great
West by 1890, settling most densely in the river valleys
of Nebraska, Kansas and California where they earned
a living mainly as farmers and miners. Next came the
Scandinavians, about two hundred and twenty-five thousand in all, overflowing from the Middle West into
the wheat lands of Dakota and Nebraska, with strong
contingents in the Pacific states. The settlers from England, one hundred and forty-five thousand strong, were
attracted by the opportunities of mining, ranching and
agriculture. Thickest in central California, they were also
to be found about Puget Sound, in the Salt Lake area,
eastern Kansas and Nebraska, and the mining districts

[1] U. S. Eleventh Census, I, lxxxii, lxxxvii, 395.

[2] L. P. Brockett, Our Western Empire (Phila., 1884), 71.

[3] James Bryce, The American Commonwealth (London, 1888), III,
86.

[4] U. S. Eleventh Census, I, 606-609, and maps 10-14.

of Denver, Leadville and Pueblo, Colorado. The
Canadians, though not quite so numerous, shared fully
in the varied economic activities of the West, being especially important in the life of the Pacific Coast. The one
hundred and thirty thousand Irish, for the most part,
continued to cling to the rims of the Great West,
half of them being found in the more settled parts
of California and most of the others in Kansas and
Nebraska.

Many of these racial groups came in family clans;
sometimes whole neighborhoods in Norway or Prussia
emptied themselves onto the prairies and plains. At least
one migration, that of the German Russians, was a
genuine folk migration. Something like an Old Testament flavor attaches to their story. In the half-century
after 1763 nearly one hundred thousand German peas-
ants—Catholic, Lutheran and Mennonite—had been
induced by the czarist government to flock over the
border into south Russia. There, exempt from military
service and allowed to preserve their German language
and religious customs, they dwelt in distinct settlements
along the Volga and the north shore of the Black Sea.[1]
By thrift and hard work they made their section the
granary of Russia. All went well until Alexander II in
1871 announced his intention of withdrawing their
special privileges. Thoroughly alarmed, the German
Russians sent small bands to the western parts of North
America to spy out the land for a new haven of refuge.
Everywhere the agents met with a cordial reception. The
Canadian government offered them large tracts of cheap
land; on the American side of the border the land-grant
railways made similar inducements, the Santa Fé even

---

[1] Konrad Keller, *Die Deutschen Kolonien in Süd-Russland* (Odessa,
1905); Gottlieb Bauer, *Geschichte der Deutschen Ansiedler an der
Wolga* (Saratow, 1908).

sending a special representative for that purpose to the Russian Mennonite districts.[1]

The organized movement began in the mid-seventies. Though many arrived with insufficient funds, one group of four hundred families brought with them over two million dollars and purchased sixty thousand acres in Marion, McPherson, Harvey and Reno counties in Kansas.[2] By 1880 twenty thousand German Russians had taken up their abode in that state, Dakota, Nebraska and Minnesota, nearly half of them in the Arkansas Valley in Kansas. During the eighties an equal number came, and colonies of Volga Germans, mostly railway laborers, were started in the Pacific states and Colorado. Their numbers would have been much greater if the czar, fearful of losing more such valuable subjects, had not restored most of the canceled privileges in 1883. Despite this concession more than fifty thousand German Russians were to be found in the West by the end of the century.[3]

By dint of thrift, enterprise and the labor of all members of the family they made themselves the most successful farming group in the Western states.[4] The hot winds and clouds of locusts created great fear in their hearts at first; yet, unlike the thousands of native-born farmers

[1] For a first-hand account of his experiences, see C. B. Schmidt, "Reminiscences of Foreign Immigration Work for Kansas," Kan. State Hist. Soc., Colls., IX, 485-497. See also Bradley, Santa Fé, 113-134.

[2] Schmidt, "Reminiscences," 495.

[3] The census figures, which do not distinguish German Russians from Slavic or Jewish Russians, have been checked against other data for these estimates. At least an equal number of German Russians settled in western Canada. U. S. Tenth Census (1880), I, 494-495; U. S. Eleventh Census, I, 608; U. S. Twelfth Census, I, 734.

[4] The two standard general treatments are C. H. Smith, The Coming of the Russian Mennonites (Berne, Ind., 1927), and Richard Sallet, Ruszlanddeutsche Siedlungen in den Vereinigten Staaten von Amerika (reprinted from Deutsch-Amerikanischen Historischen Gesellschaft von Illinois, Jahrbuch, Chicago, 1931), which deals with the Lutheran and Catholic groups.

who fled the region, they held stubbornly on.[1] Fifty-five Lutheran families, who had colonized in Clay County, Nebraska, about ten years before, owned property valued at a half-million dollars in 1882. It was a Black Sea Mennonite, Bernhard Warkentin, who a few years later introduced into Kansas the justly famed hard (or Turkey) wheat, an improved Russian variety which soon made that commonwealth the greatest wheat-producing state in the Union. Though, as in Russia, the settlers strove to live their life apart, Americanizing influences crept into the communities and imperceptibly altered many of their manners and customs.[2] Even their names began to bear testimony to the forces making for change, for in the hands of ignorant public officials and careless school teachers Grünwald became Greenwalt, Jost became Yost, Junk Young, etc.

While the racial make-up of the Great West seems sufficiently varied, in most respects the ethnic pattern would not have appeared fantastic to an American of older stock. The Teutonic and Celtic strains had, from earliest times, formed the basis of the American breed. But two other elements gave a touch of the exotic to the scene: the seventy-five thousand Spanish-speaking, adobe-dwelling Mexicans along the southern border (in-

[1] This was partly because their experience in Russia had taught them some knowledge of dry farming. M. A. Carleton, "Successful Wheat Growing in Semiarid Districts," U. S. Dept. of Agr., *Yearbook for 1900*, 531-532, 539 ff.

[2] Judge J. C. Ruppenthal made a study of the German speech used by the Kansas colonists, first, as modified by their long stay in Russia, and, secondly, as affected by their residence in America (to 1913). In the latter instance, the number of non-German words absorbed was "many times as great." See his "The German Element in Central Kansas," Kan. State Hist. Soc., *Colls.*, XIII, esp. 524-525. Striking evidence of rapid adjustment may be found in first-hand observations made of the Mennonite settlements near Newton, Kansas, in 1875 and 1882. See N. L. Prentis, *Kansas Miscellanies* (Topeka, 1889), 162-184. C. C. Regier studies the process in even more intimate terms in "An Immigrant Family of 1876," *Social Science*, VII, 250-266.

cluding Texas); and a somewhat larger body of Orientals in flapping pantaloons, basket hats and ebony queues on the Pacific Slope. Neither group, however, was sufficiently numerous or widely enough scattered to alter the general character of Western civilization.

In no part of the Great West were the contrasts of race and culture more striking than in California. Ranking next to Kansas in total population, she exceeded every other state of this section in the bewildering variety and sheer numbers of her immigrant elements. At Monterey, where the Scotchman Stevenson remained for a time, his daily companions at the little restaurant were a Frenchman, an Italian, a Mexican and two Portuguese, who were occasionally joined by a Middle Westerner, an Indian, a Chinese, a Switzer and a German.[1] But the common life of the town remained strongly Mexican in tinge. Spanish was the language of the streets; the people, dressed in gaudy colors, went about their business with true Latin leisureliness; serenaders added charm to the lingering dusks. Underneath the surface, however, this tranquil world was vibrant with new life. Not only were all the great estates of the vicinity held by Americans, but the new county seat, Salinas City, was a hustling town of pure American stamp. As for the original sovereigns of the region, the Indians, they eked out a miserable existence as hired hands on the near-by estates.

Though the Mexican coloration faded as one went north, racial heterogeneity reached its height in San Francisco, the metropolis of the state, a city which reminded Helen Hunt Jackson of New York—"a little lower of story, narrower of street, and stiller, perhaps."[2] It surpassed New York, however, as the American capital of the Chinese. Thousands of these Orientals huddled to-

[1] Stevenson, *Across the Plains*, 97-98.
[2] H. H., *Bits of Travel*, 77.

gether in the sunless rooms and alleys of Kearny, Du-
pont, Jackson and Sacramento streets, outrivaling the St.
Giles of London or its American counterpart, the old
Five Points of New York. There, in the heart of the
city, they lived, worshiped strange gods and smoked
opium; while in ill-ventilated quarters, screened from the
street with long scrolls of red paper, they carried on all
the trades of Canton and Hong Kong.[1] Their presence
was a visible reminder of a "problem" whose reverbera-
tions were still ringing through the nation. Farther to
the north, the state retained its frontier characteristics
and alien newcomers were relatively few. All told, there
were in California about three hundred and seventy
thousand foreign-born residents in 1890, a gain of
nearly seventy-five thousand in the decade.[2]

Economically, the Great West at the close of the
seventies was passing out of one era into another. The
older industries, mining and ranching, were being obliged
to assume new forms and agriculture was about to take
its dominant place in Western economy. Just as the
period opened, a silver rush to Leadville, Colorado,
transformed that place in three years from an unnamed
settlement of six log cabins in April, 1877, to a busy
hive of thirty thousand inhabitants.[3] Such stampedes,
however, occurred with rapidly diminishing violence and
frequency. Indeed, mining was losing its earlier spirit of

[1] For contemporaneous descriptions of Chinatown, see H. H., *Bits
of Travel*, 62-76; Willard Glazier, *Peculiarities of American Cities*
(Phila., 1883), 464-471; G. A. Sala, *America Revisited* (3d edn.,
London, 1883), II, chaps. xvi-xix; W. H. Barneby, *Life and Labour
in the Far Far West* (London, 1884), 40-41; C. A. Stoddard, *Beyond
the Rockies* (N. Y., 1894), 175-179.

[2] Besides 70,000 Asiatics, the total included more than 60,000 each
of Irish and Germans, about 50,000 natives of Great Britain, and
substantial contingents of Canadians, Italians, French, Swedes, Portuguese, Swiss and Danes. *U. S. Eleventh Census*, I, 608.

[3] Brockett, *Western Empire*, 671-673; Allan Nevins, *The Emergence
of Modern America* (*A History of American Life*, VIII), 374-375.

individualistic adventure. That picturesque nomad, the prospector, was giving way to the trained metallurgist employed by a mining company; the rocker, the sluice and other primitive devices for obtaining ore were yielding to the hydraulic process and great rock-crushing and smelting machines.

The new system required large investments of capital and the formation of mining corporations. Already by 1880 groups of capitalists controlled not only the Leadville district, but also the richest mines in Nevada. One gigantic California company owned all the best mines near Deadwood in the Black Hills, while similar conditions prevailed in Utah and Montana.[1] Emigrant guidebooks cautioned the tenderfoot against the hardships, risks and almost certain losses of seeking precious metals by rule-of-thumb methods, pointing out that most of the mining kings had had comfortable fortunes to begin with.[2] Such advice did not go unheeded. So far as mineral wealth was concerned, the typical American of the 1880's preferred to get his thrills vicariously, risking his money (rather than his life) by buying stock in mining corporations which, alas, too often defaulted their dividends. One hundred and forty such companies, located at San Francisco in 1880, had already assessed their stockholders forty-seven million dollars in addition to their original investment and had paid a total of but six million in dividends.[3]

No less notable was the change that took place in the conduct of the cattle industry. As the decade began, stock raising seemed to be at the noontide of its prosperity. The northerly push of longhorns along the trails

[1] Brockett, *Western Empire*, 118.
[2] L. P. Brockett, *Handbook of the United States of America* (N. Y., 1883), 120-127; F. V. Hayden, *The Great West* (Bloomington, Ill., 1880), 221-224, 247, 283-291.
[3] Brockett, *Handbook*, 116.

from Texas was as great as ever while on the north-western ranges the herds increased in size and value. Huge cattle companies were formed, often with English and Scotch capital, and in many sections of the Western range the cowboy began to receive his orders from a boss appointed by a board of directors in New York or London—a man who kept ledgers and gave serious study to cattle breeding and market conditions. As ranching sobered down to a businesslike basis, the position of the cowboy became steadily less that of a romantic hero and more that of a plain hired hand.

The abounding prosperity, however, was doomed from the outset, for it rested upon the rancher's possession of unfenced and unsettled public domain—obviously a temporary condition.[1] As the homesteader or "nester" advanced into the open range and the prairie was "cleft by skirmish lines of fence," the zone of free pasturage steadily dwindled. An angry desultory warfare occurred between the upholders of two types of civilization, the herdsman and the husbandman, with all history tilting the balance in favor of the husbandman. Each spring saw new homesteads marking the plains like a checkerboard and erecting prickly barriers against the free movement of the herds. Each year, too, the Long Drive from Texas was being slowly blotted out of existence, an event hastened by the cattle quarantines laid in 1885 by Kansas and Colorado. The federal government also sided with the farmer. Thus the tortoise once more defeated the hare. The last half of the decade witnessed the collapse of the old range industry. In order to survive, the stock raiser was obliged to reorganize his

---

[1] F. L. Paxson, "The Cow Country," *Am. Hist. Rev.*, XXII, 71-82; W. P. Webb, *The Great Plains* (Boston, 1931), 227-244; E. E. Dale, *The Range Cattle Industry* (Norman, Okla., 1930), chap. v; E. S. Osgood, *The Day of the Cattleman* (Minneapolis, 1929), chaps. iv-vii.

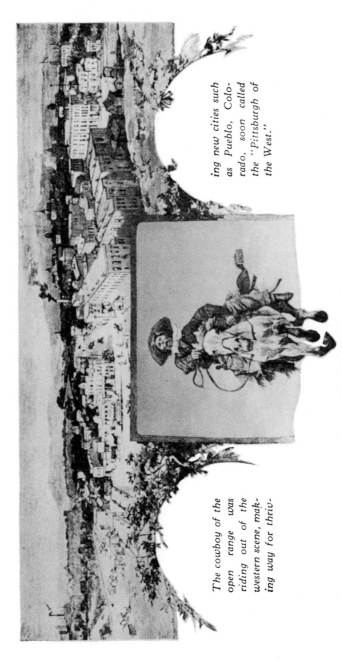

ing new cities such as Pueblo, Colorado, soon called the "Pittsburgh of the West."

The cowboy of the open range was riding out of the western scene, making way for thriv-

The Wild West Passes

business on a new basis—own his grazing grounds, fence
them, provide winter feed and breed better and fewer
cattle.[1]

As the mining and cattle industries settled down to an
orderly routine the social disorders characteristic of the
rawer early days subsided. To be sure, Leadville in the
first flush of the boom reproduced all the elements of a
tumultuous mining town—saloons, dance halls, gambling hells; ruffians, prostitutes, criminals. But the advent of the railway in 1880 quickly and quietly gave the
forces of civilization the upper hand, and the citizens
presently began to boast of their schools, churches, newspapers and banks.[2] A similar fate befell Dodge City,
Kansas, last of the border "cow towns" and magnet of
a turbulent, bird-of-passage population.[3] The settlement
of a hinterland of farming communities and the effects
of the state quarantine in keeping away the cattle drives
caused this "Bibulous Babylon of the Frontier" to lose
the chief source both of its prosperity and its wickedness.

Sporadic flare-ups of criminality continued to occur,
but generally at points remote from the centers of law
and order. The chief breeding ground was central and
eastern New Mexico, a region less accessible and less
known than Africa is today. Here in 1879 the Lincoln
County cattle war dragged to a weary and gory close
after the intervention of federal troops, though the
principal killer, Billy the Kid, escaped a violent death
for two years more.[4] Other bad men—Joel Fowler,

[1] Overstocking of the ranges and a succession of severe winters hastened
the end. Twelve great companies which in 1883 had been in a flourishing condition passed their dividends in 1887. R. A. Clemen, *The American Livestock and Meat Industry* (N. Y., 1923), 186.

[2] C. C. Davis, *Olden Times in Colorado* (Los Angeles, 1916), 114-
304.

[3] R. M. Wright, *Dodge City, the Cowboy Capital* (n.p., n.d.), chaps.
vii-xvii.

[4] He died at the age of twenty-one with the reputation of having

Jesse Evans, Billy Wilson—had their day of truculence and death-dealing before they themselves became victims of their own system of private justice or else, surprisingly enough, changed their names and localities and settled down to become respected and useful citizens.[1] Undoubtedly much of the old border wildness—the "desperado complex"—was a result of social sanction. When times changed men changed with them. A full meed of credit, however, belongs to the frontier sheriff, the good man who terrified bad men and made the country safe for law-abiding citizens.

The plague of banditry also came to an end in that part of the Mississippi Valley most exposed to lawless influences.[2] Though temporarily disorganized by their bloody repulse three years before when trying to rob the Northfield (Minnesota) bank, the most notorious gang, the James Boys, resumed their depredations in 1879 in Missouri, holding up trains and robbing or shooting the passengers. Public opinion was so aroused that in September, 1881, the governor of the state joined with various railway and express companies in setting a price on the heads of Jesse and Frank James. Tempted by the heavy reward, a member of the gang treacherously killed Jesse several months later. Frank voluntarily gave himself up and, after several futile attempts to convict him, quietly lived out the rest of his life as a decent member of society.[3]

killed one man for each of his years. Emerson Hough, *The Story of the Outlaw* (N. Y., 1907), 196-226, 256-273, 300-312; W. N. Burns, *The Saga of Billy the Kid* (Garden City, 1926), 53-289.

[1] Hough, *Story of the Outlaw*, chap. xvi.

[2] Robertus Love, *The Rise and Fall of Jesse James* (N. Y., 1926), 300-399.

[3] A recrudescence of brigandage, inspired by the example of the James Boys, occurred in Oklahoma territory in 1891-1892 when the Dalton Brothers' gang ran their swift and bloody course as train and bank robbers. Hough, *Story of the Outlaw*, 375-391.

The evil that the old West had done continued to live after it, highly romanticized in song, dime novel and cheap melodrama. The substance, however, was gone. This satisfactory condition had been hastened by the spread of agricultural life through most parts of the Great West—by the coming of people who built houses and lived in them and were not content with a blanket for a bed and the sky for a roof. The typical miner or cowboy was a bachelor and a rover, but with the farmer came his women folk, home makers, supplying the Great West for the first time with the "right kind of girls" in sufficient quantities. There were twice as many women there in 1890 as in 1880. In certain parts, such as Wyoming, Idaho and Oregon, their number tripled and, in the cases of Washington and Montana, quadrupled.[1] Quickly the family hearth took the place of the ranch house or the camp saloon as the social center of Western life. It was a change which, however much for the better, involved for men a lessening of desirable simplicities and freedoms as well as of moral laxities. We can at least spare a transient tear for the last surviving longhorn who, in the cowboy lay, declaimed with his dying breath:

> I little dreamed what would happen
>     Some twenty summers hence,
> When the nester came with his wife, his kids,
>     His dogs and his barbed-wire fence.[2]

Though by 1878 the technique of farming in the well-watered sections had been mastered by the old timers, the fresh arrivals, especially those from the wooded belts, had to learn the lessons anew.[3] Lacking

[1] In every case the rate of growth exceeded that of the population in general. *U. S. Eleventh Census*, I, 398.

[2] "The Last Longhorn," J. A. Lomax, comp., *Cowboy Songs and Other Frontier Ballads* (N. Y., 1910), 198.

[3] Finlay Dun, *American Farming and Food* (London, 1881), 424-

timber for buildings and fences, they usually had to spend their first years in dugouts or sod houses, while strands of barbed wire were made to take the place of the familiar zigzag log fences of the Middle West. As protection from the winter winds, the thrifty pioneer set about at once planting trees, selecting those which grew most rapidly, such as willows, cottonwoods, soft maples or Lombardy poplars. The thick, tough prairie sod, beaten down for ages by wind and rain and the hoofs of buffaloes, presented another problem, making deep plowing—fifteen inches or more—a necessity. It took hard work, skill and patience to "get the Indian out of the soil." Fortunately the new and constantly improving farm implements of these years came to the aid of the pioneer. Many a homestead was mortgaged to secure more efficient work tools. Without them Western agriculture must have advanced at a much slower pace.

As the better and more accessible lands were occupied, the tidal wave of migration in the early eighties pushed great numbers of prospective farmers into districts which a few years before would have been avoided. Thus the zone of settlement spread into western Nebraska, Kansas and Dakota and eastern Colorado and Wyoming, places where the soil was fertile but the rainfall uncertain and the rivers shallow and inconstant. A wet season meant smiling crops and reduction of the farmer's mortgage; but the dice of nature were loaded against him and what was won one year was wiped out the next. Harried by droughts and other afflictions and ignorant of the possibilities of dry farming, thousands abandoned their hard-earned homes in the late eighties and returned East. It was this uneven duel with nature

426; Brockett, *Western Empire*, 138-142. For descriptions of dugouts and sod houses, see anon., "Kansas Farmers and Illinois Dairymen," *Atlantic Mo.*, XLIV (1879), 718.

which injected much bitterness into the farmer's soul and helped goad him into movements of protest.

Though the small farm was everywhere the typical unit of cultivation, this accustomed American system was for a time threatened by a spectacular new development in agricultural management. This was the bonanza farm, which had first appeared when Jay Cooke's failure in 1873 dumped large quantities of Northern Pacific land on the security holders. By the early eighties scores of great tracts of from five thousand to a hundred thousand acres in Kansas, Dakota, Minnesota, Texas and California had gravitated into the hands of individuals or companies, many of them absentee owners.[1] On one such farm near Colusa in the Sacramento Valley, California, nearly ninety square miles were under cultivation, principally in wheat, most of the laborers being Chinese. One of the famous Red River farms at Casselton in Dakota, managed by Oliver Dalrymple, half-owner in partnership with some directors of the Northern Pacific, spread over one hundred and fifteen square miles. It was conducted with the efficiency of a railway. The principal buildings were connected by telephone, a central clerical staff kept accounts, and free medical service was maintained for the workers. Though only a third of the area was as yet under the plow, an army of six hundred were employed during the harvest. A formidable line of one hundred and fifteen self-binding reapers attacked the ripe wheat, cutting a swath of one fifth of a mile; then the grain, after passing through seventy-one steam threshers, was loaded into waiting trains that

[1] Three excellent accounts are Dun, *American Farming*, 199-212; W. G. Moody, *Land and Labor in the United States* (N. Y., 1883), chaps. ii-iii; and H. E. Briggs, "Early Bonanza Farming in the Red River Valley of the North," *Agricultural History*, VI, 26-37. See also Brockett, *Western Empire*, 78-79, 740-745 n., and Paul de Rousiers, *American Life* (A. J. Herbertson, tr., Paris, 1892), chap. iv.

every night puffed away toward Duluth. With land
bought at from forty cents to five dollars an acre yielding
an average of fifteen or twenty bushels, and with the
wheat grown at a minimum cost and commanding special
shipping rates, the profits were enormous.

The bonanza farm was a revival, under unexpected
conditions, of a type of agriculture reminiscent of the
plantation system of the prewar South but really allied
to the mass-production methods that were transforming
the Eastern factory system. Alarmed by the new development, students of the social trend did not hesitate to
predict that rural America was approaching the condition to which Europe had been reduced by "a thousand
years of feudal robbery and tyranny of wealth—with
the lands concentrated . . . in the hands of the few and
cultivated by a people who are dependent upon the
rich." [1] Such fears, however, proved premature. The
same decade that saw the greatest efflorescence of large-
scale farming saw its fading. After the riches were once
skimmed from the soil by the staple-crop system and
when land values began to rise, the large holders inevitably yielded to the pressure to sell their farms in
units small enough for more intensive cultivation. The
census of 1890 showed everywhere, except in the grazing
sections, a marked tendency to return to medium-sized
holdings. [2]

While the westward extension of the wheat and corn
belts was the most striking development in Western
agriculture, almost equally significant was the increasing
diversification of farming through most parts of the
region. California, for example, was in 1878 not only

[1] [W. G. Moody], "The Bonanza Farms of the West," *Atlantic Mo.*,
XLV (1880), 42-44.
[2] U. S. Dept. of Agr., *Yearbook for 1899*, 323; *U. S. Twelfth
Census*, V, xxi, xliv-xlvi, cxxv, 688; C. D. Warner, *Studies in the
South and West* (N. Y., 1889), 124-125.

the greatest wheat-growing state in the Union, but also the banner state in wool production.[1] Sheep raising, however, waned in importance as new settlers appeared, eager to invest in more intensive agriculture. Orange groves, peach farms, prune orchards, vineyards, chicken ranches, bee farms and similar undertakings attested the diverse interests of the later comers. Although fruit culture had been tried earlier, it was the decade after 1878 which, by means of irrigation and better marketing facilities, changed it from a highly speculative venture to a settled business. Through "citrus fairs," held first at Riverside in 1879, and fruit-growers' conventions, beginning a year or so later in southern California, the motley crowd of ex-sheepmen, teachers, health seekers and tired business men were taught the basic principles of scientific culture and correct standards of judging fruit. Citrus settlements or "colonies" sprang up at Redlands, Riverside, Pasadena and Pomona, organized not on any fanciful utopian principles but as the best practical way of sharing the expense of irrigation works. Irrigation colonies were also formed in the Fresno district of the San Joaquin Valley and there laid the permanent foundations for the raisin industry.

Into the midst of this varied activity there came, in 1875, a young man of Massachusetts birth named Luther Burbank, who established a nursery at Santa Rosa. From the outset he displayed an astounding wizardry in developing new forms of plant life through selection, grafting and cross fertilization. The improved varieties of fruits, berries, vegetables, grains and grasses which

[1] D. S. Jordan, "California and the Californians," *Atlantic Mo.*, LXXXII (1898), 793-801; E. J. Wickson, *Rural California* (L. H. Bailey, ed., *Rural State and Province Series;* N. Y., 1923), 79-82, 169-176, 292-297; Osgood Hardy, "Agricultural Changes in California, 1860-1900," Pacific Coast Branch, Am. Hist. Assoc., *Proceeds. for 1929*, 216-230.

Burbank produced, each involving the patient handling of countless seedlings, contributed greatly to the wealth of the state, and added variety and flavor to the diet of people the world over.[1] In fruit growing California found a Golconda which yielded greater wealth than the gold deposits Sutter first laid bare.

In other Western commonwealths, also, economic life showed a similar tendency toward greater diversity. The people of Washington, for example, turned their energies to vegetables and fruits as well as to grain growing and grazing. Alongside of these, lumbering and the fisheries with their satellite industries every year grew in importance. Even a state like Kansas, though clinging to the cultivation of corn, wheat and oats as its mainstay, devoted increasing attention to the raising of swine and domestic fowls, meat packing and the growing of flax and potatoes.

Over the broad and sometimes wrinkled face of the Great West there were two spots which, though in many respects peculiar to themselves, were nevertheless profoundly affected by the new economic forces at work. One was the religious commonwealth of Utah, which by 1878 the Mormons had transformed from a sand-girt solitude into a cultivated domain rich in flocks, herds, farms and orchards and threaded with highways and railroads.[2] The fanatical ardor which had fired the original colonists already showed signs of cooling as Brigham Young passed from the scene in 1877 and a

---

[1] In 1893 Burbank gave up his nursery business and devoted himself solely to the work in which he had already won an international reputation. W. S. Harwood, *New Creations in Plant Life* (N. Y., 1905); John Wilson, Robert John and H. S. Williams, eds., *Luther Burbank, His Methods and Discoveries and Their Practical Application* (N. Y., 1914-1915), prepared from Burbank's notes covering more than one hundred thousand experiments.

[2] Nevins tells the story of the Mormons from 1865 to 1878 in *Emergence of Modern America* 141-146, 366-367.

new generation came into control. Thanks to its ready
access by rail, Salt Lake City exhibited a lusty growth
—from twenty thousand in 1880 to nearly forty-five
thousand in 1890. While some of the newcomers were
Mormon converts from Great Britain and the Scandinavian countries, many more were "Gentiles" utterly
at variance with the Mormon creed and seeking their
share of this world's goods. Under the circumstances the
contagion of new ideas was not to be avoided. The
*Deseret News,* the church organ, dating from 1850, now
had rivals in the independent *Salt Lake Herald* and the
anti-Mormon *Tribune.* Even in the religious field proper
the Latter-day Saints, as they called themselves, were
challenged by the efforts of other sects, notably the
Presbyterians, Methodists and Congregationalists.[1]

Looked at apart from their peculiar religious beliefs,
the Mormons were a canny practical folk, hard working,
temperate and clannish.[2] The plague of saloons, brothels
and gambling dens was apparently introduced by the
non-Mormons, though the latter insisted that the Saints
were the sinners.[3] How many Mormon marriages were
polygamous it is difficult to ascertain, but the Mormon
figure of about three per cent is probably nearer the truth
than the feverish guesses of their opponents.[4] The
church, however, did not recede from its earlier attitude

[1] *Appletons' Annual Cyclopaedia,* XXI (1881), 860; D. L. Leonard,
"Six Years in Utah," *Missionary Rev.,* IX (1896), 807-813; Sala,
*America Revisited,* II, 316 n.

[2] R. T. Ely, "Economic Aspects of Mormonism," *Harper's Mag.,*
CVI (1903), 667-678, is an unusually discriminating account.

[3] H. H. Bancroft, *History of the Pacific States* (San Fran., 1882-
1890), XXI, 686-687. Cf. E. H. Murray, "The Crisis in Utah,"
*N. Am. Rev.,* CXXXIV (1882), 340-342; Sala, *America Revisited,*
II, 291-292.

[4] Compare, for example, C. W. Penrose, "Church Rule in Utah,"
*Forum,* V (1888), 673, with the charges of anti-Mormon critics: G. E.
Edmunds, "Political Aspects of Mormonism," *Harper's Mag.,* LXIV
(1882), 286, and Theodore Schroeder, "Polygamy and the Constitution," *Arena,* XXXVI (1906), 493-495.

that polygamy was a divine institution, designed by the Hebrew patriarchs to produce a eugenically superior race. It was this stubborn contention which, more than anything else, hindered the growing friendliness between Mormon and Gentile, sharpened the long-standing antagonism of the rest of America, and for many years kept Utah from statehood.

Though Congress in 1862 had prescribed fine and imprisonment as penalties for polygamy and twelve years later had strengthened the enforcement provisions, the legislation had remained virtually a dead letter. Prior to 1882, when a more drastic act was passed, only three final convictions had been secured by the government, largely because of the difficulty of obtaining proper testimony. The Edmunds law of that year aimed to cure the defects of earlier legislation and at the same time destroy the temporal power of the church.[1] While legitimating children born in polygamy before 1883, it threw safeguards about the jury system and the testimony of witnesses, and added to the previous penalties for polygamy the loss of the right to vote and hold office. An even more direct blow at the Mormon theocracy was the provision for placing the conduct of Utah elections under a federal commission. Though this stringent measure brought gratifying results—there were over a thousand convictions by 1888 [2]—public opinion was not yet appeased. As a result the Edmunds-Tucker law in 1887 empowered the United States to take over all the property of the church except such as was used for exclusively religious purposes.[3]

[1] U. S. Statutes at Large, XXII, 30-32.

[2] According to the "Report" of the Utah Commission, 50 Cong., 1 sess., House Exec. Doc., no. 447. See also Deseret News, July 8, 1888; Latter-day Saints' Millennial Star, L (1888), 568-570; W. A. Linn, The Story of the Mormons (N. Y., 1902), 599-600.

[3] U. S. Statutes at Large, XXIV, 635-641.

The resentment of the Mormon leaders knew no bounds. Despite Supreme Court decisions to the contrary they rang all the changes on the charge that they were being denied their constitutional right of freedom of worship.[1] They faced a crisis of national proportions, however, which could no longer be met either by open defiance or by passive evasion. Some of them went into hiding temporarily rather than submit; but this was a gesture of futility. It was clear that the days of polygamy were numbered and that the church must soon take the necessary steps to bring itself into harmony with the spirit of the age.

The region now known as Oklahoma presented a different kind of problem. All of it but the narrow strip, "No Man's Land," north of the Texas panhandle had been set aside as a protected area for the Indians in the period before the Civil War. The original colonizing tribes—the Cherokee, Creek, Chickasaw, Choctaw and Seminole—had developed an orderly and prosperous farming life and, by establishing schools, churches and governmental institutions, had done much to justify their name of the Five Civilized Tribes.[2] As a result of choosing the losing side in the Civil War, however, they had been forced to give up the western half of their lands. The ceded region was in part assigned to newly conquered bands of the plains and mountains, such as the Kiowa, Apache, Cheyenne and Ponca Sioux, but a great district near the heart of the present state, known to the

[1] For example, see *Latter-day Saints' Millennial Star*, XLIV (1882), 267-269, 284-286; XLIX (1887), 648-649, 809-811.

[2] Such periodicals as the *Democrat* and the *Republican* of St. Louis, *Harper's Magazine* and territorial newspapers were to be found in many Cherokee homes in the eighties. Commissioner of Indian Affairs, *Report for 1886*, 148. See also W. P. Adair, "The Indian Territory in 1878," and V. A. Travis, "Life in the Cherokee Nation," *Chronicles of Oklahoma*, IV, 255-274, and 16-30; and Brockett, *Western Empire*, 797-813.

Indians as Oklahoma ("the beautiful land") and two thirds as large as the state of Connecticut, remained unoccupied.

The existence of this vacant central tract was a constant source of irritation and temptation to land-hungry Westerners; and shrewd railway promoters, eager to hasten white occupation, helped to keep this irritation at the boiling point. Moreover, since federal laws did not apply to the Indian country and the tribal authorities lacked jurisdiction over vagrant whites, the territory had become a threat to the peace of the older Western communities by the use horse thieves and other desperate characters made of it. The Indians, on the other hand, suspicious of any move to tamper with their existing status, preferred to bear the ills they had than to fly to others they knew not of. In this position they found ardent allies in the cattlemen to whom they had leased vast unused acres for grazing purposes.[1]

In 1879 began a stubborn ten years' struggle by squatters to seize choice sites in the Oklahoma district in defiance of all the forces of law and order.[2] The early raids were led by Captain David L. Payne, a veteran of the Civil War and a former border fighter. About twice each year he and a party of "boomers," after eluding the soldiery, would squat on desirable ground, be removed by United States cavalry, and then be vainly prosecuted under a faulty federal statute. Payne had made no less than eight attempts at colonization when he suddenly died in November, 1884, under circumstances which excited ugly suspicions of poisoning by

[1] Dale, *Range Cattle Industry,* chap. vii.
[2] The best accounts are S. J. Buck, "The Settlement of Oklahoma," Wis. Acad., *Trans.,* XV, 335-342; J. B. Thoburn and I. M. Holcomb, *A History of Oklahoma* (San Fran., 1908), 148-170; and Roy Gittinger, *The Formation of the State of Oklahoma* (Univ. of Calif., *Publs.,* VI), chaps. vii-ix.

cattlemen. His work was promptly taken up by William L. Couch, who led two boomers' forays in 1885.

Meantime whites steadily sifted into the eastern half of the territory where the Five Civilized Tribes held sway. In ten years the number of whites who had not been adopted as tribal citizens grew from six thousand in 1879 to perhaps more than a hundred thousand.[1] While most of these were in the employ of the Indians or the government, one third of them were plain intruders who persistently returned when shooed off by the military. The situation was equally unsatisfactory in No Man's Land, adjoining the northwest corner of Indian Territory. Though the strip was open to legal settlement, Congress had left the five or six thousand inhabitants without a government. After resorting to vigilance committees and unofficial claims courts, the settlers assembled a convention at Beaver, the chief town, in 1887 and boldly proclaimed the formation of the territory of Cimarron. This improvisation, however, Congress refused to recognize.[2]

Each year of the decade emphasized increasingly the need of a different handling of the problem by the government at Washington. A first and very important step was taken in 1889 when President Harrison, acting under congressional authorization, gave public notice that the Oklahoma district would be thrown open to home seekers at high noon on April 22. A week or so before the appointed time eager throngs began to gather along the border until finally twenty thousand boomers awaited the signal to cross the line. "Every man was armed like a walking arsenal," declared a participant, "and many also constituted themselves walking com-

[1] The total population at the end of the ten-year period was 175,000. Gittinger, *Formation of State of Oklahoma*, 176-177.

[2] E. E. Brown, "No Man's Land," *Chronicles of Oklahoma*, IV, 89-99.

missaries."[1] At exactly twelve a shrill bugle blast rent the air, the troops stood aside, and the impatient hosts— by horseback and rail, in buggies and buckboards, even on foot—began the mad race for claims and homes. Into a few hours of intense drama was packed the whole story of American pioneering. Guthrie, which had been scarcely more than a town site six hours before, was by nightfall a tented city of more than ten thousand inhabitants. Its chief rival, Oklahoma City, thirty miles to the south, held a population of perhaps half as many. Everywhere over the countryside flickered the camp fires of the scattered homesteaders. One hundred days later Guthrie presented the appearance of a typical Western city, with banks, hotels, stores, newspapers, parks and an electric-light plant. By the end of 1889 the Oklahoma district had a population of about sixty thousand. Through some ineptitude of Congress the settlers, like those in No Man's Land, were left without any law or organized government save that established by common consent. It was clear, however, that formal territorial status could not long be withheld.

As in the South, so in the Great West the decade of the eighties was significant as marking the end of one cycle and the beginning of another. The trans-Missouri country was like a well-favored woman who, having given her adolescent years to an exciting and somewhat dubious round of gayety, decides while the conventions still permit to settle down to a life of sober respectability. The West looked back over its shoulder toward a glamorous and romantic past, cherishing memories which have become a part of the national folklore, but

[1] H. S. Wicks, "The Opening of Oklahoma," *Cosmopolitan*, VII (1889), 460-470, reprinted in *Chronicles of Oklahoma*, IV, 129-142. Good accounts may also be found in M. T. Rock, *Illustrated History of Oklahoma* (Topeka, 1890), 20-78; Buck, "Settlement of Oklahoma," 344-351; and Gittinger, *Formation of State of Oklahoma*, chap. x.

bent its energies to the rewards of a life of steady habits and prosaic toil. It was no mere coincidence that border heroes like Buffalo Bill, Texas Jack Omohundro and Wild Bill Hickok forsook the rapidly paling drama of Western life to take part in blood-curdling frontier melodramas on the mimic stage.[1]

Yet the eighties also taught the Westerner that hard work was not enough. Like his Southern brother, he was caught in the toils of an economic transition which too frequently denied him the legitimate fruits of his labors. Low crop prices, grinding debts, high freight rates, droughts and insect visitations made him feel that the hand of both man and nature was raised against him. Thus the settling down of the Great West was, paradoxically enough, attended by multiplying evidences of agrarian unrest. Just as in the South, the farmers, despite their traditional individualism, turned increasingly to organized action. The Farmers' Alliances by 1890 controlled many of the legislatures and even had spokesmen in both houses of Congress.[2]

These loudly declaimed grievances, however, did little to halt the movement of settlers into the region. As the population enlarged, demands for statehood were made with ever greater vehemence. Only the inevitable jockeying for party advantage delayed appropriate action by Congress. In the summer and fall of 1889 conventions in North and South Dakota, Washington, Idaho, Montana and Wyoming drew up constitutions reflecting the agrarian dislike of railroads and other corporations and

---

[1] M. B. Leavitt, *Fifty Years of Theatrical Management* (N. Y., 1911), chap. xi; F. J. Wilstach, *Wild Bill Hickok* (Garden City, 1926), chap. xiii. When Wild Bill took to the stage, he had behind him a record of perhaps eighty-one homicides, not all of them performed in the interests of public justice though all his victims fell in fair fight. Hough, *Story of the Outlaw*, 182-185.

[2] J. D. Hicks, *The Populist Revolt* (Minneapolis, 1931), 153-170, 179-181.

embodying sundry demands for reform.[1] In 1889 and 1890 the six new states were admitted to the Union. The economic ills of the people remained, but the Great West was now in a position to join with the South and other discontented groups in pressing for relief through national action.

[1] J. D. Hicks, *The Constitutions of the Northwest States* (Univ. of Neb., *Studies*, XXIII, nos. 1-2).

# CHAPTER III

## THE LURE OF THE CITY

IN the Middle West and the North Atlantic states rural America, like a stag at bay, was making its last stand. The clash between the two cultures—one static, individualistic, agricultural, the other dynamic, collectivistic, urban—was most clearly exhibited in the former section, for the march of events had already decided the outcome in the East. Agriculturally the Middle West, unlike the Great West, was beyond its period of growing pains. Farming was no longer pioneering and speculative; save in some of the newer districts the tendency everywhere was toward stabilization and a settled routine. Though the corn belt cut a wide swath through the lower tier of states and wheat predominated in the colder climes, the individual farmer was apt to supplement his main product with hay, orchard fruits and vegetables and to raise horses, cattle and hogs as well as crops, meantime guarding his soil resources through systematic rotation and the use of fertilizers.

The maturity of agriculture was mirrored in the physical appearance of the farms, particularly in the older regions. Neat frame dwellings housed the owners. Barns of increasing size and solidity, built of trimmed painted boards and perhaps protected below the ground line by stonework, sheltered the livestock and crops in place of the pioneer's slender framework of poles covered with straw. Instead of the old-time zigzag fences of split logs now appeared orderly rail fences or the new-fashioned wire variety. One observant Old World visitor formed a distinctly favorable impression of Middle America as it flashed by his car window. "The tall corn pleased the eye;" he wrote afterwards, "the trees were graceful in themselves, and framed the plain into long, aërial vistas; and the clean, bright, gardened townships spoke of country fare and pleasant summer evenings on the stoop." That this "flat paradise" was "not unfrequented by the devil" was suggested to him only by the billboards along the car tracks advertising cures for the ague.[1]

Economic stabilization bred political caution. Though the Granger agitation and the Greenback propaganda of earlier years had centered largely in the Middle West, the agrarian unrest which shook the trans-Missouri country and the South in the 1880's won little response. Already in the preceding decade the growth of a prosperous dairying interest in Wisconsin and Iowa had caused opposition to the demands of the wheat growers for greenback inflation.[2] Even more notable results appeared in the eighties as mixed farming became the rule and agricultural products found a ready market in near-by cities. Urban sentiment, always hostile to agrarian panaceas, also colored the farmers' thinking in countless imperceptible ways and helped confirm their new-found conservatism. In 1893 the states from Ohio to Iowa and Minnesota would vote more than seven to one in both houses of Congress for Cleveland's proposal to repeal the silver-purchase act, while the Solid South and the Great West would plump heavily in the other direction.[3]

[1] R. L. Stevenson, *Across the Plains* (N. Y., 1892), 15-17.

[2] C. O. Ruggles, "The Economic Basis of the Greenback Movement in Iowa and Wisconsin," Miss. Valley Hist. Assoc., *Proceeds.*, VI, 142-165.

[3] The Populist vote, both in 1892 and 1894, failed to reach one twelfth of the total in any Mid-Western state except Minnesota. H. C.

It should further be noted that the migration of many
sons of the Middle West into the trans-Missouri farming country and into the cities did much to relieve the
pressure on the means of rural livelihood. As we have
seen, the Far West, like another Eve, was formed out
of a rib taken from the side of Middle America. By 1890
a million native Mid-Westerners lived in Kansas, Nebraska and the Dakotas and six hundred thousand more
in the region beyond.[1] Still others were trying their luck
in the newer parts of Texas and Arkansas. This great
exodus drew off many restless and adventurous souls
whose staying might have given the politics of the home
states a distinctly radical cast. Professor Turner has
pointed out that the agrarian leadership in the new
Western commonwealths came chiefly from the ranks of
natives of the Middle West.[2]

While great numbers of immigrant farmers settled in
the section, they generally shunned the older agricultural regions, flocking rather into Minnesota, Michigan
and other of the less developed parts. Though the promise of an easier living beckoned them farther westward,
they preferred to consort with fellow countrymen who
had already firmly established themselves and were well
satisfied with the returns of their toil. State immigration
boards in Minnesota, Wisconsin, Michigan and Missouri
exerted themselves to attract alien newcomers,[3] but with

Nixon, "The Cleavage within the Farmers' Alliance Movement," *Miss.
Valley Hist. Rev.*, XV, 31, 33.

[1] *U. S. Eleventh Census* (1890), I, 560-563.

[2] F. J. Turner, "Dominant Forces in American Life," *Atlantic Mo.*,
LXXIX (1897), 440-441, reprinted in his *The Frontier in American
History* (N. Y., 1920), chap. xii.

[3] T. C. Blegen, "The Competition of the Northwestern States for
Immigrants," *Wis. Mag. of History*, III, 20-29; M. L. Hansen, "Official
Encouragement of Immigration to Iowa," *Iowa Journ. of History and
Politics*, XIX, 185-195; Kate A. Everest, "How Wisconsin Came by
Its Large German Element," State Hist. Soc. of Wis., *Colls.*, XII, 327-
330.

diminishing energy as the decade advanced. In 1884 Iowa frankly discontinued all official efforts, no longer desiring people "merely to count up in the census." Norwegians, Swedes and Danes, following the well-worn tracks of their countrymen in earlier years, came in such numbers as to make of Minnesota and Wisconsin a New Scandinavia.[1] Industrious, thrifty, law-abiding, highly literate, these descendants of the Vikings contributed materially to the prosperity and civic advancement of their adopted states. The whole family— ten children were common, twenty not unknown— toiled in the fields, at least until comparison with Yankee ways planted seeds of revolt in the daughters' breasts.[2] There were two hundred and sixty-five thousand more Scandinavians in the Middle West in 1890 than a decade before. Most of them became agriculturists, a third settling in the single state of Minnesota.

Like the Scandinavians, a majority of the four hundred thousand Germans who came in the 1880's turned farmer. But they were less imbued with the true pioneer spirit and generally bought the partly worked farms of Americans who were itching to be up and doing elsewhere. As thrifty and hard working as the Scandinavians, they were also deeply interested in education and quite as easily assimilated.[3] They were not, however, such stern Protestants, many indeed being Catholics, and they brought to rural life a *Gemüthlichkeit,* a sociability, which set them apart from all other racial elements. On

[1] K. C. Babcock, "The Scandinavian Contingent," *Atlantic Mo.,* LXXVII (1896), 660-670. See his fuller treatment, *The Scandinavian Element in the United States* (Univ. of Ill., *Studies,* III, no. 3), chaps. vii-xiii, and also G. T. Flom, "The Scandinavian Factor in the American Population," *Iowa Journ. of History and Politics,* III, 57-91.

[2] Hamlin Garland treats this theme in "Among the Corn Rows," *Main-Travelled Roads* (Cambridge, Mass., 1893), 139-174.

[3] A. B. Faust, *The German Element in the United States* (Boston, 1909), II, chaps. ii-iii, v, viii.

local political issues the two north European peoples
were often divided, particularly when the Teutonic bias
in regard to "blue laws" and the liquor traffic entered as
a factor. By 1890 more than half the Germans and
Scandinavians resided in the Middle West, about the
same proportion of the Swiss and Poles and nearly two
thirds of the Dutch and Bohemians.[1]
A traveler familiar with the great stretches of country toward the Pacific and the Gulf would have been
immediately aware that in the Middle West the traditional rural culture of America was rapidly dissolving
and a new form rising in its stead. Though occasional
cities, some of them populous and wealthy, were to be
found in the Great West and the South, their existence
merely accented the general rural character of the civilization which encompassed them. But in the great triangular central region, extending from Ohio to Missouri
and Minnesota and containing nearly one third of all
the people of the nation, the migration from the country districts had attained a momentum that was fast
giving the city a dominant position in the social organism. In 1880 one out of every five Middle Westerners
lived in urban communities of four thousand or more
inhabitants, ten years later one out of every three.[2] In
the single decade the number dwelling in such centers
doubled, attaining a total of six and a quarter million.
Illinois and Ohio boasted nearly one hundred and twenty
towns and cities, including some of the largest in the
land, while even in Minnesota and Missouri three out
of every ten persons in 1890 were townsfolk.

[1] The Dutch immigrant is given special attention in G. F. Huizinga,
*What the Dutch Have Done in the West of the United States* (Phila.,
1909).

[2] *U. S. Twelfth Census* (1900), I, lxvi, lxxxiv-lxxxv. For the same
census years, the percentage of people living in cities of eight thousand or more inhabitants was 18.5 and 27.6. *U. S. Eleventh Census,*
I, lxviii; *U. S. Twelfth Census,* I, lxxxii.

The drawbacks of life on the farm had, of course, been felt by earlier generations, but never before with such compelling force.[1] At least since the adoption of a national land policy in 1785, isolation and loneliness had been the almost inescapable conditions of country existence, for by the ordinance of that year the government rejected the New England system of farmer communities and provided for large, scattered, individual holdings. These tendencies were confirmed and strengthened by the homestead law of 1862. Thus in the less developed parts of the Middle West such as Minnesota and Wisconsin, or in the near-by territory of Dakota, country neighbors dwelt too far apart for friendly intercourse, being but four to the square mile when land was held in quarter sections and even farther away if the homesteads were larger or tracts remained unoccupied.[2] Even in the older farming districts families generally lived out of sight of other habitations; they had no mail deliveries; and the balm of a telephone was denied to all but a tiny minority.

As urban communities increased in number and importance, the farmer's feeling of isolation was deepened by a knowledge of the pleasant town life not many miles away. The craving for solitudes is not as natural as the craving for multitudes; and the companionable sense of rubbing elbows, even if anonymously, with one's fellows compensates for many of life's repulses and frustrations. If the chief historian of the Scandinavian

[1] N. H. Egleston, *Villages and Village Life* (N. Y., 1878), chaps. iv-v; same author, *The Home and Its Surroundings* (rev. edn., N. Y., 1883), chaps. i-vi, xxv; J. G. Holland, *Every-Day Topics* (N. Y., 1882), 303-309; W. L. Anderson, *The Country Town* (N. Y., 1906), esp. chap. xii.

[2] "In no civilized country have the cultivators of the soil adapted their home life so badly to the conditions of nature as have the people of our great Northwestern prairies," according to E. V. Smalley, "The Isolation of Life on Prairie Farms," *Atlantic Mo.*, LXXII (1893), 378-382.

Americans is correct, the cheerlessness and hardships of farm life accounted for the uncommonly high proportion of insanity among the Norwegians and Swedes in the Middle West.[1] Certainly where families of different nationalities occupied the same neighborhood social intercourse was at a minimum, though a homogeneous immigrant community sometimes succeeded for a time in keeping alive the friendly social customs of the home land.[2]

Despite such drawbacks many farmers valued the free open country life above all else and would not willingly have exchanged it for any other type of existence. Rural life, too, had its occasional cherished diversions for both young and old: its picnics and its gatherings at the swimming hole in summer, its nutting and hunting expeditions in the fall, its annual county fair and horse races, its family reunions at Thanksgiving, its bob-sled parties of merrymakers in winter, its country dances in all seasons of the year.[3] Even its religious revivals might be so regarded. Funerals, too, were as much social events as solemn obsequies, attracting people from miles around and affording a treasured opportunity for brushing shoulders and exchanging gossip on the doorstep of the church or under the horse sheds. For those with eyes to see, nature itself in its vagrant moods and infinite variety was a never ending source of pleasure. A field of growing wheat—"deep as the breast of a man, wide as a sea, heavy-headed, supple-stalked, many-voiced,

---

[1] Babcock, *Scandinavian Element*, 136-137.

[2] For example, see F. S. Laing, "German-Russian Settlements in Ellis County, Kansas," Kan. State Hist. Soc., *Colls.*, XI, 518-522.

[3] For such pleasures in Iowa and Dakota, see Hamlin Garland, *Boy Life on the Prairie* (N. Y., 1899); in Kansas, J. E. House, "A Boy's Job in the Eighties," *Sat. Eve. Post*, CXCVII, 10 ff. (May 16, 1925); in Wisconsin, Grant Showerman, *A Country Chronicle* (N. Y., 1916) —fictional autobiography—and Joseph Schafer, *A History of Agriculture in Wisconsin* (*Wis. Domesday Book, General Studies*, I), 172-178.

full of multitudinous, secretive, whispered colloquies"—
was to the æsthetic "a meeting-place of winds and of
magic." [1]

But such pastimes and diversions paled before the
bright attractions of the city, for, after the manner of
human nature, the country dweller was apt to compare
the worst features of his own lot with the best aspects
of urban life. Nor, in the thinking of many, especially
the younger folk, did these occasional pleasures repay
for the drudgery and monotony which attended much
of the daily toil, only to yield in the end a modest living. Farm work in former days had been spiced with
greater variety. Now the advent of railroads and the
lowered cost of manufactures led the farmer to buy
over the store counter or through the mail-order catalogue multifarious articles which he had once made for
himself. With no apparent reduction in the amount of
labor, the kinds of tasks were fewer and often less ap-
pealing to his special interests and aptitudes. In contrast
the city offered both better business openings and a
greater chance for congenial work.

The parents of Hamlin Garland, after a taste of Iowa
village life, returned to the farm, to the resentful disap-
pointment of their two sons (one of whom had clerked
in an "ice-cream parlor"), who compared unfavorably
the "ugly little farmhouse" and the "filthy drudgery of
the farm-yard" with the "care-free companionable existence" of the town. Herbert Quick's mother pleaded
in vain with her husband to leave their Iowa homestead
for a place where their children might attend better
schools. About the same time in Wisconsin Grant
Showerman's farmer father told him, "I hope you won't

---

[1] Garland, *Boy Life*, 273. For further expressions of this lyric mood,
see his *Prairie Songs* (Cambridge, Mass., 1893) and Herbert Quick,
*One Man's Life* (Indianapolis, 1925), chaps. ix-x.

have to drudge the way I've had to . . . . I want you
to be a lawyer. I might have been a lawyer if I'd only had
an education." [1] Men and boys, however, were probably less sensitive to the shortcomings of rustic life than
the women who, as Herbert Quick recorded in after
years, "in many, many cases . . . were pining for
neighbors, for domestic help, for pretty clothes, for
schools, music, art, and the things tasted when the magazines came in." [2] It was the city rather than the unpeopled wilderness that was beginning to dazzle the
imagination of the nation. The farmer, once the pride
of America, was descending from his lofty estate, too
readily accepting the city's scornful estimate of him as a
"rube" and a "hayseed." [3]

Different from Australia, where a few great centers
gathered in the city-wending throng, the tendency was
to move from the countryside to the nearest hamlet,
from the hamlet to the town, and from the town to the
city. [4] The reasons that impelled a person to leave the
farm to go to a crossroads village were likely to cause
the ambitious or maladjusted villager to remove to a
larger place, or might in time spur the transplanted
farmer lad himself to try his fortunes in a broader
sphere. The results were seen in the records of city
growth. The pyramid of urban population enlarged at
every point from base to peak, and the countryside
found itself encroached upon by hamlet, town and city.

[1] Hamlin Garland, *A Son of the Middle Border* (N. Y., 1917), 204-
206; Quick, *One Man's Life*, 240-241; Showerman, *Country Chronicle*, 148-149.

[2] "The 'drift to the cities,' " Quick added, "has been largely a woman
movement." "Women on the Farms," *Good Housekeeping*, LVII
(1913), 426-436.

[3] Eugene Davenport, "The Exodus from the Farm," U. S. Dept. of
Agr., *Experiment Station Bull.*, no. 41 (1897), 84-86.

[4] H. J. Fletcher, "The Drift of Population to Cities," *Forum*, XIX
(1895), 737-745.

The typical Mid-Western urban community was a small town varying in size from a few thousand to ten or fifteen thousand people.[1] Amidst such surroundings, it may be noted, youths like George Ade, Charles A. Beard, Meredith Nicholson and Charles H. Mayo grew up and had their first taste of life's sweets and bitters with no foreknowledge of that greater world where their names were to gain repute.[2]

Such a town, for instance, was Xenia with its seven or eight thousand inhabitants, the county seat of a rich agricultural community in southwestern Ohio. The well-shaded dirt streets, running at right angles, were lined with trim two-story houses set well back from the brick sidewalk behind neat picket fences and looking out on the world from under the screen of pleasant, if over-ornate, porches. Deep backyards with a stable and other outhouses and an occasional fruit tree allowed ample space for children's play and, through a back gate, opened onto a highway of dust and dark adventure known to matter-of-fact grown-ups as "th' alley."

Except for a ropewalk, paper mill and lumber yard on the outskirts, the chief business activity centered at the intersection of Main and Detroit streets. Here within a few minutes' walk were situated the only shops of the town: the "notion" store, a hardware store, two or three groceries, the drug store displaying great bottles of colored liquid in its windows, the odorous harness shop fronted with a huge dapple-gray wooden Percheron, the cigar store with its undersized wooden Indian on guard. Here the Little Miami train came puffing through two or three times a day, the shrill whistle of the "eight-

---

[1] There were 1028 towns ranging in population from 1000 to 8000 in the year 1890, 102 cities of from 8000 to 25,000 and 32 of 25,000 or over. *U. S. Twelfth Census*, I, lxvi.

[2] Ade recalls his childhood in "The Dark Ages," *Hearst's International and Cosmopolitan*, LXXXI (1926), 80 ff.

thirty" serving as a sort of curfew for the youngsters. Here, too, overlooked by the upstairs offices of the lawyers along Main Street, the stone courthouse reared its bulk, surrounded by trees and lawn, with a band stand and commodious hitching rails in the rear. Behind the courthouse grounds, around the corner from the Y. M. C. A. quarters and the *Gazette* office, stood the only other civic building—a barnlike brick structure sheltering the jail, the mayor's office and an auditorium and stage. The "op'ry house" it was called by official decree.

Signs abounded of the important place the horse occupied in the doings of the town. A hitching block or post hospitably reposed in front of nearly every store or house, while at important street corners municipal watering troughs offered refreshment. For the accommodation of the citizen who lacked his own horse and buggy a half-dozen livery stables plied a brisk trade. Blacksmith shops—dark caverns of enchantment to passing juveniles—replaced the horses' worn or cast shoes. For six days of the week life was uneventful enough; but on Saturday the streets took on an unwonted stir and bustle, for then the country people hitched up Nelly or Dobbin and invaded the town— whiskered adults self-conscious in their Sunday "best," young swains beauing bashful sweethearts, thin-chested mothers herding restless broods. It was a gala occasion for the farmers and their families, a day of hard work and many sales for the merchants.

The morals of the townspeople were safeguarded less by the single blue-clad policeman or the lively concern signified by the six or eight steepled churches than by the intimate knowledge which everyone had of everyone else's affairs. City sophistication was conspicuous for its absence; yet the people enjoyed advantages of education and social commingling which made them the envy of their country cousins. For many a young man, however, Xenia was not a spacious enough world, and there was a constant drift of the young people to larger places.

The extraordinary growth of its bigger cities was one of the marvels of Middle Western life in the eighties. Chicago, which best represented the will power and titanic energy of the section, leaped from a half million in 1880 to more than a million ten years later, establishing its place as the second city of the nation. The Twin Cities trebled in size; places like Detroit, Milwaukee, Columbus and Cleveland increased by from sixty to eighty per cent.[1] Of the fifty principal American cities in 1890 twelve were in the Middle West.

The rapid urbanization was, of course, accelerated by the swarming of foreigners into the section. During the eighties the immigrant population of Middle America increased nearly nine hundred thousand, reaching a total at the close of the decade of three and a half million.[2] Every fifth or sixth person in 1890 was of alien birth. Though the Scandinavians, as we have seen, generally preferred the farm to the city, seventy thousand of them were working in Chicago in 1890, the men as mechanics or factory hands, the daughters usually as domestic servants. Fifty thousand more dwelt in the Twin Cities. The Germans also divided their allegiance. James Bryce heard German commonly spoken on the streets of Milwaukee; the Teutonic element in Chicago, while thrice as numerous, was less conspicuous because of the babel of other tongues. As skilled workers the newcomers from the *Vaterland* were generally found in such trades

[1] *U. S. Eleventh Census*, I, lxvii.
[2] *U. S. Eleventh Census*, I, lxxxiii, lxxxvii-lxxxviii, xc, cxxxviii-cxxxix.

as photography, tailoring, baking, locksmithing and lithography.[1] The nationalities which most thoroughly identified themselves with city life, however, were the Irish and particularly the increasing stream of Russian and Polish Jews and Italians who constituted the "new immigration."

So great was the influx of all races into Chicago that its foreign-born inhabitants in 1890 numbered nearly as many as its entire population in 1880. A writer in the nineties, analyzing its school census, pointed out that "only two cities in the German Empire, Berlin and Hamburg, have a greater German population than Chicago; only two in Sweden, Stockholm and Göteborg, have more Swedes; and only two in Norway, Christiania and Bergen, more Norwegians."[2] If the "seacoast of Bohemia" was a figment of the poet's imagination, the third largest city of Bohemians in the world could at least boast an extended lake front.

These and other immigrant groups huddled together in dense colonies like islands in a sea of humanity. They jealously maintained their own business institutions, churches, beneficial societies, foreign-language newspapers and often their own parochial schools. In the small district about Hull House on South Halsted Street eighteen nations were represented. As individuals ventured forth from these racial fastnesses into the bewildering world outside, they generally found it their lot to perform the disagreeable or arduous work which Americans of older stock disdained. The sweatshops in the garment industry were recruited largely from Bohe-

[1] J. F. Willard (Josiah Flynt, *pseud.*), "The German and the German-American," *Atlantic Mo.*, LXXVIII (1896), 655-664.
[2] Quoted by Turner, "Dominant Forces in American Life," 438. See also G. W. Steevens, *The Land of the Dollar* (N. Y., 1897), 144, and J. C. Ridpath, "The Mixed Populations of Chicago," *Chautauquan*, XII (1891), 483-493.

mians and Russian Jews; the rough unskilled jobs in
the building trades fell chiefly to Irish and Italians;
while the business of peddling became a specialty of
Jews.

Assimilation went on at an uneven pace, being
notably slow in the case of the new arrivals from southern Europe and Russia. Timidity and ignorance on the
part of the immigrant, suspicion and contempt on the
part of the native-born, constantly retarded the process.
Even the American-born children, if reared in an Old
World atmosphere and taught their school lessons in an
alien tongue, were more apt to be second-generation immigrants than first-generation Americans. But sooner or
later the influences of the new land began to penetrate.
Perhaps unusual business success or the liberalizing effect
of membership in a labor union helped break down the
barriers. More often, however, the change reflected the
influence of the public school carried into the immigrant
home by the children. Though a regrettable breach
sometimes resulted between the older and younger generations, the democratic school system was a major force
for rapid Americanization. The number of American-
born immigrant children in Chicago in 1890 nearly
equaled that of the total alien-born, thus increasing,
though not by that proportion, the foreign character of
her population.[1]

As was Chicago, so in a measure were Cleveland,
Minneapolis and Detroit. Yet Chicago's four hundred
and fifty thousand foreign-born, Cleveland's one hundred thousand, Detroit's eighty thousand and Minneapolis's sixty thousand formed only two fifths of all
the people in those cities in 1890. In places like Columbus and Indianapolis seven eighths of the population
continued to be of American nativity. Many of the

[1] *U. S. Eleventh Census*, I, clxii-clxiii.

native-born, however, were of alien parentage and still in the process of learning American ways.

In so far as the swiftly growing urban localities drew population away from the countryside, the effects were severe enough to threaten many rural districts with paralysis. A map of the Middle West, shading the counties which suffered the chief losses between 1880 and 1890, would have been blackest across central Missouri and in the eastern half of Iowa, northern and western Illinois, central and southeastern Indiana, southern Michigan and central and southern Ohio.[1] Though some of the depletion, particularly in Iowa and western Illinois, was connected with the building up of the agricultural country to the west, much of it was due to the cityward flight. In Ohio 755 townships out of 1316 declined in population; in Illinois 800 out of 1424. Yet during the same decade every Middle Western state gained substantially in total number of inhabitants— Ohio about one seventh and Illinois nearly a quarter— an advance only in part to be accounted for by immigrant additions and the natural increase of population.

Such indications of rural decay, however, were mild as compared with conditions in the North Atlantic states. In this great seaboard section stretching from the Potomac to the St. Croix the city had completed its conquest. Already in 1880 about half the people—seven and a half million—lived in towns and cities of four thousand or more inhabitants; within a decade the proportion grew to nearly three fifths or eleven million.[2]

[1] For this purpose the Census Bureau classifies as urban any compact community of one thousand or more. *U. S. Eleventh Census*, I, lxix-lxxi. See also E. W. Miller, "The Abandoned Farms of Michigan," *Nation* (N. Y.), XLIX (1889), 498; H. J. Fletcher, "The Doom of the Small Town," *Forum*, XIX (1895), 214-223; anon., "The City in Modern Life," *Atlantic Mo.*, LXXV (1895), 552-556.

[2] *U. S. Twelfth Census*, I, lxxxiv-lxxxv. In terms of cities of eight

In 1890 about two out of every three persons in New
York and Connecticut were townsfolk, four out of every
five in Massachusetts and nine out of every ten in Rhode
Island. Only the states of northern New England preserved their essentially rural character. In the East, too,
most of the nation's great cities were to be found. New
York City, with already more than a million people in
1880, reached a million and a half in 1890 without the
help of Brooklyn which contained eight hundred thousand more. Philadelphia attained a million in 1890,
though since the previous census Chicago had supplanted
her as the second city of the United States. Boston, Baltimore and Washington had about half a million each,
Buffalo and Pittsburgh a quarter million each. Countless
smaller places spotted the landscape and gave to the
entire region a strongly urban cast.

In striking contrast were the rural backwaters.
"Sloven farms alternate with vast areas of territory,
half forest, half pasturage;" an observant foreign traveler wrote of Pennsylvania and New England, "farm
buildings, partly in ruins, testify at once to the former
prosperity of the agricultural industry and to its present
collapse." Then, "all at once, on rounding a hill, one
comes upon a busy valley, its slopes dotted with charming cottages, while at the further end rise the immense
blocks of buildings and chimneys that tell of the factory." [1]

The census of 1890 first revealed the extent of the
rural exodus. [2] Two fifths of Pennsylvania, a good quar-

thousand or more inhabitants the urban percentages for the two years
were 43.1 and 51.8. *U. S. Eleventh Census*, I, lxviii.

[1] Paul de Rousiers, *American Life* (A. J. Herbertson, tr., Paris,
1892), 189.

[2] *U. S. Eleventh Census*, I, lxviii-lxxi. See also M. A. Veeder, "Deserted
Farms in New York," *Nation*, XLIX (1889), 431; Clarence Gordon,
"The Revival of Agriculture," same vol., 498-499; J. R. Elliott, *American Farms* (*Questions of the Day Series*, LXII, 2d edn., N. Y., 1890),
46.

ter of New Jersey, nearly five sixths of New York state and much of New England had fallen off in population during the decade. The eclipse of the Eastern countryside had, of course, been long in process, indeed ever since the old farming districts of the Atlantic states first felt the competition of the virgin lands of the interior.[1] After the Civil War the pressure became even greater, for the opening of new railway lines enabled the prairie farmers, with the aid of favoring freight rates, to undersell Eastern farmers in their own natural markets. The normal drain on the older agricultural districts was intensified by the drift of country boys and girls to the towns and cities as industry boomed and the lure of the near-by metropolis captured their imaginations. Far removed from the free lands of the Great West, the rural youth was now less inclined to ask "Where is the fittest farm?" than "Where is the fitter vocation?"

New England was hardest hit of all, especially those parts in which agricultural retrogression was not offset by corresponding urban development. Three fifths of Connecticut, three fourths of Vermont and nearly two thirds of New Hampshire and Maine declined in population. Out of 1502 townships in all New England 932 had fewer people in 1890 than at the start of the decade.[2] Cellar holes choked with lilac and woodbine, tumble-down buildings, scrubby orchards, pastures bristling with new forest growths, perhaps a lone rosebush—these mute, pathetic memorials of once busy farming communities attested the reversal of a familiar

[1] Thus in 1857 Professor J. W. Patterson estimated that that very season had seen an exodus to the West of 300,000 "from the impoverished hillsides and valleys of New England." *Address before the Grafton County Agricultural Society* (Hanover, N. H., 1857), 7.

[2] Josiah Strong, *The New Era* (N. Y., 1893), 167. See also J. D. Long and others, "The Future of the New England Country," *New England Mag.*, n.s., III (1890-1891), 661-673.

historic process, with civilization retreating before the advancing wilderness.

Official inquiries at the end of the eighties revealed more than a thousand farms in Vermont abandoned for agricultural purposes, over thirteen hundred in New Hampshire, nearly fifteen hundred in Massachusetts and more than thirty-three hundred in Maine.[1] Vermont farms with good buildings went begging at five dollars or less an acre. Nor did the upland villages escape the general *debâcle*. "The proportion of abandoned wagon-shops, shoeshops, saw-mills and other mechanical businesses has far outstripped the abandonment of farms," wrote one contemporary.[2] Judge Nott of Washington, D. C., happening upon a stricken village in southern Vermont, found that

> the church was abandoned, the academy dismantled, the village deserted. The farmer who owned the farm on the north of the village lived on one side of the broad street, and he who owned the farm on the south lived on the other, and they were the only inhabitants.

All others had fled—"to the manufacturing villages, to the great cities, to the West." Where once had dwelt "industry, education, religion, comfort, and contentment," there remained "only a drear solitude of forsaken homes."[3]

---

[1] F. H. Fowler, "Abandoned Farms," L. H. Bailey, ed., *Cyclopedia of American Agriculture* (N. Y., 1909), IV, 102-106; Anderson, *Country Town*, 66-69; Elliott, *American Farms*, 42-43, 60-64.

[2] G. F. Wells, "The Status of Rural Vermont," *Twenty-Third Ann. Vt. Agricultural Rep.*, 621.

[3] C. C. Nott, "A Good Farm for Nothing," *Nation*, XLIX (1889), 406. A. F. Sanborn, "The Future of Rural New England," *Atlantic Mo.*, LXXX (1897), 74-83, also presents a striking picture of a decayed town—its outward dilapidation and the emptiness of its inner life. Even more lugubrious is R. L. Hartt, "A New England Hill Town," *Atlantic Mo.*, LXXXIII (1899), 561-574, 712-720.

Generally the people of push and initiative migrated while the less enterprising stayed at home. Thus Yankee energy, though continuing to contribute vitally to the upbuilding of America, did so at a terrible cost to the stock it left behind. Ministers and humanitarian workers in the country districts were appalled by the extent of inbreeding, the prevalence of drunkenness, bastardy and idiocy, the lack of wholesome amusements and the almost universal poverty. In nearly the same words two Congregational preachers reported, "My people are degenerates; the people all through my district are degenerates." [1] It may well be believed that such characterizations applied to the most neglected communities rather than to typical ones. Yet everywhere the process of folk depletion was going on at an alarming rate, lending color to the assertion that New England's woods and templed hills were breeding their own race of poor whites.

Dismayed by the trend of the times, the close of the eighties saw the several state governments engaged in frantic efforts to promote a back-to-the-country movement. Few literate Americans were allowed to remain ignorant of the bargains in land and farm buildings that might be found in New England's rustic parts. Vermont even tried the expedient of colonizing three small groups of Swedish immigrants on deserted tracts. The situation, however, had to grow worse before it could become better. Once the nation-wide agricultural sickness of the early nineties had run its course, rural New England would discover sources of new wealth in dairying, truck gardening, the expansion of wood-working industries

[1] Comments quoted in R. L. Hartt, "Our Rural Degeneracy," *Boston Transcript*, May 17, 1899. On this subject, see also R. L. Hartt, "The Regeneration of Rural New England: Social," *Outlook*, LXIV (1900), 577-583, the article by A. F. Sanborn already cited, Anderson, *Country Town*, chaps. v-vi, and Strong, *New Era*, chap. viii.

based on second forest growths and, last but not least, the rapid development of the summer-boarder business.[1]

Despite the decline of rural population in New England and other parts of the East the attractions of city life were so great that from 1880 to 1890 the section in general gained twenty per cent in number of inhabitants. By the latter year nineteen million, or somewhat less than a third of all the nation, lived there. Urban growth, even more than in Middle America, was nourished by foreign immigration.[2] A larger proportion of the alien arrivals settled in the East and fewer of them took up farming as a livelihood. The census of 1890 disclosed a million more immigrants than a decade earlier. In the section as a whole one out of every five persons was foreign-born.

Nor could one assume, as ten years before, that any immigrant he met was likely to belong to the older racial strains that had fused into the historic American stock. The Eastern commonwealths with their great ports and thriving industries were the first to feel the impact of the new human tide that was setting in from southern and eastern Europe. While in 1890 they contained more Irish and Britons than did any other section—a total of two and a third million—and with nine hundred thousand Germans ranked in that respect next to the Middle West, they also embraced more Italians, Russians and Hungarians than any other section, to the number of a quarter million.

A fourth of the people of Philadelphia and a third

---

[1] F. H. Chase, "Is Agriculture Declining in New England?," *New England Mag.*, n.s., II (1890), 449-452; J. W. Sanborn, "Comparison of Eastern and Western Farming," Mass. State Bd. of Agr., *Forty-Second Ann. Rep., 1894*, 161-218; G. W. Atherton, "The Future of New England Agriculture," Mass. State Bd. of Agr., *Forty-Fourth Ann. Rep., 1896*, 118; Anderson, *Country Town*, 83-85; U. S. Industrial Commission, *Reports* (Wash., 1900-1902), XIX, 116-120.

[2] *U. S. Eleventh Census*, I, cxviii-cxix, clv, 606-609.

of the Bostonians were in 1890 of alien birth. New
York-Brooklyn was the greatest center of immigrants
in the world, having half as many Italians as Naples,
as many Germans as Hamburg, twice as many Irish as
Dublin and two and a half times as many Jews as War-
saw.[1] Four out of every five residents of Greater New
York were foreigners or of foreign parentage. Different
from Boston and Philadelphia, the newer type of immigrant had become a considerable element in the city's
population though the Germans and Irish still greatly
predominated.

These latest arrivals, ignorant, clannish, inured to
wretched living conditions, gravitated naturally to the
poorest quarters of the city toward the tip of Manhattan and gradually pushed the older occupants into the
better sections to the north.[2] Lower New York was like
a human palimpsest, the writings of earlier peoples
being dimmed, though not entirely effaced, by the
heavier print of the newest comers. Through the eighties
the Italians crowded into the old Irish neighborhoods
west of Broadway, while the Russian and Polish Jews
took possession of the German districts to the east with
the tenth ward as their center.[3] The Hungarians settled
thickly east of Avenue B, about Houston Street, and

---

[1] Compared with Chicago, Greater New York in 1890 possessed
more Irish, English, Germans, Russians and Italians, but Chicago had
a larger number of Scandinavians, Bohemians, Poles and Canadians.
Thirty-nine per cent of the population of New York-Brooklyn was
foreign-born in 1890.

[2] Kate H. Claghorn, "The Foreign Immigrant in New York City,"
U. S. Industrial Comn., *Reports*, XV, 465-492. See also J. A. Riis,
*How the Other Half Lives* (N. Y., 1890), chap. iii.

[3] The specialized character of Italian clannishness is shown by the
fact that Neapolitans and Calabrians clung to the Mulberry Bend district, a colony of Genoese lived in Baxter Street, a Sicilian colony in
Elizabeth Street, between Houston and Spring, while north Italians
predominated in the eighth and fifteenth wards west of Broadway, and
south Italians in "Little Italy" between 110th and 115th streets in
Harlem.

the Bohemians near the river on the upper East Side
from about Fiftieth to Seventy-sixth Street. Smaller
groups like the Greeks and Syrians also had their special
precincts where picturesque Old World customs and
trades prevailed; and in the heart of the lower East Side
grew up a small replica of San Francisco's Chinatown.

Quite as strange to Americans as the south Europeans
were the French Canadians who began their mass invasion of New England shortly after 1878. For over
two centuries these descendants of the pioneers of New
France had tilled the soil of the province of Quebec
where, intensely race-conscious and devoted to Catholicism, they had stubbornly maintained their identity and
language apart from the conquering English. Harried,
however, by hard times from the 1860's on and tempted
by better opportunities elsewhere, many of them sought
escape in migration.[1] Some moved westward to set up
farm colonies in Ontario and Manitoba. Others, feeling
the pull of the busy mill towns across the international
border, succumbed to le mal des États-Unis. Presently
the trickle of population into New England became a
flooding stream. About fourteen thousand had removed
to Rhode Island by 1875, sixty-four thousand to Massachusetts ten years later. Northern New England made
less appeal though occasional settlements of farmers and
lumberjacks were to be found. By 1890 the French
Canadians, then numbering two hundred thousand,
formed approximately a sixth of the entire immigrant
population of New England.[2] Nearly half of them were
in Massachusetts.

[1] D. M. A. Magnan, Histoire de la Race Française aux États-Unis
(Paris, 1912), 250; Alexandre Beslisle, Histoire de la Presse Franco-
Américaine (Worcester, 1911), 4-9.

[2] Before 1890, when the federal enumerators (Eleventh Census, I,
clxxiii-clxxv) first took cognizance of French Canadians as distinguished
from Anglo-Canadians, statistics of settlement must be based on state
census reports.

Hiving in the manufacturing towns, they were eagerly welcomed by employers who found them not only hard workers but also slow to give trouble even when conditions were galling. The opprobrium of being the "Chinese of the Eastern states," however, they scarcely deserved, although their ready acceptance of low living standards naturally roused the ire of organized labor.[1] Religiously, too, they were viewed askance by the older elements. Added to the already large Irish Catholic contingent, their presence seemed to threaten the traditional Puritan and Protestant character of the section. "Protestant New England will soon have within itself, a Roman Catholic New France, as large as, if not larger than itself," cried one alarmist.[2] As a matter of fact, the language barrier and the desire of the newcomers to import their own priests caused more friction than friendship between them and the resident Irish-American clergy.[3] It was said that French-Canadian support of the Republican party at the polls was due to no reason so good as that the Irish preferred the Democrats.

A race so resistant could hardly be expected to adopt new ways of life overnight. Yet, scattered in a hundred different communities and obliged constantly to rub elbows with people unlike themselves, the chemistry of Americanization worked as quickly with them as with most other alien groups. Intermarriage, while not com-

---

[1] Massachusetts Bureau of Labor Statistics, *Twelfth Annual Report* (1881), 469. This document should be read in the light of the record of the public hearings held in 1882. See *Thirteenth Ann. Rep.* (1882), 3-92.

[2] C. E. Amaron, *Your Heritage; or New England Threatened* (Springfield, Mass., 1891), 116.

[3] Édouard Hamon, *Les Canadiens-Français de la Nouvelle-Angleterre* (Quebec, 1891), 57, 60, 175; Magnan, *Histoire*, 255-261, 266, 273-274, 296-297; Prosper Bender, "A New France in New England," *Mag. of Am. History*, XX (1888), 391.

mon, took place most readily with Anglo-Canadians.[1]
Less adept politically than the Irish, they nevertheless
gradually found their way into local offices and by 1890
thirteen French Canadians were members of New England legislatures.[2] Different from other immigrant peoples, however, they massed themselves in New England,
few of them going into the Middle West or even into
other parts of the East.

As a lodestone for both immigrant and native-born
the city had decisively placed the East under thrall. Its
hand already lay heavily upon the Middle West. Even
in the farther West and the South its power and distant
allure were strongly felt though society as yet lingered
in an agricultural state. Through the nation in general
every third American in 1890 was an urban dweller,
living in a town of four thousand or more inhabitants.[3]
Cities of from twelve to twenty thousand people had
since 1880 increased in number from 76 to 107; cities
of from twenty to forty thousand from 55 to 91;
larger places up to seventy-five thousand inhabitants
from 21 to 35; cities of yet greater size from 23 to 39.[4]

Moreover, the concentration of population had been
attended by a significant concentration of wealth. This
latter circumstance furnished ample basis for the agrarian contention that the rural districts were not sharing
proportionately in the advancing national wealth. In
1880, according to the census, the value of farms was
equal to that of urban real estate, about ten billion dollars for each. In 1890 the value of farms was returned
as thirteen billion while other real estate—mostly urban

[1] *U. S. Eleventh Census*, I, 698-701; *U. S. Twelfth Census*, I, 850-
853; *Mass. Census of 1895*, III, 152-154.
[2] Adélard Desrosiers and P. A. Fournet, *La Race Française en Amérique*
(Montreal, 1910), 240.
[3] *U. S. Twelfth Census*, I, lxxxiv-lxxxv.
[4] *U. S. Eleventh Census*, I, lxvii.

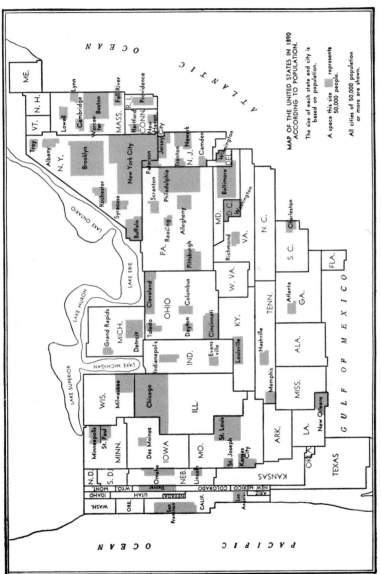

MAP OF THE UNITED STATES IN 1890
ACCORDING TO POPULATION.

The size of each state and city is based on population.

A space this size ▪ represents 50,000 people.

All cities of 50,000 population or more are shown.

*The Populous States in 1890*

—was listed at twenty-six billion. Nor did the people on the farms and in the rural hamlets of the East fare better than those of the West and South. On the contrary, the farms in the Eastern states declined in absolute value during the decade.

If personalty were included, the contrast between city and country became even sharper, particularly since the tangible personalty on the farms was in considerable degree offset by mortgages held in the towns and cities. The most careful contemporary student of the subject estimated that in 1890 the average wealth of families in the rural districts did not exceed $3250 while the average wealth of city families was over $9000.[1] The wider implications of urban growth, however, reached far beyond exigent considerations of wealth and income. These, as they affected the character of American civilization for good or ill, remain yet to be examined.

[1] The data for the above discussion are derived from C. B. Spahr, *An Essay on the Present Distribution of Wealth in the United States* (N. Y., 1896), 46-49, which concludes the passage with the observation: "When American political parties shall again divide upon issues vitally affecting the distribution of wealth, the clearly marked line of division will not be between East and West, but between city and country."

# CHAPTER IV

## THE URBAN WORLD

THE clash of country and city was not a phenomenon peculiar to America. All over the civilized globe the rural regions lay under a cloud—in Great Britain, France, Germany, Russia, Italy, Belgium.[1] The introduction of farm machinery and the opening up of virgin fields in the Argentine and Australia, added to those of the new American West, rendered unprofitable much of the agricultural labor of the Old World, stirred rural conservatism into fierce discontent and enhanced the attractions of the near-by city for the peasant toilers. Everywhere there was an exodus from the soil while the trading and industrial centers waxed by leaps and bounds. Between 1881 and 1891 Prussia added two million to her cities while her countryside barely increased a half million; rural France lost a half million at the same time that her urban places gained well over a million; the rural population of England and Wales declined over two hundred thousand while the towns and cities advanced by three and a quarter million.[2] By 1891 London and Paris had doubled their population of mid-century and Berlin had more than quadrupled hers.

From earliest times the painful, upward march of mankind had beaten a path through the streets of the town. The cities, not the country districts, had been—

[1] See the authorities cited by A. F. Weber, *The Growth of Cities in the Nineteenth Century* (Columbia Univ., *Studies*, XI), 210-211 *n*.
[2] Weber, *Growth of Cities*, 46, 68, 73, 82, 84.

in Theodore Parker's phrase—"the fireplaces of civilization whence light and heat radiated out into the dark cold world." Memphis, Thebes, Nineveh, Babylon, were the great capitals of early civilized man. In Greek and Roman times the city was the state itself. The revival of a vigorous urban life in the eleventh century, along the shores of the Mediterranean and in northern Germany, hastened the breakdown of feudalism and paved the way for the Renaissance and modern times. Unregarded by all but etymologists, the age-long contrast between city and country survives in the very language we speak—that language which townsmen coined with such glib facility. The well-mannered *civis* living in *urbs* was, for that reason, civil and urbane as well as civic and urban; his manner of life was epitomized in the very word, civilization. His rude rural neighbor, on the other hand, was a pagan or a rustic (from the Latin words, *paganus* and *rusticus,* for peasant), a boor (from the Dutch *boer,* a farmer), or a heathen (that is, a dweller on the heaths).

In America in the eighties urbanization for the first time became a controlling factor in national life.[1] Just as the plantation was the typical product of the *antebellum* Southern system and the small farm of the Northern agricultural order, so the city was the supreme achievement of the new industrialism. In its confines were focused all the new economic forces: the vast accumulations of capital, the business and financial institutions, the spreading railway yards, the gaunt smoky mills, the white-collar middle classes, the motley wage-earning population. By the same token the city inevitably became the generating center for social and

[1] For a contemporary appreciation of the dynamic rôle of the city, see F. J. Kingsbury, "The Tendency of Men to Live in Cities," *Journ. of Social Sci.,* XXXIII (1895), 1-19.

intellectual progress. To dwell in the midst of great affairs is stimulating and broadening; it is the source of a discontent which, if not divine, is at least energizing. In a populous urban community like could find like; the person of ability, starved in his rural isolation, might by going there find sympathy, encouragement and that criticism which often refines talent into genius.

Moreover the new social needs created by crowded living stimulated inventors to devise mechanical remedies—appliances for better lighting, for faster communication and transit, for higher buildings—which reacted in a thousand ways on the life of urban folk. Density of population plus wealth concentration also facilitated organized effort for cultivating the life of mind and spirit.[1] In the city were to be found the best schools, the best churches, the best newspapers, and virtually all the bookstores, libraries, art galleries, museums, theaters and opera houses. It is not surprising that the great cultural advances of the time came out of the city, or that its influence should ramify to the farthest countryside.

As the cradle of progress the city, in some manner or other, seemed to favor persons born within its walls over those born on the farm. One investigator, basing his conclusions on *Who's Who in America*, found that towns of eight thousand and more people produced nearly twice as many men of distinction as their numerical importance warranted.[2] A study of the antecedents

---

[1] U. S. Commissioner of Education, *Report for 1894-95*, I, 3-8.

[2] The names under the first five letters of the alphabet in *Who's Who* for 1908-1909 were analyzed. F. A. Woods, "City Boys versus Country Boys," *Science*, n.s., XXIX, 577-579. For similar conclusions, see S. S. Visher, *Geography of American Notables* (Indiana Univ., *Studies*, XV, no. 79), esp. pt. v; and R. H. Holmes, "A Study in the Origins of Distinguished Living Americans," *Am. Journ. of Sociology*, XXXIV, 670-685. Alfred Odin, *Genèse des Grands Hommes* (Paris, 1895), made a study of over six thousand French men of letters during five centuries

of leading American scientific men disclosed that a dis-
proportionate number of these were likewise of city
birth. "The main factors in producing scientific and
other forms of intellectual performance," concluded
the investigator, "seem to be density of population,
wealth, opportunity, and institutions and social traditions and ideals." [1]

But the heirs of the older American tradition did not
yield the field without a struggle. To them, as to Jefferson, cities were "ulcers on the body politic." In their
eyes the city spiritual was offset by the city sinister,
civic splendor by civic squalor, urban virtues by urban
vices, the city of light by the city of darkness. In politics they sought to preserve or restore their birthright
of equality by stoutly belaboring their capitalistic foe
embattled in his city fortress; but against the pervasive
lure of metropolitan life, felt by their sons and daughters, they could do no better than invent sensational
variations of the nursery tale of the country mouse and
the city mouse. Urban growth evoked a voluminous
literature of bucolic fear, typified by such titles as *The
Spider and the Fly; or, Tricks, Traps, and Pitfalls of
City Life by One Who Knows* (N. Y., 1873) and J. W.
Buel's *Metropolitan Life Unveiled; or the Mysteries and
Miseries of America's Great Cities* (St. Louis, 1882).
It may be questioned, however, whether such exciting
accounts with their smudgy but realistic pictures did
more to repel than entice their breathless readers to
partake of the life they depicted.

To traveled persons familiar with the distinctive personalities of European centers American cities presented

and found that the cities produced thirteen times as many in proportion
to population as the rural districts.

[1] J. M. Cattell, "A Statistical Study of American Men of Science:
III. The Distribution of American Men of Science," *Science*, n.s., XXIV,
esp. 735.

a monotonous sameness. Apart from New York, Boston, Washington, New Orleans and a few other places Bryce believed that "American cities differ from one another only herein, that some of them are built more with brick than with wood, and others more with wood than brick." [1] Most places possessed the same checkerboard arrangement of streets lined with shade trees, the same shops grouped in much the same way, the same middle-class folk hurrying about their business, the same succession of unsightly telegraph poles, the same hotels with seedy men lounging in the dreary lobbies. Few foreign visitors stopped to think, however, that American cities were the handiwork not of many national states but of a fairly uniform continent-wide culture. If they lacked the colorful variety of ancient European foundations, they also lacked the physical inconveniences and discomforts which picturesqueness was apt to entail. But it could not be gainsaid that a tendency toward standardization, as well as toward higher standards, was one of the fruits of American urban development.

While in the European sense there was no single dominant city in America—no city both metropolis and capital—yet all agreed in according the foremost position to New York. Nowhere else were there such fine buildings, such imposing financial houses, such unusual opportunities for business and recreation. No other place had such an air of rush and bustle, the streets constantly being torn up, dug up or blown up. To New York an unending stream of visitors discovered some pretext to go each year; in it many foreign travelers, going no further, found material for pithy, if ill-informed, com-

---

[1] James Bryce, *The American Commonwealth* (London, 1888), III, 621. See also E. Catherine Bates, *A Year in the Great Republic* (London, 1887), I, 248, and Paul Blouët (Max O'Rell, *pseud.*), *A Frenchman in America* (N. Y., 1891), 244-245.

ments on the whole American scene. "The streets are narrow," wrote one observer in 1883, "and overshadowed as they are by edifices six or more stories in height, seem to be dwarfed into mere alley-ways." [1] At that time the well-populated district did not extend much beyond Fifty-ninth Street; and Madison Square at the intersection of Broadway and Fifth Avenue had recently supplanted Union Square as the nerve center of New York life. But the period of growth and expansion was at hand. The corporate limits, which before 1874 had not reached beyond Manhattan Island, spread rapidly until in 1898, as Greater New York, they embraced Bronx County, Kings County (Brooklyn), Richmond County (Staten Island), and a portion of Queens County (on Long Island).

As earlier, Broadway was the main artery of New York life, lending itself successively to wholesale trade, newspaper and magazine publishing, retail shopping, hotels and theaters, as it wended its way northward from the Battery. Manhattan's other famous thoroughfare, Fifth Avenue, offered a continuous pageant of "palatial hotels, gorgeous club-houses, brownstone mansions and magnificent churches." [2] Different from most American cities, the finest residences stood side by side without relief of lawn or shrubbery; only on the striking but as yet unfinished Riverside Drive, with its noble view of the Hudson, was architecture assisted by nature.

[1] Willard Glazier, *Peculiarities of American Cities* (Phila., 1883), 290. On New York, see also Paul de Rousiers, *American Life* (A. J. Herbertson, tr., Paris, 1892), chap. xiii; W. G. Marshall, *Through America* (London, 1881), chap. i; G. J. Holyoake, *Among the Americans* (Chicago, 1881), chap. ii; G. A. Sala, *America Revisited* (London, 1883), I, chaps. ii-vi; S. R. Hole, *A Little Tour in America* (N. Y., 1895), chaps. iv-vi.

[2] Glazier, *Peculiarities of American Cities*, 301; J. F. Muirhead, *The Land of Contrasts* (N. Y., 1898), 193-197; H. C. Brown, *In the Golden Nineties* (*Valentine's Manual of Old New York*, XII, Hastings-on-Hudson, 1927), 25-48.

Merchant princes and Wall Street millionaires vied with one another to sustain Fifth Avenue's reputation of being the most splendid thoroughfare in America, "a very alderman among streets." During the 1880's a dark brown tide swept up the avenue. The late A. T. Stewart's marble palace at the corner of Thirty-fourth Street, long a magnet for sightseers, was eclipsed by the newer brownstone mansions of the Vanderbilts and others farther up the avenue, inclosed by forbidding iron fences. In the late afternoon Fifth Avenue churned with "a torrent of equipages, returning from the races or the park: broughams, landaus, clarences, phætons, . . . equestrians in boots and corduroys, slim-waisted equestriennes with blue veils floating from tall silk hats." [1]

Yet New York was a city of contradictions, reminding one visitor of "a lady in ball costume, with diamonds in her ears, and her toes out at her boots." [2] Against the splendors of Fifth Avenue and the show places of the metropolis had to be set the rocky wastes of Shantytown, extending during the 1880's along the East Side from Forty-second to One Hundred and Tenth Street and inhabited by Irish squatters, goats and pigs living promiscuously together. Contrasting with the pillared citadels of wealth in Wall Street was the near-by slum section, a festering spot of poverty and immorality, finding a tawdry outlet for its life in the notorious Bowery. [3]

The New Yorker was already famed for his provincialism: his proud ignorance of the rest of the nation

[1] Raymond Westbrook, "Open Letters from New York," *Atlantic Mo.*, XLI (1878), 92.

[2] Muirhead, *Land of Contrasts*, 193.

[3] H. C. Brown, *New York in the Elegant Eighties* (*Valentine's Manual of Old New York*, XI, Hastings-on-Hudson, 1926), 11-16; anon., "Along the Bowery, When Vice Stalked Openly," *Police Gazette*, Nov. 29, 1930.

and lofty condescension toward cities of lesser note.[1]
Yet foreign tourists found much to interest and detain
them in these other centers, and at least one felt a native
New Yorker to be "less American than many Westerners
born on the banks of the Oder or on the shores of some
Scandinavian *fjord.*" [2] Boston charmed with the quiet
tenor of her life, her atmosphere of intellectuality, her
generally English appearance.[3] With the reclamation of
the Back Bay, a great engineering project completed in
1881, the city acquired over a hundred acres of filled
land which made possible its expansion southward and
the development of straight, wide thoroughfares to
Copley Square and beyond.

Even more than Boston, Philadelphia impressed her
visitors as a city of homes, with row upon row of prim
brick houses with white wooden shutters, owned by
their occupants. "If there are few notable buildings,
there are few slums." [4] In Washington the traveler
found America's most beautiful city, "one of the most
singularly handsome cities on the globe." [5] Its parks and
wide shaded avenues, its spacious vistas, the dazzling
white of its public edifices, were reminiscent of great
European capitals. In the absence of an army of factory

---

[1] This attitude was one of the certain symptoms of *Newyorkitis,* a malady amusingly described by J. H. Girdner in a small volume so titled (N. Y., 1901).

[2] Rousiers, *American Life,* 242.

[3] See Emily Faithfull, *Three Visits to America* (Edinburgh, 1884), chap. viii; G. W. Steevens, *The Land of the Dollar* (N. Y., 1897), 50-53; O'Rell, *Frenchman in America,* chaps. xvi-xvii.

[4] Steevens, *Land of the Dollar,* 115-116. See also Rousiers, *American Life,* 209-214, and Ephraim Turland, *Notes on a Visit to America* (Manchester, 1877), 21.

[5] Muirhead, *Land of Contrasts,* 218. See also H. L. Nelson, "Social Washington," *Atlantic Mo.,* LII (1883), 818-825; Hole, *Tour in America,* chap. xxi; Paul Blouët (Max O'Rell, *pseud.*) and Jack Allyn, *Jonathan and His Continent* (Madame Paul Blouët, tr., N. Y., 1889), 39-42; A. M. Low, "Washington: the City of Leisure," *Atlantic Mo.,* LXXXVI (1900), 767-778.

workers the general tone was one of dignified ease in pleasing contrast to the feverish anxiety typical of other cities. "The inhabitants do not rush onward as though they were late for the train . . . or as though the dinner-hour being past they were anxious to appease an irritable wife . . . ." [1]

Farther to the west lay Chicago, "the most American of American cities, and yet the most mongrel," a miracle city risen Phœnix-like from its great fire of 1871. [2] Its business and shopping district, rivaling New York's in high buildings, noise and impressiveness, was fringed by three residential areas: the north side, its broad streets lined with handsome abodes, churches and club houses overlooking the lake; the south side, a newer and hardly less aristocratic section, studded with stately mansions and spacious parks; and the vast west side, more populous than the other two combined, where dwelt the immigrants and laboring folk. Like every other great city, Chicago offered a study in contrasts: squalor matching splendor, municipal boodle contending with civic spirit; the very air now reeking with the foul stench of the stockyards, now fresh-blown from prairie or lake. A "splendid chaos" indeed, causing the roving Kipling to exclaim, "Having seen it, I urgently desire never to see it again." [3]

No better example could be found of what one contemporary called "urban imperialism." The surrounding prairie was for miles laced with railroads, and a

[1] Hole, *Tour in America*, 246.

[2] Steevens, *Land of the Dollar*, 144-145. See also Finlay Dun, *American Farming and Food* (London, 1881), chap. xii; William Archer, *America To-day* (N. Y., 1899), chap. ix; Hole, *Tour in America*, chap. xviii; Marshall, *Through America*, chap. iv; Sala, *America Revisited*, II, chap. ix; C. D. Warner, *Studies in the South and West* (N. Y., 1889), 184-186, 200-201; Glazier, *Peculiarities of American Cities*, chap. ix.

[3] Rudyard Kipling, *American Notes* (Boston, 1899), esp. 91.

large portion of the city and its suburbs was made up
of a series of huge stations, car yards, grain elevators,
cattle pens and storehouses. As the world's greatest corn,
cattle and timber market Chicago completely dominated
the Mississippi Valley and, to some degree, the farther
West as well. Other places like Milwaukee, Kansas City,
Detroit and the Twin Cities rose and flourished largely
by its sufferance or favor. Even the older *entrepôts*—
Cincinnati, St. Louis, New Orleans—lay under tribute
to the Lake city, and Denver and San Francisco were
not too remote to escape its influence.[1] Yet these and
other cities had their own economic and cultural spheres
of influence, and astonished Europeans found in them
a level of material comfort typical only of the principal
foreign centers.

Certain problems growing out of crowded living conditions vexed all municipalities, differing among them
in degree rather than in kind. None was more important
in 1878 than that of adequate traffic facilities. Even in
the major cities streets were ill paved, if paved at all,
and in the business sections were apt to be choked with
rushing, jostling humanity. "The visitor is kept dodging, halting and shuffling to avoid the passing throng
. . . ," asserted one timid contemporary. "The confusing rattle of 'busses and wagons over the granite pavement in Broadway almost drowns his own
thoughts, and if he should desire to cross the street a
thousand misgivings will assail him . . . although he
sees scores of men and women constantly passing through
the moving line of vehicles . . . ." [2] Cobblestones and

[1] A Chicagoan of these times, being asked his opinion of New York,
which he had just visited, replied, "Wal, I guess it's too far away from
Chicago to do any partic'lar amount of business!" Marshall, *Through
America,* 103.

[2] J. W. Buel, *Metropolitan Life Unveiled* (St. Louis, 1882), 26.
For similar reactions, see Rousiers, *American Life,* 240; Hole, *Tour in
America,* 43-45; Marshall, *Through America,* 7.

granite blocks were the favorite paving materials in the East because of their local availability, just as wood blocks were in the Middle West.

But streets so constructed soon wore rough and uneven, and the eighties marked an era of experimentation with more satisfactory types of surfacing.[1] The discovery of natural beds of pitch on the Island of Trinidad directed attention to asphalt, already widely used in Paris and London. When Washington laid four hundred thousand square yards of it between 1878 and 1882, that city set a pace soon followed by Buffalo, Philadelphia and other places. By 1898 the United States possessed nearly thirty million square yards of asphalt paving. The imported material, however, was rivaled by a native product, brick. Charleston, West Virginia, and Bloomington, Illinois, had tried it in the previous decade, but it was not until the mid-eighties that it came into general use, notably in the Middle West. By 1898 Des Moines, Columbus and Cleveland stood first in the proportion of brick paving to population, though Philadelphia with its two million square yards had more than any other one city. In most cities macadam, a much cheaper material, was deemed sufficiently durable for residential and suburban roadways. Smaller towns contented themselves with dirt or gravel.

In the twenty years the streets of America were greatly improved, though the civic conscience did not regard it essential that good streets should be kept clean.[2]

[1] G. W. Tillson, *Street Pavements and Paving Materials* (N. Y., 1900), chaps. ix-x; N. P. Lewis, "Modern City Roadways," *Pop. Sci. Mo.,* LVI (1899-1900), 524-539.

[2] European cities were far ahead in the cleanliness of their streets. Emmons Clark, "Street-Cleaning in Large Cities," *Pop. Sci. Mo.,* XXXVIII (1890-1891), 748-755. However, in 1895-1898, when Colonel Waring was commissioner of street cleaning in New York under the anti-Tammany administration, he actually kept the streets clean and set an example for other American cities. Among other things, he dressed the street sweepers in white, from which the term, "white wings,"

By the end of the century Washington and Buffalo had become the best-paved cities in the world while Boston and the borough of Manhattan in New York were not far behind.[1] Chicago remained the Cinderella of great American municipalities, closely rivaled by Baltimore. In 1890 only 629 of Chicago's 2048 miles of streets were paved at all, about half with wood block, the rest with macadam, gravel, stone block, asphalt, cinders or cobblestones. Despite the civic lift given by the World's Fair of 1893 the situation was but little better at the close of the decade.

Since most large cities were intersected by waterways, the needs of rapidly growing municipalities required an adequate system of bridges. The problem appeared in its most acute form in New York where hordes of people must cross over each day to their places of work on Manhattan Island. After thirteen years in course of construction, a great bridge connecting New York with Brooklyn was completed in 1883. Its designer, John A. Roebling, had died from an injury before the work had more than started, leaving the actual construction to be directed by his son, Colonel Washington A. Roebling, who worked out the details as the enterprise proceeded.[2] All the riveting of steel in the structure was done by hand, pneumatic tools and compressed air being as yet unknown. Falling ill from overwork in December, 1872, Colonel Roebling supervised the operations from a wheel chair on the roof of his home, directing the progress with field glasses as a general might a battle.

When finished, Brooklyn Bridge was the longest suspension bridge in the world. The formal opening on

---

derives. G. E. Waring, *Street-Cleaning* (N. Y., 1897), chaps. i-v; Charles Zueblin, *American Municipal Progress* (N. Y., 1902), 78-81.

[1] J. A. Fairlie, *Municipal Administration* (N. Y., 1901), 234-235.

[2] Allan Nevins, *The Emergence of Modern America* (*A History of American Life*, VIII), 80; *N. Y. Times*, May 24, 1883.

May 24 was attended by President Arthur and his cabinet, the governors of near-by states and many other distinguished persons. The only discordant note in the chorus of rejoicing came from Hibernian New Yorkers who denounced the choice of Queen Victoria's birthday for the grand occasion. Majestic in the sweep of its great cables from tower to tower, the completed structure was over a mile long, with a central river span of nearly sixteen hundred feet and a passageway wide enough for two rail lines, two double carriage lanes and a footpath.

Though the traffic relief was considerable it was not sufficient. Between 1886 and 1889 Washington Bridge was built over the Harlem River, its two great steel arches each over five hundred feet in span. and in 1896 a second bridge, the Williamsburg, was begun to link Brooklyn and New York.[1] Other cities wrestled with the same problem. Thus Pittsburgh built the Seventh Street suspension bridge over the Allegheny River in 1884, Philadelphia completed a cantilever bridge carrying Market Street over the Schuylkill two years later, and Richmond, Indiana, spanned the Whitewater River with a suspension bridge in 1889.[2]

Horse cars, omnibuses, cabs and other similar vehicles had suited the needs of simpler days, but the age of the great city called for swifter conveyance. The old "bobtail" cars, modeled on the stagecoach and pulled by horses or mules, did not suffice for moving an enormous mass of people to and from their places of work at about the same hours of the day. Already New York had shown the utility of an overhead railway, four-car trains being drawn by diminutive steam locomotives

[1] Anon., "The New East River Bridge," *Scientific Am.*, LXXV (1896), 213, 218.

[2] For these and many other examples, see H. G. Tyrrell, *History of Bridge Engineering* (Chicago, 1911), chaps. xii-xiii.

which scattered oil and live ashes on the heads of unwary pedestrians.[1] In 1878 a second unit, the Sixth Avenue Elevated, extending nearly the length of the island, was added to the original line. The "L" three years later was transporting one hundred and seventy-five thousand passengers daily or, if you prefer, "12,000 tons of human flesh, averaging each person at 140 lbs."[2] Under the spur of faster transit population spread rapidly northward. New lines were projected and built, reaching beyond the Harlem River into the northern suburban districts.[3] Kansas City also elevated some of her tracks in the mid-eighties and Brooklyn built an extensive system the same decade. But Chicago did not open her first line until 1892, and Boston, which meantime had begun to burrow underground, not until 1901.

The slow adoption of the overhead system was due partly to its ugliness and noise, but even more to the initial cost of construction. Of greater popularity in the eighties was the cable car, first contrived by a Scotch immigrant, Andrew S. Hallidie, in 1873 to solve the problem of transit over the hilly streets of San Francisco. The car moved by means of a grappling device which descended from the floor to an endless steel cable moving in a slotted trench between the tracks.[4] After a few years the system was taken over by cities which lacked San Francisco's peculiar need. In 1882 Charles T. Yerkes laid a cable road in Chicago, achieving not only a success for the city but a fortune for himself. Philadelphia followed the next year and New York in 1886.

[1] Nevins, *Emergence of Modern America*, 82.

[2] Marshall, *Through America*, 26. At the formal opening the trip from Trinity Church to Central Park took twenty-two minutes. *N. Y. Tribune*, May 1, 1878.

[3] Bureau of the Census, *Street and Electric Railways, 1902* (*Special Rep.*), 36.

[4] *Appletons' Annual Cyclopaedia*, XXVI (1886), 122-125, gives a technical description.

By the mid-nineties Eastern cities had one hundred and fifty-seven miles in operation, the Middle West two hundred and fifty-two, the Far West two hundred and seventeen and the South six.[1] While the cable system was yet in its heyday, this generation made its most substantial contribution toward solving the problem of urban transit. For many years— at least since 1835—inventors in America and abroad had been working on the idea of an electrical railway. Until the development of a practicable dynamo in the 1870's, however, they had been baffled by the lack of an adequate supply of cheap current. The 1880's saw the launching of trial lines at points as far removed as Boston and Denver,[2] but the credit for the first American electric railway successfully operated for profit over city streets belongs to Lieutenant Frank J. Sprague. In 1887-1888 he installed two and a half miles of track in Richmond, Virginia, the cars securing their current from an overhead trolley wire fed from a central power house.

Its instant success started a veritable revolution in urban transit. Not only were electric-propelled cars fast and comfortable but they were relatively cheap to construct and maintain. Fifty-one cities installed the new system by 1890, and five years later eight hundred and fifty lines were in operation, mostly in the East and Middle West, with a total mileage of ten thousand.[3]

[1] H. H. Vreeland, "The Street Railways of America," C. M. Depew, ed., *One Hundred Years of American Commerce* (N. Y., 1895), I, 141-143.

[2] By T. A. Edison at Menlo Park, C. J. Van Depoele in Chicago and elsewhere, Leo Daft in Boston and elsewhere, E. M. Bentley and W. H. Knight in Cleveland, J. C. Henry in Kansas City (where the term, trolley, probably originated), S. H. Short in Denver, and by others. Germany really led the way, Berlin having constructed a line in 1867 on the third-rail principle. T. C. Martin, "History and Development of Electric Traction," *Street and Electric Railways, 1902*, 160-167.

[3] Anon., "A Retrospect of the Year 1895," *Scientific Am.*, LXXIV (1896), 2; Vreeland, "Street Railways," 144. Steps were also taken

Though horse and cable cars lingered on many streets, their doom was sealed. European cities lagged far behind those of America in adopting electric transit. At the close of the century Germany, with a trackage as great as all other European countries combined, possessed only one ninth the mileage of the United States.[1]

Traffic congestion, however, kept even pace with the new facilities for dealing with it. The tangled situation in down-town Boston, whose narrow crooked streets exemplified the old adage that one good turn deserves another, led to the final effort of this generation. Taking a leaf from the experience of London and Budapest, Boston between 1895 and 1897 constructed a subway line a mile and a half long under Tremont Street.[2] It was a notable engineering feat costing the city four and a quarter million dollars. Plans were at once made for extensions, and New York, as was fitting, projected a much more ambitious tunnel system which, however, did not open to the public until 1904.[3] Except for these last two instances, the varied and heroic endeavors made during these twenty years to clear the city streets were all carried out under private auspices.

Hardly less urgent than the need for better transit was the need for readier communication. In 1878 the recently invented telephone was hardly more than a scientific toy.[4] To use it a person, after briskly turning a crank, screamed into a crude mouthpiece and then, if

to electrify the elevated systems, though New York did not do so until 1901-1903. For an explanation, see Brown, *New York in Elegant Eighties*, 16-17.

[1] Fairlie, *Municipal Administration*, 296.

[2] *Street and Electric Railways, 1902*, 37-39.

[3] J. B. Walker, *Fifty Years of Rapid Transit* (N. Y., 1918), chaps. xii-xiii.

[4] Nevins, *Emergence of Modern America*, 88-89; G. M. Shaw, "The Telephone and How It Works," *Pop. Sci. Mo.*, XII (1877-1878), 559-569.

the satanic screechings and groanings of static permitted, faintly heard the return message. There was no central exchange station, telephone users being directly connected with one another by separate wires. Besides these disadvantages the sheer novelty of Bell's miracle made it unpopular. People felt "a sense of oddity, almost of foolishness," in using the instrument. "The dignity of talking consists in having a listener and there seems a kind of absurdity in addressing a piece of iron . . . ."[1] For a number of years Bell traveled about the country exhibiting his invention. On one such trip he offered Mark Twain stock in the enterprise at twenty-five, but that usually gullible humorist "didn't want it at any price," though before the year was out he put up the first telephone wire in Hartford, Connecticut, connecting his home with the *Courant* office.[2]

As population centers grew, social and business needs caused the telephone to be perfected rapidly and made the public forget its earlier prejudices. An important obstacle to success was removed in 1879 when the Western Union Telegraph Company, which had bitterly fought the Bell group by fair means and foul, came to terms and sold out its own telephone interests to the Bell Company.[3] Had the Western Union been able to invalidate Bell's claims as prior inventor before the courts, it is almost certain that the development of the telephone would have been sacrificed to that of the telegraph and hence its extension greatly retarded. Under the circumstances, however, mechanical improvements

[1] Edit., "Some Teachings of the Telephone," *Pop. Sci. Mo.*, XII (1877-1878), 626.

[2] He believed it was "the *first* one that was ever used in a private house in the world." A. B. Paine, *Mark Twain* (N. Y., 1912), II, 726.

[3] A. B. Paine, *In One Man's Life* (N. Y., 1921), chap. xxiii; Bureau of the Census, *Telephones and Telegraphs, 1902* (*Special Rep.*), 66-67; J. W. Stehman, *The Financial History of the American Telephone and Telegraph Company* (Boston, 1925), 13-18.

quickly ensued.[1] Francis Blake's invention of a carbon transmitter in 1878, an advance over Emile Berliner's and Edison's devices of the year before, greatly improved the carrying qualities of the voice. Five years later another young man, J. J. Carty, exorcised the mysterious noises of the wires by a simple mechanical arrangement known as the metallic-circuit system.

Hardly less important was the contriving of a central switchboard, the work principally of George W. Coy who installed the first commercial board at New Haven, Connecticut, in January, 1878, for the use of twenty-one subscribers.[2] When L. B. Firman followed in 1879 with the invention of a multiple switchboard, the nerve center of the telephone was complete. At first boys were employed at "central," but being addicted to fighting one another and swearing at their unseen customers, they were soon superseded by girls who thus found a new vocation.[3]

The rapid expansion of the Bell system owed much to the business genius of Theodore N. Vail, general manager of the company from 1878 to 1885. Grandnephew of Stephen Vail, who had built the engines for the first transatlantic steamship, and a cousin of Alfred Vail, who had worked with Morse on the telegraph, young Vail came naturally by his interest in the latest mechanical marvel. He threw himself into the work with boundless enthusiasm, overcoming innumerable obstacles

[1] H. N. Casson, *The History of the Telephone* (Chicago, 1910), 118-125; E. W. Byrn, *The Progress of Invention in the Nineteenth Century* (N. Y., 1900), 82-85; Paine, *One Man's Life*, 161-162.

[2] Other exchanges, established the same year, were Meriden, Connecticut, San Francisco, Albany, Chicago, Wilmington, Delaware, St. Louis, Detroit and Philadelphia. Casson, *History of the Telephone*, 143-147; anon., *Things Worth Knowing about the Telephone* (N. Y., 1929), 43.

[3] Casson, *History of the Telephone*, 153-155; Katherine M. Schmitt, "I Was Your Old 'Hello' Girl," *Sat. Eve. Post*, CCV, 18 ff. (July 12, 1930).

and in the end making the telephone an indispensable adjunct to every business house.[1] By insisting that equipment should be uniform and leased, not sold, to the subscriber, he saved the United States from the chaos which exists in certain other countries, notably France, where each customer buys his own instrument from a selection of about forty different varieties.

In 1880 eighty-five towns had telephone exchanges with nearly fifty thousand subscribers and about thirty-five thousand miles of wire. Ten years later the number of subscribers had grown fivefold and the wire mileage sevenfold.[2] From the first intercity line joining Boston and Lowell in 1879, the reach of the telephone grew constantly greater until by 1892 Boston and New York were talking with Washington, Pittsburgh, Chicago and Milwaukee and a few years later with Omaha.[3] As presidential candidate McKinley sat in his home at Canton, Ohio, and talked with his campaign managers in thirty-eight states. When in 1893 the patents owned by the Bell Company expired, many independent companies sprang up, especially in the smaller towns of the Middle West where the Bell system had not found it worth while to extend its service.[4]

Nearly eight hundred thousand phones were in use by 1900, one for every ninety-five persons as compared with one for every nine hundred and twenty-three twenty years before; the United States had twice as many telephones as all Europe. In two decades Bell's invention had, from a mechanical curiosity, become a

[1] Paine, One Man's Life, chaps. xx-xxviii.

[2] Anon., "The Telephonic Exchange in the United States," Nature, XXIV (1880), 495; Telephones and Telegraphs, 1902, 5.

[3] Anon., "Progress of the Bell Telephone," Scientific Am., LXX (1894), 250.

[4] K. B. Miller, "Merits of Independent and Industrial Telephone Systems," Engineering Mag., XVIII (1900), 550-557; Telephones and Telegraphs, 1902, 9-11, 67.

necessity of American life. That it added to the speed of living and the breaking down of personal privacy cannot be doubted. That it helped make the American people the most talkative nation in the world is likewise clear. On the credit side of the ledger, however, must be put the enormous gains resulting from the facilitation of social and business intercourse and from the extension of urban influences into areas of rural isolation.

Largely because of the greater utility of the telephone the telegraph expanded slowly during these years. In 1874 Edison had doubled the carrying capacity of the wires by his invention of quadruplex telegraphy, which allowed two messages to be sent simultaneously from opposite ends of the same line.[1] Actual wire mileage, however, grew but fourfold between 1878 and 1898. By the mid-nineties only one telegram per person per year was being sent in the United States while the people were using the telephone ten times as much.[2] The telephone far outstripped its elder sister even for long-distance use; only in submarine communication did the telegraph continue to reign unchallenged. In the closing years of the decade, however, new vistas opened for it in a field in which it was thought the telephone could never compete. This was wireless telegraphy, the invention in 1896 of Guglielmo Marconi, an Italian engineer. Still in the experimental stage, the chief use of "wireless" before the coming of the new century was for ocean vessels.[3]

[1] F. L. Dyer and T. C. Martin, *Edison* (N. Y., 1910), I, 154-160; *Telephones and Telegraphs, 1902*, 99-105, 115.
[2] T. C. Martin, "Electrical Manufacturing Interests," Depew, *American Commerce*, II, 377-378.
[3] J. A. Fleming, "Scientific History and Future Uses of Wireless Telegraphy," *N. Am. Rev.*, CLXVIII (1899), 630-640; P. B. Delaney, "The Development of Wireless Telegraphy," *Engineering Mag.*, XVIII (1900), 747-754; Guglielmo Marconi, "Origin and Develop-

Meantime the slower communication afforded by the postal service had shown steady improvement as city populations thickened.[1] In 1883 the rate for single letters was cut from three to two cents a half-ounce and, two years later, to two cents an ounce, with a provision for special-delivery service to secure swifter transmission. In 1887 free delivery was extended to towns with as few as ten thousand people, increasing the number of places so served by one hundred and sixty-nine.[2] The sale of ordinary postage stamps leaped from seven hundred and forty-two million in 1878 to nearly two billion in 1888 and to three billion ten years later.[3] Despite the quickened pace of American life the post office with its cheaper rates remained the basic means of intercommunication, being supplemented by the faster services of the telephone and telegraph.

Improved lighting was almost as great a necessity as improved communication, for the new conditions of city life required something better than the dim rays shed from gas lamp-posts on the streets and the yellow glow of kerosene lamps or open-flame gas jets indoors. For years inventors in many countries had been seeking to harness electricity to the service of illumination, but success, as in the case of the trolley car, had to await the development of the modern dynamo.[4] Though the Rus-

ment of Wireless Telegraphy," *N. Am. Rev.*, CLXVIII (1899), 625-629; anon., "Recent Development of Wireless Telegraphy," *Nature*, LXI (1899), 78.

[1] D. C. Roper, *The United States Post Office* (N. Y., 1917), 75, 141-142, 178, 206, 371-372.

[2] Eighty-seven cities had free-carrier service in 1877-1878; 358 in 1887-1888; and 688 in 1897-1898. In the same years the number of mail carriers increased from 2275 to 6346 to 13,696. Postmaster-General, *Report for 1900*, 108-109.

[3] Postmaster-General, *Report for 1878*, 6; for *1888-89*, 704; for *1899*, 30.

[4] Bureau of the Census, *Central Electric Light and Power Stations, 1902 (Special Rep.)*, 86-92.

sian engineer, Paul Jablochkoff, in 1876 devised an arc lamp which was used with some success to light the boulevards of Paris, his achievement was quickly eclipsed by the ingenuity of Charles F. Brush, a young Ohio engineer, who in 1879 illuminated the public squares of Cleveland, Ohio, by means of a system which could maintain sixteen arc lamps on a single wire.[1] The superiority of the new device won immediate public favor. Soon the hissing, sputtering noise of the carbons and the brilliant glare of the lamp were familiar sights on American city streets, San Francisco leading the way by setting up a central power plant the same year as the Cleveland trial. The Brush system quickly spread across the Atlantic and presently, too, to the cities of Japan and China.

Satisfactory as was the arc lamp for outdoors it proved of little use for interior illumination. For this purpose some method had to be found of minutely subdividing the electric current so as to produce lights corresponding to gas jets in size and cheapness. Inventors on both sides of the Atlantic labored at the problem;[2] but success came first to Thomas A. Edison, whose wizardry in the domain of electricity was already presaged by his improvements on the telegraph and the telephone. Edison was at this time thirty-two years old, "a pleasant looking man, of average size . . . with dark hair slightly silvered, and wonderfully piercing gray eyes," who was apt to be found "with acid-stained garments, dusty eyebrows, discolored hands and dishevelled hair."[3] Since

[1] Brush has a number of American rivals in the invention of arc lighting. See Henry Schroeder, *History of the Electric Light* (*Smithsonian Miscel. Colls.*, LXXVI, no. 2), 33-41.

[2] Notably Swan, Lane-Fox and Crookes in England and Edison, W. E. Sawyer, M. G. Farmer, Edward Weston and H. E. Maxim in the United States. *Central Electric Light and Power Stations, 1902,* 92-94; Schroeder, *Electric Light,* 42.

[3] J. B. McClure, ed., *Edison and His Inventions* (Chicago, 1879),

1876 he had been conducting his experiments in a great laboratory at Menlo Park, New Jersey; but this establishment had been acquired only after years as a tramp telegrapher and mechanical tinker had led him by devious paths from his native town of Milan, Ohio, to Boston and New York, where his inventions won generous financial backing.

The problem of incandescent lighting quickly reduced itself, in Edison's mind, to finding a suitable filament which, when sealed in a vacuum bulb, would burn more than a few hours.[1] After patiently trying many substances he succeeded in October, 1879, in getting a carbonized cotton thread to last forty-five hours. Soon after, he attained even better results from a bamboo strip torn from a palm-leaf fan. Now began a search of the world for the most suitable fiber. One of his agents made his way to the Malay Peninsula, Burma and south China; others tried Ceylon, India, the West Indies and South America. Out of six thousand specimens Edison found three varieties of bamboo and one of cane exactly suited to his purpose. His incandescent lamp was patented on January 27, 1880. It not only gave a steadier, cooler and brighter light than gas, but he had also solved the problem of switching lamps off without affecting others on the same circuit.[2]

The public gazed with wonder at the new illuminant

15-16. See also W. H. Bishop, "A Night with Edison," *Scribner's Mo.*, XVII (1878-1879), 88-99, and F. A. Jones, *Thomas Alva Edison* (N. Y., 1908), chaps. i-vii. From 1878 to 1898 inclusive Edison took out 613 patents. Dyer and Martin, *Edison*, II, 947-965.

[1] Jones, *Edison*, chap. viii; Schroeder, *Electric Light*, 43-50; Dyer and Martin, *Edison*, I, chaps. xi-xv.

[2] By 1894 manufacturers were substituting cellulose for bamboo or vegetable-fiber filaments. The price of globes fell from one dollar or more apiece in the early eighties to eighteen cents in 1900. For these and other improvements, see *Central Electric Light and Power Stations, 1902*, 94-95; Byrn, *Progress of Invention*, 73; Schroeder, *Electric Light*, 50-62, 93-94.

in Edison's showroom at 65 Fifth Avenue. In 1882 central lighting stations were erected in London and New York. Perhaps no mechanical invention ever spread so swiftly over the world.[1] The new light first entered American homes at the residence of J. Hood Wright in New York; it began to burn in American hotels at the Blue Mountain House in the Adirondacks; it first appeared in a theater when six hundred and fifty bulbs lighted up a performance of Gilbert and Sullivan's opera "Iolanthe" at the Bijou in Boston on December 12, 1882. The number of central electric stations for all purposes—incandescent and arc lighting, traction power, etc.—rose from thirty-eight in 1882 to nearly six hundred in 1888 and to approximately three thousand in 1898.

The greater convenience and safety of incandescent lighting put gas-light producers at a serious disadvantage, but they did what they could to meet the competition by lowering the cost of their product, at the same time improving its quality.[2] Gas made from coal was supplemented in Pennsylvania and other parts of the country by natural gas drawn from underground reservoirs. An even greater advance came in 1875 when T. S. C. Lowe discovered that a successful illuminant could be made at extremely low cost by decomposing steam and mixing it with carbonic acid and other gases. In less than a dozen years one hundred and fifty cities were using water gas, as it was called, and soon it prevailed over the other varieties. The need of achieving a steady white flame comparable to the Edison lamp was also met when Carl Auer von Welsbach of Vienna in 1885 invented a net-like conical mantle which gave forth an intense incan-

---

[1] Dyer and Martin, *Edison*, chaps. xvi-xvii; *Central Electric Light and Power Stations, 1902, 7,* 106-107.

[2] Byrn, *Progress of Invention*, chap. xxvi.

descent light. After the United States patent was granted in 1890, Americans developed a new skill in adjusting the fragile Welsbach mantles without breaking them. The gas-light industry, though steadily losing ground, achieved a new lease of life. Only in the field of heating, however, was it as yet able to breast electricity without fear of failure.

Improved lighting not only dispelled much of the darkness of urban night life but also many of its dangers. By helping erase the difference between day and night it lengthened the working hours for intellectual toilers, made possible continuous operation of factories and, at the same time, gave an enormous stimulus to after-dark amusements and the theater. Better illumination also meant less eye strain, though this advantage may have been offset by the constant temptation to overwork on the part of the studious. The vastly increased productivity of mind and mill in this period owes more than has ever been recognized to the services of Brush, Edison and Welsbach.

Municipalities were less successful in coping with the problem of waste elimination. Since the middle of the century and earlier, places like New York, Boston and Chicago had had public underground conduits for discharging sewage into near-by bodies of water. But their facilities lagged behind the growth of population and most other cities employed village methods of surface-draining their streets and of using private vaults and cesspools for family wastes. In 1877 Philadelphia had eighty-two thousand such vaults and cesspools, Washington fifty-six thousand and Chicago, despite its sewerage system, thirty thousand.[1] Two years later a noted sanitary engineer called proper sewage disposal "the

[1] Azel Ames, "Removal of Domestic Excreta," Am. Public Health Assoc., *Public Health*, IV (1877), 74.

great unanswered question of the day." [1] Its solution
involved grave problems of community health, for dense
populations made private uncleanliness increasingly a
public concern.

In the two decades following, however, sewerage
facilities were greatly extended, while important improvements were effected in sewer construction and in
methods of ultimate disposal.[2] This last problem was an
especially difficult one. Cities with water fronts usually
discharged their sewage into sea or river with always a
danger of water pollution, especially where there was a
tidal backwash; elsewhere filter beds and farm irrigation systems were commonly used. Progress was very
uneven. While Boston and Washington spent millions
in improving their sewerage works during these years,
Philadelphia and St. Louis had at the close of the period
little more than half as great a mileage of sewers as of
streets, and Baltimore, New Orleans and Mobile continued to rely for drainage mainly on open gutters.[3]
The allied problem of garbage disposal was taken care
of hardly better.[4] In New York, Boston and other ports
such matter was carried in scows and barges several miles
out to sea and discharged upon an outgoing tide. A common practice in inland towns was to contract for its collection by farmers who fed it to swine. Since animals so
fed were subject to trichinæ, with a consequent danger
to meat eaters, after 1885 furnaces began to be intro-

[1] G. E. Waring, "Recent Modifications in Sanitary Drainage," Atlantic Mo., XLIV (1879), 62.
[2] G. E. Waring, Modern Methods of Sewage Disposal (N. Y., 1894) ;
G. W. Rafter and M. N. Baker, Sewage Disposal in the United States
(N. Y., 1894).
[3] Zueblin, American Municipal Progress, 120-126; Fairlie, Municipal
Administration, 250-251.
[4] N. S. Shaler, ed., The United States of America (N. Y., 1894),
III, 1235-1237; M. N. Baker, Municipal Engineering and Sanitation
(R. T. Ely, ed., The Citizen's Library of Economics, Politics, and Sociology; N. Y., 1901), chap. xx.

duced, especially in Middle Western cities, for the reduction of garbage by fire.[1]

The growing volume of urban wastes complicated the problem of a potable water system. This generation, however, gave less heed to the quality of the water than to its quantity. Only about six hundred cities had public waterworks in 1878, but in the next two decades their number grew nearly sixfold. At the same time some of the greater cities enlarged their existing facilities.[2] Thus between 1885 and 1892 New York, at a cost of twenty-four million dollars, constructed the New Croton Aqueduct with a carrying capacity of nearly three hundred million gallons a day.

Gradually, however, as a result of European example and the advance of the germ theory of disease, attention was also given to the purity of the water. The Massachusetts board of health in 1886 was granted by law general oversight of all inland waters of the state with power to advise municipal authorities in regard to water supply, sewage disposal and methods of preventing pollution.[3] Within the next few years careful investigations were also made by the state health boards of Connecticut, Minnesota, New Jersey, New York, Ohio and Rhode Island.[4] Cities differed greatly as to the purity of their water supplies, and public-health guardians were not slow in pointing out corresponding differences as to mortality from typhoid fever. Between 1880 and 1890 about half as many people proportion-

[1] About ninety cities had installed furnaces by the end of 1898. W. F. Morse, *The Collection and Disposal of Municipal Waste* (N. Y., 1908), 99-116.

[2] Zueblin, *American Municipal Progress*, chap. iv.

[3] W. T. Sedgwick, "Notable Sanitary Experiments in Massachusetts," *Forum*, XX (1895-1896), 752-756; G. C. Whipple, *State Sanitation* (Cambridge, Mass., 1917), I, 125-128.

[4] C. V. Chapin, *Municipal Sanitation in the United States* (Providence, 1901), 298.

ately died of typhoid fever in New York and Boston, where the water was comparatively pure, as in Philadelphia and Chicago, where the supply was contaminated.[1] Pollution by sewage and manufacturers' wastes was especially serious in the case of cities drawing their water from rivers or other natural sources.

The activity in developing municipal water plants was in part caused by the greatly increased fire risks which resulted from the crowding together of buildings and the extensive use of electric wiring. This generation was resolved to have no such conflagrations as those of Chicago and Boston in the early seventies.[2] Though they succeeded in this aim, scarcely a year passed without one or more million-dollar fires and the waste of thousands of lives. The estimated total fire losses in 1878 were over sixty-four million dollars. In 1883 they passed permanently beyond the hundred-million-dollar mark and in 1892 and 1893 rose above one hundred and fifty million.[3]

That the situation was no worse was due to the new methods devised for combating the danger. While small towns and the more backward cities still clung to the volunteer system of fire fighting, with sometimes a nucleus of professional firemen, the large places possessed full-time paid·departments, though Philadelphia's

[1] The death rate per ten thousand inhabitants was: New York 3.36; Boston 3.5; Chicago 6.25; Philadelphia 6.8. Shaler, *United States,* III, 1230.

[2] See Nevins, *Emergence of Modern America,* 84-85.

[3] *World Almanac for 1929,* 375. A letter of Dec. 3, 1925, from R. S. Moulton of the National Fire Protection Association, Boston, says: "During the period 1875 to 1900, while there were no large conflagrations, the total amount of the fire loss was larger in proportion to the then national wealth than it is today, being variously estimated at from three to four dollars per thousand dollars of burnable wealth as compared with from one dollar and a half to two dollars today." See also Clifford Thomson, "The Waste by Fire," *Forum,* II (1886-1887), 27-39.

dated only from 1871 and St. Paul did not have one until ten years later.[1] With more efficient organization appeared improved apparatus and equipment.[2] Swinging harness for hitching the horses to the fire wagons came into use in the seventies, as did also the fire boat, the fire-alarm signal box and the water tower. In the next decade chemical engines were introduced in Chicago, Milwaukee, Springfield, Ohio, and elsewhere. The invention of the Grinnell automatic fire sprinkler in 1877, added to the widening use of fire-resistant building materials—concrete, terra cotta, brick, steel, asbestos—helped further to reduce fire hazards, particularly in factories and office buildings. Though wide differences continued to exist among cities, the fire departments in general compared favorably with those of any other country. Chicago, for example, had twice as many men and horses and half again as many steam fire engines as London, a city three times as populous.

Conditions of lodging varied as widely as types of people and differences in income. For well-to-do transients the great cities offered hotels constantly increasing in number, size and sumptuousness.[3] Already famous in the eighties were such hostelries as the Grand Union, Park Avenue and Murray Hill in New York, the Stratford and the Lafayette in Philadelphia, Young's and the Vendôme in Boston, the Grand Pacific, Palmer

---

[1] Scranton was the only city in the hundred-thousand class which at the close of the century still relied mainly upon call men. Fairlie, *Municipal Administration*, 154-155; Zueblin, *American Municipal Progress*, 65-66.

[2] Fairlie, *Municipal Administration*, 152-154; Zueblin, *American Municipal Progress*, 68; Helen Campbell and others, *Darkness and Daylight* (Hartford, 1891), chap. xxvii; P. J. McKeon, *Fire Prevention* (N. Y., 1912), esp. 6-7; C. J. H. Woodbury, "Conflagrations in Cities," Franklin Inst., *Journ.*, CXXXII (1891), 209-223.

[3] Hiram Hitchcock, "The Hotels of America," Depew, *American Commerce*, I, 153-155; Alexander Craib, *America and the Americans* (London, 1892), chap. xxvii; Brown, *Golden Nineties*, 311-323.

House and Auditorium in Chicago, the Brown Palace Hotel in Denver and Baldwin's in San Francisco. Among the new ones in the last decade of the century were the Plaza, Savoy and Waldorf-Astoria in New York, the Jefferson in Richmond, Virginia, and the Raleigh in Washington. Such hotels, gorgeously decorated and furnished, with a steadily diminishing emphasis on the "steamboat style," made a special appeal with their private baths, electric elevators, electric-call service and other up-to-the-minute conveniences. Though the incessant "tinkle, tinkle, tinkle of the ice-pitcher" proved "positively nauseous" to the British compiler of *Baedeker*, he otherwise thought well of the American institution and had even a word of praise and commiseration for that "mannerless despot," the hotel clerk.[1] Every large city also had hotels of second and third class or of no class at all, falling as low in New York as lodging places in Chatham Street (now Park Row) and the Bowery where one could secure sleeping space for a few pennies a night.[2] In general, hotels in the South were apt to be poorer than in any other section, while in the West, even in the newer towns, they were unexpectedly good.

If the traveler did not wish to patronize his own hotel dining room, he could usually find in the larger cities excellent restaurants at hand. In Delmonico's at Fifth Avenue and Twenty-sixth Street he could eat the best meals in America, at the highest prices. There important political conferences were held, college societies celebrated their reunions and distinguished foreigners

[1] Muirhead, *Land of Contrasts*, 255-257. See also [J. F. Muirhead], *The United States* (Karl Baedeker, ed., *Handbook for Travellers;* 2d rev. edn., Leipsic, 1899), xxvi-xxvii.

[2] Over four and a half million cheap lodgings were provided in such houses in the single year 1888 in New York. H. L. Myrick, *The Importance of the Scientific and Practical Study of Crime* (N. Y., 1895), 25; J. A. Riis, *How the Other Half Lives* (N. Y., 1890), chap. viii.

were fêted. The Brunswick and the Brevoort were hardly less fashionable, the former receiving its summer patrons in an attractive garden in the rear. While other centers were not as well served as New York, Chicago boasted of the Richelieu and Kingsley's, and the French restaurants in New Orleans—Moreau's, Mme. Venn's, Flêche's, Victor's—were justly famed the country over.

City dwellers who wished to escape the drudgery and responsibility of housekeeping usually lived in boarding houses. With the opening of the Buckingham Hotel in New York in 1877, however, an increasing number of attractive apartment hotels for private families made their appearance. At the same time the swifter means of transit and communication caused a flow of population into suburban districts where shaded streets, ample lawns and neighborly friendliness gave everyday living something of a bucolic flavor. This dispersion was particularly noticeable in the last ten years of the period, far outdistancing the rapid extension of official municipal limits.[1] By the end of the nineties New York's suburbs held over a million people, one third as many as the city proper, while more people actually lived on Boston's outskirts than within her corporate confines. Pittsburgh, Providence and Cincinnati had similarly acquired strong satellite colonies.

In contrast to this agreeable picture must be placed another, that of the living conditions of the less prosperous classes and particularly of the immigrants. Of the great cities of the land Philadelphia and Chicago were least scarred by slums. Boston, Cincinnati, Jersey City and Hartford had badly diseased spots, but the evil was most deeply rooted in New York City, where land rentals

[1] *U. S. Thirteenth Census* (1910), I, 73-75; *Street and Electric Railways, 1902*, 26-29; Brown, *New York in Elegant Eighties*, 69-73; A. F. Weber, "Suburban Annexations," *N. Am. Rev.*, CLXVI (1898), 612-617.

were highest and the pressure of immigrants strongest.[1]
In all Europe only one city district, in Prague, was half
as congested as certain parts of Manhattan. Bad as conditions had been earlier in New York, they became worse
in 1879 with the advent of a new type of slum, the
"dumb-bell" tenement, so called because of the outline
of the floor plan. This became virtually the only kind
erected there in the next two decades.

Five or six stories high, the bleak narrow structure
ran ninety feet back from the street, being pierced
through the center by a stygian hallway less than three
feet wide.[2] Each floor was honeycombed with rooms,
many without direct light or air and most of them
sheltering one or more families. Almost at once such
barracks became foul and grimy, infested with vermin
and lacking privacy and proper sanitary conveniences.
The sunless, ill-smelling air shafts at the sides of the
building proved a positive menace during fires by in-
suring the rapid spread of flames. In rooms and hall-
ways, on stairs and fire escapes, in the narrow streets,
dirty half-clad children roamed at will, imbibing soiled
thoughts from their soiled surroundings. The dense slum
district bounded by Cherry, Catherine, Hamilton and
Market streets was known as "lung block" because of
the many deaths from tuberculosis. No wonder such
rookeries were nurseries of immorality, drunkenness,
disease and crime. The real surprise is, as the state tenement-house commission pointed out in 1900, that so
many of the children grew up to be decent, self-respecting citizens.

[1] R. W. De Forest and Lawrence Veiller, eds., *The Tenement House
Problem* (N. Y., 1903), I, 57, 131-170. For the situation earlier, see
Nevins, *Emergence of Modern America*, 319-320.
[2] A New York invention, the dumb-bell tenement was unknown in
any European city. De Forest and Veiller, *Tenement House Problem*,
I, 8-14, 100-102; Riis, *How the Other Half Lives*, 18-19.

In 1879 the total number of tenements in New York was estimated at twenty-one thousand, their inhabitants at more than half a million. A census taken in 1888 showed over thirty-two thousand tenements with a population exceeding a million. By 1900 the number of buildings had grown to nearly forty-three thousand and their occupants to over one and a half million.[1] From time to time philanthropic citizens like Ellen Collins and Alfred T. White built model tenements in New York and Brooklyn to demonstrate that decent lodgings for the poor comported with fair profits for the landlord. Organizations like the State Charities Association and the Association for Improving the Condition of the Poor insistently agitated for stricter housing laws. To their aid came a young Danish American, Jacob A. Riis. As police reporter on the *Sun* he had gained a first-hand knowledge of slum conditions, which he used with great literary effect in a series of newspaper and magazine articles beginning in the eighties. His first book, *How the Other Half Lives,* published in 1890, came to Theodore Roosevelt as "an enlightenment and an inspiration for which . . . I could never be too grateful."[2]

Remedial legislation, following the first tenement-house statute of 1867, was passed in 1879, 1887 and 1895.[3] But in spite of the reformers the laws contained loopholes and enforcement was sporadic. The tenement-house commission of 1900 felt that, on the whole, conditions were worse than they had been fifty years before. Yet one year later a comprehensive statute was adopted

[1] For various estimates, see Riis, *How the Other Half Lives,* 275, 300; De Forest and Veiller, *Tenement House Problem,* I, 5, 37; II, 78.
[2] Theodore Roosevelt, *An Autobiography* (N. Y., 1919), 169. Riis's *The Battle with the Slum* (N. Y., 1902) is autobiographical.
[3] De Forest and Veiller, *Tenement House Problem,* I, 5, 95-115; II, 207-345.

which showed that the humanitarian energies of this generation had not been spent in vain. The act of 1901 not only insured real housing reform in New York, but prompted other states and municipalities to a fundamental attack on the evil.[1]

The problem of urban lawlessness and crime was deeply rooted in that of the slums. Vile places like "Misery Row," "Poverty Lane" and "Murderers' Alley" were both continuous recruiting grounds for juvenile delinquents and hiding places for criminal bands. Lacking normal outlets for play, the tenement waifs naturally drifted into gangs in which what might have been a laudable spirit of group loyalty was twisted into an ambition to emulate the lawless exploits of their elders. Beginning as beggars, sneak thieves and pickpockets, they graduated all too quickly into the ranks of shoplifters, robbers and thugs.[2] The foreign origin of many of the slum dwellers made this transition all the easier because of prior unfamiliarity with American traditions and laws. In particular, the Irish and Italians contributed more than their proportionate share of the country's prison population, though it was the American-born immigrant children, lacking proper parental guidance and wholesome surroundings, who turned most readily to underworld life.[3] One student of the problem, observing that most of the men, women and children in the jails and penitentiaries he had visited were native-born, concluded: "We have ourselves evolved as cruel and cunning

[1] H. U. Faulkner, *The Quest for Social Justice* (*A History of American Life*, XI), 158-159.

[2] W. F. Howe and A. H. Hummel, *Danger!* (Buffalo, 1886), chap. iii; Campbell and others, *Darkness and Daylight*, chap. vi; Herbert Asbury, *The Gangs of New York* (N. Y., 1927), 238-246.

[3] W. M. F. Round, "Immigration and Crime," *Forum*, VIII (1889-1890), 428-440; S. G. Fisher, "Immigration and Crime," *Pop. Sci. Mo.*, XLIX (1896), 625-630; F. H. Wines, *Report on Crime, Pauperism, and Benevolence in the United States* (*U. S. Eleventh Census, 1890,* XXII), I, 23-43, 131-133.

criminals as any that Europe may have foisted upon us."[1]

Other than New York the great criminal centers of the nation were Chicago, Boston, Philadelphia, Pittsburgh, Buffalo, Detroit, Cleveland, Cincinnati, St. Louis and San Francisco.[2] The freemasonry of crookdom made it possible for evildoers to pass quickly from city to city as self-preservation required, or to congregate like birds of prey when crowds gathered for such occasions as the Philadelphia Centennial or the Chicago World's Fair of 1893. In San Francisco lawlessness in the 1880's still possessed a strong frontier flavor, being characterized by the depredations of youthful hoodlums who brandished large knives and six-shooters and did not hesitate to use them.[3] In the older American centers crime for profit had fallen into the hands of professionals who constantly devised new traps for the unwary. Pickpockets, badger-game experts, knock-out-drop artists, green-goods men (who circulated worthless money), bunco steerers (swindlers), gamblers, hold-up men—all these prospered in such a hotbed of evil as New York's Tenderloin, bounded by Twenty-fourth and Fortieth streets and Fifth and Seventh avenues.[4]

In particular, New York was the national base for bank robbers. One band led by George L. Leslie was credited by Chief of Police Walling with being responsible for four fifths of the bank burglaries in Amer-

---

[1] J. F. Willard (Josiah Flynt, *pseud.*), *Notes of an Itinerant Policeman* (Boston, 1900), 10.

[2] Flynt, *Notes*, 33.

[3] Marshall, *Through America*, 269-272.

[4] The very name, Tenderloin, is a product of these turbulent years. Being in 1876 transferred from an obscure precinct to West Thirtieth Street, Police Captain A. S. Williams exclaimed, "I've been having chuck steak ever since I've been on the force, and now I'm going to have a bit of tenderloin." H. L. Mencken, *The American Language* (N. Y., 1919), 163, *n.* 64. Taken up by the newspapers, the term was soon applied to gay, wicked districts in any city.

*Broadway and John Street, New York City, in 1890.*

*A farmer's bitter memory of his visit to the city: a "green goods" swindle on the Bowery*

*In the Metropolis*

ica until "Western George's" murder in 1884. His greatest coup was the looting of the Manhattan Savings Institution in New York on October 27, 1878, to the extent of nearly three million dollars, the result of three years' careful planning.[1] In order to protect the financial district from other similar maraudings Inspector Thomas Byrnes established his famous Dead Line on March 12, 1880, at Fulton Street, south of which a known criminal would be arrested on sight. While not usually of the professional ilk, absconding bank cashiers were perhaps the most elegant culprits of the time, though this form of law breaking became less frequent with the conclusion of extradition arrangements with Canada in 1889. Of the new swindles contrived during these years probably the most successful was the gold brick, introduced into New York in 1880 by Reed Waddell, a native of Springfield, Illinois. In ten years' time he is believed to have made more than two hundred and fifty thousand dollars from the sale of his gilded lead bricks and from green goods.[2]

Organized crime was the special product of the slum districts where such bands as the Hartley Mob, the Molasses Gang, the Dutch Mob, the Potashes and the Stable Gang flourished in the dives along the Bowery and its sordid byways.[3] The Whyos, the most powerful gang of all, had their principal base in Mulberry Bend whence they sallied forth on their missions of pillage and death

[1] Two of his accomplices were sentenced to long prison terms, but the police could not find enough evidence against Leslie to bring him to trial. G. W. Walling, *Recollections of a New York Chief of Police* (N. Y., 1887), chap. xix; Asbury, *Gangs of New York*, 203-211; T. F. Byrnes, *Professional Criminals of America* (N. Y., 1886), 81-82.

[2] Waddell met a violent death in 1895 as a result of a thieves' quarrel. Asbury, *Gangs of New York*, 194-197.

[3] Riis, *How the Other Half Lives*, chap. xix; Asbury, *Gangs of New York*, chaps. xi-xii; Howe and Hummel, *Danger!*, chap. ii; Walling, *Recollections*, chap. xxxv; Campbell and others, *Darkness and Daylight*, chap. xxiv.

until their own destruction in the early nineties. Fortunately for the general safety these bands spent a part
of their murderous energy in fighting one another.

Criminologists and publicists pointed with alarm to
the portentous increase of lawlessness in the United
States. A census inquiry disclosed a fifty-per-cent rise
in the number of prison inmates from 1880 to 1890.[1]
Statistics collected by the *Chicago Tribune* revealed a
growth of murders and homicides from 1266 during the
year 1881 (24.7 to a million people) to 4290 in 1890
(or 68.5 to the million) and to 7840 in 1898 (or
107.2 to the million).[2] Such figures were all the more
startling since most other civilized countries showed a
declining homicide rate, the ratio in England and Germany being less than half that of the United States.
Students of the subject were agreed in placing the fundamental blame on unhealthy urban growth, unrestricted
immigration, the saloon and the maladjusted Negro.[3]
In addition, Lombroso pointed to the lingering habits of
frontier lawlessness even in the more settled states, the
new opportunities for crime afforded by discoveries in
chemistry and toxicology, and the evil effects of sensation-mongering newspapers. Another writer stressed the

---

[1] Wines, *Report,* I, 11, 124. In general, crime statistics need to be
used with considerable caution because of lack of registration in most
states, divergent legal definitions of crime in the United States and
abroad, differences in law enforcement as between states and from time
to time within the same state, and other similar circumstances.

[2] Figures cited in S. S. McClure, "The Increase of Lawlessness in the
United States," *McClure's,* XXIV (1904), 168. For the same years
suicides numbered 605, 2640 and 5920.

[3] See, for example, H. M. Boies, *Prisoners and Paupers* (N. Y.,
1893), chaps. i, vi-xi; I. C. Parker, "How to Arrest the Increase of
Homicides in America," *N. Am. Rev.,* CLXII (1896), 667-673; W. D.
Morrison, *Juvenile Offenders* (N. Y., 1897), esp. chap. ii; Cesare
Lombroso, "Why Homicide Has Increased in the United States," *N. Am.
Rev.,* CLXV (1897), 641-648; CLXVI (1898), 1-11; James
O'Meara, "Concealed Weapons and Crimes," *Overland Mo.,* XVI
(1890), 11-16.

undoubted fact that violence and criminality had come to be regarded "as a sort of natural and inevitable concomitant" of every great labor disturbance.[1]

Yet it seemed to an acute observer like James Bryce that the Americans were at bottom a law-abiding people.[2] Indeed, in the absence of adequate data for earlier periods, it is possible that crime, being mainly concentrated in the cities, had become merely more conspicuous rather than greater in volume. However this may be, all agreed that the evil was accentuated by lax law enforcement. The official guardians of society only too often were in league with the antisocial elements, passively or actively. In most large centers a crook could secure police "protection" provided he agreed to hunt his prey elsewhere or, if operating locally, to share his profits with the authorities.[3] It was the opinion of the widely experienced Josiah Flynt that, from Maine to California, the aim of police departments was merely "to keep a city superficially clean, and to keep everything quiet that is likely to arouse the public to an investigation."[4] Beyond that point they felt no genuine concern.

Yet now and then conditions became intolerable, and official inquests laid bare a state of affairs almost too vile for belief. Such was the outcome of the courageous war against vice waged by the Reverend Charles H. Parkhurst, of the Madison Square Presbyterian Church in New York, with the help of the New York Society for the Prevention of Crime. The ensuing legislative inquiry, conducted in 1894 under Senator Clarence Lexow as chairman, caused the overturn of the Tammany gov-

---

[1] G. C. Holt, "Lynching and Mobs," *Journ. of Social Sci.*, XXXII (1894), 76-81.

[2] Bryce, *American Commonwealth*, III, 312.

[3] Flynt, *Notes*, chaps. iv, vi; J. F. Willard (Josiah Flynt, *pseud.*), *The World of Graft* (N. Y., 1901), *passim*.

[4] Flynt, *Notes*, 101.

ernment the following year and the appointment of Theodore Roosevelt to a strenuous administration as main police commissioner.[1] Among other things the Lexow investigation revealed that appointments and promotions in the police force were for sale and that police officials, besides collecting monthly blackmail from gamblers, saloonists and bawdyhouse keepers, exacted percentages of the profits of "street walkers," pickpockets and gun men.[2]

In various states efforts were made from time to time to divorce police administration from corrupt municipal politics, the favorite scheme being to head the city forces with officials appointed by the governor. This plan was tried in cities as widely separated as Boston, Charleston, South Carolina, Cincinnati, Detroit, Minneapolis, Omaha and Denver. But in most cases it resulted merely in transferring political control from one group of self-seeking overlords to another, without real improvement from the standpoint of the public.[3] The judiciary also shared responsibility for the bad conditions. In the opinion of one judge at least, "the greatest cause of the increase of crime is the action of the appellate courts, which . . . make the most strenuous efforts, as a rule, to see not when they can affirm but when they can reverse a case." [4]

Discouraging as was the situation, it was less so than it seemed. Individual police chiefs and officers were noted

[1] C. H. Parkhurst, *Our Fight with Tammany* (N. Y., 1895) ; Roosevelt, *Autobiography*, chap. vi.

[2] One woman who owned a chain of brothels testified that she paid $30,000 annually for protection. For a summary of the findings, see N. Y. State Committee Appointed to Investigate the Police Department of the City of New York, *Report and Proceedings* (Albany, 1895), I, 3-61. The commission paid by criminals in Chicago was ten per cent of their earnings, according to L. W. Moore, a reformed bank robber, in *His Own Story* (Boston, 1892), chap. xl.

[3] R. B. Fosdick, *American Police Systems* (N. Y., 1920), 90-102.

[4] Parker, "How to Arrest Increase of Homicides," 670.

for their bravery and rectitude; and every city now and then, under reform pressure, treated its wrongdoers with Draconian severity. Moreover the path of the wicked was rendered increasingly thorny by by-products of American inventive genius.[1] To overcome the difficulties presented by improvements in vault and safe construction and the constantly spreading use of Yale locks, burglars had to be ever on the alert. Likewise, electricity aided the law-abiding citizen not only by means of better-lighted streets but also through its application to burglar-alarm wiring and to emergency street boxes for summoning police help. The utility of the "rogues' gallery," in limited use since mid-century, was also greatly extended by a free exchange of photographs with other cities; and beginning in 1887 the whole method of identifying criminals was revolutionized by the introduction, first in Illinois, then in Massachusetts and elsewhere, of the Bertillon system of the Paris police, whereby detailed measurements of the culprit's body were taken and recorded.

Unfortunately urban delinquency had its repercussions on the countryside, most notoriously in the case of the "tramp evil," which had first appeared in America in the hard years following 1873.[2] While the return of prosperity after 1878 somewhat diminished the number of such vagrants, habit, uncertainties of work, difficulties of personal adjustment, *Wanderlust* and the ease of stealing rides on the railroads caused many to continue in their old ways. Pitiful caricatures of the restless hardy pioneers of earlier times, these aimless wanderers were freely spawned by the great urban centers, particularly in years of unemployment and industrial con-

[1] B. P. Eldridge and W. B. Watts, *Our Rival, the Rascal* (Boston, 1896), chap. xviii; *Telephones and Telegraphs, 1902*, 146-148.
[2] See Nevins, *Emergence of Modern America*, 301-302.

flict like 1885-1886 and 1892-1894.[1] An unofficial tramp census taken in the year 1893 indicated that three out of five were between twenty and fifty years of age, about the same proportion were native-born and trained to skilled trades, five out of six enjoyed good health, and nearly all were literate and unmarried.[2] If, as the investigator estimated, the total number of tramps then in the nation was 45,845, they represented an army larger than Wellington's at Waterloo and their vagabondage involved the withdrawal of a quarter of one per cent of the male population from productive work, not to mention the burdens thrown on the public in the form of alms, police supervision and hospital care.

These nomads developed a manner of living, a culture, peculiar to themselves. A well-marked caste system distinguished between the hobo, forced temporarily "on the road" by lack of work, and the habitual tramp in his ascending social scale from "gay-cat" (tenderfoot) and harmless wanderer to expert criminal.[3] By cabalistic chalk marks on gate posts the elect were informed as to chances for a "hand-out"; a rigid code of ethics governed their conduct toward one another; and an argot, characterized by such expressions as doss (sleep), elbow (detective), mooch (beg) and shack (brakeman), marked their common speech.[4]

[1] For the marching columns of the jobless in 1894, see D. L. McMurry, *Coxey's Army* (Boston, 1929).

[2] J. J. McCook, "A Tramp Census and Its Revelations," *Forum,* XV (1893), 753-766. 1349 tramps were interviewed. Their ages averaged younger than those of tramps in England and Germany. Nearly half of them said they had taken to the road within a week of losing their last real job. Of immigrant elements the Irish were the most prominent, accounting for one fifth of all the tramps.

[3] E. L. Bailey (an ex-tramp), "Tramps and Hoboes," *Forum,* XXVI (1898-1899), 217-221; Flynt, *Notes,* 49-53, 118-140; Jack London, *The Road* (N. Y., 1907).

[4] J. F. Willard (Josiah Flynt, *pseud.*), *Tramping with Tramps* (N. Y., 1899), 381-398, contains a glossary with comments. This student of trampdom estimated that at least three thousand distinctive

In the 1880's a gang of itinerant criminals, known as the Lake Shore Push, working out of Cleveland, forcibly monopolized the "empties" of the Lake Shore line to the exclusion of other wanderers; and in 1886 bands, numbering a hundred or more, seized trains for temporary use in Mississippi and Tennessee. But, for the most part, tramps went about alone or by twos and threes, their occasional presence and overindulgence in drink increasing the hazards of solitary rural living. Beginning with New Jersey in 1876, a wave of anti-tramp legislation swept over the nation so that by 1893 twenty-one or more states had passed such acts.[1] Varying in severity—from a short jail sentence to public whipping or even (in two Southern states) sale into temporary servitude—these laws varied even more greatly in the degree of their enforcement. Local communities often found it necessary to improvise their own remedies; town authorities in Massachusetts attained the desired object by exacting manual work from vagrants.[2] The nuisance showed no abatement during the life of this generation; there were probably more tramps abroad at the close of the period than at its beginning.[3] Improvement awaited a better adjustment of wages and employment to available labor supply and a less indulgent attitude on the part of railroads toward the unbidden occupants of "side-door Pullmans." [4]

expressions had been in vogue in the previous twenty years. *Cf.* Flynt's glossary in *World of Graft*, 219-221.

[1] Samuel Leavitt, "The Tramps and the Law," *Forum*, II (1886-1887), 190-200; McCook, "Tramp Census," 764-765.

[2] Committee of the Massachusetts Association of Relief Officers, "Tramps and Wayfarers," Am. Stat. Assoc., *Publs.*, n.s., VII (1900), 74-84—a report on the practices of 184 Massachusetts towns and cities.

[3] Flynt in *Tramping with Tramps*, 304, estimated their number in 1898 as sixty thousand; Bailey's guess in "Tramps and Hoboes," 220, was one hundred thousand.

[4] The lenience of the railroads was considered by Flynt a major factor in the situation. See *Tramping with Tramps*, 291-314, 355.

If we consider only the sordid aspects of urban life the American city of the period seems a cancerous growth. But the record as a whole was distinctly creditable to a generation which found itself confronted with the phenomenon of a great population everywhere clotting into towns. No other people had ever met such an emergency so promptly or, on the whole, so successfully. The basic facilities of urban living—transit, lighting and communication—were well taken care of by an outburst of native mechanical genius which helped make these years the Golden Age of Invention. Some places moved forward faster than others, of course, and all lagged in some respects while advancing in others. If the rural spirit of neighborliness was submerged in the anonymity of city life, there developed in its place a spirit of impersonal social responsibility which devoted itself, with varying earnestness and success, to questions of pure water, sewage disposal and decent housing for the poor, sometimes taking the extreme form of municipal ownership. Moreover, what the great cities felt obliged to do under the whip of necessity, smaller towns undertook in a spirit of imitation, so that the new standards affected urban life everywhere. What most impresses the historical student is the lack of unity, balance, planfulness, in the advances that were made. Urban progress was experimental, uneven, often accidental: the people were, as yet, groping in the dark. A later generation, taking stock of the past and profiting by its mistakes, would explore the possibilities of ordered city planning, not only in the interests of material welfare and community health but also with an eye to beautification.[1]

[1] See P. W. Slosson, *The Great Crusade and After* (*A History of American Life*, XII), 407-408.

# CHAPTER V

## THE AMERICAN WOMAN

THE American woman reigned if she did not govern. She was in transition—as she always has been—and while the American man was too gallant to regard her as a "problem," her unusual restlessness in the eighties and nineties proved a constant source of worry to the old-fashioned of both sexes. It was as mistress of the home and dispenser of its hospitality that she was most favorably known; and in this rôle she inspired masculine visitors from Europe to a catalogue of such adjectives as vivacious, fascinating, candid, unaffected, intelligent, self-reliant. With an effort at statistical restraint the musician Offenbach at the opening of the era declared, "Out of a hundred women, ninety are perfectly ravishing"; while another artist, Soissons, observing America twenty years later, could agree that the "modern American woman is charming and almost superior to the majority of European women." [1] Even Matthew Arnold, who saw little to relieve the drab monotony of the transatlantic scene, accounted the unusual measure of feminine charm as an authentic touch of civilization. [2]

Nothing more sharply set off the American woman from her sisters abroad than the deference paid her by men and the unaffected social relations between the

[1] Jacques Offenbach, *America and the Americans* (London, 1876), 43-44; S. C. de Soissons, *A Parisian in America* (Boston, 1896), 8.
[2] Matthew Arnold, *Civilization in the United States* (Boston, 1888), 168-169.

121

sexes. "It is the pride of Americans," noted one foreign
observer, "that a woman, unaccompanied, can travel
from one end of their country to the other without
being subjected to any unpleasantness or to a vestige of
impertinence." [1] This attitude, of course, had long been
a national characteristic; but as a product of frontier
and rural influences it was subjected during these years
to a new and unexpected strain as greater numbers of
people came to live under urban conditions and women
entered the world of men as breadwinners.

In correct social circles of the Eastern cities the practice of chaperonage took root during the 1880's, stimulated by the example of the Old World with which an
increasing number of traveled Americans had become
acquainted. "The duties of a chaperon are very hard
and unremitting, and sometimes very disagreeable,"
wrote an editor of *Harper's Bazar* in 1884.

> She must accompany her young lady everywhere; she
> must sit in the parlor when she receives gentlemen; she
> must go with her to the skating rink, the ball, the
> party, the races, the dinners, and especially to theater
> parties; she must preside at the table, and act the part
> of a mother, so far as she can; she must watch the
> characters of the men who approach her charge, and
> endeavor to save the inexperienced girl from the dangers
> of a bad marriage, if possible. [2]

Three years later another authority noted that the
chaperon was "slowly but surely extending her sway,"
and in 1898 it was announced that the practice was
so generally observed in the East that "a girl of the

[1] William Saunders, *Through the Light Continent* (London, 1879),
401. See also Emily Faithfull, *Three Visits to America* (Edinburgh,
1884), 323, and E. Catherine Bates, *A Year in the Great Republic*
(London, 1887), II, 281-283.

[2] Mrs. John Sherwood, *Manners and Social Usages* (N. Y., 1884),
147.

present generation would not venture to combat it without the risk of sharp criticism from alien tongues." [1]

Despite the undoubted spread of the new custom its well-wishers overstated the facts. As Mrs. Sherwood ruefully acknowledged, the "vivacious American girl, with all her inherited hatred of authority, is a troublesome charge. All young folks are rebels." Not appreciating "what Hesperidean fruit they are," they "dislike being watched and guarded." [2] And the young lady found an ally in her young man who, besides sharing her libertarianism, objected to the extra drain on his purse which the presence of a third party at dinner or the theater entailed. In the smaller towns and rustic parts of the nation the two sexes continued to mingle socially, go buggy riding in the moonlight and pay court unvexed by the attentions of a duenna. Even in the cities spinsters or "elderly girls" of twenty-five years or more were generally regarded as exempt from the requirement, for "with the assumption of years" had they not safely left behind them "the wild grace of a giddy girlhood"? Yet an "elderly girl," though of thirty-five, was deemed to act unwisely if she visited an artist's studio alone, even though "there is in art an ennobling and purifying influence which should be a protection." [3]

On none did the yoke of Victorian convention lie so heavily or so unreasonably as on affianced lovers.

A chaperon is indispensable to an engaged girl. . . . Nothing is more vulgar in the eyes of our modern society than for an engaged couple to travel together or

[1] Florence H. Hall, *Social Customs* (Boston, 1887), 177; Mrs. Burton Harrison, *The Well-Bred Girl in Society* (N. Y., 1898), 39. See also Mrs. Burton Kingsland, "A Daughter at Sixteen," *Ladies' Home Journ.*, XI (1894), no. 10, 10.

[2] Sherwood, *Manners and Social Usages*, 147 (rev. edn., 1900, 196).

[3] Sherwood, *Manners and Social Usages*, 153-154 (rev. edn., 1900, 202-203).

to go to the theatre unaccompanied, as was the primitive custom. . . . Society allows an engaged girl to drive with her *fiancé* in an open carriage, but it does not approve of his taking her in a close carriage to an evening party.[1]

While the young lady was not expected to abstain entirely from social contacts, she must be extremely circumspect in her relations with the other sex, for even the "shadow of a flirtation" constituted a breach both of manners and morals.[2] Once the wedding cards were issued, it was *"de rigueur"* for the bride-to-be to withdraw from the public gaze, allowing herself only the occasional privilege of a quiet walk with her future husband during the day.[3]

Despite new social and economic conditions marriage continued to be the cherished goal of the majority of women, all the more so as the numerical excess of females over males steadily climbed in the urban parts of America.[4] Nevertheless the growing practice of seeking matrimonial mates through the advertising columns of the newspapers was generally frowned upon as betraying an unmaidenly zeal. Though in a few Eastern cities the "woman bachelor," as she called herself, gained steadily in standing and public respect, in most parts of the country the "elderly girl" was looked upon as a

[1] Sherwood, *Manners and Social Usages*, 148-149 (rev. edn., 1900, 197-198). See also Hall, *Social Customs*, 171.

[2] Clara S. J. Moore (Mrs. H. O. Ward, *pseud.*), *Sensible Etiquette* (16th rev. edn., Phila., 1878), 334-335; A Lounger in Society (*pseud.*), *The Glass of Fashion* (N. Y., 1881), 43; Frances Stevens, *The Usages of the Best Society* (N. Y., 1884), 175; J. H. Young, *Our Deportment* (Springfield, Mass., 1881), 190.

[3] Ward, *Sensible Etiquette*, 337. One regrets to note, however, that on one occasion "A young lady at the sea-shore greatly shocked public opinion by going down to the surf beach and bathing on the morning of her wedding day." Hall, *Social Customs*, 171.

[4] *Supplementary Analysis and Derivative Tables* (U. S. Twelfth Census, *Special Rep.*), 86, 89.

creature of frustrated purpose.[1] A fragile clinging vine was the ideal of an age which little dreamed a later generation would prefer the rambler.

The Americans were, in fact, one of the most married peoples in the world, being surpassed in Western Europe only by the French. There was a difference, however, between city and country. Matrimony generally took place earlier in the rural districts, was likely to endure longer and, whether ended by death or divorce, was more often followed by fresh nuptials.[2] In the cities the higher cost of living, together with the greater economic independence of women and the many substitutes for the sociability of the fireside, served to delay marriage or to prevent it entirely. Higher education also proved a deterrent, at least so far as women were concerned. It was widely noted that fewer college-bred girls married proportionately than did their less educated sisters, though the graduates of coeducational institutions showed less reluctance in this respect than those of women's colleges.[3]

From the later marriages of middle-class urban folk came smaller families, due partly to an increasing resort to the practice of birth control. One medical authority dared assert openly that such conduct was "not only not in itself sinful" but even "under certain circumstances commendable."[4] The result, as Bryce and others pointed

---

[1] Mary G. Humphreys, "Women Bachelors in New York," *Scribner's Mag.*, XX (1896), 626-636. See also anon., "The Old Maid," *Harper's Bazar*, XII (1879), 251; anon., "Old Maids," *Harper's Bazar*, XV (1882), 434. Mrs. Burton Harrison's novel, *A Bachelor Maid* (N. Y., 1894), is a gentle satire on the "new woman."

[2] *Supplementary Analysis and Derivative Tables*, 386, 395-402.

[3] Milicent W. Shinn, "The Marriage Rate of College Women," *Century*, L (1895), 946-948; Horace Davis, "Collegiate Education of Women," *Overland Mo.*, XVI (1890), 337-344; Mary R. Smith, "Statistics of College and Non-College Women," *Am. Stat. Assoc., Publs.*, n.s., VII, 1-26.

[4] J. S. Billings, "The Diminishing Birth Rate in the United States,"

out, seemed a reversal of the principle of natural selection, for the progeny of poor and undernourished parents multiplied while the better-nurtured classes barely held their own. In general, the membership of the average household steadily shrank. In 1890 the most usual size was four members; in 1900 three.[1]

All the moral preachments of the time pointed to the wife and mother as the one upon whom rested the chief responsibility for connubial bliss. Hers it was "to embellish the home, and to make happy the lives of the near and dear ones who dwell within it." [2] Addressing her in the *Christian Herald*, the Reverend T. DeWitt Talmage declared:

> Whether in professional, or commercial, or artistic, or mechanical life, your husband from morning to night is in a Solferino, if not a Sedan. It is a wonder that your husband has any nerves or patience or suavity left. . . . If he come home and sit down preoccupied, you ought to excuse him. If he do not feel like going out that night . . . , remember he has been out all day. . . . Remember, he is not overworking so much for himself as . . . for you and the children.[3]

Nevertheless the law, more charitable, it would seem, than the pulpit, accorded married women larger rights than they had ever before enjoyed in America. The

*Forum*, XV (1893), esp. 475-477. Contraceptive information and devices had been excluded from the mails under heavy penalties by a federal act of 1873. Anthony Comstock, *Frauds Exposed* (N. Y., 1880), 401.

[1] James Bryce, *The American Commonwealth* (London, 1888), III, 676; *Supplementary Analysis and Derivative Tables*, 376, 379, 408-409.

[2] Ward, *Sensible Etiquette*, 353.

[3] That a husband with a slatternly wife "stays at home as little as possible is no wonder," he added. "It is a wonder that such a man does not go on a whaling voyage of three years, and in a leaky ship." Reprinted in T. DeW. Talmage, *The Wedding Ring* (N. Y., 1896), 80-81, 83.

old common-law discriminations, already beginning to crumble prior to the Civil War,[1] continued to fall before the assaults of new legislation. By 1898 the special disabilities of wives had been wholly removed in Mississippi, Oregon and Washington; and in most other states they could own and control their property, retain their earnings, make contracts, sue and be sued.[2] Here and there, however, inequalities of civil status remained. Thus in Georgia, Louisiana, New Mexico, the Dakotas and California the law still expressly designated the husband as head of the family and the wife subject to him. Furthermore, in all but seven states, the father continued to enjoy prior authority in the guardianship of minor children; and a few commonwealths—North Carolina, Kentucky and Texas—ordinarily permitted divorce for adultery only when the wife was the offender. So widely was the principle of civil equality recognized, however, that only time was required to remove the few remaining discriminations from the statute books.

If woman's chief sphere were the home, complaint was general that she had failed badly in one department of her duties, that of training her children. European visitors invariably described them as "pert and disrespectful," one Frenchman maintaining that a composite photograph of American youth would reveal *"le plus terrible de tous les enfants terribles."* [3] Even American

[1] See C. R. Fish, *The Rise of the Common Man* (*A History of American Life*, VI), 271.
[2] Annie N. Meyer, ed., *Woman's Work in America* (N. Y., 1891), 271-274, 446-448; H. C. Whitney, *Marriage and Divorce, the Effect of Each on Personal Status and Property Rights* (Phila., 1894) ; G. J. Bayles, *Woman and the Law* (N. Y., 1901).
[3] Anon., *America and the Americans* (N. Y., 1897), 222. See also Bates, *Year in Great Republic*, I, 52; Hugo Münsterberg, *American Traits from the Point of View of a German* (Boston, 1902), 129; Paul de Rousiers, *American Life* (A. J. Herbertson, tr., Paris, 1892) 254-260; edit., *Ladies' Home Journ.*, IX (1892), no. 7, 12.

writers admitted that filial irreverence was "the greatest blemish that exists on the childhood of this country today," and one suggested that "the present problem of the children is the painless extinction of their elders."[1] Nevertheless the gradual disappearance of corporal punishment from the home was regarded even by such critics as a sign of increasing civilization.[2] Whether the slump in manners was due to parental indulgence, or to a desire to give children a freer and more self-reliant start in life, the experts were not agreed, though doubtless both elements entered into the situation. One thoughtful European was obliged to confess that "the fruit does not by any means correspond to the seed. . . . The unendurable child does not necessarily become an intolerable man."[3]

Perhaps no factor affected child life more than the growth of cities. In the rural districts boys and girls continued to live in the customary manner, close to nature's bosom; but not so in the urban centers. An investigation conducted in 1880 by G. Stanley Hall, then a lecturer in psychology at Harvard, showed that over half the children entering Boston's primary schools had never seen a plow or spade, a robin, squirrel, snail or sheep; they had never observed peaches on a tree or growing grain and could not distinguish an oak tree from a willow or poplar.[4] In place of these traditional

[1] Martha B. Mosher, *Child Culture in the Home* (N. Y., 1898), 168; Kate Douglas Wiggin, *Children's Rights* (Boston, 1892), 3. See also Hall, *Social Customs*, chap. xi; Mary V. Terhune (Marian Harland, *pseud.*), *The Secret of a Happy Home* (N. Y., 1896), chaps. xxi, xxiii; anon., "The Next Generation," *Harper's Bazar*, XV (1882), 754; E. W. Bok, "The Blot on Our American Life," *Ladies' Home Journ.*, XII (1895), no. 8, 14.

[2] Edit., *Ladies' Home Journ.*, X (1893), no. 8, 12.

[3] J. F. Muirhead, *The Land of Contrasts* (Boston, 1898), 70.

[4] G. S. Hall, "The Contents of Children's Minds on Entering School," *Pedagogical Seminary*, I (1891), 139-173. See also C. D. Kellogg, "Child-Life in City and Country," *Journ. of Social Sci.*, XXI (1885),

experiences of American childhood the city youth must arrange his play with reference to paved streets, telegraph poles and iron lamp-posts. Instead of collecting birds' eggs he collected the small picture cards of burlesque queens and prize fighters, which came in cigarette packages. His greatest thrills centered in the clang and clatter of the passing patrol wagon, fire engine or ambulance.

While the swift panorama of the streets more or less colored the manners and outlook of all city children, it was, of course, the center of existence for the waifs of the tenement districts. With such homes particularly in mind, many cities in the 1880's followed New York's earlier example by forming societies for the prevention of cruelty to children. It was due to the activity of such bodies, for instance, that the vicious practice of selling Italian children into the slavery of *padroni*, who compelled them to become beggars or strolling musicians, was stamped out or driven under cover.[1]

Less successful were humanitarians in coping with the growing evil of child labor in factories and sweatshops. Though the census undoubtedly understated the facts, the number of boys and girls from ten to fifteen years old engaged in gainful work was recorded as having increased from a million in 1880 to a million and three quarters in 1900. They were employed mostly in the textile industry, and in the new Southern mill towns often began work as young as seven or eight. In Northern cities children also thronged the streets as newsboys and, with their mothers, formed the mainstay of the

207-223; Stewart Culin, "Street Games of Boys in Brooklyn, N. Y.," *Journ. of Am. Folk-Lore*, IV (1891), 221-237; R. A. Woods, ed., *The City Wilderness* (Boston, 1898), 198.

[1] U. S. Commissioner of Education, *Report for 1879*, ccxi-ccxii; *for 1882-83*, ccvi; Helen Campbell and others, *Darkness and Daylight* (Hartford, 1892), 398-400.

sweating trades. In Chicago large numbers of them toiled as meat packers in the stockyards. State legislation, somewhat more restrictive than in the previous generation, ordinarily forbade child labor under the ages of twelve or fourteen; but even such laws were lacking in most Southern states and in few parts of the Union were they effectively enforced.[1]

In an effort to recover for childhood a part of its natural heritage of outdoor recreation, a Boston society in 1885 tried the experiment of providing sand gardens for youngsters. The success of the undertaking led to an ampler provision of public playgrounds there and to imitation on the part of other municipalities. By the end of 1898, however, the movement had spread to but thirteen cities, mostly in the East.[2] As a special provision for poor and invalid children, the Reverend Willard Parsons of Sherman, Pennsylvania, devised the scheme of "country week" in 1877 to secure a blessed respite of blue sky and pure air during the stifling hot season—a plan quickly taken up by charitable organizations in leading cities and assisted by the "fresh-air funds" of enterprising newspapers.[3] For sons of the well-to-do, summer camps began to be established where city-bred boys were taught the ways of the woods under skilled instruction. The success of the first camp, at Squam Lake, New Hampshire, in 1881, caused others to be set up in New England, New York, Pennsylvania and elsewhere until by the close of the period nearly a score were in operation.[4] If this generation did little more than

[1] Bureau of the Census, *Occupations at the Twelfth Census* (*Special Rep.*), lxvi-lxviii; U. S. Industrial Commission, *Reports* (Wash., 1900-1902), XIX, 917, 922; Campbell, *Darkness and Daylight*, chaps. iv-v.

[2] C. E. Rainwater, *The Play Movement in the United States* (Chicago, 1921), chap. ii.

[3] Campbell, *Darkness and Daylight*, 313-317; R. A. Woods and others, *The Poor in Great Cities* (N. Y., 1895), 131-150.

[4] Porter Sargent, *A Handbook of Summer Camps* (Boston, 1925),

glimpse the problem of conserving childhood under the new conditions of American life, at least it laid foundations upon which its successors were to build more soundly.

One pleasure the city could give young America which the country could not rival. This consisted in the variety and savoriness of the comestibles at hand.[1] Nor was the child specialist yet come to judgment, intent on turning into Dead Sea fruit the dainties most appetizing to juvenile palates. On the Northern farm the long winter usually meant an uninterrupted routine of heavy foods without fresh fruit or green vegetables, followed by a general "spring sickness" which sent the people helter-skelter to the village druggist for tonics and "molasses 'n' sulphur." The city, on the other hand, with its concentration of wealth and population, supplied a market for the ready sale of myriad food products brought from all parts of the world by means of ever swifter transportation and improved methods of refrigeration.[2]

Moreover, the sedentary habits of many urban dwellers, calling for a diet less burdened with meat, made them eager to diversify their fare and caused them to rely more on vegetables, salads, fish and fruit. In the mid-century fresh fish had been available only to persons living near bodies of water; but in the eighties and nineties fish, caught in the Northern Pacific and transported several thousand miles, was daily supplied fresh to the markets of the Middle West and the Atlantic

---

17-31; Louis Rouillon, "Summer Camps for Boys," *Am. Rev. of Revs.*, XXI (1900), 697-703.

[1] "No other people existing, or that ever did exist, could command such a variety of edible products for daily consumption as the mass of the American people habitually use to-day." C. D. Warner, *The Relation of Literature to Life* (N. Y., 1897), 264. See also N. S. Shaler, ed., *The United States of America* (N. Y., 1894), III, 1243.

[2] W. A. Taylor, "The Influence of Refrigeration on the Fruit Industry," U. S. Dept. of Agr., *Yearbook for 1900*, 561-580.

Coast.[1] Most tropical fruits—oranges, lemons, red-skinned bananas—were as abundant and cheap in the city as domestic fruits, sometimes cheaper, and their consumption increased greatly throughout the period.[2] After the attractive exhibit of grapefruit at the Chicago World's Fair epicures began tentatively to add that dish to their breakfast menu.

Steadily the factory invaded the precincts of the city kitchen, lightening the drudgery of the home and enriching the family dietary. Quaker Oats, Wheatena and other package cereals began to take the place of cornmeal mush and similar concoctions at the breakfast table. The prejudice against baker's bread as the mark of a lazy housewife waned in face of the greater convenience of commercially prepared loaves, though even town women usually continued to make their own cakes and cookies. Factory-canned foods also came, for the first time, to occupy an important place in the housewife's activities. After 1878 canning factories multiplied in the East and the Middle West while improved machinery cheapened the cost and increased the variety of the foods packed.[3] By the mid-nineties the principal canned goods, in the order of their importance, were tomatoes, corn, milk, oysters, corned beef, salmon, sardines, peaches, peas and beans. "Housekeeping is getting to be ready made, as well as clothing," rejoiced one

[1] C. M. Depew, ed., *One Hundred Years of American Commerce* (N. Y., 1895), II, 390, 393; D. A. Wells, *Recent Economic Changes* (N. Y., 1889), 340.

[2] For instance, from 1880 to 1887 the importation of bananas into the United States grew fortyfold. Wells, *Recent Economic Changes,* 339; anon., "Bananas," *Good Housekeeping,* VIII (1889), 112. See also Depew, *American Commerce,* II, 603-605, and Arnold, *Civilization in United States,* 165.

[3] Depew, *American Commerce,* II, 398-399; J. H. Collins, *The Story of Canned Goods* (N. Y., 1924), esp. 38, 80-82, 126-127, 155, 166, 187; anon., "Canned Goods," *Good Housekeeping,* X (1890), 105 ff.

woman, who predicted that "Even the cook book may yet be obsolete, for every can of prepared food has a label with directions how to cook."[1] At the same time synthetic food products made their appearance. The rapid spread of the use of oleomargarine in place of butter threatened a serious rift in the ranks of the Farmers' Alliance movement in the 1880's, with the dairy farmers opposing the cattle raisers and the Southern cottonseed crushers.[2] Not content with the restrictive measures adopted by nearly twenty states, the dairy interests induced Congress in 1886 to pass a law taxing oleo and regulating its sale.[3]

Though the antagonism to oleo was based on economic rather than sanitary grounds, the increasing part played by outside agencies in preparing food for the home made governmental supervision important as a health measure. The Supreme Court's decision in the Slaughter House cases (1873) breathed new life into the efforts of states and municipalities to regulate the slaughtering of meat. Thanks to agitation by medical and health associations, pure-food laws were passed in 1881 by New York, New Jersey, Michigan and Illinois, and before the end of 1895 twenty-three other states had followed their lead.[4] Milk came in for special attention because of its relation to infant mortality. Not only did

[1] Anon., "Ready-made Housekeeping," *Good Housekeeping*, V (1887), 266.

[2] H. C. Nixon, "The Cleavage within the Farmers' Alliance Movement," *Miss. Valley Hist. Rev.*, XV, esp. 25-26. For the similar strife over compound lard and vegetable shortening, see 26-31.

[3] R. A. Clemen, *By-Products in the Packing Industry* (Chicago, 1927), 170-180.

[4] Modeled on the English laws of 1875 and 1879. W. M. Ravenel, ed., *A Half Century of Public Health* (N. Y., 1921), 213-214; W. K. Newton, "The Sanitary Control of the Food Supply," Am. Public Health Assoc., *Public Health*, IV, 151-154; Shaler, *United States*, III, 1232; C. O. Bates, "Pure Food Laws," Iowa Acad. of Sci., *Proceeds.*, VIII, 206 ff.

the principal cities provide for systematic inspection of their sources of supply, but by 1900 twenty-nine states had pure-milk laws on their statute books. Aside from milk inspection, such laws were usually not well enforced, though Wisconsin, Michigan, Ohio and Connecticut stand out as shining exceptions.

American cooking was not favorably regarded by foreign travelers though their opinion may have been influenced by national prejudices. The worst conditions prevailed in the country where the frying pan remained the mainstay of all cooking. But even in the cities the ordinary American family cared more about the quantity than the quality of the food set before them. In such centers, however, inherited frontier culinary habits were becoming modified by contact with foreign peoples. Italian spaghetti and olives, Hungarian goulash and Chinese chop suey (unknown in China) were gastronomic contributions of the newer immigrant stocks as surely as the white potato and sauerkraut had been of earlier ones. More important was the attention which Americans began to give to the subtleties of seasoning. In the five years following the removal of the tariff on unground spices in 1883 the amount of pepper, pimento, cloves and nutmegs imported into America doubled.[1]

That cooking was a subject worthy of scientific study was recognized when the New York Cooking School was opened in 1874 and the Boston Cooking School three years later. The former had twelve hundred students enrolled in the winter of 1877-1878.[2] Other schools were established in Philadelphia, Washington and elsewhere and courses were even introduced into the high schools. At the same time dietary studies were

---

[1] Wells, *Recent Economic Changes*, 384-385.
[2] U. S. Comr. of Educ., *Rep. for 1878*, cxcv.

undertaken by official and private agencies and the printing press groaned with the production of new and improved manuals and cookbooks.[1] Nor did the pleasures of between-meal eating escape attention, especially on the part of commercial caterers to the popular palate. The simple candies of yore— peppermint sticks, gum drops, candy hearts inscribed with sentimental mottoes—were supplemented by boxed confections such as Gunther's (Chicago) and Lowney's (Boston). Chewing gum won an army of addicts, notably among children and the vulgar classes.[2] Ginger beer, pop and other "soft" drinks acquired a new popularity, partly as a result of discoveries which made the artificial production of ice a commercial success.[3] Soda fountains, introduced by the previous generation, grew rapidly in number until, at the close of the period, perhaps sixty thousand were in use.[4] Constructed imposingly of marble, onyx and various decorative metals, some of them cost as much as ten thousand dollars. Few courtships lacked the odorous adjunct of the soda fountain. The young lady and her escort, having made their choice of syrups, waited in palpitant ecstasy while the attendant pulled the faucet first this way for the broad,

[1] See A. P. Bryant, "Some Results of Dietary Studies in the United States," U. S. Dept. of Agr., *Yearbook for 1898*, 439-452, and A. C. True and R. D. Milner, "Development of the Nutrition Investigations of the Department of Agriculture," U. S. Dept. of Agr., *Yearbook for 1899*, 403-414. Fannie Merritt Farmer's *The Boston Cooking-School Cook Book*, which quickly became standard, was first published in 1896.

[2] In *As We Were Saying* (N. Y., 1891), 80-85, C. D. Warner amusingly deplores the wasted energy resulting from the "gum habit" of "the last ten years."

[3] Ice-making plants first appeared in the South in the 1870's and, after the failure of the natural-ice crop in the two mild winters of 1888-1890, spread rapidly through the North. T. M. Prudden, "Our Ice Supply," *Pop. Sci. Mo.*, XXXII (1888), 668-682; F. A. Fernald, "Ice-Making and Machine Refrigeration," *Pop. Sci. Mo.*, XXXIX (1891), 19-20.

[4] Depew, *American Commerce*, II, 470-474.

silvery, foaming stream of soda and then that for the
sharp hissing spurt which crowned the glass with irides-
cent bubbles.

As the cost of manufactured tobacco steadily declined
and its quality improved, the tobacco habit affected an
ever greater proportion of people. Red-blooded men
smoked cigars and pipes and chewed tobacco, the latter
habit being shared by men otherwise so dissimilar as
James Whitcomb Riley, President Cleveland and the
eminent zoologist, Professor W. K. Brooks of Johns
Hopkins. The new-fangled cigarette, on the other hand,
bore the taint of the dude, the sissy and the underworld. Notwithstanding this stigma and the belief that
the "insane asylums . . . are being constantly recruited from excessive smokers of the cigarette," its use
grew nearly nine times as fast as that of the cigar during the period.[1] Perhaps as a quick nervous smoke it
accorded better with the increasing tension of urban life.
In the world of fashion smoking in any form was
frowned upon as a reprehensible masculine habit not to
be practised in the presence of the other sex. It was even
"bad form for a gentleman to smoke on streets . . . at
the hours at which he will be likely to meet many ladies." [2] At the dinner parties of the 1890's, however, an
increasing number of hostesses permitted their male guests
to smoke, though any woman who ventured to join
them would at once have placed herself beyond the pale.

The interior of the home showed signs of emerging
from the reign of terror which had afflicted it in the
preceding generation.[3] In the early 1880's the typical

---

[1] Mosher, *Child Culture*, 202-203; Depew, *American Commerce*,
II, 420-421; Meyer Jacobstein, *The Tobacco Industry in the United
States* (Columbia Univ., *Studies*, XXVI, no. 3), 45-52.

[2] Hall, *Social Customs*, 290-291.

[3] See Allan Nevins, *The Emergence of Modern America* (*A History
of American Life*, VIII), 205-208.

middle-class abode was still likely to be a museum of æsthetic horrors, the choicest rooms cluttered up with easels, bamboo stands, gilded rams' horns, hand-painted rolling pins, and inverted glass domes sheltering wax flowers and china statuettes. To complete the chaos, Japanese lanterns often hung from the ceiling and a painted iron heron stood one-legged amidst cat-tails beside the marble mantel. Such a home, for example, the Marches in Howells's *A Hazard of New Fortunes* found themselves obliged to take after six weary chapters of house hunting in New York.[1] But better things portended. While Mrs. John A. Logan, writing from Washington in the decorous traditions of senatorial conservatism, continued to hymn the advantages of turning cupid-decorated tambourines into photograph frames, another widely read authority, the sister of President Cleveland, was announcing that "every room in the house should be arranged for occupancy, having nothing too good for use," and no room should be overcrowded.[2]

American taste was steadily improving as Americans traveled more widely, as art museums and art schools multiplied, and as women's magazines like the *Ladies' Home Journal,* founded in 1883, and *Good Housekeeping,* dating from 1885, devoted increasing space to sanity in household decoration. The Philadelphia Centennial in 1876 gave an important stimulus to better standards of home furnishing, particularly in the East, equaled only by the influence of the far superior exhibits of the World's Fair of 1893 on the minds of countless

[1] W. D. Howells, *A Hazard of New Fortunes* (N. Y., 1889), I, 58-60. For other descriptions, see anon., "Forty Years Ago, and Now," *Harper's Bazar,* XIII (1880), 514, and anon., "N. Y. Fashions: House-Furnishing," *Harper's Bazar,* XV (1882), 323.

[2] Mrs. J. A. Logan, *The Home Manual* (Boston, 1889), 267-268; Rose E. Cleveland, ed., *The Social Mirror* (St. Louis, 1888), 345, 348.

thousands of Middle Westerners.[1] At the same time the æsthetic doctrines of the Englishmen Charles L. Eastlake and William Morris swept like a fresh breeze through American drawing rooms, helping to clean out much of the débris; and the efforts—not always successful—of manufacturers in Grand Rapids, Chicago and New York to duplicate the superior furniture at lower cost brought better-designed pieces into the homes of the masses.

Undoubtedly, too, the servant problem—"the great unsolved American Question," according to one domestic authority—had a wholesome effect on the situation.[2] Whether, as some maintained, the arrogant mistress was the problem rather than the impertinent maid, servants were hard to get and harder to keep despite the enormous immigration of these years.[3] Accordingly, common sense dictated greater simplicity in furnishings and the adoption of labor-saving devices to lighten housework. The introduction of courses in domestic science in high schools and universities helped also to raise housekeeping from a traditional folk exercise to somewhat the dignity of a profession. Whatever the causes, the results were so marked that Judge Robert Grant described the typical American home of the mid-nineties as

---

[1] See, for example, J. L. Ford, *Forty-Odd Years in the Literary Shop* (N. Y., 1921), 75-77; C. D. Warner, *Studies in the South and West* (N. Y., 1889), 153; F. A. Fernald, "Household Arts at the World's Fair," *Pop. Sci. Mo.*, XLIII (1893), 803-812.

[2] M. E. W. Sherwood, *The Art of Entertaining* (N. Y., 1892), 206-220. See also Julia M. Wright, *The Complete Home* (Phila., 1879), chap. xviii; Helen Campbell, *Household Economics* (N. Y., 1897), chap. xi; Lucy M. Salmon, *Domestic Service* (N. Y., 1897), esp. chaps. vi-ix.

[3] Among the Cleveland Papers in the Library of Congress are protests against the proposed literacy test of 1897 on the ground that thereby the incoming stream of domestic servants would be seriously reduced. Mr. J. L. Norton has called my attention especially to letters of J. H. Semmes to J. G. Carlisle, Feb. 18, 1897, and C. S. Hamlin to H. T. Thurber, Feb. 23, 1897.

"intended for every-day use by rational beings." [1] He was referring, of course, primarily to city abodes because in smaller towns and in the country the older customs still held sway.

The changes can be followed in greater detail. Nothing was more revolutionary, perhaps, than the widespread abolition of the parlor, a ceremonial room which, darkened with drawn shades and closed doors, had hitherto served as a sort of mortuary chapel for the reception of guests. As the normal life of the family reached into all parts of the house other improvements were inaugurated. More and larger windows made the home cheerier, as did also the replacement of dark gloomy wallpaper with pale tints and simple chintz designs, and the substitution of lighter furniture for ponderous mahogany and black walnut. Upholstery of glossy black horsehair, once the pride of every middle-class household though always a mortification to the flesh, gave way rapidly to rep coverings or even to cretonne and plush. [2] In many homes metal bedsteads, for better or worse, replaced the old top-heavy wooden ones with their elaborately carved headboards reaching almost to the ceiling. Carpets continued to stretch from wall to wall in the average house, but as the rough board floors were succeeded by evenly joined, polished ones, rugs became increasingly popular, commending themselves by reason of greater cleanliness and the possibility of more artistic effects. [3]

At the same time better arrangements for plumbing

[1] Robert Grant, "The Art of Living," *Scribner's Mag.*, XVII (1895), esp. 308 (later printed in book form under the same title). See also Florence R. Simmons, "Superannuated Trash," *Good Housekeeping*, XII (1891), 41.

[2] Campbell, *Household Economics*, 113-114.

[3] Mrs. M. J. Plumstead, "Sweeping Day," *Good Housekeeping*, III (1886), 51; Sarah B. Thayer, "A Reconstructed Household," same mag., XII (1891), 11.

and heating enhanced both comfort and safety. The primitive plumbing of the 1870's, by conveying noxious odors into the rooms, was often a threat to the family health,[1] but with the introduction of improved methods and appliances, adopted under the prod of state and municipal inspection laws, a great change resulted in domestic sanitary equipment in the 1880's.[2] Plumbing could no longer be installed in a first-class dwelling for about two hundred and fifty dollars, as in Civil War times, but was more apt to cost from two to four thousand dollars. Nowhere was the change more welcome than in the bathroom, which at the beginning of the period was usually small and gloomy, its atmosphere tainted with sewer gas. As plumbing fixtures became more tasteful and the bath tub shed its zinc lining for white enamel or porcelain, the mistress of the house began to take a special delight in keeping this room spotless and airy.

Less alteration occurred in methods of heating. The base burner, with funereal urns on top and mica windows showing the blaze within, continued to be the chief resort of most homes; and any woman considered herself fortunate who owned a Crown Jewel, a Hub or an Art Garland. Yet well-to-do families usually aspired to a hot-air furnace and, as the price of steam-heating and hot-water systems fell with the expiration of the basic patents, there was a notable expansion in the use of such furnaces as well.

[1] Clarence Cook, "Beds and Tables, Stools and Candlesticks," *Scribner's Mo.*, XIII (1876-1877), 86; C. F. Wingate, "The Unsanitary Homes of the Rich," *N. Am. Rev.*, CXXXVII (1883), 172; Campbell, *Household Economics*, 75-77.

[2] G. E. Waring, jr., "Recent Modifications in Sanitary Drainage," *Atlantic Mo.*, XLIV (1879), 56-62; W. P. Trowbridge, "Modern Sanitary Engineering," *Harper's Mag.*, LXVIII (1884), 761; W. T. (*pseud.*), "Some Common Facts about Plumbing," *Architectural Record*, I (1891), 97-108.

In the kitchen the housewife learned to rely increasingly upon a wide assortment of new conveniences, such as the steam cooker, double boiler, Dover egg beater, gas toaster, asbestos stove mat, triple saucepans and cake tins with removable bottoms. More important perhaps was the introduction of aluminum ware shortly after 1890 in place of the iron or tin or granite variety. New metallurgical processes had made the metal almost as cheap as tin, and it won quick favor by reason of its lightness, durability and freedom from poisonous alloys.[1] Improved makes of washing machines also appeared and, thanks to the genius of Mrs. Potts, a practicable flatiron with a detachable handle was added to the equipment of the laundry. Even greater relief was promised by the enlarging patronage of commercial laundries by private families.[2] One form of drudgery, however, resisted all efforts at abatement: the washing of dishes.

The progressive liberation from household routine left the middle-class woman with more leisure on her hands than ever before and opened the way for a wider participation in the world that lay beyond domestic walls. The wives and daughters of the poor had long been swelling the ranks of industry, and the five-year depression following 1873 had shown that women even of the comfortable classes might unexpectedly be obliged to supplement the family income. At the same time the colleges and universities were training increasing numbers for pursuits hitherto followed chiefly by men, while the new conditions of American life were opening employments to them wholly unknown to previous generations.

Though the old prejudice against self-support for

[1] J. W. Richards, "Recent Progress in the Aluminum Industry," Franklin Inst., *Journ.*, CXLIX, 451, 454.

[2] Edith Minister, "Ironing Day," *Good Housekeeping*, XVII (1893), 20.

women lingered, its doom was rendered more certain with the passage of each year. "We have reached a new era," declared a women's magazine in 1883. "Slowly as woman has come to her inheritance, it stretches before her now into illimitable distance, and the question of the hour is rather whether she is ready for her trust than whether that trust is hampered by conditions." [1] Never before had such attractive and multifarious occupations been within reach. Women who would have shrunk from factory work and domestic service or even from teaching trooped forth with a sense of adventure to become typists, telephone girls, typesetters, bookkeepers, nurses, librarians, journalists, lecturers, social workers, doctors, lawyers, artists. Even in the realm of mechanical invention, a time-honored monopoly of men, they were displaying surprising capacity in a variety of fields. [2] Miss Faithfull reported that in Massachusetts alone there were in 1882 nearly three hundred branches of business and industry in which women could earn from one hundred to three thousand dollars a year. [3] It is not surprising that the number of feminine breadwinners in the United States rose from two and a half million in 1880 to four million in 1890 and to five and a third million in 1900, or that legislatures in the chief industrial states began in the 1880's to give serious attention to acts for regulating factory conditions of female toil. [4]

[1] Anon., "The Promise of the Dawn," *Harper's Bazar*, XVI (1883), 18. See also Robert Burdette, "Woman Yesterday and Today," *Ladies' Home Journ.*, IX (1892), no. 2, 11.

[2] Anon., "Women as Inventors," *Good Housekeeping*, VIII (1889), 119.

[3] Faithfull, *Three Visits to America*, 275. See also Mary P. Jacobi, *"Common Sense" Applied to Woman Suffrage* (N. Y., 1894), 16, 118-119, 201.

[4] *Occupations at the Twelfth Census*, lxxxvi; Bayles, *Woman and the Law*, 257-260; F. J. Stimson, *Handbook to the Labor Law of the United States* (N. Y., 1896), 55, 71, 79-80.

THE LADIES HOME JOURNAL

*The woman in business, a new phenomenon.*

## The New Woman

Nowhere was the change in the position of the sex more striking than in the old Confederacy. There the "nobility of helplessness in woman" was still cherished as an ideal by many survivors of the old régime; but postwar realities—the goad of poverty, the opportunities of city life, the shiftlessness of hired help—caused the younger generation to discover the ideal of self-reliance and self-support. "The crowning glory of the present age is that every woman is free to develop her own personality," proclaimed one daughter of Dixie in the early 1890's. In contrast to former times, "a woman is respected and honored in the South for earning her own living, and would lose respect if . . . she settled herself as a burden on a brother" or hard-working father.[1] It was noted that a larger proportion of girls, even of the poorer classes, were going to college than formerly and that more of them stayed on to take their degrees.

Not all American women used their new-found time in bread-winning pursuits: many of them, especially of the upper middle class, found an outlet in club activities. "We have art clubs, book clubs, dramatic clubs, pottery clubs. We have sewing circles, philanthropic associations, scientific, literary, religious, athletic, musical, and decorative art societies," testified one writer.[2] "The absence of men," observed a visiting French woman, "would make French women feel . . . as if they were eating bread without butter."[3] But such extramural contacts were the best means the average housewife had of learning about the complex world in which circumstances were forcing her to play a part; and

[1] W. F. Tillett, "Southern Womanhood as Affected by the War," Century, XLIII (1891-1892), 9-16.

[2] "Contributors' Club," Atlantic Mo., XLVI (1880), 724-725.

[3] Thérèse Blanc, The Condition of Woman in the United States (Abby L. Alger, tr., Boston, 1895), 107.

though the clubs often served as mere excuses for evading domestic responsibility, they proved to be an indispensable training school for countless women who became active civic and humanitarian leaders in their respective communities. By 1889 the clubs were so numerous and influential that they became linked together in a great national system under the name of the General Federation of Women's Clubs.[1]

Conservative folk were not at all certain that the widening range of feminine activity denoted progress. "What is this curious product of to-day, the American girl or woman?" asked one woman writer. ". . . is it possible for any novel, within the next fifty years, truly to depict her as a finality, when she is still emerging from new conditions . . . , when she does not yet understand herself . . . ?" She added, "The face of to-day is stamped with restlessness, wandering purpose, and self-consciousness." [2] As the years passed the note of disapprobation was sounded more and more frequently. "The great fault of the girl of to-day," declared another member of the sex in 1890, "is discontent. She calls it by the more magnificent sounding name of ambition, but in reality she is absolutely restless and dissatisfied with whatever may be her position in life." [3]

Nothing more excited both male and female disapproval than the energetic attempts of certain women to claim for their sex equal political rights with men. In the opening years of the period even the historian Park-

[1] By 1896 the membership consisted of 495 individual clubs and 20 state federations. Ellen M. Henrotin, "The General Federation of Women's Clubs," *Outlook*, LX (1897), 443-444.

[2] Kate G. Wells, "The Transitional American Woman," *Atlantic Mo.*, XLVI (1880), 817-818 (reprinted in her *About People*, Boston, 1885).

[3] Ruth Ashmore, "Side-Talks with Girls," *Ladies' Home Journ.*, VII (1890), no. 4, 10. See also her "The Restlessness of the Age" in same mag., XII (1895), no. 2, 16; and editorials in VII (1890), no. 11, 10; X (1893), no. 5, 18.

man was tempted away from his cloisters long enough
to deliver some smashing blows against this effort to
overleap "Nature's limitations," disrupt the home and
give women excitements and cares "too much for their
strength." Especially in the "crowded cities," he pointed
out, woman suffrage would be "madness," a certain
means of making bad government worse.[1] Five leading
feminists joined in a powerful counterblast: Julia Ward
Howe, Thomas Wentworth Higginson, Lucy Stone
(Blackwell), Elizabeth Cady Stanton and Wendell
Phillips.[2] Reaffirming the principles of the Declaration
of Independence, they declared that women as well as
men had contributions to make to public life and denounced the failure to accept the consequences of woman's altered position as an effort to "put the bird back
into the egg." "One of two things is true:" asserted the
forthright Phillips, "either woman is like man—and if
she is, then a ballot based on brains belongs to her as
well as to him; or she is different, and then man does
not know how to vote for her as well as she herself
does."

This widely read debate marked the lines on which
the great battle over the ballot was fought in periodicals,
public gatherings, legislative halls and constitutional
conventions. While the majority of women remained
somewhat indifferent spectators, the militant "antis" did
not feel that their disapproval of feminine political
activity precluded them from organizing committees and
societies in opposition. In effectiveness of organization,
however, they were completely outdone by their an-
tagonists, many of whom had been trained in the old

[1] Francis Parkman, "The Woman Question," *N. Am. Rev.*, CXXIX
(1879), 303-321. See also his reply to his critics, "The Woman Question Again," in same mag., CXXX (1880), 16-30.

[2] Anon., "The Other Side of the Woman Question," *N. Am. Rev.*,
CXXIX (1879), 413-446.

days of the antislavery struggle and the Sanitary Commission. Already two strong woman-suffrage associations were in the field, the American and the National, one seeking the ballot through state action, the other through a federal amendment.[1] New branches of these bodies were organized in the various states; and in 1890, when it became clear that the parent societies were but two blades of the same scissors, they united under the name of the National American Woman Suffrage Association.

Meantime campaigns were being hotly waged on every front and with many weapons. As Colonel Higginson pointed out, "Mrs. Stowe helps to free Uncle Tom in his cabin, and then strikes for the freedom of women in her own 'Hearth and Home.' Mrs. Howe writes the 'Battle Hymn of the Republic,' and keeps on writing more battle-hymns in behalf of her own sex. Miss Alcott not only delineates 'Little Women,' but wishes to emancipate them." [2] Prominent men lent their pens and voices to the cause: George W. Curtis, Senator G. F. Hoar, the venerated Whittier and others. Both the Knights of Labor and the American Federation of Labor rallied to the banner. In 1878 Senator A. A. Sargent of California introduced into Congress an equal-suffrage amendment, drafted by Susan B. Anthony in the very language which forty-two years later was to find lodgment in the Constitution.[3] In the next two decades Senate committees reported five times and House committees twice in favor of the proposal, but action went no further. The platforms of the major parties ignored the issue, and the Prohibitionists perhaps hurt

[1] See Nevins, *Emergence of Modern America*, 340.

[2] T. W. Higginson, *Common Sense about Women* (Boston, 1881), 329.

[3] Susan B. Anthony and others, *History of Woman Suffrage* (Rochester and N. Y., 1881-1926), V, 623.

it by associating it in the public mind with their battle against rum. In 1884 a group of suffragists launched a political party of their own, the Equal Rights party, defiantly nominating for president a woman lawyer, Mrs. Belva A. Lockwood of Washington, D. C. Though the outcome scarcely justified it, she was put forward in the next election as well.[1]

The policy of divide-and-conquer brought more encouraging results. Campaign after campaign was conducted in state after state under the inspiration of veteran leaders like the angular Miss Anthony and the motherly Mrs. Stanton, aided by such new recruits as Dr. Anna Howard Shaw and Mrs. Carrie Chapman Catt.[2] The initial gains, as in Britain and the Scandinavian countries during these same years, took the form of obtaining the vote in school elections and sometimes also in regard to municipal or taxation questions. Thus in 1878 New Hampshire and Oregon, following the earlier example of a few other states, authorized school suffrage. Massachusetts, New York and Vermont acted in the next two years, and by the close of 1898 thirteen additional states and territories, representing all parts of the Union but the old Confederacy, had fallen into line.[3]

The cause of full equality in voting, on the other hand, showed signs of losing ground when Congress by the Edmunds law of 1887 deprived the women of Utah territory of the ballot as a means of destroying polygamy and when, two years later, the voters of

[1] T. H. McKee, ed., *The National Conventions and Platforms of All Political Parties* (3d edn., Balt., 1900), 226-228, 256.

[2] Ida H. Harper, *The Life and Work of Susan B. Anthony* (Indianapolis, 1898-1908), II, *passim*.

[3] Montana, Iowa and Louisiana established a form of taxation suffrage, respectively in 1887, 1894 and 1898; Kansas municipal suffrage in 1887 and Michigan in 1893 (declared unconstitutional). E. A. Hecker. *A Short History of Women's Rights* (N. Y., 1910), 167.

Washington refused to authorize the reëstablishment of
equal suffrage at the election for adopting a state constitution.[1] The next year, however, Wyoming was admitted into the Union with the universal suffrage she
had practised since 1869; and three of her neighbors
after achieving statehood—Colorado in 1893 and Utah
and Idaho in 1896—ranged themselves by her side.
Nevertheless the closing years of the decade showed an
apparent decline of interest in the movement. For some
years to come most Americans were to regard "ballots
for both" as an aberration of the wild and woolly
West.

Feminism, with considerably less success, sought to
play a rôle in the reform of women's clothing. In this
domain Paris ruled supreme, and the law and the proph-
ets required that the human figure be used to display
clothes, not clothes the figure. Most American women
in the late 1870's, tightly imprisoned in wasplike
waists, reveled in flounces and frills, their long, trail-
ing skirts, drawn in at the bottom, making a quick gait
impossible. The "street-cleaning-department style" it
was called by a writer in *Harper's Bazar*.[2] Underneath
they were stuffed out with layers of garments known
collectively as "unmentionables." Young women dressed
like their elders and, by a natural law of descent, even
the children were clad to look like premature grown-
ups.[3] About 1880 began the vogue of the pannier, an
overskirt draped up at the hips or back by means of a
bustle. With each season pannier draperies grew more
"bouffant," dress extenders or cushion bustles with

[1] Mary A. Greene, "Results of the Woman-Suffrage Movement,"
*Forum*, XVII (1894), esp. 414-416.

[2] Anon., "Clothed and in Her Right Mind," *Harper's Bazar*, XIV
(1881), 562.

[3] See, for example, anon., "Childish Children," *Harper's Bazar*, XIV
(1881), 663; Isabel A. Mallon, "Dressing a Growing Girl," *Ladies'
Home Journ.*, X (1893), no. 9, 21.

steel springs being used to produce the desired effect. A walking costume, described in the *Cosmopolitan* for October, 1887, called for fifteen and a half yards of material twenty-two inches wide; a stylish frock for eighteen and a half yards. But at the close of the decade the pannier was on the decline, while the skirt was worn wider at the bottom and the sleeves, hitherto tight, had become high and full.[1] The new mode reached its climax in 1896 in the leg-o'-mutton sleeve, puffed out balloonlike from a tight band below the elbow and projecting beyond the shoulder.

Recurrent protests against the tyranny of fashion were based partly upon considerations of cost,[2] but much more on the presumed unhealthful effects of long, heavy skirts, tight, high-heeled shoes and, worst of all, the breath-taking, steel-reënforced corsets. "Woman by her injurious style of dress," asserted one physician, "is doing as much to destroy the race as is man by alcoholism." "Niggardly waists and niggardly brains go together," agreed Miss Frances Willard.[3] In the 1870's the New England Women's Club, led by Elizabeth Stuart Phelps, had raised the banner of revolt, declaring war in particular against the corset, and had even opened

[1] Modish skirts in 1890 were from four and a half to five yards wide at the bottom. *Ladies' Home Journ.*, VII (1890), no. 7, 15.

[2] One well-known pulpiteer, calling attention to the fact that "Arnold of the Revolution proposed to sell his country in order to get money to support his home wardrobe," announced that a similar cause had "sent prominent business men to the watering of stocks, and life insurance presidents to perjured statements about their assets, and some of them to the penitentiary, and has completely upset our American finances." Talmage, *Wedding Ring*, 103-104.

[3] Dr. R. L. Dickinson of Brooklyn estimated the pressure exerted by corsets as varying, in given cases, from 21 to 88 pounds. Helen G. Ecob, *The Well-Dressed Woman* (N. Y., 1892), 27-29, 34-35. See also B. W. Richardson, "Dress in Relation to Health," *Pop. Sci. Mo.*, XVII (1880), 182-199. But Mrs. Terhune declared: "Women will wear corsets; they always have and they always will. We may as well consider this a settled fact." Mary V. Terhune (Marion Harland, *pseud.*), *Talks upon Practical Subjects* (N. Y., 1895), 119.

a shop for the sale of "dress-reform garments."[1]
Though a limited number of women, presumably in the
vicinity of Boston, adopted the new "health waists,"
evidence is overwhelming that, in general, the corset
continued to hold its own.

Yet each year, by emphasizing anew the cramping
effects of the prevailing styles upon the enlarging activities of women, prepared the way for a new rebellion.
In 1891 the National Council of Women of the United
States, meeting in Washington, gave the matter of
rational attire particular consideration. Its committee
reported the following year in favor of a model based
upon the "Syrian costume adopted by the English Society for Rational Dress, the short-skirted gown with leg-
gins, and the new gymnastic suit."[2] While no change
so radical could hope for adoption, a wider vogue of
"mannish styles" such as tailored suits and shirt waists,
an increasing use of discreetly shorter skirts for business
and even, in some cases, the wearing of divided skirts
for bicycling gave promise of a better day.[3]

By none were the caprices of fashion more hypnoti-
cally followed than by the leaders of society. But this
generation remained more or less puzzled as to who were
the leaders and just what was Society. Culture, wealth,
family—no single criterion was conclusive. In Boston,
it was said, the question was, "How much do you
know?"; in New York, "How much are you worth?";
in Philadelphia, "Who was your grandfather?" In Chicago, social life remained "more fluid and undetermined

[1] Julia A. Sprague, *History of the New England Women's Club*
(N. Y., 1894), 19-20; Julia Ward Howe, "Dress and Undress," *Forum*,
III (1887), esp. 315; Ecob, *Well-Dressed Woman*, 130-132.

[2] Ecob, *Well-Dressed Woman*, 143-146. A series of articles favorable
to the movement appeared in the *Arena*, VI-VIII (1892-1893).

[3] May R. Kern, "Dressing without the Corset," *Ladies' Home Journ.*,
X (1893), no. 8, 17; C. H. Crandall, "What Men Think of Women's
Dress," *N. Am. Rev.*, CLXI (1895), 251-254.

than in Eastern large cities," with the newly rich aspiring to inherit the kingdom.[1] San Francisco was noted for its "terribly fast so-called society set, engrossed by the emptiest and most trivial pleasures . . . ."[2] Yet even in Boston and Philadelphia the forward thrust of postwar millionaires, merchant princes and railway barons was upsetting established values and introducing the gold standard. Throughout the country in fact, even in the urban parts of the South, social gradations were rapidly taking the form expressed by the Englishman who said that "all humanity is divided into pounds, shillings and pence."

The aspirations of social climbers were reflected in the appearance of a plethora of etiquette books, bearing such titles as *The Social Etiquette of New York* (1878), *The P. G., or, Perfect Gentleman* (1887) and *Success in Society* (1888).[3] How should socially inexperienced but well-to-do nobodies manipulate a fork, wear a dress coat, know when and on whom to leave cards?[4] How could they attain that lofty distinction of manner which would permit them to be ill-bred in a well-bred way? Invited to dine at the Coreys' on the water side of Beacon Street, the ladies of Silas Lapham's household consulted not one but several etiquette books to prepare for the great occasion. The social game usually was played by the deft hands of women who often developed a skill of strategy and execution which exceeded that of their husbands on the Rialto. Palatial mansions and liveried retinues helped obscure the rise from humble origins; liberal patronage of fashionable

---

[1] Warner, *Studies*, 196.

[2] Faithfull, *Three Visits to America*, 216-217.

[3] Many others are referred to in footnotes earlier in this chapter.

[4] See the frank recognition of this situation in the preface of Mrs. John Sherwood, *Manners and Social Usages* (N. Y., 1884; rev., 1887, 1897).

charities might provide the magic key; a busy guild of
genealogists stood ready to furnish "ancestors." Even
Mrs. Mary Baker Eddy for a time paraded a coat of
arms until her right to it was protested by the representative of the family in Scotland.[1] If such measures
failed, there was always the possibility of a brilliant
international marriage.

To upholders of a more genteel tradition American
society seemed to smack too much of the marriage mart.
"The parents launch their offspring as well as possible,
and display their wares to the greatest advantage, but
the business of the market is carried on chiefly by the
young girls themselves, instead of by their mothers as
in England and Europe." [2] "Care should be taken in
presenting foreigners to young ladies," cautioned one
authority on etiquette, for "sometimes titles are dubious." [3] Yet a surprising number of the sensationally rich
families which came to the fore in the 1870's and
1880's succeeded in annexing a genuine foreign title by
marriage.[4] It was estimated toward the end of the century that over two hundred million dollars had by this
means been exported to replenish the coffers of impoverished European nobility. The year 1895 was especially
glamorous in New York social annals by reason of three
such alliances: the Paget-Whitney, the Castellane-Gould
and the Marlborough-Vanderbilt. When it was learned
that the Duke of Marlborough and his new American
duchess would attend the horse show, a frantic mob
early choked the entrances, eager to render that uproar-

---

[1] J. D. Champlin, jr., "The Manufacture of Ancestors," *Forum*, X
(1890-1891), 565-572; Sibyl Wilbur (O'Brien), *The Life of Mary
Baker Eddy* (N. Y., 1908), 4-5 *n*.

[2] Unsigned comment in *Atlantic Mo.*, LI (1883), 558.

[3] Sherwood, *Manners and Social Usages* (1884), 45.

[4] See the imposing list in W. T. Stead, *The Americanization of the
World* (N. Y., 1902), 318-329.

ious acclaim which only a democracy can accord the hereditary distinctions of effete monarchy.

In every great city the citadels of exclusiveness were being assailed by the gold rush. The Vanderbilt fancy-dress ball of March 26, 1883, the most sumptuous entertainment that had yet been given in America, marked the entry into New York society of the William K. Vanderbilts, whose grand-uncle, the "Commodore," had begun his career as a ferryboat master.[1] Yet society, in the high and holy sense of the word, could not survive if the wife of every successful captain of industry should gain a place within the sacred portals. In order to maintain a judicious blend of patrician and parvenu, Ward McAllister, self-styled "Autocrat of the Drawing-Rooms," organized in 1872 the Patriarchs, a group of twenty-five socially impeccable men who assumed the function of censoring the guest lists at select gatherings.[2]

A chance remark of McAllister in 1890 that about four hundred people in New York comprised the inner circle gave coinage to an expression which became synonymous the country over for the smart set. Every considerable city soon had its "Four Hundred," and local newspapers vied with their New York contemporaries in giving prominence to society news. As a matter of fact, the moneyed element was definitely setting the tone of New York society by the 1890's.[3] A ten-thousand-dollar dinner for seventy-two guests at Delmonico's no longer excited comment; pretentious winter residences in the city must be supplemented by

[1] Harold Seton, "How the Vanderbilts Crashed Society Gates," *Boston Herald*, Feb. 12, 1928.

[2] Ward McAllister, *Society as I Found It* (N. Y., 1890), esp. 214-252. See also Moran Tudury, "Ward McAllister," *Am. Mercury*, VIII (1926), 138-143; and Arthur Train, "The Perfect Goldfish," *Sat. Eve. Post*, CCII, 25 ff. (Sept. 28, 1929).

[3] Mrs. John K. Van Rensselaer and Frederick Van de Water, *The Social Ladder* (N. Y., 1924), chaps. v-viii.

luxurious summer homes at Newport, Bar Harbor, Lenox or Tuxedo; the courtly Knickerbocker strain had lost most of its influence. Even Ward McAllister himself had become a butt of ridicule—"Would Make All-a-stir," as someone derisively called him.

The growing absorption of women in interests outside the home, whether as social butterflies or as breadwinners or reformers, seemed to some a sufficient explanation of the waning sanctity of the marriage relation. Whatever the reason there could be no doubt as to the fact. With sixteen thousand divorces granted in 1878, the number rose to nearly twenty-nine thousand in the year 1888 and to almost forty-eight thousand in 1898. The rate of increase was far greater than the rate of population growth—indeed, in the last decade of the century, three times as great—and the proportion of divorces granted in the United States far exceeded that of any foreign country except Japan.[1] In 1890 one divorce was granted for every sixteen marriages solemnized, in 1900 one for every twelve. Since the practice was forbidden Roman Catholics, the frequency of divorce among those not of that faith was even greater than these figures indicate.

The situation excited the widespread alarm of press and pulpit. As a result of the activity of the National Divorce Reform League, formed in 1881, the federal government undertook in 1887-1888 a comprehensive collection of data concerning marriage and divorce. The findings confirmed a cherished notion of the reformers that one fruitful source of the evil was the diversity of state legislation. In some states marriage was permitted as early as twelve or fourteen years; in most a civil cere-

[1] The divorce rate in Switzerland, which was the highest of any European country, was about three sevenths that of the United States at the close of the century. Bureau of the Census, *Marriage and Divorce, 1867-1906 (Special Rep.)*, pt. i, 12-13, 19, 54-55, 62-64.

mony would suffice; and, in perhaps half, a ceremony could be dispensed with altogether under the general principles of the "Scotch law of marriage," which required merely mutual consent.[1]

Divorce might be made an equally simple matter provided the proper jurisdiction were sought. South Carolina denied divorce on any ground whatever; but elsewhere the causes varied from the single one of adultery, in the case of New York, to a list of ten or more, including, in the case of Washington, "any other cause deemed by the court sufficient"—the so-called "omnibus clause." While residence of a year or more was usually necessary to secure a divorce in most states, in Nevada and Wyoming only six months were demanded and in the Dakotas but ninety days. As a result "large divorce colonies" were to be found in the Dakotas, and in all four commonwealths a majority of the defendants were residents of other states.[2] The fruits of such a system were scandalous and demoralizing. As one writer expressed it, "a husband who has obtained a divorce in one State on trivial grounds . . . may marry again, and with his new wife and children travel through the United States, and in some places his new relations will be considered legal and proper, while in others he will be a bigamist, his new wife a paramour, and their children illegitimate." [3]

The lax standards of the law were largely an inheri-

---

[1] E. H. Bennett, "National Divorce Legislation," *Forum*, II (1886-1887), 429-438; same author, "Marriage Laws," *Forum*, III (1887), 219-229; E. J. Phelps, "Divorce in the United States," *Forum*, VIII (1889-1890), 349-364; Duncan Convers, *Marriage and Divorce in the United States* (Phila., 1889); Whitney, *Marriage and Divorce*, chaps. iii-iv, xxix-xlv; Bayles, *Woman and the Law*, 55-119; *Marriage and Divorce, 1867-1906*, pt. i, chaps. ii-iii.

[2] South Dakota changed her residence requirement to one year in 1893. *Marriage and Divorce, 1867-1906*, pt. i, 33, 305, 312, 318, 327.

[3] Bennett, "National Divorce Legislation," 434.

tance from a rural age when early and easy marriage was
desired for population growth and community disapproval prevented reckless recourse to the divorce courts.
The phenomenal increase of divorce was largely an outgrowth of urban conditions: the anonymity of city life,
its distractions and temptations, the growing practice of
living in boarding houses and flats, the harsh struggle
for existence, the opportunities for self-support afforded
women.[1] Not only was the divorce rate higher in large
cities than in small ones and country districts, but the
rate of increase was also greater there than elsewhere.[2]
Since twice as many divorces in the period 1878-1898
were granted upon the wife's complaint as on the husband's, it is likely that the increase reflected, in part, a
greater self-respect among women and an unwillingness
to put up with conditions which their mothers would
have accepted in silence.[3] Legislative changes during the
period were in the direction of greater strictness, Connecticut leading the way in 1878 by repealing her "omnibus clause." But the gains were not impressive, and
no headway was made toward the reformers' goal: a
uniform divorce law for all the states.[4] The more
thoughtful perceived that what was needed was not so
much a change of legislation as of ethical attitudes.

Even more shocking to most people was the growth
of commercialized immorality. Primarily an urban phenomenon, it throve most extensively in the great pop-

---

[1] Whitney, *Marriage and Divorce*, 10-12; S. G. Fisher, *The Cause
of the Increase of Divorce* (Phila., 1890), esp. 19-20.

[2] *Marriage and Divorce, 1867-1906*, pt. i, 19.

[3] In the South, where cities were fewer and women less accustomed
to the idea of earning their own living, wives were less active in seeking
to sever the marriage tie. In four Southern states, indeed, more divorces
were granted to husbands than to wives. *Marriage and Divorce, 1867-
1906*, pt. i, 24-25, 94-95.

[4] S. E. Dike, *A Review of Fifteen Years* (Natl. Divorce Reform
League, *Rep. for 1895*), esp. 11-12.

ulation centers where unmarried men congregated in
largest numbers and out-of-town visitors were numerous. In New York, for example, vice catered to all tastes
and purses—in "palatial bagnios" as well as in widely
scattered medium-class houses and places of assignation,
not to mention basement dives on the Bowery where, we
may well believe, the business was "divested of the gas-
light glare and tinsel of the high-toned seraglios." [1]
As in the seaboard metropolis, "sporting houses" existed in all parts of Chicago, though the traffic was most
boldly carried on in the district between Harrison and
Polk and between Clark and Dearborn streets.[2] There,
as in the red-light districts of other cities, the male
passer-by after dark was almost certain to be hailed from
curtained windows or accosted on the street by pert
sauntering women.

The number of such wretched females cannot be
known, but the circumstances which brought them to
their life of shame and eventual disease are not difficult
to understand.[3] As one brothel keeper in Chicago told
W. T. Stead, the English journalist, "Prostitution is
an effect, not a careless, voluntary choice on the part of
the fallen." Some of them were country newcomers to

---

[1] W. F. Howe and A. H. Hummel, *Danger!* (Buffalo, 1886), chap.
xii. See also Herbert Asbury, *The Gangs of New York* (N. Y., 1927),
chap. ix.

[2] See frontispiece map and first appendix of W. T. Stead, *If Christ
Came to Chicago!* (Chicago, 1894). For Boston, see Woods, *City
Wilderness*, 159-173, and F. A. Bushee, *Ethnic Factors in the Popula-
tion of Boston* (Am. Econ. Assoc., *Publs.*, IV, no. 2), 107-116.

[3] Police Inspector Thomas Byrnes in 1893 believed there were forty
thousand prostitutes in New York City. National Purity Congress,
*Papers* (N. Y., 1896), 113. Stead's estimate for Chicago about the
same time was ten thousand. *If Christ Came to Chicago*, 35. The census
figures possess even less reliability; thus in 1890 Indianapolis was credited with nearly as many brothels as New York, and Baltimore with
three times as many as either Philadelphia or Washington. *U. S. Eleventh
Census* (1890), XXIII, 1024-1035. For the 1880 figures, see *U. S.
Tenth Census* (1880), XXI, 566.

the city, starved for companionship and lacking the wholesome restraining influence of neighborhood opinion. Others were shopgirls or housemaids eager for the pretty clothes and good times which their meager wages denied them. Many more perhaps were the hapless victims of evil youthful surroundings in the slums, while still others were girls of feeble mentality who in a better-ordered society would have been under institutional care. In the opinion of Stead's informant, "the real cause lies not in the girls who fall, but in the social conditions that make the fall easy and the men who tempt to the step . . . ."[1] The situation was made worse by the growth of an organized traffic in "white slaves," intercity in character, which often involved forcible induction into a life of vice.

Everywhere in the nation the law placed a ban on prostitution; but while municipalities outlawed the evil to prove themselves respectable, they condoned lax enforcement to prove themselves liberal.[2] In some places the authorities raided the vice resorts every month or so, imposing fines that amounted to an irregular license fee. Elsewhere the police were apt to be in collusion with the keepers of disorderly houses, levying blackmail on them for their private gain. As we have seen, the Lexow investigation revealed such a system at work in New York, and Stead exposed a similar situation in Chicago. Though without warrant in law, segregation was permitted or required in many cities; and in a few isolated cases, like that of Cleveland, the experiment was briefly tried of introducing the Continental European system

[1] Stead, *If Christ Came to Chicago*, 252. Cf. W. F. Garrison, "The Relation of Poverty to Purity," Natl. Purity Congress, *Papers*, 398-405.
[2] D. F. Wilcox, *The American City* (N. Y., 1904), 127-133; Stead, *If Christ Came to Chicago*, 37, 382; G. W. Hale, ed., *Police and Prison Cyclopaedia* (rev. edn., Boston, 1893), 189 ff. See also a series of articles on "Official Complicity with Vice" in six different cities, in *Christian Union*, XLVI (1892).

of police registration and medical inspection. The recurrent upheavals of civic reform generally disclosed the alliance of commercialized vice with corrupt politics and the liquor interests, and brought about a temporary improvement of conditions. In general, community sentiment upheld the time-honored double standard of morality, which conceived of sexual promiscuity as permissible only for the male. Few reform officials were willing to emulate Police Commissioner Roosevelt in treating the men taken in vice raids precisely as their female companions, so far as the law allowed him to do so.[1]

Serious as was the social evil, there was little spread of licentiousness upward through society; and foreign observers were justified in rating American standards of sexual morality as superior to those of most European countries. Indeed, in spite of the whips and buffetings of circumstance, the American woman had substantial cause for pride in the advances made by her sex. Though, as the writer in the *Atlantic Monthly* had said, she might not yet understand herself, she was responding to her highest instincts in struggling toward an easier, more self-respecting and self-reliant footing in American society. Her failures, though disheartening at the time, were not irreparable, while her successes formed a lasting heritage to those who were to follow.

[1] Theodore Roosevelt, *An Autobiography* (N. Y., 1919), esp. 196.

# CHAPTER VI

## THE EDUCATIONAL REVIVAL

THE closing decades of the century saw an educational renaissance comparable in many respects to the great days of Horace Mann and Henry Barnard.[1] While the cities were the chief beneficiaries, the country also shared in the movement and the South for the first time became a part of the national educational order. Nor was the awakening one of the schools alone, for countless other agencies of a less formal sort began to play a significant rôle in shaping popular culture. Lewis Miller, Frederick W. Poole, S. S. McClure, Joseph Pulitzer and Edward W. Bok, no less than the professional educators, helped instruct the people and mold their outlook on life.

The ideal of free tax-supported elementary schools had been accepted in the North already by mid-century, but even there practice had lagged behind theory while in the South such facilities hardly existed at all. In the dozen years after the Civil War, though enrollments grew, operating expenses were generally held down in the North, school buildings kept simple, and few new features added to the curriculum. The South, obliged by the Reconstruction constitutions to set up public-school systems, was handicapped by poverty, Carpetbag exploitation and the very magnitude of the task.[2] But

[1] See C. R. Fish, *The Rise of the Common Man* (*A History of American Life*, VI), 216-224.

[2] E. P. Cubberley, *Public Education in the United States* (Boston, 1919), 252-253; E. W. Knight, *The Influence of Reconstruction on Education in the South* (Teachers College, *Contribs. to Educ.*, no. 60), esp. 99.

with the widespread economic recovery following 1878 and the end of Republican meddling in Southern affairs, a new era opened for both sections. Though the North and West now faced the duty of caring for hordes of immigrant children, the vast accumulation of taxable wealth and the growth of cities facilitated accomplishment. If the visible progress was less spectacular in the old slave states, the difficulties overcome were even greater.

Taking the nation as a whole, improvement of the educational system occurred at every point from top to bottom. Congress had evidenced its interest in 1867 by creating a special department (later bureau) of education which, under able leadership, served as a national clearing house, gathering statistics, disseminating information and holding up the torch for the more backward commonwealths. After 1870 compulsory-attendance laws began to spread over the North and West, nineteen states and territories taking this step by 1881, and twelve more by 1898.[1] Rhode Island, for example, had been notorious as a haven for immigrant parents who preferred their children's wages to their education, but this condition was corrected in 1883.[2] The typical statute required children from eight to fourteen years old to attend school from twelve to sixteen weeks a year; as late as 1890 Connecticut was the only state to exact attendance for the full session. Enforcement, however, was another thing. With notable exceptions it was only the older, well-established communities which compelled parents and children to observe the law.[3] Elsewhere so-

[1] Though such laws were to be found in Massachusetts (enacted in 1852), Vermont and the District of Columbia before 1870, they were of a crude and unsatisfactory character. For their spread after 1870, see *Reports* of the U. S. Commissioner of Education: for *1882-83*, xxx-xxxvi; for *1886-87*, 56; for *1888-89*, I, 15-16, 475-531; for *1894-95*, I, 1118-1121; for *1896-97*, II, 1525.

[2] U. S. Comr. of Educ., *Rep. for 1888-89*, I, 501.

[3] U. S. Comr. of Educ., *Rep. for 1897-98*, II, 1695.

cial custom and parental pride were more influential than legal coercion in keeping youngsters at their tasks.

The number of pupils in the common schools of the nation rose from nine and a half million in 1878 to twelve million a decade later and to fifteen in 1898, somewhat outstripping the growth of population. Kindergartens, public and private, increased from less than two hundred in 1878 to nearly three thousand at the close of the period when perhaps two hundred thousand children were tasting the delights of learning through play-activities.[1] Even more remarkable was the growth of high schools from less than eight hundred in 1878 to fifty-five hundred in 1898. For the first time, the American public, at least in the North and West, squarely accepted the responsibility of extending the benefits of free education upward from the elementary grades. With less than one hundred thousand pupils in the secondary schools in 1878, over half a million were so accommodated in 1898.[2]

Educational development, of course, varied from section to section and even more between country and city. The concentration of wealth and population in urban centers and the greater spirit of progress insured higher salaries for teachers, longer school terms, better buildings and, in general, superior organization and methods of instruction. It was the cities which promoted the kindergarten movement and were most active in providing high schools. Some places like St. Louis under the superintendency of William T. Harris (1867-1880) became the generating centers of ideas that helped revolutionize the theory and practice of teaching throughout the land.

---

[1] U. S. Comr. of Educ., *Rep. for 1897-98*, II, 2537; E. G. Dexter, *A History of Education in the United States* (N. Y., 1904), 166-169.
[2] U. S. Comr. of Educ., *Rep. for 1898-99*, II, 1842, 1844.

In the rural districts, on the other hand, ungraded schools were the rule. The single schoolmaster shepherded students of all ages and degrees of advancement and, in intervals between chastising unruly charges, listened to the halting recitations of individual pupils whenever they were ready. The rural schoolmaster in his value to the community might be compared to the country doctor, but he seldom enjoyed the same neighborhood respect and, if opportunity offered, he fled his employment for something more rewarding. The school year also ended sooner than in the cities and large towns, where in 1891 the typical session lasted from one hundred and eighty to two hundred days as compared with from seventy to one hundred and fifty in the country.[1]

In the North and West the rural school situation was the subject of constant recommendation by state commissioners of instruction. A basic difficulty was the dissipation of meager resources among many small, independent school districts. Under a Massachusetts law of 1882 abolishing the district system, such schools began to be consolidated, the scattered pupils being daily carried by wagon to a centrally located, graded school. Before 1898 the idea made some headway elsewhere—in Ohio, New York, New Jersey and a few other places—but, in general, rural conservatism was slow to yield and the country schools remained in an unsatisfactory condition.[2]

The rural school problem in the South was, in a sense, the problem of the entire section. With relatively few cities and a country population more thinly distributed than in most parts of the North, the South had

[1] U. S. Comr. of Educ., *Rep. for 1890-91*, I, x. "The increase in urban population is accompanied by increase in the length of the school year," remarked the commissioner. *Rep. for 1898-99*, I, x.

[2] U. S. Comr. of Educ., *Rep. for 1883-84*, xxxiv; for *1899-1900*, I, x-xi.

also a greater number of children in proportion to adults than did the North and a net taxable wealth considerably less.[1] The burden of educational support on adults in such a state as Mississippi was about twice as heavy as in Vermont. The situation was further complicated by the lingering financial effects of Reconstruction and the fact that the cost of maintaining separate racial schools rested almost wholly on the whites. For these and other reasons, little or no trace of a state school system existed in Virginia, South Carolina, Georgia, Mississippi and Texas until 1870 or 1871. In several other commonwealths public schools were confined chiefly to the larger towns.

To get the new system under way, women of the impoverished gentry helped by promptly enlisting as teachers.[2] Northern philanthropy, notably the fund of $3,500,000 established by George Peabody in 1867 and 1869, quickened the spread of town and city schools and also made provision for systematic teacher training.[3] Between 1881 and 1889 repeated appeals were made to Congress for aid in bearing the burden. A proposal by Senator Henry W. Blair of New Hampshire, himself a victim of poor rural schools, to distribute federal funds among the states in proportion to their illiteracy passed the Senate on three different occasions. But the measure

[1] In 1880 the eighteen Northern states had 909 minors for every thousand adults; the sixteen ex-slave states 1242. The net wealth per capita of minors in the North was $2225; in the South $851. U. S. Comr. of Educ., *Rep. for 1887-88*, 22-29.

[2] A. D. Mayo, "Southern Women in the Recent Educational Movement in the South," U. S. Bur. of Educ., *Circular of Information for 1892*, no. 1.

[3] There was not a normal school in the entire South in 1868. For the work of the Peabody Fund, see E. W. Knight, *Public Education in the South* (Boston, 1922), chap. xi; E. A. Alderman and A. C. Gordon, *J. L. M. Curry* (N. Y., 1911), chaps. xv, xvii; and J. L. M. Curry, *A Brief Sketch of George Peabody and a History of the Peabody Education Fund* (Cambridge, Mass., 1898).

died in the House because of opposition from members who were unwilling to have the lion's share of the money go to the South.[1]

Despite the failure of this badly needed assistance and notwithstanding the many other handicaps, the expansion of the common-school system in the South was characterized by the federal commissioner of education in 1890 as probably "without a parallel." The enrollment grew from two million seven hundred thousand in 1878—less than one quarter Negroes—to nearly four and a half million in 1888, including a somewhat larger proportion of Negroes. "At present," the commissioner asserted, "the schools of the South, taken as whole, enroll a larger percentage of the population than those of the older States of the North, and furnish to every child an opportunity to acquire at least the essential rudiments of a school education." [2] The rise of the agrarian elements to political power in the late eighties and the nineties gave added momentum to the cause of free education, especially in the rural districts. By 1898 the total enrollment had risen to more than five million.[3]

However bright the picture may appear against the former darkness, the South throughout the period lagged behind the rest of the nation. Its chief energies were necessarily absorbed in the basic task of abolishing illiteracy, the curse of the white masses as well as of the colored race. In many rural districts schoolhouses were often mere log shacks without windows, desks, maps

[1] *What is the Blair Bill?* (Charleston, 1887), a pamphlet reprinting articles from the *News and Courier;* P. B. Plumb, *The Blair Education Bill* (Wash., 1890), esp. 4.

[2] U. S. Comr. of Educ., *Rep. for 1889-90,* I, xviii, 11-12. This statement needs to be read in light of the fact that, though enrolling a larger proportion of the whole population, the South did not enroll a larger proportion of the population of school-going age. Also, the school term was much shorter. *Rep. for 1886-87,* 89.

[3] U. S. Comr. of Educ., *Rep. for 1898-99,* I, xiv.

or blackboards. The school term averaged about a hundred days in 1890 as compared with one hundred and fifty in the Middle West and one hundred and seventy-four in the North Atlantic states. When the assertion might still be heard that "it is robbery to tax one man to educate another man's children,"[1] the time was not yet ripe for a forward thrust along all lines as in the North. At most, education was regarded in the South as an opportunity for the individual child and not as a civic obligation, for not one of the states of the former Confederacy applied the principle of compulsion to attendance.

Even in the North teachers were often badly underpaid, the worst conditions prevailing in the rural regions and among women. The state superintendent of Iowa reported in 1883 that teachers of ungraded schools did not average a hundred and fifty dollars a year, though an ordinary farmhand with no obligation to dress well or pay institute fees received two hundred with board.[2] For the country as a whole the average monthly salary for a male teacher in 1888-1889 was $42.43, for a woman $34.27; by 1898-1899 these amounts had advanced to $45.25 and $38.14.[3] The displacement of men by women teachers, already marked in Civil War days, continued at an accelerating rate, partly because of the

---

[1] Cited from report of the North Carolina superintendent of education, by U. S. Comr. of Educ., *Rep. for 1887-88*, 161. In a somewhat similar spirit Governor F. W. M. Holliday of Virginia declared to the legislature in 1878, "Public free schools are not a necessity. The world, for hundreds of years, grew in wealth, culture, and refinement, without them." Knight, *Public Education in the South*, 347-348.

[2] U. S. Comr. of Educ., *Rep. for 1882-83*, xxix.

[3] The wide variation among sections is indicated by the average monthly salary of $136.23 paid in 1898-1899 to men teachers in Massachusetts as contrasted with $50.00 in Ohio and $25.07 in North Carolina. In these same states women were paid $51.41, $40.00 and $22.24 respectively. U. S. Comr. of Educ., *Rep. for 1888-89*, I, 8; for *1898-99*, I. lxxix-lxxx.

lower price at which women would work and partly because of the higher rewards for men in the business world. In 1878 about three out of every five teachers were women; in 1898 two out of three.[1] Women won recognition also as educational administrators. By 1897 over two hundred were county superintendents, while twelve were city superintendents and two were state commissioners of instruction.[2] For better or for worse—and educational writers were not certain which—the youth of the nation were receiving their instruction increasingly from that sex which hitherto had had least contact with the world of affairs.

For both men and women, teaching was too apt to be a mere stepping-stone to something more congenial or profitable. The federal commissioner of education, noting in 1887 that twenty-six changes occurred yearly in every one hundred positions, estimated the average term of service at less than four years.[3] Such conditions militated against the conception of teaching as a life career, a profession to be cultivated as was law or medicine. Another deterrent to the attainment of professional standards was the active meddling, not only of politicians but also of schoolbook publishers, in teaching appointments and the selection of textbooks.[4]

Nevertheless, the increase of normal schools, the

[1] U. S. Comr. of Educ., *Rep. for 1888-89*, I, 23, 319, 327-328; for *1891-92*, II, 669; for *1898-99*, I, lxxviii.

[2] The state superintendents were Grace E. Patton in Colorado and Estelle Reel in Wyoming. U. S. Comr. of Educ., *Rep. for 1896-97*, II, 1528-1533.

[3] In the Middle West the changes ran as high as sixty-five. J. T. Prince, "American and German Schools," *Atlantic Mo.*, LXVI (1890), esp. 415.

[4] G. S. Hall, "The Case of the Public Schools," *Atlantic Mo.*, LXXVII (1896), esp. 405-407; anon., "Confessions of Public School Teachers," *Atlantic Mo.*, LXXVIII (1896), 97-110. The extent of the corrupt activities of schoolbook publishers will never be known, but the fact was generally admitted. In the case of Washington in 1890 a

progressiveness of city systems and the waxing strength of teachers' associations helped offset some of these baneful influences. As public schools grew nation-wide in their reach, the American people were exalted by a lyric faith in education which rivaled an earlier generation's zeal for democracy. In a time of low political morality it was expected to be the solvent of all governmental ills. Indeed, reformers urged that its precepts be directly applied to officeholders through the examination system of appointment.

The period was marked not only by a physical expansion of the school system, but also by a spread of new ideas, the addition of fresh subjects to the curriculum and a marked improvement in textbooks. In the late 1880's a number of young Americans who had studied under Professor William Rein at the University of Jena brought back with them the Herbartian conception of instruction.[1] Charles De Garmo's *Essentials of Method* (1889) and C. A. McMurry's *General Method* (1892), by popularizing the new ideas for American educators, did much to change the teacher from a mere drillmaster and disciplinarian to a person charged with the responsibility of interesting his pupils through an effective presentation of subject matter.

Due less to Herbartianism perhaps than to humanitarianism, a setback was given to those pedagogues who, as a wag put it, thought of the hickory stick as the chief board of education. Many city systems—in New York, Albany, Cleveland, Chicago and elsewhere—forbade corporal punishment, New Jersey going so far as to

member of the state board of education exposed a prominent book concern (which he named) which had paid him $5000 in the expectation of receiving help in securing state-wide adoptions. *Publishers' Wkly.,* XXXVII, 793 (June 14, 1890).

[1] S. C. Parker, *History of Modern Elementary Education* (Boston, 1912), chap. xvii.

forbid it by state law.[1] New studies—drawing, nature lore, sewing, cooking, manual training—were introduced here and there into city elementary schools, while high-school courses were broadened to include sciences, commercial subjects and the manual and household arts. As the new offerings multiplied, it became necessary to add a fourth year to the high school (common everywhere by 1890 except in the South), and the curriculum was often arranged in alternative four-year courses.

Though the new studies and methods were designed to fit children better for the life of the new America, educational "advance" impressed some critics as a mere succession of "crazes—the method craze, the object-lesson craze, the illustration craze, the 'memory-gem' craze, the civics craze . . . , the phonics craze, the word-method craze, the drawing and music craze," not to mention the "craze" for "business forms, picture study, and physics."[2] In a somewhat similar fashion the federal commissioner of education in 1885 felt obliged to combat the charge of "communism" leveled against the growing practice of providing free textbooks for pupils. Begun by New York City some years before, the plan spread to other centers in the 1880's and was made obligatory throughout Massachusetts by a law of 1884. By 1898 free textbooks were provided for by state action in ten Northern and Western commonwealths while ten other states empowered local communities to decide the question for themselves.[3]

Though the complex racial situation raised many difficulties for educators, German communities could gen-

[1] U. S. Comr. of Educ., *Rep. for 1886-87*, 228; *for 1896-97*, II, 1537; *for 1897-98*, II, 1701-1702.

[2] *N. Y. Eve. Post*, quoted by U. S. Comr. of Educ., *Rep. for 1888-89*, I, 597.

[3] U. S. Comr. of Educ., *Rep. for 1884-85*, cix-cx; *for 1896-97*, II, 1538; *for 1897-98*, I, 894.

erally be counted on as sturdy champions of better schools. The Swedes, Danes and Norwegians, accustomed to popular education at home, also gave them hearty support. The language question, however, caused trouble in the late 1880's, particularly in the case of the more recent Scandinavian arrivals. In Dakota territory they openly defied the law requiring the teaching of English. When in 1889 Wisconsin and Illinois declined by statute to recognize schools in which English was not the language of instruction, the Scandinavians successfully united with other racial groups to force through a repeal.[1]

The Catholic parochial schools, relatively few and poorly equipped at the opening of the period, were ill prepared to take care of the many immigrant children who sought their doors. To remedy this lack the third plenary council of Catholic bishops in Baltimore in 1884 laid down detailed regulations for the management of such schools, requiring their establishment wherever possible and directing Catholic parents to send their children to them. From this action dated the rapid growth of the parochial system, especially notable in New England and only less so in the Middle Atlantic states and the newly formed dioceses of the West.[2]

It is easier to record the outer aspects of educational development than to appraise its results. Like religion, the influence of education cannot be gauged by a count of buildings, the amount of capital invested or the sheer number of persons reached. European visitors were deeply interested in the unfolding American experiment, and no less a person than James Bryce believed that, due

[1] Board of Education of Dakota, *First Biennial Report* (1888), xxxvi; K. C. Babcock, *The Scandinavian Element in the United States* (Univ. of Ill., *Studies*, III, no. 3), 166-169.

[2] M. M. Sheedy, "The Catholic Parochial Schools of the United States," U. S. Comr. of Educ., *Rep. for 1903*, I, esp. 1083-1089.

to its effects, "the average of knowledge is higher, the habit of reading and thinking more generally diffused, than in any other country."[1] Of course, many members of this generation owed their formal training to the schools of an earlier time and, by the same token, the schoolrooms of the 1880's and 1890's were cradling the intellectual life of the early twentieth century.

Certainly, in accomplishing their primary task, the schools made an impressive record, for the proportion of illiteracy in the nation declined from seventeen per cent in 1880 to thirteen in 1890 and to less than eleven in 1900.[2] The large cities made a better showing than the small towns and country districts, the North and West better than the South, and the children of immigrants better than their parents. Indeed, the American-born children of the European newcomers were more literate than the white children of native parentage, chiefly perhaps because of their concentration in cities. If the ability to read and write may be supposed to have any relationship to political intelligence, conservative folk must have been dismayed to observe that, of the nine states that stood highest in literacy, all but one voted for Bryan and free silver in the notable "campaign of education" of 1896.

Despite the remarkable growth of educational facilities since the 1830's, the comparative newness of the system in many parts of the country left vast numbers of adults with a pitifully inadequate share of systematic instruction. In 1880 the total amount of schooling received by the average person in his entire lifetime was less than

[1] James Bryce, *The American Commonwealth* (London, 1888), III, 52. See also Emily Faithfull, *Three Visits to America* (Edinburgh, 1884), 219-220.

[2] The corresponding figures for native-born whites were: 8.7%, 6.2% and 4.6%; for foreign-born whites: 11.9%, 13% and 12.8%. J. A. Hill, "Illiteracy," *Supplementary Analysis and Derivative Tables* (U. S. Twelfth Census, *Special Rep.*), 328-375.

four years; in 1898 it amounted to exactly five.[1] In other words, the average American had not advanced, in his formal training, beyond the attainments of the fourth or fifth grade of the elementary school. As we shall see, the varied literary aspirations and attainments of the time were conditioned by this fundamental fact. Fortunately the constant tendency to pull literature down to the level of the half-educated masses was somewhat offset by the fact that more people than ever before were pouring from the halls of the high schools and colleges.

If the schools were primarily concerned with the instruction of children, their elders had a special opportunity of their own in the contagious spread of the Chautauqua movement. This novel institution gave countless middle-class folk a chance to make up for the deficiencies of their youthful education. Founded in 1874 by an Ohio manufacturer, Lewis Miller, and a Methodist minister, John H. Vincent, as a sort of camp meeting for the training of Sunday-school teachers, the annual summer gatherings on the forested shores of Lake Chautauqua, New York, quickly developed broader educational functions whose influence ramified to many parts of the country.[2] "Any man who loves knowledge and his native land," observed Professor G. H. Palmer of Harvard,

> must be glad at heart when he visits a summer assembly of Chautauqua: there . . . attends the swiftly

[1] All kinds of schooling, whether in public or private schools or colleges, are included. These statistical years consist of ten months of twenty school days each. U. S. Comr. of Educ., *Rep. for 1899-1900*, I, xvi.

[2] H. B. Adams, "Chautauqua: a Social and Educational Study," U. S. Comr. of Educ., *Rep. for 1894-95*, I, 977-1077; J. H. Vincent, *The Chautauqua Movement* (Boston, 1886) ; Ellwood Hendrick, *Lewis Miller* (N. Y., 1925), chaps. xxi-xxiii; L. H. Vincent, *John Heyl Vincent* (N. Y., 1925), chaps. xi-xiii; J. L. Hurlbut, *The Story of Chautauqua* (N. Y., 1921).

successive Round Tables upon Milton, Temperance, Geology, the American Constitution, the Relations of Science and Religion, and the Doctrine of Rent; perhaps assists at the Cooking School, the Prayer Meeting, the Concert, and the Gymnastic Drill; or wanders under the trees among the piazzaed cottages, and sees the Hall of Philosophy and the wooden Doric Temple shining on their little eminences.[1]

At the annual assemblies the best scholars of this and other countries gave courses, and for many years Professor William Rainey Harper of Yale, later president of the University of Chicago, served as director of instruction. To supplement the summer offerings the Literary and Scientific Circle was formed in 1878, involving a plan of reading and study lasting four years and carried on in books most of which were especially written for the purpose. By 1892 one hundred thousand students were enrolled in the Circle, half of them between thirty and forty years of age. These and innumerable others were reached also by the *Chautauquan,* a monthly magazine established in 1880. For more ambitious students the Chautauqua College of Liberal Arts was organized in 1888 to afford an opportunity to secure a bachelor's degree by means of a four-year combination of resident, extension and correspondence study.

The parent Chautauqua proved to be a prolific mother. Led by Petoskey, Michigan, and Clear Lake, Iowa, in 1877, outdoor assemblies of one or two weeks' duration were conducted in various localities until about seventy were in operation at the close of the century, representing nearly every state in the Union. "To find a popular movement so composite and aspiring," declared Professor Palmer, "we must go back to the mediaeval

[1] G. H. Palmer, "Doubts about University Extension," *Atlantic Mo.,* LXIX (1892), esp. 369-370.

Crusades or the Greek mysteries."[1] If these minor Chautauquas presented somewhat less serious programs than their progenitor, they nevertheless served as yeast to small-town intellectual life and inspired many a parent to "pathetic sacrifices . . . in the next generation to send the boys and girls to a real college."[2]

During the winter "star courses" or lecture series— survivals of the once powerful lyceum movement—were offered in most small and many large towns, featuring a wide variety of inspirational speakers, authors, politicians and entertainers.[3] On such programs no one was more welcome than John L. Stoddard whose "travel talks" afforded fascinating glimpses of foreign peoples and customs and whose colored lantern slides were rivaled only by the lecturer's splendor of diction. Stoddard it was who introduced the now familiar double stereopticon by which each picture dissolves magically into the one succeeding. Other favorites were the humorists Mark Twain, Edgar Wilson ("Bill") Nye and James Whitcomb Riley; George W. Cable who interspersed his Creole tales with haunting Creole melodies; the Norwegian violinist Ole Bull; and the Reverend Russell H. Conwell of Philadelphia, whose fame was inseparably identified in the public mind with his lecture, "Acres of Diamonds."[4]

[1] These supplementary Chautauquas are listed, with brief historical accounts, in U. S. Comr. of Educ., *Rep. for 1891-92*, II, 937-945. See also Vincent, *Chautauqua Movement*, 289-301; Hurlbut, *Story of Chautauqua*, chap. xxiv; H. A. Orchard, *Fifty Years of Chautauqua* (Cedar Rapids, 1923), chaps. iii-iv.

[2] Palmer, "Doubts about University Extension," 370.

[3] C. F. Horner, *The Life of James Redpath and the Development of the Modern Lyceum* (N. Y., 1926), chap. xv; W. M. Emery, "John L. Stoddard of Yesterday and Today," *Boston Transcript*, Feb. 5, 1927.

[4] The theme of "Acres of Diamonds" was that people listening to tales of "easy money" to be had far away are apt to neglect the opportunities at their very door. Between 1861 and 1913 it was delivered five thousand times. Says his admiring biographer, "Little did he foresee how it would affect the lives of thousands upon thousands of people;

Of more lasting value for the diffusion of culture was the multiplication of public libraries. Though dating back to mid-century, tax-supported free libraries had remained few in number outside of certain Eastern cities. Neither in these nor in college and society libraries did proper catalogues exist to indicate the contents of the collections, and the tired ex-teacher or ex-preacher who served as librarian was usually more interested in hoarding books than in having them used. But all this was forced to change as an eager public stormed the reading rooms and demanded untrammeled access to the republic of the printed word. In 1876 a group of progressive librarians, meeting in Philadelphia, formed the American Library Association, which thereafter proceeded aggressively to foster the ideal of providing "the best reading for the largest number at the least expense."[1] Leaders in this body—such as Justin Winsor of the Harvard Library, F. W. Poole of the Chicago Public, Charles Cutter of the Boston Athenaeum and Melvil Dewey, librarian at Columbia—were responsible for developing those ingenious methods of cataloguing, shelf classification and book circulation, which have helped make the American library the most efficient in the world.

At the same time the establishment of new libraries was promoted by both public and private agencies. Between 1878 and 1898 eighteen commonwealths authorized the use of taxation for such purposes, and in 1895 New Hampshire went so far as to make its permissive law obligatory.[2] Private munificence for library

nor the influence it would have upon the industries of this country." Agnes R. Burr, *Russell H. Conwell and His Work* (Phila., 1917), chaps. xxxi-xxxiv, 405-438.

[1] Melvil Dewey, "The American Library Association," *Library Journ.* (N. Y.), I (1876-1877), 247.

[2] Sixteen states already had permissive laws before 1878, most of them enacted after 1871. Dexter, *History of Education*, 484-485.

construction is inseparably connected with the name of
the steel magnate, Andrew Carnegie, whose first benefactions went in 1881 to the city of Pittsburgh and near-
by towns. Widening his field of activity, he presently
paid for the erection of buildings in many parts of the
country, stipulating only that a site be furnished and
maintenance provided by taxation. By the end of 1898
he had given nearly six million dollars to the cause, a
mere hint, however, of what was to follow.[1] Carnegie,
though the greatest giver, was not the only one. During
the two decades a total of not less than thirty-six million
dollars was contributed for library purposes. Some
donors, like Enoch Pratt who gave a million to Baltimore and Samuel J. Tilden who in 1886 bequeathed
most of his estate to New York City, helped create new
foundations. Others, like Mrs. John M. Reid who presented the German historian Leopold von Ranke's
library of twenty thousand books and manuscripts to
Syracuse University, greatly enriched existing collections.[2]

The climax of this age of unexampled library expansion came in the closing years. In 1895 the Astor,
Lenox and Tilden libraries—each the product of private
bounty—united to form the great New York Public
Library and plans were made for adequate housing of
the collections. The same year Boston opened its new
two-million-dollar building to the public, a pleasing
edifice in Roman Renaissance style facing Richardson's
noble Trinity Church across Copley Square. Chicago
followed in 1897 with an impressive building in the
classical mode, erected on the lake front at a cost of two

[1] T. W. Koch, *A Book of Carnegie Libraries* (White Plains, 1917);
H. U. Faulkner, *The Quest for Social Justice* (*A History of American
Life*, XI), 279-280.
[2] Adolph Rein, "Nachricht über Rankes Bibliothek," *Historische Vier-
teljahrsschrift*, XXIV (1928), 253-254.

million. The same year the Library of Congress was removed from its cramped quarters in the Capitol to a splendid new structure built in Italian Renaissance style, costing over six million dollars and possessing a floor space of over thirteen acres.[1] It was the largest and costliest library building in the world—a generous, if somewhat belated, recognition by the federal government of the central importance of books in American culture.

By 1900 the total number of free circulating libraries of all kinds, possessing three hundred or more volumes, had grown to over nine thousand, more than half of them being located in the Middle and Far West.[2] The number of volumes in these collections had increased in twenty-five years from twelve million to nearly forty-seven. A Massachusetts inquiry revealed that library patrons, especially in rural towns, were generally young people, and that in such places the taste ran more strongly to "books of a high class" than in large centers.[3] When Luther Burbank in 1868, at the age of nineteen, read a book by Darwin, which he had discovered at the Lancaster, Massachusetts, public library, he received an impulse which, he tells us, was "probably the turning point of my career in fixing my life work in the production of new species and varieties of plant life." [4] Thirty years later there was scarcely an American community, save in parts of the South, in which the library did not stand ready to perform a similar service for eager and talented youths. It had "come to be recognized as no less im-

[1] Herbert Putnam, "The Library of Congress," *Atlantic Mo.*, LXXXV (1900), 145-158.

[2] U. S. Comr. of Educ., *Rep. for 1899-1900*, I, 939.

[3] E. B. Tillinghast, "Books and Readers in Public Libraries," *Forum*, XVI (1893-1894), 61.

[4] Emma B. Beeson, *The Early Life and Letters of Luther Burbank* (San Fran., 1927), 74.

portant than the schoolhouse in the system of popular education." [1]

Although libraries spread the habit of reading books, most people did not freely patronize bookstores. This situation was ascribed by publishers to lack of enterprise on the part of retailers, but a more important cause was the antiquated system of distributing books to the trade. Semiannual auctions were held in New York where large purchasers were able to buy their supplies from publishers at extremely low figures and subsequently sell the volumes to the public at cut-rate prices. This system was a special boon to department stores whose practice of "book butchering" caused a running fire of complaint throughout these years in the pages of the *Publishers' Weekly*, the main trade organ. [2] Such stores often sold books at an actual loss in order to attract customers for other articles. In smaller places like Madison, Wisconsin, and Los Angeles people had no choice but to buy their books at shops dealing mainly in other wares. In the latter city a drygoods store in 1885 announced that every purchaser of six pair of lisle hose might, for ten cents additional, have his selection of their stock of novels. [3]

Bad methods of distribution accounted also for the continued vogue of subscription selling by house-to-house canvassers. The largest of such firms was Baird & Dillon of Chicago whose sales in 1883 amounted to over a million dollars. [4] They employed fifteen hundred canvassers and had agents in fifteen thousand towns

[1] R. G. Thwaites, "Ten Years of American Library Progress," *Library Journ.*, XXV (1900), no. 8, 3. In 1875 there were in libraries twenty-five volumes per hundred of population; in 1900, fifty-nine.

[2] See also J. H. Dingman, "American Bookselling and Booksellers," *Dial*, XXVIII (1900), 345-346.

[3] C. D. Warner, *Studies in the South and West* (N. Y., 1889), 173-175; *Publishers' Wkly.*, XXVII, 733 (June 27, 1885).

[4] *Publishers' Wkly.*, XXVI, 33 (July 12, 1884).

and cities. While the business was ordinarily confined to standard sets, dictionaries and encyclopedias, Mark Twain had found the method paid so well in the case of his earlier books that in 1884 he organized his own subscription house. His first offering, *The Adventures of Huckleberry Finn,* had forty thousand orders before it was ready for delivery. His greatest coup, U. S. Grant's *Memoirs,* written or dictated by the old warrior as he lay slowly dying, sold more than three hundred thousand sets of two volumes each, and netted the ex-president's widow around four hundred and twenty-five thousand dollars.[1]

Both subscription selling and book auctions declined in importance in the last years of the century. As the trade became better organized through a system of fixed discounts, retailers developed the habit of ordering from traveling salesmen or through one of the great jobbing houses, such as A. C. McClurg & Company of Chicago or the Baker & Taylor Company in New York. While the department store continued to hamper an extensive development of independent bookshops, on the other hand, by its hustling salesmanship, it accustomed this generation to think of literature as ordinary merchandise —something within the reach of all—and thus greatly stimulated book buying.

Though book knowledge had never before constituted so large a part of the common intellectual stock, the mental world of the average man continued in large measure to consist of a *mélange* of information, lore and gossip culled from the periodical press. Even the magazines catered to the most diverse tastes. If the score of years from 1878 to 1898 did little to increase their

---

[1] "The first check of $200,000, drawn Feb. 27, 1886, remains the largest single royalty check in history." For Clemens's publishing activities and the eventual failure of the firm in 1894, see A. B. Paine, *Mark Twain* (N. Y., 1912), II, chaps. cxlix, cliii-clvi, clix, clxiv.

variety, it added to their number and adapted their manner and matter better to the stratified reading public. Monthly periodicals increased from about twelve hundred to eighteen hundred, while their more sedate quarterly contemporaries grew from about one hundred to well over two hundred.[1] The chief gains occurred in periodicals devoted to transportation, business (including trade journals) and fraternal organizations. Magazines for general readers were less remarkable for their growth in number than, as we shall see, for their greatly expanded circulations.

Of the better-class periodicals this generation could hardly improve upon those it had inherited from earlier years: *Harper's Monthly,* the *Atlantic* and *Scribner's Monthly* (changed to the *Century* in 1881 when the Scribner interests withdrew). An enlarging clientèle, however, made it possible for Charles Scribner's Sons to launch in 1887 a new monthly of similar appeal, *Scribner's Magazine.* Distinguished in typography, dignified in tone, careful in diction, these journals, the *Atlantic* excepted, also took special pride in their illustrations. Indeed, the triangular rivalry was responsible for important improvements in the art of engraving and the technique of printing pictures. On the literary side they were aided by continuity of editorial policy, Richard Watson Gilder serving throughout these years as editor of the *Century,* as did H. M. Alden and E. L. Burlingame respectively of *Harper's* and *Scribner's Magazine.*[2] A citizen attained a certain prestige merely by having one of these periodicals on his library table.

---

[1] W. S. Rossiter, "Printing and Publishing," *U. S. Twelfth Census* (1900), IX, 1045, gives these and other data cited.

[2] Though the *Atlantic* had three editors—W. D. Howells (1871-1881), T. B. Aldrich (1881-1890) and H. E. Scudder (1890-1898) —an examination of its files reveals no change in editorial policy or standards.

Though clearly partial to long serialized biographies and heavy descriptive articles, the editors were yet ever on the alert for new writers and fresh themes. George W. Cable, Frank R. Stockton, Charles Egbert Craddock (Mary N. Murfree), W. D. Howells, F. Marion Crawford, Joel Chandler Harris, Henry James, Thomas Nelson Page, Ruth McEnery Stuart, Richard Harding Davis and, among foreign contributors, Rudyard Kipling, Joseph Conrad and Gilbert Parker—such a list suggests the throng of authors whose fictional wares were retailed to the public by these journals. All contributors, however, were required to conform to certain canons of "good taste," difficult to define but natural to persons of fastidious breeding; editorial lapses in this regard brought prompt reprisals from indignant subscribers.[1] Even the manuscripts of Howells, James and Edmund C. Stedman, and of course those of the irrepressible Mark Twain, were subjected to such treatment, usually without protest from the authors. When, however, Gilder cut out certain dubious passages in "Pudd'nhead Wilson," the long-suffering author burst into a torrent of wrath.

A sudden access of prosperity came to the *Century* when in November, 1884, it began the publication of a succession of Civil War narratives by leading commanders on the two sides, a feat which required two

[1] On this whole subject, see L. F. Tooker, *The Joys and Tribulations of an Editor* (N. Y., 1924), chap. vi, 180-188; R. U. Johnson, *Remembered Yesterdays* (N. Y., 1923), 124-131; Richard Watson Gilder, *Letters* (Rosamond Gilder, ed., Boston, 1916), chap. xi; Algernon Tassin, *The Magazine in America* (N. Y., 1916), 321-336; J. L. Ford, *Forty-Odd Years in the Literary Shop* (N. Y., 1921), 118-121; Bernard DeVoto, "Mark Twain and the Genteel Tradition," *Harvard Graduates' Mag.*, XL (1931), 155-163. Once when Gilder wrote a commencement poem for Smith College, some wags in the *Century* office gave him an uncomfortable half-hour by sending him a telegram, purporting to come from a Smith professor, which read: "Faculty doubt morality of fourth stanza. Can it be changed?" Johnson, *Remembered Yesterdays*, 93-94.

years for completion. Whether due to the appeal to half-forgotten memories, the fame of the contributors or the curiosity of a new generation grown old since Appomattox, the series was a spectacular success, swelling the circulation from one hundred and twenty-five thousand to two hundred and fifty. But in the fall of 1886, when the elated editors sought to repeat the coup with the first installment of Nicolay and Hay's monumental life of Lincoln—paying fifty thousand dollars for the full serial rights—the subscription list steadily shrank as the ponderous narrative, "apparently facing eternity," clogged its pages for nearly three and a half years.[1]

Magazines for special constituencies were legion. For critical literary appraisals the reader found one of his ablest mentors in a Chicago publication, the *Dial*, founded in 1880 under the editorship of Francis F. Browne. The *Overland Monthly*, revived in 1882 after six years' suspension, served the wide reaches of the Pacific West with reading matter of a robust type. *Outing*, begun the same year, performed a similar function for lovers of sport. For those seeking a longer-range view of current events than that afforded by the newspapers, four well-conducted magazines appeared: *Public Opinion* in 1886, *Current Literature* two years later, and in 1890 the *Literary Digest* and the *American Review of Reviews*, the last an American version of a British journal. Older weeklies like the *Nation, Independent* and *Outlook* (known until 1893 as the *Christian Union*) continued to survey analytically the passing scene, the two latter from a religious angle.[2] But in impatience and crusading zeal they were outstripped by two new monthlies, the

---

[1] Tooker, *Joys and Tribulations*, 45-46, 77-79, 255-257, 304-308; Johnson, *Remembered Yesterdays*, 189-208.

[2] J. F. Muirhead considered these three weeklies superior to any of a similar kind in England. *The Land of Contrasts* (N. Y., 1898), 159.

*Forum* (1886) and the *Arena* (1889), whose ardent course prepared the way for the Muckrakers of the twentieth century.

A flock of new publications bespoke the widening interests of women who no longer needed to content themselves with old-fashioned journals of the *Godey* type. Of such magazines none was so influential as the *Ladies' Home Journal.* Established in 1883 by Cyrus H. K. Curtis, it began its astonishing success six years later when Edward W. Bok, an aggressive journalist of Dutch birth, took the editorial helm.[1] Bok, without neglecting familiar household concerns, introduced many fresh features: fiction by the best writers, articles on interesting personalities of the world, attractive illustrations, inexpensive house plans, and special departments like "Ruth Ashmore's Side Talks with Girls" which brought an average of ten thousand letters a year from maidens troubled with affairs of the heart. And for such riches the reader paid but ten cents a copy. A feminine rather than a feminist magazine, the *Ladies' Home Journal* not only kept in stride with the intelligent middle-class woman, but walked several paces ahead.

Bok's success called attention to the existence of a mass of readers, suckled largely on newspapers, whom fiction magazines selling at twenty-five and thirty-five cents had never been able to reach. What Bok had done to interest women, might not others do for this greater public of both sexes? New manufacturing processes, large-scale production and the possibility of unusual advertising revenues suggested the means of accomplishment. Armed with this bold idea and savings of seventy-three hundred dollars, Samuel S. McClure in 1893 launched a new periodical, *McClure's,* which sold for

[1] E. W. Bok, *The Americanization of Edward Bok* (N. Y., 1920), chaps. xv-xviii.

but fifteen cents a copy. Within a few months *Munsey's* and the *Cosmopolitan* went him one better, lowering their rates to ten cents.[1] The great popularity which all of them achieved rested almost as much on their ability to attract able authors and illustrators and on the crisp manner of writing as on the low cost to readers. Ida M. Tarbell's careful articles on Napoleon and Abraham Lincoln in 1894 and 1895 helped increase the circulation of *McClure's* by the tens of thousands. By 1898 the popular-priced magazine had enlarged the number of magazine buyers from about five hundred thousand to nearly three million.[2]

The cheap periodical emphasized a tendency noticeable in the more expensive journals, a trend away from pedantic prose and literary attitudinizing toward a warmly human treatment of life and its interests. A review of magazine literature for the two decades reveals a marked decline of the polite essay and of the old-fashioned travel sketch, a gain in the number of timely articles, and a notable increase of short stories.[3] To magazines was largely due the rise of the short story to its significant place in American letters. Moreover, there was hardly an important novel which did not first find publication in their pages. By this means the author not only reached a wider audience but also assured himself a competence. As Howells and others pointed out, literary earnings came mainly from serialization, and "the prosperity of the magazines has given

[1] S. S. McClure, *My Autobiography* (N. Y., 1914), chap. vii; same author, "An Open Letter," *Haldeman-Julius Wkly.*, no. 1475, 4 (March 8, 1924). The *Cosmopolitan* had been founded by John Brisben Walker in 1886; *Munsey's* by Frank A. Munsey in 1891.

[2] F. A. Munsey, "Advertising in Some of Its Phases," *Munsey's*, XX (1898-1899), 480.

[3] See A. R. Kimball, "The Invasion of Journalism," *Atlantic Mo.*, LXXXVI (1900), esp. 123-124; W. D. Howells, *Literature and Life* (N. Y., 1902), 26-27; also later, 199, 201.

a whole class existence which, as a class, was wholly unknown" in America before the Civil War. The return
from book sales was merely "so much money found in
the road."[1]

Just as more people read magazines than books, so a
greater number read newspapers than magazines. The
nineteenth-century American had long since come to regard the newspaper as second only to the church and
the school in importance; indeed, in many a pioneer
settlement it leaped into lusty manhood while the other
two were still gasping for birth. The sweep of population into the Great West, the gargantuan growth of
cities and the increasing literacy of the masses now afforded newspapers new areas for conquest. The result
was seen in a multiplication of papers, tremendous competition in news gathering and a growing vulgarization
of the press. Between 1880 and 1900 the number of
dailies advanced from 971 to 2226, and the weeklies
and semiweeklies—published chiefly in rural towns—
from less than nine thousand to nearly fourteen thousand. At the latter date the United States was fathering
more than half the newspapers in the world. Yet the
growth of subscribers outstripped even the increase of
journals.[2]

While the newspapers clustered most thickly in the
states possessing large cities, the two new commonwealths
carved out of Dakota contained twenty-five dailies and
three hundred and fifteen weeklies at the close of the

[1] Toward the close of the period magazine remuneration to authors
varied from five or six dollars a thousand words for beginners to $150
for veterans. Howells, *Literature and Life*, 7-9, 11. See also edit., "Authors' Incomes," *Publishers' Wkly.*, XXVII, 732 (June 27, 1885); and
G. P. Lathrop, "Reward of Authorship in America," same mag., XXX,
523-524 (Oct. 9, 1886).

[2] In 1880 there were two copies of a newspaper issued for every
three persons; twenty years later there were two copies for each individual. For these and other data cited in the text, see Rossiter, "Printing
and Publishing," 1037-1119.

century, and even Oklahoma territory could boast of
nine daily papers and nearly a hundred weeklies. Indeed
it is worth recalling that, though the dynamic forces in
journalism emanated from the cities, the average American remained addicted to a weekly or semiweekly journal. As late as 1900 forty-two and a half million took
such papers as compared with fifteen million who bought
dailies.[1] The country weekly of 1900 was, however, a
far different sheet from its counterpart of twenty years
before.

The character of metropolitan journalism was determined in part by the rapid pace and high tension everywhere manifest in city life and in part by the presence
of vast multitudes who had but freshly mastered the art
of reading. To command a large circulation the presentation of news must be terse, colorful, entertaining,
dramatic. It must interest, but not too long detain, and,
withal, afford the reader a romantic respite from the
daily grind. Equally important was the discovery that, as
a source of revenue, subscribers were less important than
advertisers. At the opening of the period income from
subscriptions and sales still provided well over half the
total; but with the tremendous growth of retail stores
and nation-wide merchandising, advertising had by the
early 1890's come to provide the major share.[2] Not that
the newspapers could afford to neglect subscribers, but
big circulations were more important as a means
of prying up advertising rates than for their own
sake.

As vast business undertakings the larger papers grew
more and more to reflect the opinions of the intrenched
interests represented by their owners and leading ad-

[1] The figures for 1880 were sixteen and a half million for weeklies
and semiweeklies and three and a half million for dailies. Rossiter,
"Printing and Publishing," 1046.

[2] Rossiter, "Printing and Publishing," 1042, 1044.

vertisers. The journalism of these two decades thus presents the apparent paradox of an editorial policy tending to become spineless or conservative while the treatment of day-by-day news became increasingly sensational. No generalization, however, could fit so diversified a world. Organs like the *New York Evening Post* and the *Boston Transcript* made few concessions to the moronic mentality of the enlarged reading public, journals like the *Chicago Daily News* and the *Kansas City Star* battled for the common weal without regard to advertising revenue, while the advent of persons like Pulitzer, Hearst and Melville E. Stone showed it was still possible for vigorous men to imprint their personalities on even mammoth newspaper enterprises.

Of the new generation of editors Joseph Pulitzer occupied the center of the stage for most of the period. His career illustrates some of the best as well as some of the worst phases of journalistic practice.[1] Born in Hungary, Pulitzer had come to America in 1864 at the age of seventeen, penniless and friendless. Going soon after to St. Louis, he quickly made himself a force in the community, doing newspaper work for Carl Schurz, mixing in politics and being ever active for civic betterment. In 1878 he acquired the *Post-Dispatch* which under his militant direction became the principal evening paper of the city and earned him the money with which to try his fortunes in a wider field. In 1883 he bought the rundown *New York World* from Jay Gould—an event from which dates the rise of modern American journalism.

Declaring in the first issue that his efforts would be "dedicated to the cause of the people rather than that of

[1] D. C. Seitz, *Joseph Pulitzer* (N. Y., 1924), chaps. iv-x; J. L. Heaton, *The Story of a Page* (N. Y., 1913), chaps. i-xii; Alleyne Ireland, *Joseph Pulitzer* (N. Y., 1914)—a personal portrait by his secretary.

purse-potentates," [1] he frankly directed his appeal to the toiling masses, shrewdly suiting the form and content of his paper to their mental capacity and tastes. "Human interest" was emphasized in the day's news; illustrations, including diagrams showing "X—where the body was found," lent variety; headlines such as "Death Rides the Blast" and "Baptized in Blood" arrested attention. An ardent supporter of Cleveland in 1884, he published the first series of political cartoons ever appearing in an American newspaper, "picturized editorials" four or five columns wide, drawn by Walt McDougall and Valerian Gribayédoff.

He plunged with crusading zeal into every manner of humanitarian cause. In the years 1885 and 1886, for instance, the *World* exposed the bribery of New York aldermen in connection with the Broadway street-car franchise, it bared the white-slave traffic carried on by a self-styled astrologer and, when Congress failed to make an appropriation, it induced one hundred and twenty thousand persons to subscribe a hundred thousand dollars for a pedestal for Bartholdi's colossal Statue of Liberty in New York Harbor.[2] His addition of a colored supplement to the Sunday edition in 1893 caused another leap in sales and, by means of R. F. Outcault's portrayal of "The Yellow Kid" and child

[1] Signed statement in *N. Y. World*, May 11, 1883. His platform of reform, announced on May 17, called for taxation of luxuries, inheritances, large incomes and privileged corporations; reform of the tariff and of the civil service; and the punishment of corrupt officials, vote buyers and employers who coerced employees in elections.

[2] Pulitzer also set a new pace for journalism in the grand manner when he commissioned a reporter "Nellie Bly" (Elizabeth Cochrane) to outdo Jules Verne's hero in *Around the World in Eighty Days*. Leaving Hoboken on Nov. 14, 1889, she girdled the globe in 72 days, 6 hours, 11 minutes and 14 seconds, her return on Jan. 25 being greeted by the screeching of sirens and the booming of cannon. She lost one day by stopping to interview Verne at his home in Amiens. See Elizabeth Cochrane, *Nellie Bly's Book: Around the World in Seventy-Two Days* (N. Y., 1890).

life in "Hogan's Alley," paved the way for the coming of colored comics. It was largely due to Pulitzer that the Sunday newspaper became the remarkable cyclopedia of fact, fiction, fun and folly so characteristic of our own era.[1] Even when ill health and increasing blindness forced him to spend much time abroad, he nevertheless continued aggressively to direct the *World's* policies.

When Pulitzer acquired the *World* it had à daily circulation of fifteen thousand. Within a year this number grew to more than sixty thousand, and by 1898 it passed the million mark.[2] Pulitzer's course was a beacon light to newspapers in all parts of the country. In Detroit the *Evening News,* launched in 1873 by James E. Scripps, found sensational methods so effective that between 1878 and 1881 his brother, E. W. Scripps, set up journals of the same type in Cleveland, St. Louis and Cincinnati. By somewhat similar means the *Chicago Daily News,* established in 1875, advanced its circulation from fifty thousand in 1881 to one hundred and thirty thousand in 1890. As evening papers, moreover, such journals were able to make a special appeal to office workers and wage-earners when the long day's work was done, thus opening up a fresh field for newspaper enterprise.

Meanwhile a wealthy young Californian, enrolled at Harvard from 1883 to 1885, had been so captivated by the success of Pulitzer's methods that on his return home he induced his father to buy him the *San Francisco Examiner.* Emboldened by the results, he invaded

[1] The credit, or responsibility, really belonged to Morrill Goddard, Pulitzer's Sunday editor. Anon., "The Man Who Invented the Sunday Newspaper," *Am. Rev. of Revs.,* XXII (1900), 619.

[2] In September, 1886, when the circulation went beyond 250,000, a silver medal was struck off to commemorate "the largest circulation ever attained by an American newspaper."

the New York field in 1895 with the purchase of the *Morning Journal*. William Randolph Hearst, this latest gale out of the West to agitate Eastern journalism, there set himself to outdo Pulitzer at his own game.[1] As Pulitzer's *World* marked an advance in sensational methods over Charles A. Dana's *Sun*,[2] so Hearst's sensationalism now surpassed Pulitzer's in spite of all efforts of the latter to keep pace. The struggle of the giants over the publication rights of "The Yellow Kid"—resulting in two series by different cartoonists being run simultaneously—gave coinage to the term by which their brand of newspaper enterprise has ever since been known, "yellow journalism."

The battle royal raged fiercely through the campaign of 1896, Pulitzer condemning free silver while Hearst's cartoonist, Homer Davenport, inflamed popular prejudice against the Republicans by portraying Mark Hanna, McKinley's chief backer, as an ogrelike figure plastered over with dollar signs. Their efforts reached a feverish pitch as the Spanish-American War approached.[3] The mysterious destruction of the *Maine* in Havana Harbor caused the rival papers to break out in a rash of inch-high type, page-wide streamer headlines, and blood-curdling full-page pictures showing alleged Spanish atrocities in Cuba. In the second week following the explosion the *World's* circulation passed five million. Hearst insistently called for armed intervention; and though Pulitzer earlier had rebuked Cleveland for jingo-

[1] J. K. Winkler, *William Randolph Hearst* (N. Y., 1928), chaps. iii-vii; Faulkner, *Quest for Social Justice*, 251-252.

[2] See Allan Nevins, *The Emergence of Modern America* (*A History of American Life*, VIII), 240-241.

[3] In 1897 a party organized by the *Journal* effected the escape from a Havana prison of Evangelina Cisneros, a young Cuban girl convicted of treason. Winkler, *Hearst*, 147-151. The incident of the De Lôme letter, published by the *Journal*, is too well known to require further comment here. See J. F. Rhodes, *The McKinley and Roosevelt Administrations* (N. Y., 1922), 48-49.

# NEW YORK JOURNAL

AND ADVERTISER.

SATURDAY WAS 1,408,760

HOW DO YOU LIKE THE JOURNAL'S WAR?

HOW DO YOU LIKE THE JOURNAL'S WAR?

NEW YORK, SUNDAY, MAY 8, 1898.—84 PAGES. PRICE FIVE CENTS

OUR VICTORIOUS FLEET

## TWO DETAILED AMERICAN ACCOUNTS OF THE
## GREAT BATTLE AT MANILA.

FROM JOURNAL CORRESPONDENT JOHN T. M'CUTCHEON ON BOARD THE UNITED STATES GUNBOAT M'CULLOCH
FROM JOURNAL CORRESPONDENT HENRY G. LADD, OF HONG KONG, ALSO ON THE M'CULLOCH

(Copyright, 1898, by W. R. Hearst.)
Special Cable to the New York Journal.
By *John T. McCutcheon, Journal Correspondent with Admiral Dewey's Squadron.*

HONG KONG, May 7.—This is the result of the great fight in Manila Bay:
Eleven Spanish ships destroyed.
Eight Spanish ships captured.
Four shore batteries at Cavite demolished.
Three forts on Corregidor Island reduced.
Four hundred Spaniards killed.
Six hundred Spaniards wounded.
Spanish supplies lost and captured to the amount of $5,000,000.
American loss:
Eight men slightly wounded.
One thousand dollars damage.
Those are the figures of victory. The story of the battle will live forever. The
its heroes can never die.
The fighting began at 5 o'clock in the morning.
and surrendered at 12:40 in the afternoon.

*New Journalism*

ism at the time of the Venezuela boundary crisis, he now also demanded a "short and sharp" war.[1] "Nothing so disgraceful as the behavior" of these two papers, commented E. L. Godkin, "has been known in the history of American journalism." [2] Undoubtedly such melodramatic tactics, pursued primarily to boost sales, pushed the peace-loving McKinley into a war for objects which were already on the point of being gained untheatrically through the channels of diplomacy.

Enormous circulations with frequent editions and "extras" could not have been achieved without great improvements in the mechanics of manufacture. These years saw the introduction of larger and ever faster presses, color printing, quicker and cheaper methods of reproducing pictures (photolithography, the line-cut and half-tone processes), and a sharp reduction in the cost of print paper. By 1878 the typewriter was perfected, equipped at last to print both small and large letters,[3] and six years later L. E. Waterman placed on the market the first successful fountain pen—two conveniences which the new generation of reporters quickly adapted to their uses. Newspaper composition was transformed from a hand to a machine process in 1885 through Ottmar Mergenthaler's invention of the linotype, a mechanical marvel which, under the fingers of a skilled operator, cast from molten lead solid lines

[1] Signed edit. in *N. Y. World*, April 10, 1898.

[2] W. M. Bleyer, *Main Currents in the History of American Journalism* (Boston, 1927), 377. Pulitzer's sober second thought is revealed by instructions given to his editors in 1907 when President Roosevelt proposed to send battleships into the Pacific to impress Japan: "Show that Spain had granted to Cuba all that we demanded, but passion in Spain and here forced the hands of government. . . . Give further details of jingoism causing Cuban War after Spain had virtually granted everything . . . ." Seitz, *Pulitzer*, 312-313.

[3] This improvement was devised by Byron A. Brooks, a public-school teacher in New York City, and was at once bought by the Remingtons who incorporated it in a new model, Remington No. 2.

of type ready for printing, thus shortening the time required to put news into type.[1]

To secure greater efficiency and economy in "covering" the world's happenings newspapers found it advantageous to pool their resources. Though the New York Associated Press, which sold its service also to out-of-town papers, was already in the field, several news-gathering agencies arose and waged hot war with one another. One of these, the Western Associated Press, after a temporary alliance with the Eastern body, broke away in 1892, forming the Associated Press of Illinois. With Melville E. Stone as general manager it soon established its dominance in the national news-distributing field, driving its chief rival to the wall five years later.[2] Newspaper chains, foreshadowed by the activities of Pulitzer, took definite form when a league of Mid-Western papers was organized in the 1880's by the Scripps brothers.[3] The establishment of the Scripps-McRae Press Association in 1897 marked the entry of a new competitor of the Associated Press.

Hardly less important was the growth in the amount of syndicated material used by the press, a practice begun in 1884 when S. S. McClure, then on the *Century Magazine*, formed the first American agency for the purpose. By the early nineties the "S. S. McClure Newspaper Features" consisted of novels and short stories, articles on current topics by men in the public eye, a woman's page and a juvenile department; and there were rival syndicates in the field, notably one belonging to Edward

[1] Rossiter, "Printing and Publishing," 1092-1097; G. E. Barnett, "The Introduction of the Linotype," *Yale Rev.*, XIII (1904-1905), 251-273.

[2] The present-day Associated Press dates from a reorganization in 1900 under a New York charter. M. E. Stone, *Fifty Years a Journalist* (Garden City, 1921), 207-218, 235.

[3] M. A. McRae, *Forty Years in Newspaperdom* (N. Y., 1924), 21-79.

Bok.[1] Politicians were not slow to take the hint. In the campaign of 1896 it is estimated that the Republican national committee, by organizing its own syndicate service, reached five million families every week with arguments and caricatures against Bryanism and bimetallism.[2]

As a result of these various developments, newspaper readers were kept abreast the passing show as never before in American history. If a fifty-mile radius represented the approximate distance to which a city daily had a general sale, there were twenty-one principal newspaper-distribution areas in the United States, embracing a population of nearly nineteen and a half million or about a third of all the people in the nation. Here were found three fourths of the dailies with the greatest circulation.[3] At the same time the country press moved closer into the orbit of metropolitan journalism, and, seconded by the magazines, city standards and interests were ceaselessly dinned into the ears of the rural audience—a telling example of urban imperialism in the cultural sphere and indirectly the source of much rustic unhappiness.

To foreigners the new journalism seemed a peculiarly American phenomenon. "The whole character of the nation is there: spirit of enterprise, liveliness, childishness, inquisitiveness, deep interest in everything that is human, fun and humor, indiscretion, love of gossip, brightness," wrote Paul Blouët.[4] A more thoughtful European ob-

[1] McClure, *Autobiography*, 164-206; Rossiter, "Printing and Publishing," 1103-1104.

[2] W. B. Shaw, "Methods and Tactics of the Campaign," *Am. Rev. of Revs.*, XIV (1896), esp. 555.

[3] Based on the census of 1890. See D. F. Wilcox, "The American Newspaper," Am. Acad. of Polit. and Social Sci., *Annals*, XVI (1900), 59-61.

[4] Paul Blouët (Max O'Rell, *pseud.*), *A Frenchman in America* (N. Y., 1891), 110.

server, however, deemed the ordinary journal fit only for the servants' hall.[1] Undoubtedly prying sensationalism robbed American life of much of its privacy to the gain chiefly of morbid curiosity. As an American journalist charged, from dieting on the press the "mind loses the power of discrimination, the taste is lowered, and the appetite becomes diseased." [2] Such sweeping appraisals, however, left out of account the enormous additions to the newspaper-reading public. Fifty years earlier the only literate class was that which in the 1880's and 1890's read papers like the *New York Times* and the *Boston Transcript;* the audience corresponding to that addressed by the yellow press did not read at all.

Nor was sensation-mongering without advantages to civic welfare. Pulitzer's zeal in exposing corruption and jarring public complacency was matched by the efforts of editors in scores of other cities. Bryce himself testified that in the war against boodling politicians "the newspapers of New York, Boston, Philadelphia and Chicago have been one of the most effective battalions." [3] Journalism, moreover, for the first time began to provide an important training school for authors. In the last two decades of the century the *New York Sun,* for example, numbered among its reporters Julian Ralph, David Graham Phillips, Will Irwin, Samuel Hopkins Adams, Jacob Riis and Richard Harding Davis.[4] These and many other young men in all parts of the country

---

[1] Herbert Spencer, *Civilization in the United States* (6th edn., Boston, 1900), 177-180. See Muirhead's similar verdict in *Land of Contrasts,* chap. ix.

[2] C. D. Warner, *The Relation of Literature to Life* (N. Y., 1897), 268-269 (an essay first published in 1890).

[3] Bryce, *American Commonwealth,* III, 41.

[4] On the staff of the *Chicago News* were George Harvey, George Ade, Slason Thompson, Finley Peter Dunne, Eugene Field, James Whitcomb Riley, Henry Guy Carleton and others. Stone, *Fifty Years,* 111-112.

climbed the first rungs of the literary ladder while grubbing for the day's news.

If income from advertising was one of the prime factors in remaking the periodical press, advertising also deserves notice for its own sake as a potent influence in American culture. Hitherto, outdoor signs and billboards had been the chief means of catching the eye of a people, many of whom did not regularly read newspapers.[1] "America is daubed from one end of the country to the other with huge white-paint notices of favorite articles of manufacture," wrote one observer.[2] The great cities were plastered and painted and papered with blaring notices, while the rural landscape where "every prospect pleases and only man is vile" suffered from the same misguided zeal. Bret Harte in 1876 wrote of one energetic concern:

> One Sabbath morn, as heavenward
> White Mountain tourists slowly spurred,
> On every rock, to their dismay,
> They read the legend all the way—
> SAPOLIO.[3]

Outdoor publicity showed no decline in the 1880's and 1890's, but advertisers centered their energies on reaching the hordes of newspaper and magazine readers.[4] Between 1880 and 1900 the amount of newspaper advertising increased from about forty million dollars

[1] Frank Presbrey, *The History and Development of Advertising* (Garden City, 1929), 366.

[2] G. W. Steevens, *The Land of the Dollar* (N. Y., 1897), 49-50. Similar comments may be found in O'Rell, *Frenchman in America*, 263; W. G. Marshall, *Through America* (London, 1882), 111-113; Muirhead, *Land of Contrasts*, 136.

[3] In a booklet designed to explain to dealers the unflagging enterprise of this particular soap company. Bret Harte's name did not appear. Presbrey, *Advertising*, 374.

[4] Other avenues were not neglected, however, such as mail-order catalogues, street-car signs, gas and electric signs and the use of novelties.

to nearly ninety-six.[1] An analysis of an ordinary week-day issue of ten leading dailies in different sections of the country in the mid-nineties showed that advertising occupied from twenty-five to seventy per cent of the space, or an average of forty per cent.[2] From the start the *Century* was an active advertising medium; and in 1882 *Harper's Magazine*, yielding its earlier compunctions, swung into line. By October, 1888, *Harper's* was carrying one hundred and ninety-three ads—a total of fifty-four pages—and by October, 1898, three hundred and thirty ads filling eighty-three pages.[3] The new *Scribner's* was one of the first to entice readers into the vast hinterland of its advertising section by spreading the disjected members of an illustrated comic through its length. Strangely enough, the several hundred religious journals found their most profitable source of revenue in the space devoted to patent medicines.

On the part of merchants and manufacturers, the new age entailed unprecedented and ever mounting expenditures of money and brains to capture and retain the fickle public. The makers of Sapolio, for instance, while content with an appropriation of fifteen thousand dollars in 1871, were spending seventy in 1885 and four hundred by 1896.[4] The old bill-posting traditions taught advertisers the importance of a crisp, striking phrase to

[1] Rossiter, "Printing and Publishing," 1042. In the early 1890's about a fourth of all advertising expenditure was still going into outdoor display. Presbrey, *Advertising*, 366, 394.

[2] F. W. Ayer, "Advertising in America," C. M. Depew, ed., *One Hundred Years of American Commerce* (N. Y., 1895), I, 78.

[3] See tables in S. A. Sherman, "Advertising in the United States," Am. Stat. Assoc., *Publs.*, n.s., VII, 122, 142-143. Sherman also analyzes periodical advertising in 1898 from the standpoint of number and distribution of general advertisers.

[4] Presbrey, *Advertising*, 394. It is to be noted, however, that the increase of advertising was attended by a decline in the number of drummers or traveling salesmen, though this was partly a result of the merger of competing companies. Sherman, "Advertising," 129, 157-158.

impale the fleeting attention of possible patrons. Even people who professed never to look at ads knew of Ivory Soap that "It Floats," of Castoria that "Children Cry for It," of the Eastman Kodak that "You Press the Button; We Do the Rest," and that Schlitz was "The Beer that Made Milwaukee Famous." The lineaments and fame of Dr. Munyon—"I Am for Men"—were familiar to many an illiterate mountaineer or foreign immigrant who might have fumbled at naming the chief executive of the nation.[1]

For the most part, both the advertising agencies and the publications in which the announcements appeared assumed the attitude of *caveat emptor*. This was frankly the position, for instance, of George P. Rowell & Company, a leading New York agency, though a certain measure of discretion resulted when they inadvertently inserted a notice of H. R. Stiles's *Bundling, Its Origin, Progress and Decline* in the pages of the *Churchman*.[2] A few men like John E. Powers, who in the 1880's directed publicity for Wanamaker's in Philadelphia, discovered that honesty in advertising pays. But the fact was not so evident to a periodical which derived its heaviest revenues from patent-medicine sources—and as late as 1898 such firms still comprised the most important group of general advertisers.[3] A different attitude, however, was evinced by the *Farm Journal*, founded at Philadelphia in 1877, which from the outset declined "quack medical advertisements at any price" and, three years later, inaugurated the first known guarantee against

---

[1] The devices of the advertiser were endless. When a canning establishment found that its salmon would not sell because of the whitish color, it reversed its fortunes by advertising: "Positively Guaranteed Not to Turn Pink."

[2] G. P. Rowell, *Forty Years an Advertising Agent* (N. Y., 1906), 382-383, and *passim*.

[3] Presbrey, *Advertising*, 295, 303-310, 363-364.

fraudulent representations.[1] After the *Ladies' Home
Journal* in 1892 banned such ads, others of its contemporaries adopted the same policy. But no widespread
benefit resulted until the early years of the next century
when the Muckrakers began their career of pitiless
exposure.[2]

Partly for weal and partly for woe, the new age of
commercial publicity made a deep impress on American
life. With advertising "playing upon the brain of man
like a musician does upon a piano,"[3] the average citizen
learned the blessings of frequent applications of soap
and dentifrice, his dietary habits were influenced, and
his standards of home decoration improved. He learned,
in fact, what merchants with wares to sell thought
should constitute the American standard of living. At
the same time he was constantly being inveigled into
ill-advised expenditures, when not actually gulled by
misrepresentations, and his notions of personal therapy
were violently distorted by the extravagant claims made
for worthless or injurious medicines.

The American of the period could not escape being
educated whether by the school or the multifarious other
instrumentalities seeking to woo his thought and mold
his will. What, then, was the content of the average
American's mind in the 1880's and 1890's? What subjects excited his attention and what shifts of interest
took place? In so far as a highest common denominator
existed, it was probably implied by the way the newspaper press divided its space among various categories
of news. This may be assumed whether one argues that
newspapers reflect or seek to direct public opinion.

The accompanying table, though confined to an

[1] Wilmer Atkinson, *An Autobiography* (Phila., 1920), 161, 180.
[2] See Faulkner, *Quest for Social Justice*, 237-238, 255-256.
[3] Jacques Offenbach, *America and the Americans* (London, 1876),
51-52.

*A testimonial advertisement.*

*The Hall of Philosophy—Chautauqua—The Golden Gate.*

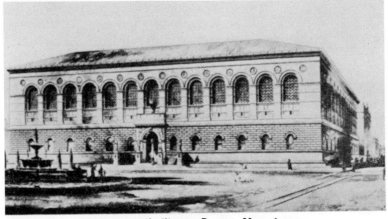

*A great public library, Boston, Massachusetts.*

Influencing the American Mind

ANALYSIS OF CONTENT OF SELECTED METROPOLITAN
DAILIES, 1878-1898 [1]

SHOWING THE ORDER OF IMPORTANCE AND PERCENTAGE OF SPACE
DEVOTED TO VARIOUS CATEGORIES OF NEWS

| 1878 | % | 1888 | % | 1898 | % |
|---|---|---|---|---|---|
| 1. Advertising | 21.5 | 1. Advertising | 29.8 | 1. Advertising | 28.2 |
| 2. Government and politics | 14.8 | 2. Government and politics | 19.2 | 2. Government and politics | 18.5 |
| 3. Foreign affairs | 10.0 | 3. Business and finance | 8.7 | 3. Business and finance | 11.2 |
| 4. Business and finance | 9.6 | 4. Editorials | 6.1 | 4. Foreign affairs | 6.5 |
| 5. Editorials | 8.5 | 5. Transportation | 4.7 | 5. Cultural interests | 6.2 |
| 6. Cultural interests | 7.9 | 6. Cultural interests | 4.4 | 6. Editorials | 5.0 |
| 7. Crimes and disasters | 5.2 | 7. Crimes and disasters | 4.1 | 7. Sports | 4.2 |
| 8. Transportation | 5.1 | 8. Foreign affairs | 3.5 | 8. Women | 3.2 |
| 9. Religion | 2.5 | 9. Sports | 3.2 | 9. Transportation | 3.1 |
| 10. Education | 2.1 | 10. Religion | 3.1 | 10. Education | 2.6 |
| 11. "Society" | 1.8 | 11. Social welfare | 2.2 | 11. Crimes and disasters | 2.0 |
| 12. Labor | 1.3 | 12. "Society" | 2.1 | 12. Religion | 1.6 |
| 13. Social welfare | 1.1 | 13. Education | 1.6 | 13. Social welfare | 1.4 |
| 14. Agriculture | 0.8 | 14. Labor | 1.3 | 14. "Society" | 1.2 |
| 15. Sports | 0.6 | 15. Agriculture | 0.8 | 15. Labor | 0.4 |
| 16. Women | 0.6 | 16. Women | 0.3 | 16. Agriculture | .2 |

[1] Based upon an unpublished study made by Mr B. B Bouton of Howe School, Howe, Indiana. The issues of the *New York Tribune*, *Chicago Tribune* and *Boston Transcript* for Jan. 1, April 1, July 1 and Oct. 1 were examined for each of the years 1878, 1888 and 1898. When articles belonged to more than one category an appropriate division was made. Cultural interests include the fine arts, literary items, poetry and theatrical notices. In general, allowance needs to be made for the fact that hard times directed unusual attention to business and finance in 1878, that 1888 was a presidential-election year, and that war news (the Balkans in 1878 and Cuba in 1898) temporarily increased the space given to foreign affairs.

analysis of metropolitan dailies, reveals certain well-marked trends.[1] Through the two decades business and finance bulked ever larger in the common consciousness. Along with governmental and partisan interests these items accounted for from a fourth to almost a third of the time which the ordinary person gave to extramural concerns.[2] Foreign affairs were of small import save in times of war and rumors of war. Religion retreated before the rush of other interests, as did also the attention given labor questions, though the latter circumstance was probably due to the growing alliance of the press with the employing class. Urban cerebration in regard to agriculture sank almost to the vanishing point. On the contrary, consideration of women's concerns increased fourfold and of sports sevenfold. In general, the mental universe of the newspaper-reading citizen seemed more and more occupied with matters of material welfare, comfort and pleasure; and it is clear that the great energy which special groups were devoting to humanitarian reform, education, science, literature and the fine arts had as yet made relatively little dent on the mass mind.

These impressions are in large measure supported by the tendencies displayed in the better magazines. Designed for leisure-time perusal and for a more restricted clientèle, such periodicals, of course, gave their lion's share of space to fiction, poetry, literary criticism,

---

[1] If allowance is made for differences of classification, much the same conclusions are sustained by certain content studies made at the time: H. R. Elliot, "The Ratio of News," *Forum*, V (1888), 99-107, which analyzes issues of current newspapers in selected cities; J. G. Speed, "Do Newspapers Give the News?," *Forum*, XV (1893), 705-711, which compares Sunday editions of four New York dailies in 1881 and 1893; Wilcox, "American Newspaper," 56-92, an elaborate sampling analysis of the content of 240 different dailies in 1898 and 1899.

[2] From a third to over two fifths, if the space occupied by advertisements be disregarded.

history and travel.[1] Where their subject matter over-
lapped that of the newspaper press, however, similar
drifts of reader interest appear: an increasing absorption in current business and political affairs and in feminine welfare, variability in regard to foreign affairs, and
a declining curiosity as to religion, cultural subjects
(fine arts, music and the drama) and agriculture. Education, labor, science and invention, on the other hand,
fared somewhat better than in the dailies, while the vicarious excitement afforded by fiction may perhaps account
for the relative neglect of sports.

Despite all setbacks and shortcomings the educational
advance during the 1880's and 1890's was astonishing.
All parts of the country and all classes of society were
affected. Through the spread of schools, bookstores,
libraries, magazines and newspapers America had become, in Freeman's phrase, "the land of the general
reader," the home of the greatest reading public hitherto known in the history of the world.[2] If cultural
progress in a democracy depends upon a continuous
process of recruitment from the ranks of the many,
never before had America so ample an opportunity for
a forward push along all lines of intellectual endeavor.

[1] These categories account for about seventy per cent of the contents
in 1878 and 1888 and a little more than sixty per cent in 1898. This
analysis is based on an unpublished study of all issues of *Harper's Mo.,
Atlantic Mo., N. Am. Rev., Lippincott's Mag., Scribner's Mo.-Century*
and the *Overland Mo.* for the years 1878, 1888 and 1898, made by
Dr. R. L. Welty of Texas Christian University.

[2] E. A. Freeman, *Some Impressions of the United States* (N. Y.,
1883), 184-185.

# CHAPTER VII

## INCREASING THE WORLD'S KNOWLEDGE

NEW forces were at work in the colleges and universities as well as in the wider reaches of popular education. Not only did institutions of higher learning grow in number, endowment and quality of instruction, but for the first time they began to take seriously their obligation to enrich the world's store of knowledge. "Nothing more strikes a stranger who visits the American universities," declared an English scholar familiar with Oxford and Cambridge, "than the ardour with which the younger generation has thrown itself into study, even kinds of study which will never win the applause of the multitude." [1] By way of historical parallel observers were reminded of the brilliant days of the Italian Renaissance.

Colleges and universities increased from three hundred and fifty-odd in 1878 to nearly five hundred in 1898, the combined student body from about fifty-eight thousand to approximately one hundred thousand.[2] Mere growth in number of institutions, however, did not necessarily denote progress except on the theory of the misguided patriot who exulted, "There are two universities in England, four in France, ten in

---

[1] James Bryce, *The American Commonwealth* (London, 1888), III, 571. See also anon., "The American College," *Atlantic Mo.*, LXXV (1895), esp. 703.

[2] This was a more rapid growth of enrollment than of total population. U. S. Commissioner of Education, *Report for 1887-88*, 632, and later *Reports, passim.*

Prussia and thirty-seven in Ohio." Particularly in the rural South and the Middle West, the country was wretchedly overstocked with institutions making pretensions to the name of college or university, at a time when higher standards of instruction and research called for a concentration of funds. In 1881 the total income of all the colleges and universities in Ohio fell considerably short of that of Harvard alone.[1] Most institutions of this kind had been planted by denominational zeal, and catered to local rural constituencies. Once pioneers in the westward march of higher culture, they were now fallen on bitter times, for the state universities, with constantly increasing legislative support, superior equipment and richer curricula, were drawing away their students and undermining their position of influence. In many a Western and Southern state legislature the tax-maintained university won its appropriations only in the teeth of hardy opposition from those who decried its "godless" character.

But in an age of the glorification of public education such die-hards contended against the spirit of the times. Between 1885 and 1895 the number of students in eight representative state universities—Michigan, Illinois, Wisconsin, Minnesota, Iowa, Kansas, Nebraska and California—trebled, while the gain in eight equally reputable church schools of the Middle West was scarcely fifteen per cent. In the latter year there were more Presbyterian students in seventeen state universities than in the thirty-seven best Presbyterian colleges.[2]

[1] C. F. Smith, "Southern Colleges and Schools," *Atlantic Mo.*, LIV (1884), 544-547. Ohio was not the only sinner: Illinois had 25 colleges, Iowa 18, Indiana 16, Michigan 10. U. S. Comr. of Educ., *Rep. for 1887-88*, 1040-1041.

[2] F. W. Kelsey, "State Universities and Church Colleges," *Atlantic Mo.*, LXXX (1897), 826-832. See also A. A. Johnson, "The State Universities and Denominational Colleges," *Educ.*, XVI (1895-1896), 435-437.

Moreover, ten commonwealths of the West and South which, for one reason or another, had not earlier seen fit to set up their own universities now proceeded to do so.[1] To the University of Michigan more than any other was due the constant improvement in state-university standards during these years. One of the first to free herself from the hampering influence of politics, she vied with Eastern institutions in introducing new educational methods and was the first to link the public schools with the university by admitting graduates of accredited high schools without examination.[2]

When Emily Faithfull, the English social worker, visited the University of Michigan in 1883, she was told by President J. B. Angell that, though coeducation was still on trial in the East, the question was definitely settled in the West. Moreover, he assured her, "none of the ladies had found the curriculum too heavy for their physical endurance . . . ."[3] All the new state universities in the West and South, as a matter of course, were coeducational and the strength of the tide was such that most of the Southern state institutions which had hitherto held aloof now succumbed.[4] While the practice continued to be less common in the older parts of the nation than in the West, the proportion of mixed colleges in the United States grew from fifty-one per cent

[1] South Dakota, 1882; North Dakota and Texas, 1883; Nevada and Wyoming, 1886; Idaho, 1889; Arizona and New Mexico, 1891; Oklahoma, 1892; and Montana, 1895.

[2] G. E. Howard, "The State University in America," *Atlantic Mo.*, LXVII (1891), esp. 340; Sara A. Burstall, *The Education of Girls in the United States* (London, 1894), chap. vi.

[3] Emily Faithfull, *Three Visits to America* (Edinburgh, 1884), 56-58. Thomas Woody, *A History of Women's Education in the United States* (J. M. Cattell, ed., *Science and Education*, IV, N. Y., 1929), bk. ii, chaps. iv-vi, is the fullest treatment of the subject.

[4] Only the state universities of Virginia, Georgia and Louisiana declined to change. E. G. Dexter, *A History of Education in the United States* (N. Y., 1904), 446-447.

in 1880 to seventy per cent in 1898, and the number of women students from twenty-seven hundred and fifty to more than twenty-five thousand.[1]

To meet the challenge of coeducation the East established new women's colleges of high rank and improved existing ones. Thus Bryn Mawr, near Philadelphia, was opened in 1885 with ample resources and excellent scientific equipment, while three years later Mount Holyoke Seminary was converted into a college with degree-granting powers. Most interesting of all was the grudging compromise by certain men's institutions, of setting up affiliated colleges for the other sex—coöperation without entanglement—after the manner of Oxford and Cambridge. Starting in 1879 with twenty-seven students, an organization, informally known as the Harvard Annex, enrolled studious young women who, under the guidance of such professors as William James, John Knowles Paine and Ephraim Emerton, were enabled to take the same courses as the men at Harvard, though not in their company. By the time this undertaking ripened into Radcliffe College (1894), Tulane University, Western Reserve and Columbia had created coördinate women's colleges and Brown University was in the course of so doing. By 1898 four out of every five colleges, universities and professional schools in the United States admitted women. Their right to as complete and diversified an education as men was no longer seriously questioned.

Meanwhile the old-fashioned, hard-and-fast college course was everywhere rapidly crumbling under the hammering blows inflicted by President Charles W. Eliot of Harvard and his like. However valid were the

[1] In calculating the proportions, separate women's colleges were not included. U. S. Comr. of Educ., *Rep. for 1889-90*, II, 764; *for 1900-01*, I, xlix.

pedagogical reasons for the elective system, the reform was in any case inevitable because of the great advances in science and scholarship and the sheer impossibility of a student's taking in four years all the courses offered. The world had changed; and as life itself became more diverse, more complex, it was fitting that education, as a preparation for life, should take on greater richness and variety. The elective system, moreover, was the practice of German universities where many American professors had studied. At Harvard freedom of election went farthest; in most other places the principle of liberty in the choice of subjects was introduced gradually, the first two years being largely prescribed with options thereafter.[1]

Under the new plan the college curriculum offered a variety of appeal which accounts in part for the swelling stream of students.[2] The time-honored courses in Latin, Greek and mathematics lost favor in competition with such newer subjects as English literature, certain laboratory sciences, modern languages, history, economics and political science.[3] While critics deplored an irrational scattering of choices by students and a tendency to concentrate on "snap" courses, Dean LeB. R. Briggs maintained, after many years' experience, that, "as a body, the students of Harvard College use the elective system with some sense of responsibility and with reasonable

[1] U. S. Comr. of Educ., *Rep. for 1883-84*, clviii; D. R. Phillips, "The Elective System in American Education," *Pedagogical Seminary*, VIII (1901), 206-230.

[2] The elective system took the curse off coeducation for many parents who would have been unwilling to let their daughters take the traditional prescribed course for men. Annie N. Meyer, ed., *Woman's Work in America* (N. Y., 1891), 76-77. A synoptic view of courses of study in over a hundred colleges is given in U. S. Comr. of Educ., *Rep. for 1888-89*, II, 1224-1361.

[3] C. F. Thwing, *A History of Higher Education in America* (N. Y., 1906), 439-445; same author, *A History of Education in the United States since the Civil War* (Boston, 1910), chap. v.

intelligence."[1] The system had one unanticipated result: by making possible greater specialization of teaching by the faculty, the diversity of offerings contributed indirectly to the increase of productive scholarship.

Further flexibility was given higher education by the development of summer schools and extension work. Though Harvard had initiated summer courses a few years earlier, the success of the New York Chautauqua and the needs of school teachers prompted a fuller development of the plan both there and elsewhere.[2] Under President Harper's leadership the University of Chicago in 1892 made the summer session an integral part of the academic year. In a somewhat similar fashion the example of Chautauqua, fortified by English experience, led universities in the 1890's to offer off-campus courses to special audiences, sometimes in other cities.[3] Less popular than summer study in residence, nevertheless certain institutions like Rutgers, Chicago, Wisconsin and Kansas succeeded in developing extension work as an important phase of their educational contribution.

Curricular changes were attended by changes in student life and conduct. While hazing continued to make the first months of the Freshman year a rough apprenticeship, in other respects there was greater soberness, a less excitable class spirit, fewer outbreaks of rowdyism and violence, than in former times.[4] The effect of the

[1] President and Treasurer of Harvard College, *Annual Report for 1899-1900*, esp. 120.

[2] W. W. Willoughby, "The History of Summer Schools in the United States," U. S. Comr. of Educ., *Rep. for 1891-92*, II, 893-959. See also U. S. Comr. of Educ., *Rep. for 1894-95*, II, 1483-1503; for *1899-1900*, I, 303-313.

[3] U. S. Comr. of Educ., *Rep. for 1891-92*, II, 945-55; for *1894-95*, II, 1483-1484; J. E. Russell, *The Extension of University Teaching in England and America* (Univ. of State of N. Y., *Extension Bull.*, no. 10, 1895), 176-184.

[4] H. D. Sheldon, *Student Life and Customs* (W. T. Harris, ed., *International Education Series*, LI, N. Y., 1901), chap. v.

elective system in destroying class unity, together with
the greater age at which students were entering college,
was partly responsible.[1] Equally important was the increasing absorption in intercollegiate athletics. The ancient loyalty to one's class was supplanted by loyalty
to the college as a whole. Typical displays of undergraduate spirit thus took the form of mass meetings,
athletic celebrations, rooting on the side lines and perhaps pitched battles after the game with supporters of
the other team. The growing sense of responsibility
encouraged colleges to experiment with plans of student
self-government. At the University of Illinois such a
scheme prevailed from 1868 to 1883, only to be abandoned by vote of the undergraduates themselves. The
student senate at Amherst, continuing from 1883 to
1894, might have lasted longer but for the opposition
of the incoming college administration. Elsewhere the
attempts ran a fluctuating course, being usually most
successful in small homogeneous institutions.[2]

Next to athletics, the chief focus of undergraduate interest was to be found in the clubs and fraternities. The
older institutions in the East had their exclusive local
societies of long standing, while throughout the West
and generally in the South the Greek-letter fraternity
system dominated student social life and, to a considerable extent, campus politics as well. To meet the needs
of ever expanding enrollments the national fraternities
increased the number of their chapters from four hun-

[1] The average age at Harvard rose from 18 years 9 months in 1878
to 19 years 6 months in 1889; during the years 1856-1860 it had
been 17 years 11 months. See U. S. Comr. of Educ., *Rep. for 1889-90*,
II, 799-803, for various colleges.

[2] See J. M. Gregory, "An Experiment in College Government," *International Rev.*, X (1881), 510-518 (for Illinois); John Bigham, "An
Instructive Experiment in College Government," *Educational Rev.*, III
(1892), 162-167 (for Amherst); Sheldon, *Student Life*, 256-271
(for a variety of experiments, including the honor system in examinations).

dred and sixty-two in 1879 to seven hundred and eighty-one in 1898 and their total membership from about sixty-three thousand to over one hundred and thirty thousand.[1] Ex-President White of Cornell defended the Greek-letter system as a means of developing group responsibility and higher personal standards, but others deplored its snobbish tendency and objected to the brutality of the initiation ceremonies.[2] The intrenched position of the fraternities is indicated by the fact that the efforts of the University of California in 1879 and of Purdue in 1881 to ban them were thwarted by an appeal to the courts. On the whole, it seems fair to say that, while fraternities generally exalted social above intellectual attainments, leadership in undergraduate activities usually came from their ranks, and their worst features were accentuated where college authorities were hostile.[3]

Virtually every institution also had a numerous array of literary, oratorical, debating, musical and dramatic societies, often, like the fraternities, bearing Greek names though lacking their exclusiveness. Student publications multiplied, the advent of the *Daily Illini* at the University of Illinois in 1871 and of the *Lampoon* at Harvard in 1876 marking the appearance respectively of the first undergraduate daily and the first humorous

[1] W. R. Baird, *American College Fraternities* (N. Y., 1879), 160-161; (5th edn., 1898), 424-431. See also J. A. Porter, "College Fraternities," *Century*, XXXVI (1888), 749-760; E. H. L. Randolph, "Greek-Letter Societies in American Colleges," *New England Mag.*, n.s., XVII (1897), 70-82; P. F. Piper, "College Fraternities," *Cosmopolitan*, XXII (1897), 641-648.

[2] A. D. White, "College Fraternities," *Forum*, III (1887), 243-253.

[3] According to Baird, writing in 1898, within the past twenty years "the Universities of California, Missouri, Alabama, North Carolina, Georgia, Iowa, Harvard and Vanderbilt have either repealed their antifraternity laws or allowed them to drop into disuse." In 1897, however, the South Carolina legislature succeeded in driving fraternities from the state university. Baird, *American College Fraternities* (5th edn.), 410, 415.

sheet. Oratory assumed an intercollegiate aspect with the formation of the Northwestern Interstate Collegiate Association in 1875; it was perhaps not without significance to the future of American politics that the contest at Iowa City in 1879 was won by a youth from the University of Wisconsin named Robert M. La Follette.[1] Interest in debating also took on new life with the beginning of intercollegiate rivalry. Harvard sent the first challenge to Yale in 1889; soon regional leagues sprang up in many parts of the country.

Denominational institutions were pervaded with an intense evangelical fervor; and everywhere the college Y. M. C. A. grew lustily, increasing its branches from twenty-six in 1877 to four hundred and seventy-five in 1895. While the drinking habit was on the wane, especially in the West, in the East high-spirited colts like the Harvard youths Bertie and Billy in *Philosophy Four* sought occasional bibulous adventure in near-by taverns. Seldom, however, it may be presumed, did such roisterers succeed in minting their experiences into satisfactory grades in the next day's examination, like those obtained by Owen Wister's heroes. Where girls attended classes with men, their presence had a refining influence on masculine manners and apparel; but the college authorities, alert to anticipate hostile outside criticism, saw to it that co-education did not become co-recreation. A quasi-inquisitorial discipline usually prevailed. In the first decade of the University of North Dakota (opened in 1884), dancing with the other sex was forbidden, chaperonage strictly enforced, and not a dress suit or evening gown was to be found in the whole student body.[2] Though in mixed colleges annual class "proms"

[1] Pauline Grahame, "La Follette Wins," *Palimpsest*, XII (1931), 179-188.
[2] Mattie G. Massee, "Student Life during the First Decade of the

and cotillions came gradually into favor, the "coeds" continued to find their chief social outlet in sororities, Greek-letter societies patterned after those of the men. Beginning with Kappa Alpha Theta founded at De Pauw in 1870, seven were in existence by the early 1880's, with a membership in 1898 totaling nearly twelve thousand scattered among one hundred and twenty-two chapters.

Only a relatively few college graduates went on to more advanced study. Postgraduate instruction represented the culmination of the Teutonic influence in higher education. The graduate school was the American counterpart of the *philosophische Facultät*. Its quick and firm rooting in the national soil attested the missionary zeal of hundreds of young scholars who, returning home with German doctorates, resolved to replace American superficiality with the Teutonic ideal of patient thoroughness. During the 1880's over two thousand Americans were studying in German universities, twice as many as in the preceding ten years and considerably more than in the next decade.[1] Berlin, Leipzig, Heidelberg, Jena, Halle—these were the chief academic springs at which their thirsty young minds drank deep of the learning of such great masters as Bluntschli, Ranke, Wagner, Schmoller, Wolf, Weismann, Johannes Müller, Ehrlich, Koch, Gauss, Helmholtz and Bunsen.

It was not hope of material reward that fired these youthful pilgrims, for the highest salary they could hope

University of North Dakota," Univ. of N. Dak., *Quar. Journ.*, XIII, esp. 373-374.

[1] C. F. Thwing, *The American and the German University* (N. Y., 1928), 42. Much smaller numbers of students were to be found in Austria, Switzerland and the University of Paris. U. S. Comr. of Educ., *Rep. for 1897-98*, II, 1702-1703; for *1902*, I, 617. See also Samuel Sheldon, "Why Our Science Students Go to Germany," *Atlantic Mo.*, LXIII (1889), 463-466.

to attain was two thousand dollars in a small college, in a large one perhaps three or four.[1] It was something different, something which never before had had so ample an expression in American life: a passion for truth born of knowledge; an eagerness to do a few things supremely well instead of many things well enough; perhaps also an unconscious withdrawal of sensitive spirits from the soiling materialism which characterized the ethics of the great captains of industry and colored the whole business world. Moreover, the broad diffusion of worldly goods made it possible for middle-class sons to take advantage of opportunities which an earlier day had restricted to the wealthy few.

These returning Americans made their influence felt in faculties far and wide.[2] The Johns Hopkins University, which had opened in Baltimore in 1876 primarily for the promotion of graduate study in the Teutonic sense, had scarcely anyone on its staff of fifty-three in 1887 who had not studied in Germany. To this bracing center went troops of youths who in turn were to help spread the new ideals to all corners of the land: Josiah Royce, John Dewey, Joseph Jastrow, in philosophy and psychology; Henry C. Adams, Davis R. Dewey, John R. Commons, in political economy; Charles H. Haskins, J. Franklin Jameson, Woodrow Wilson, Frederick J. Turner, Charles M. Andrews, in history and political science; Albion W. Small and E. A.

---

[1] Even college presidents received only from two to six thousand dollars. Bryce, *American Commonwealth*, III, 437; W. R. Harper, "The Pay of American College Professors," *Forum*, XVI (1893-1894), 96-109; One of Them (*pseud.*), "The Status of the American Professor," *Educational Rev.*, XVI (1898), 417-434.

[2] In some instances, Germans themselves were translated to American faculties, notably in the case of the historian Hermann von Holst and the neurologist Adolf Meyer at the new University of Chicago and of Kuno Francke at Harvard.

*A worried artist's vision of a future Commencement.*

*A great teaching hospital, Johns Hopkins University.*

## The Higher Learning

Ross in sociology; Edmund B. Wilson, T. H. Morgan, E. G. Conklin, in biology; and Edwin H. Hall, Joseph S. Ames and A. L. Kimball in chemistry.[1]

Spurred by the example of Johns Hopkins, the older foundations of the East placed their graduate work on a stronger basis.[2] Not a few state universities made starts in the same direction, the interest in research there usually spreading outward from the department of agriculture. Assisted by an increasing provision of fellowships, the number of students pursuing nonprofessional graduate work in American universities rose from a little over four hundred in 1878 to nearly five thousand in 1898. So rapid and sound was the development that before the end of the eighties the primacy of Hopkins was already seriously challenged and by the mid-nineties she was outstripped in number of registrants by Chicago, Harvard and Yale. It was no longer necessary for talented young men to seek their higher specialized training across the sea, for a dozen American institutions now offered as rich opportunities as could be found anywhere in the world.

Of the newly established universities three emulated Johns Hopkins by stressing graduate work. One of these, the Catholic University of America, which received its apostolic constitution from Leo XIII, threw open its doors in Washington, D. C., in 1889, offering instruc-

[1] Of the first holders of fellowships at Hopkins, one became professor of political economy at Michigan, another of natural history at Williams, a third of physics in New York University, a fourth of Greek at the University of Virginia, a fifth of political science at Middlebury College; two were called to chairs at Harvard; and three were retained on the Hopkins faculty. Other American graduate centers were, of course, performing a similar service. Between 1870 and 1890 the Cornell graduate school furnished fourteen college professors and twenty-four college presidents.

[2] In recognition of its transformed character Yale College assumed the name of Yale University in 1887, Columbia did likewise in 1896, and in the same year the College of New Jersey changed to Princeton University.

tion in divers fields.[1] Clark University, founded by a
million-dollar gift of Jonas G. Clark, was launched the
same year under the presidency of G. Stanley Hall, formerly a Hopkins professor. Gathering a small but choice
faculty about him, Hall limited instruction to psychology and a few closely related subjects. Though but the
"torso of a university," in Von Holst's famous phrase,
the band of scholars at Worcester, Massachusetts, came
to wield an influence altogether incommensurate to their
number. As administrator, however, Hall had to face
many difficulties: inadequate funds, the idiosyncrasies of
a living donor and, on one memorable occasion, the lar-
ceny of a majority of his faculty by a still newer and
much wealthier institution, the University of Chicago.

Though bearing the name of an older foundation, the
University of Chicago was virtually a fresh creation.
Backed by the Rockefeller millions and Chicago's hustling enterprise, and headed by William Rainey Harper
of Yale, a former captain of the Chautauqua movement,
the new university at its opening in 1892 stood already
at a point which it had taken the old Eastern institutions
generations to reach.[2] Its faculty was distinguished not
only for erudition but also for the fact that Chicago
salaries greatly overtopped any paid elsewhere. One can
understand President Hall's bitterness in characterizing
President Harper's surreptitious raid on his faculty "an
act of wreckage . . . comparable to anything that the
worst trust had ever attempted against its competitors,"
but Hall could hardly blame his colleagues for welcom-

[1] A. S. Will, *Life of Cardinal Gibbons* (N. Y., 1922), I, 254-257,
447-452.

[2] The original faculty contained eight members who had formerly
been presidents of other colleges and universities. H. P. Judson, "The
University of Chicago," *Educ.*, XVI (1895-1896), 278-289; T. W.
Goodspeed, *William Rainey Harper* (Chicago, 1928), chap. iv; same
author, *A History of the University of Chicago* (Chicago, 1916),
chaps. i-x.

ing salaries twice as high as he could offer.[1] While vigorously developing graduate instruction, Harper was almost equally interested in all other phases of education, undergraduate and professional.

Whatever other elements entered into Chicago's success its location in a great and growing city was an important factor. Its sensational rise was a tribute to the cultural power of population centers and served to emphasize the fact that, save for one or two state universities, all the large, progressive, prosperous institutions of higher learning were to be found in or near urban districts.[2] The closing years of the century found Columbia and New York University crowded beyond capacity and obliged to acquire, at extraordinary expense, new and larger sites.

Fortunately the new forces shaking the academic world were felt also in the departments devoted to technological and professional training. Already well established when the period opened, progress in technical education during these two decades consisted chiefly in its extension and in improved standards of instruction.[3] The East emphasized engineering; the Far West mining and metallurgy; the South and Middle West agriculture and horticulture. Agricultural education underwent the greatest expansion, due partly to the formation of additional land-grant colleges under the Morrill act of 1862 and partly to new federal bounties.[4] In 1887 the Hatch

[1] G. S. Hall, *Life and Confessions of a Psychologist* (N. Y., 1923), 295-297.

[2] C. F. Thwing, *The American College in American Life* (N. Y., 1897), 203-207; W. R. Harper, *The Trend in Higher Education* (Chicago, 1905), 156-160.

[3] T. C. Mendenhall, "Scientific, Technical and Engineering Education," and C. W. Dabney, "Agricultural Education," N. M. Butler, ed., *Education in the United States* (Albany, 1900), II, 551-592, 593-652.

[4] A. C. True, "Agricultural Education in the United States," and "Agricultural Experiment Stations in the United States," U. S. Dept. of Agr., *Yearbook for 1899*, 157-190, 513-548.

law dispensed financial aid for agricultural research through the establishment of experiment stations in connection with land-grant institutions; and three years later a second Morrill act provided annual subsidies for instruction. The law of 1890 was badly needed because of the improvidence of many colleges in wasting their original patrimony, and was designed to enable them to improve both their faculties and their equipment.

Notwithstanding the reforms introduced at Harvard and a few other places, professional education in 1878 still lingered in the dark ages.[1] Diploma selling was a regular business in several large cities. In 1880 John Norris, a Philadelphia newspaper editor, publicly exposed one nest of offenders after he had obtained, with no effort but that of loosening his purse, two M.D. degrees, two doctorates in law, one "master in electrotherapeutics" and a doctorate of sacred theology from a half-dozen duly incorporated institutions.[2] The traffic could not be easily downed, however. Despite an increasingly watchful professional censorship such fraudulent practices survived in certain states to the end of the century and after.[3]

More serious, of course, were the lax standards prevailing in reputable universities. At most institutions in 1878 a medical student, after absorbing atmosphere in a doctor's office for a time and taking a lecture course of four or five months, repeating it the second year, could obtain his degree and start practising on the innocent

[1] See Allan Nevins, *The Emergence of Modern America* (*A History of American Life*, VIII), 276-279.

[2] U. S. Comr. of Educ., *Rep. for 1880*, clx-clxv; *for 1882-83*, clxxiii.

[3] The Illinois state board of health was particularly active in the work of exposure in the 1890's. When in 1899 the state supreme court revoked the charter of the Independent Medical College of Chicago, it was discovered that in one Michigan town twenty-three physicians held its diplomas. U. S. Comr. of Educ., *Rep. for 1892-93*, II, 1622-1623; *for 1898-99*, II, 1681-1683.

public. Before 1898, however, pressure from without the profession and leadership from within wrought a gratifying change. For the protection of the community, state after state set up boards of medical examiners, empowered to license properly qualified candidates.[1] At the same time medical schools, partly to meet the new legal standards, tightened their entrance requirements and added graded subjects and laboratory and clinical instruction, while lengthening their course to three or even four years.[2] The medical school at Johns Hopkins set an even higher standard by requiring a college degree for admission, but Harvard was the only one to follow its lead before the period ended.

Legal education, unhappily, was a different story. Throughout these years the law continued to be, as a contemporary ruefully remarked, "a learned profession which requires little learning." [3] With a few praiseworthy exceptions like Columbia and Harvard, law schools had virtually no entrance conditions. The great majority required two years rather than three for the degree, the work of instruction being left to busy practitioners who preferred sonorous lectures to a laborious use of the case method. Nor did many states have effective regulations for admission to the bar. If a speaker before the American Bar Association may be believed, "an inundation of incompetency . . . has in recent years

[1] By 1895 twenty-one commonwealths had the examination system, and fourteen others allowed only graduates of accredited medical schools to practise. U. S. Comr. of Educ., *Rep. for 1885-86*, 561-569; *for 1892-93*, II, 1617-1619; *for 1894-95*, II, 1230-1232. After 1878 there was an astonishing increase of dental schools and dental students, due to the action of many states in requiring graduation from a dental school as a condition for license. J. R. Parsons, "Professional Education," Butler, *Education*, II, 527, 531-533.

[2] Parsons, "Professional Education," 506-525; Dexter, *History of Education*, 327-340; C. F. Thwing, "Better Training for Law and Medicine," *Educational Rev.*, XVI (1898), 49-60.

[3] U. S. Comr. of Educ., *Rep. for 1894-95*, II, 1248.

deluged our profession." [1] Yet in public esteem the law continued to rank as one of the most honorable of the professions, and Bryce was told of individuals whose incomes were quite as large as those of leaders of the English bar.[2]

Theological training was on a sounder basis, maintaining good standards and experiencing little change except as new religious conceptions penetrated the classroom and caused trouble for those who harbored them. While business had not yet taken on the pretensions of a profession, later times were foreshadowed by the establishment of the Wharton School of Finance and Economy in 1881 at the University of Pennsylvania. Of all the professions medicine attracted the most students, with theology second until the early 1890's when it was overtaken by law. It is worth noting that the number of professional students grew faster than did the population in general. Despite the tempting opportunities offered by business and finance, despite the thornier path which confronted the neophyte, the lure to professional service increased rather than diminished its hold on American youth.

If to the moralist the educational achievements of the 1880's and 1890's seem to offset the sinister practices of the world of big business, it should not be forgotten that, without the wealth made possible by the latter, such progress could hardly have been accomplished. Cornelius Vanderbilt's death in 1877 had revealed to an amazed public the unprecedented private fortune of one hundred million dollars, while the next two decades

---

[1] U. S. Comr. of Educ., *Rep. for 1894-95*, II, 1247. For a description of conditions, see *Rep. for 1880*, cl-clii; *for 1890-91*, I, 383-385, 414-433; *for 1893-94*, I, 997; *for 1896-97*, II, 1191; Dexter, *History of Education*, 316-327; Parsons, "Professional Education," 495-505.

[2] Bryce, *American Commonwealth*, III, 380.

produced at least two score others who were rated as multimillionaires and, if shrewd guesses may be credited, some three thousand millionaires.[1] Without inquiring here into the noxious effects of such a huge concentration of riches, suffice it to say that from sources like these and from men of lesser means a golden stream flowed into the coffers of colleges and universities and turned what would otherwise have been fantastic dreams into attainable realities. By critics of the social order this largess was cynically attributed to a frantic love of display, an anxiety for social approval or perhaps a sedative to an uneasy conscience.[2] Yet, since most of the money came in the form of bequests, there is evidence also of a developing sense of *richesse oblige*, an altruistic desire of those who had, to share with those who had not.

Between 1878 and 1898 private benefaction added no less than one hundred and forty million dollars to the revenues for higher education, affecting all its branches, undergraduate, graduate, professional and technical.[3] Scientific apparatus was improved, professorships were established, dormitories provided, libraries enlarged, fellowships endowed, additional buildings constructed. Most spectacular of all was the out-of-hand

[1] See M. C. Stevens, "Great Fortunes in New England," E. F. Gay and A. A. Young, eds., *The New England Economic Situation* (Chicago, 1927), 17-24, and authorities cited. The average annual income of the one hundred richest Americans was estimated as $1,200,000 by T. G. Shearman, "The Owners of the United States," *Forum*, VIII (1889-1890), 262-273.

[2] There is little indication that college authorities hesitated to accept "tainted money"—a phrase which Washington Gladden was to coin in 1905. In 1899, when John D. Rockefeller offered $100,000 to Wellesley, eighteen professors demanded a prior investigation of his business methods. But the money was accepted without an investigation and with gratitude. *New International Year Book for 1900*, 911.

[3] This is a conservative estimate based on U. S. Comr. of Educ., *Reps.*, esp. for *1899-1900*, II, 2596, and on J. B. Sears, *Philanthropy in the History of American Higher Education* (U. S. Bur. of Educ., *Bull.* for 1922, no. 26), 55-56, 62.

creation of a series of new institutions by princely gifts
from single donors. Besides Clark and the new University of Chicago, their number included the Case School
of Applied Science (1880), Leland Stanford Junior
University (1885), Drexel Institute (1891) and the
Armour Institute of Technology (1893).

Amply equipped for the first time with tools of research—laboratories, instruments of precision, libraries,
museums, observatories, hospitals—scholars and scientists in the United States were enabled to make a contribution to the world's learning fully comparable to
that of the first nations of Europe. Minute specialization
was the investigator's aim and his achievement. Only at
rare intervals has a great genius appeared in the history
of intellectual advance—a Newton, a Linnæus, a Comte.
Rather, science and learning, especially in modern times,
have been carried forward by myriad workers, each of
whom, in President Eliot's phrase, has sought to "pierce
with his own little search-light, if only by a hand's-
breadth, the mysterious gloom which surrounds on every
side the area of ascertained truth." [1] Withdrawn from
the marketplace and the forum, closeted with the idea,
brooding and moiling in monkish seclusion, the specialist wedded a skeleton bride whose osseous kiss and rat-
tling embrace rewarded him with an ecstasy beyond
Helen's.

Conversant with the trends and methods of investigation abroad, the research experts faced their greatest
peril in a loss of contact with their fellow workers at
home. In order to overcome this difficulty, and affected
no doubt also by the human desire for comradeship with
one's kind, the leading men brought about the formation of nation-wide associations in all the principal
branches of research endeavor. America had never before

[1] C. W. Eliot, *Educational Reform* (N. Y., 1898), esp. 233.

witnessed such a banding together for the advancement of knowledge.[1] Though the American Social Science Association had been actively cultivating its broad field since 1865, the demands of specialists led to the organization of the Archaeological Institute of America in 1879, the American Historical Association and the American Catholic Historical Society in 1884, the American Economic Association in 1885, the American Society of Church History in 1888 and the American Academy of Political and Social Science in 1889, along with a vast array of local or more specialized societies. Though the all-inclusive American Association for the Advancement of Science dated from 1848, the new requirements of scientific work brought into being the American Chemical Society (1876), the American Society of Mechanical Engineers (1880), the American Forestry Association (1882), the American Ornithologists' Union (1883), the American Society of Naturalists (1883), the American Climatological Society (1884), the American Institute of Electrical Engineers (1884), the Geological Society of America (1888), the National Statistical Association (1888), the American Mathematical Society (1888), the American Physical Society (1889), the Association of Economic Entomologists (1890) and the American Psychological Association (1892), not to mention countless regional and local bodies. Similarly, the Modern Language Association, founded in 1883, began at once to yield off-

[1] S. B. Weeks, comp., "A Preliminary List of American Learned and Educational Societies," U. S. Comr. of Educ., *Rep. for 1893-94*, II, 1493-1661; J. M. Cattell, "Scientific Societies and Associations," Butler, *Education*, II, 865-892; H. R. Steeves, *Learned Societies and English Literary Scholarship in Great Britain and the United States* (Columbia Univ., *Studies in English and Comparative Literature*, 1913), chap. vii. An incomplete enumeration shows that 79 learned societies, national and local but excluding teachers' associations, were formed in the 1870's, 121 in the 1880's and 45 in the 1890's. Dexter, *History of Education*, 552.

shoots in the American Folklore Society (1888), the American Dialect Society (1889) and the American Dante Society (1890). The tendency went so far in medicine as to bring about a union of the various specialized groups under the name of a congress.

Such organizations through their annual gatherings not only provided mutual stimulus but, by means of their publications and printed proceedings, made possible ready intercommunication among widely scattered students.[1] Including the numerous research series conducted by Johns Hopkins, Columbia and other graduate centers, nearly fifty thousand printed pages were being produced annually in the 1890's by men who, as Eliot said, cared to be known "not to millions of people, but to five or six students of the Latin dative case, . . . or of fossil beetles, or of meteorites, or of starfish." [2] If mere pedantry or antiquarian curiosity marred some of this enormous output, the gain to society was still beyond computation.

In history the seminar was the characteristic ordeal of training, the monograph the typical product. So much had been left undone or misunderstood by earlier writers, so much conceived in a spirit of partisanship or treated primarily for literary effect, that the professionally trained student had virtually a free field for applying his canons of thorough and accurate research and rigorous objectivity. History, if not a science, at least became consciously scientific. Even those who, not trained in historical seminars, essayed the broader canvas, were imbued with the new spirit; and the breadth and excellence of their work helped make this the Augustan age of American historiography.

[1] R. R. Bowker, comp., *Publications of Societies* (N. Y., 1899); E. D. Perry, "The American University," Butler, *Education*, I, 298-300; Cattell, "Scientific Societies and Associations," 880-884.

[2] Eliot, *Educational Reform*, 233.

In 1880 the legal scholar James Schouler inaugurated his seven-volume survey of American public life from 1783 to 1865. About the same time Richard Hildreth and George Bancroft revised their long-standard histories in the light of new evidence, and Francis Parkman added *Montcalm and Wolfe* (1884), the great historian's greatest achievement, to his saga of the American forest. Influenced by the example of the Englishman J. R. Green, the clergyman-novelist Edward Eggleston in 1880 projected his unfinished *History of Life in the United States,* and J. B. McMaster, then an instructor in civil engineering at Princeton, produced in 1883 the initial volume of his vast *History of the People of the United States from the Revolution to the Civil War,* based mainly on newspapers, pamphlets and other hitherto neglected sources. The next decade brought the first volumes of James Ford Rhodes's *History of the United States from the Compromise of 1850,* a sober, scholarly narrative written by an ex-captain of industry and marked by measured judgments which won ready acceptance from a generation tired of the warmed-over controversies of the Civil War.[1]

More characteristic of the scientific school were the large-scale histories constructed by piecing together the contributions of specialists. The most significant undertaking of this sort was Justin Winsor's coöperative *Narrative and Critical History of America* (published from 1884 to 1889), in eight mastodontic volumes covering the period from 1000 to 1850, a massive feat of erudition, enduring in value because of its critical bibliographical notes. An interesting variant was Hubert Howe Bancroft's *History of the Pacific States* in thirty-four

---

[1] Hermann von Holst's *The Constitutional and Political History of the United States* (J. J. Lalor and Paul Shorey, trs., Chicago, 1876-1892), an able work but marred by a strong antislavery bias, was written before the author became an American professor.

volumes (1882-1890). The self-styled author, a San Francisco publisher who had amassed a remarkable collection of books and manuscripts bearing on the past of the region, employed a staff of copyists, note takers, cataloguers and research workers to organize the material for publication under his general direction.[1] Despite a method smacking more of the business than the academic world, the mountainous product contained much scholarly merit.

Of more particularized works Henry Adams's nine-volume *History of the United States* was widely influential, partly because of its detailed treatment of the years 1800-1817 in the light of European high politics and even more so because of its rare literary charm. The pioneer efforts of McMaster and Eggleston, reënforced by the example of the German Ratzel, meantime had a quickening effect on the minds of brilliant young students like Frederick J. Turner and Ellen C. Semple who in the 1890's started to extend the outposts of historical inquiry to areas beyond the Freemanesque confines of statecraft, war and diplomacy.[2] No longer could it fairly be said that American history was written "as if Plymouth Rock underlay the whole geological formation of the United States," for students from all sections contributed to the new illumination.[3] Outside the

[1] See H. H. Bancroft, *Literary Industries* (same author, *Works*, San Fran., 1883-1890, XXXIX), chap. xxiv. This account, however, needs to be checked with *"Literary Industries" in a New Light* (San Fran., 1893) by H. L. Oak, who wrote seven or more volumes of the history, and with W. A. Morris, "The Origin and Authorship of the Bancroft Pacific States Publications," *Ore. Hist. Quar.*, IV, 287-364.

[2] The clarion note of the new departure was sounded in Turner's "The Significance of the Frontier in American History," an address before the American Historical Association, printed in its *Annual Report for 1893*, 199-227, and elsewhere. See also H. U. Faulkner, *The Quest for Social Justice* (*A History of American Life*, XI), 247.

[3] Anon., "The Dutch Influence in America," *Atlantic Mo.*, LXX (1892), 698.

sphere of national history the activity, though less notable, was not without significance. Thus, Charles Gross, whose Göttingen dissertation (1883) on the gild merchant demolished prevailing theories, prepared a monumental critical bibliography of English history. The chief large-scale work was a series of studies of ecclesiastical institutions, culminating in a *History of the Inquisition in the Middle Ages* (1888), made by Henry C. Lea, a retired Philadelphia book publisher.

The evolutionary concept, so momentous in its influence upon the natural sciences, was reflected in the historians' emphasis on continuity and growth as the key to understanding human development. Few writers, however, went so far as John Fiske, that skillful popularizer of other men's researches, who commenced his narrative of the *Beginnings of New England* with the year 476 A.D. In the related social sciences the Darwinian hypothesis had equally salient consequences— Stanley Hall called it "the greatest intellectual stimulus of the modern age." [1] The umbilical cord connecting history and political science, while retarding the latter's growth as a separate discipline, insured a knowledge of the historical and comparative development of institutions. Systematic theoretical treatises like John W. Burgess's *Political Science and Comparative Constitutional Law* (1890) and W. W. Willoughby's *An Examination of the Nature of the State* (1896) scorned the easy rationalizations of earlier native writers. Deeply influenced by the German historico-juristic approach, these men broke boldly with their American past by throwing overboard the whole cargo of natural rights' philosophy and declaring for an active employment of governmental powers for the common weal. Of descriptive and analytical studies the most important were Woodrow

[1] Hall, *Life and Confessions*, 362.

Wilson's *Congressional Government* (1885), a realistic inquiry into the system of checks and balances, written while the author was yet a student at Hopkins; and F. J. Goodnow's *Comparative Administrative Law* (1893), the first work of its kind in English.

Sociological writing, though largely in the hands of amateurs and sentimentalists in the opening years, found its master in 1883 when Lester F. Ward, turning aside from his studies in paleobotany, published his *Dynamic Sociology*.[1] This seminal work, strongly Comtean in its antecedents, formulated a complete system of cosmic philosophy. Sharply opposed to Herbert Spencer's fatalism, Ward called for a conscious direction of the forces of social evolution; and his great deliverance stimulated and colored the studies of young men like F. H. Giddings, Albion W. Small and E. A. Ross who would in the future be leaders in the field. Meantime the collection of basic data on primitive life was being advanced by the bureau of American ethnology, set up by the government in 1879. The foremost field investigator perhaps was A. F. A. Bandelier, of Swiss birth, who explored aboriginal sites and studied ways of life in the American Southwest, Mexico and South America. By shattering many ancient fables he did much to substitute critical investigation for romantic preconceptions.[2]

Imbued with the German spirit, returning students of economics took sharp issue with the abstract doctrinaire teachings of the so-called classical school. One of the avowed objects of the newly formed American Economic Association was to foster historical and statistical investigation of economic phenomena. Only less manifest was the ardent desire of certain founders like Rich-

[1] A. W. Small, "Fifty Years of Sociology in the United States," *Am. Journ. of Sociology*, XXI, 721-864.

[2] F. W. Hodge, "A. F. A. Bandelier," *Am. Anthropologist*, n.s., XVI, 349-358.

ard T. Ely, E. J. James and H. C. Adams to employ the powers of the state to convert the "dismal science," with its emphasis upon untrammeled individualism, into an active agency for general economic welfare. The rapid success of the new ideals owed much to the weighty support of President Francis A. Walker of the Massachusetts Institute of Technology, the foremost economist and statistician of the day. Though not himself German-trained, his acute and catholic intelligence cast him inevitably for the rôle of "champion and emancipator"—Ely's phrase—and his treatise *Political Economy,* published in 1883, marked the transition from the old to the new.[1] Unless it be history, no other branch of the social sciences attracted so many able minds; and the multitudinous treatises they produced illuminated all phases of the subject, particularly those to which the increasing complexity of the economic order called attention. Not of least importance was the fact that the professionally trained, academic students of society performed an essential service in providing a philosophical sanction for the strivings of reformers and humanitarians.[2]

In the effort to lift the study of social relations to the dignity of a science, scholars and teachers offended many cherished notions of the comfortable classes and excited the disapproval of powerful beneficiaries of the *status quo.* Tariff protectionists repeatedly tried to oust W. G. Sumner from Yale, almost worrying him into a resig-

[1] J. P. Munroe, *A Life of Francis Amasa Walker* (N. Y., 1923), chaps. xiv, xvi. On the new economics, see also L. L. Price, "The Present Condition of Economic Science," *Forum,* XXIV (1897-1898), 422-431; R. T. Ely, "The American Economic Association, 1885-1909," Am. Econ. Assoc., *Publs.,* ser. 3, XI, 47-111; L. H. Haney, *History of Economic Thought* (rev. edn., N. Y., 1920), 612-629.

[2] A brilliant exception to the rule was Professor William G. Sumner of Yale, who continued a champion of extreme *laissez-fairism.* See, for example, his pungent essay *What Social Classes Owe to Each Other* (N. Y., 1883).

nation in 1880 on the charge of using Spencer's textbook of sociology. Six years later H. C. Adams was forced out of Cornell because of a frank expression of his views on the Gould strike. In 1894 Ely was haled before the regents of the University of Wisconsin on charges of economic heresy, and the following year brought E. W. Bemis's resignation from the University of Chicago as a result of criticizing certain public-utility corporations.

In 1897 the entire faculty of the Kansas Agricultural College was dismissed for their failure to subscribe to Populist tenets, while J. A. Smith was driven from Marietta College because of antimonopoly utterances. The same year, when E. Benjamin Andrews tendered his resignation as president of Brown rather than yield his free-silver convictions, the editor of the *St. Louis Globe-Democrat* (July 30) spoke for most Americans in declaring: "He was only a servant; and a servant must do as his employers wish, or quit their service." But the Brown faculty and alumni, seconded by college presidents and professors elsewhere, rallied to the cause of academic freedom and secured Andrews's vindication.[1] History professors were not in so exposed a position; but if or when their new findings got into school textbooks, the authors were likely to find themselves subjected to a cross fire, on the one hand, between the Grand Army of the Republic and the United Confederate Veterans and, on the other, between militant Catholics and Protestants. In the popular mind propaganda was still the main function of history, and textbook

[1] The other signal victory for academic freedom was the action of the Wisconsin regents in asserting Ely's right "to follow the indications of the truth wherever they may lead." An incomplete list in T. E. Will, "A Menace to Freedom: The College Trust," *Arena*, XXVI (1901), 244-257, names fifteen professors who by that time had lost positions because of unorthodox social or economic views. See also *Encyclopaedia of the Social Sciences*, I, 348.

publishers solved the dilemma by broad-mindedly issuing versions to suit all tastes.[1]

Humanistic scholarship was strongly colored by the German preoccupation with the scientific study of philology. Americans, thought Bryce, showed an almost excessive anxiety to master all that had been written even by third-rate German scholars, and he noted also a tendency to imitate the Teutonic fault of neglecting form and style.[2] In Greek studies Basil L. Gildersleeve was the foremost leader, his seminar at Johns Hopkins being a training school for a multitude of coworkers. A great stimulus resulted from the establishment of the American School of Classical Studies at Athens in 1882; and the manifold benefits to students from making excavations and carrying on research in a classical land led to the founding of a similar center at Rome in 1895.[3] Minton Warren's seminar in Latin at Johns Hopkins was second only to Gildersleeve's in its influence on classical scholarship. Equally significant in ancient philology were the thoroughgoing studies of William Dwight Whitney of Yale and his followers in Sanskrit and Indo-European linguistics.

Whitney also made important contributions to general linguistics, while A. M. Elliott at Hopkins was the pioneer in organizing the scientific study of modern languages and literatures. Literary scholarship was further enriched by achievements like the *New Variorum*

---

[1] Bessie L. Pierce, *Public Opinion and the Teaching of History* (N. Y., 1926), 146-170, 175-176; anon., "The Anti-Catholic Spirit of Certain Writers," *Catholic World*, XXXVI (1883), 658-667; G. W. Cooke, "How the Catholic Church Teaches History," *Unitarian*, IV (1889), 156-161.

[2] Bryce, *American Commonwealth*, III, 568-569. See also H. E. Shepherd, "English Philology and English Literature in American Universities," *Sewanee Rev.*, I (1893), 153-159.

[3] B. L. Gildersleeve, "Classical Studies in America," *Atlantic Mo.*, LXXVIII (1896), 728-737; J. E. Sandys, *A History of Classical*

*Shakespeare,* edited by H. H. Furness, which had begun publication in 1871; Charles Eliot Norton's critical writings on the fine arts and Dante; and F. J. Child's definitive collection of *English and Scottish Popular Ballads* (1883-1898). If most of such work little touched the common life, the new erudition made contact with the lay world through the production of three great dictionaries: a thorough revision of Webster's, entitled, in disregard of the original author's uncompromising Americanism, the *International* (1890); the *Century* (1889-1891); and the *Standard* (1890-1895). These enterprises, involving years of painstaking labor by myriad experts, set a new standard for dictionary making.

In recording the growth of the language these lexicons incidentally paid impressive tribute to the advance of the pure and applied sciences. "The prominence given to . . . scientific, technological and zoölogical terms," said the editor of *Webster's International,* "will attract the attention of every critic." Even the few years between the appearance of the *Century* and the *Standard* made it possible for the latter to include terms like appendicitis and antitoxin, unknown to the former. The extraordinary progress of science owed much to generous governmental support, especially for geology, meteorology and agriculture, much also to private beneficence, and a very great deal to the immediate practical value which a considerable amount of the research possessed for the country's industrial life. Though the general public esteemed science chiefly for its utilitarian results, the specialists themselves strove to uphold the German academic ideal of science pursued for its own sake. Yet,

*Scholarship* (Cambridge, Eng., 1908), III, chap. xli; T. D. Seymour, *The First Twenty Years of the American School of Classical Studies at Athens* (School of Classical Studies at Athens, *Bull.,* V, 1902).

Americans under the skin, it was seldom they failed to assert in almost the same breath that without pure science applied science would not be possible.[1]

The echoes of the evolution controversy lingered but faintly in scientific halls in the 1880's. In all branches the hypothesis served as a salient working principle and the scientist's mind remained unruffled save when he ventured to tilt lances with orthodox religionists.[2] Broadly speaking, American science in this new era was less concerned with the mere collection of data and more with the determination of relations. The zoologist Spencer F. Baird became secretary of the Smithsonian Institution in 1878 and, under his direction and that of S. P. Langley, who followed him in 1887, that agency strengthened its leadership in the scientific world.[3]

Contributions to pure mathematics were not numerous. With a few notable exceptions like J. J. Sylvester and E. H. Moore, those capable of pursuing this difficult and abstract subject soon turned their attention to physics, astronomy, engineering and other branches where mathematical laws were applied to visible realities. In physics three Americans won international fame. J. Willard Gibbs of Yale, whom Henry Adams esteemed "the greatest of Americans, judged by his rank in science," was a classic example of the unassuming, self-sacrificing seeker for truth. Devoting himself to research in thermodynamics, he extended the fundamental laws of heat and energy to the most varied departments of

[1] See, for example, J. J. Stevenson, "The Debt of the World to Pure Science," R. M. La Follette, ed., *The Making of America* (Chicago, 1906), VII, 24-39; and Addison Brown, "Endowment for Scientific Research," Smithsonian Inst., *Ann. Rep. for 1892*, 621-638.

[2] See, for example, Asa Gray, *Natural Science and Religion* (N. Y., 1880), and W. N. Rice, *Twenty-Five Years of Scientific Progress* (N. Y., 1894). Nevins, *Emergence of Modern America*, 286-288, describes the earlier attitude of American scientists.

[3] Baird was father of the great National Museum which Congress housed in a fine new building in 1882.

physics and provided the theoretical basis for the new science of physical chemistry, which Europeans quickly proceeded to cultivate.[1] Wrote a former student in 1931, "The scientific world has been and still is writing the biography of Gibbs's mind in expounding, amplifying, and applying his ideas."[2] H. A. Rowland at Johns Hopkins performed basic experiments on the formation of magnetic fields by the rotation of static charges and, in another phase of his work, revolutionized spectroscopy by his exquisitely delicate diffraction gratings and his ingenious mechanism for producing them. Younger than either of these, A. A. Michelson of Case, Clark and Chicago was already well launched on his brilliant career, inventing the inferential refractometer and, in 1879 and 1882, measuring the velocity of light.[3]

Simon Newcomb, attaining the summit of his achievements in the 1880's and 1890's, gained recognition as the world's foremost astronomer, preëminent for his researches in mathematical astronomy. Dividing his time between the government *Nautical Almanac* office and Johns Hopkins, he made a recomputation of the elements

[1] For his contributions to physical chemistry, see particularly his epoch-making paper, "On the Equilibrium of Heterogeneous Substances," published obscurely in the *Transactions* of the Connecticut Academy of Arts and Sciences in 1876 and 1878. It consisted of three hundred pages with over seven hundred equations. The best known of the formulas is his famous phase rule, which served to classify and explain in a logical manner experimental facts of much apparent complexity.

[2] E. B. Wilson, "Josiah Willard Gibbs," *Dict. of Am. Biog.*, VII, esp. 251.

[3] Apart from invention and applied mechanics, the life of the masses was most vitally touched by physics in its application to the study of weather, the special branch known as meteorology. The federal weather bureau, founded in 1870, rapidly expanded until it became the largest and best equipped in the world. Carrying on scientific studies, it also elaborated its system of warning farmer, shipper and navigator against the hazards of storm, flood and sudden climatic change, saving millions of dollars annually for the public. F. H. Bigelow, "Work of the Meteorologist for the Benefit of Agriculture, Commerce and Navigation," U. S. Dept. of Agr., *Yearbook for 1899*, 71-92.

of the solar system, which marked an epoch. In the words of a fellow scientist, "the sun and moon and planets have been weighed as exactly as sugar and tea at the grocer's and their paths measured as precisely as silks and woolens at the draper's." [1] His contributions won him membership in nearly all the national academies of science in the world.

Yet he was only one among a brilliant group of American astronomers. At the Harvard Observatory E. C. Pickering and his staff, drafting photography into the service of science, mapped the heavens from the north to the south pole by means of thirty thousand glass plates, taken partly in Cambridge and partly in Peru. S. C. Chandler at Harvard reconciled the discrepancies in latitude records of European and American observatories and elucidated a new law of planetary motion expressed in the periodic wandering of the terrestrial poles. In 1877 Asaph Hill at the Naval Observatory in Washington detected the two satellites of Mars, the most remarkable event since the discovery of Neptune in 1846, but one exceeded in 1892 by the announcement of a fifth satellite of Jupiter, observed by E. E. Barnard at the Lick Observatory.[2] America's achievements were facilitated by the establishment of observatories such as Lick in California in 1887 and the Yerkes Observatory of the University of Chicago in 1895, possessing the most powerful refracting telescopes in the world.

[1] W. H. McGee, "Fifty Years of American Science," *Atlantic Mo.,* LXXXII (1898), 309. See also Marcus Benjamin, "Simon Newcomb," D. S. Jordan, ed., *Leading American Men of Science* (N. Y., 1910), 363-390; and R. C. Archibald, "Simon Newcomb," *Science,* n.s., XLIV, 871-878. Newcomb's versatile genius is indicated by the fact that he also made significant contributions to economic theory.

[2] C. A. Young, "The Latest Astronomical News," *Forum,* X (1890-1891), 83-93; E. S. Holden, "America's Achievements in Astronomy," *Forum,* XIII (1893), 744-752; Simon Newcomb, "Recent Astronomical Progress," *Forum,* XXV (1898), 109-119.

Chemistry remained a monument chiefly to European genius. In the absence of laboratories comparable to the great observatories and natural-history museums, little theoretical work of import was done in America save for Willard Gibbs's contributions from the standpoint of thermodynamics and perhaps Wolcott Gibbs's researches upon complex inorganic acids.[1] Applied chemistry, on the other hand, had never before been so central to the national effort in industry and agriculture.[2] Where earlier only a few dye houses and steel mills had employed chemical experts, the practice now became general. To meet increasing competition, their aid was indispensable in oil refineries, soap and candle works, glass factories, paint works and metallurgical plants. Many such concerns maintained their own laboratories. Yet, even in this respect, the United States lagged behind older industrial countries, especially Germany. It was only in agricultural chemistry—concerned with soil analysis, the use of plant foods, principles of animal nutrition, etc.— that America set the pace for the world. For this, the importance of farming in the national economy, together with the scientific competence of the newly established experiment stations, was largely responsible.

Geology likewise was closely identified with the nation's material development. Most of the principal advances stemmed from the work of a score of state geological surveys and particularly of the United States survey created in 1879. Besides disclosing and describing natural resources, progress was made in unlocking

[1] E. F. Smith, *Chemistry in America* (N. Y., 1914), 264-272, 343-349.

[2] F. W. Clarke, "Chemistry in the United States," La Follette, *Making of America*, VII, 84-90; H. W. Wiley, "The Relation of Chemistry to the Progress of Agriculture," and Milton Whitney, "Soil Investigations in the United States," U. S. Dept. of Agr., *Yearbook for 1899*, 201-258, 335-346.

the secrets of earth history by applying the evolutionary principle to the study both of land forms and fossil life.[1] T. C. Chamberlin, N. S. Shaler, W. M. Davis, R. D. Salisbury and others, using America's incomparable drift plains, drumlins and moraines as their library, solved the riddle of loess and shed new light upon the glacial period. Instead of a single great ice sheet, as had been supposed, they established the existence of five definite glacial epochs.

Meantime other geologists, notably O. C. Marsh and E. D. Cope, enriched the world's knowledge of paleontology.[2] As a result of excavations of vast fossil beds in Kansas, Dakota, Colorado and Wyoming, a glow of antique romance was cast over the sobering West. In scientific eyes at least, grasshoppers and chinch bugs paled into insignificance beside the discovery of leviathan remains of the reptilian and mammalian ages: great flesh-eating lizards, flying serpents eighty feet long, and enormous, ungainly beasts, with swaying necks, whose fearsome aspect may be sufficiently suggested to the layman by the scientific name *elasmosaurus platyurus*. Many of the finds supplied visible evidence of the transitional stages in the evolution of animal life, notably in the case of the winged beast which scientists accept as the ancestor of all hoofed animals.[3] If America continued to follow after Europe in mineralogy and petrography, the relation was reversed in other branches of geology and in its underlying principles. More and more European

[1] Geological progress is summarized in G. P. Merrill, *The First One Hundred Years of American Geology* (New Haven, 1924), chaps. viii-xiii, and E. S. Dana and others, *A Century of Science in America* (New Haven, 1918), chaps. ii-viii.

[2] G. B. Grinnell, "Othniel Charles Marsh," and Marcus Benjamin, "Edward Drinker Cope," Jordan, *Leading American Men of Science*, 283-340; Merrill, *American Geology*, 528-530.

[3] See E. D. Cope, *The Primary Factors of Organic Evolution* (Chicago, 1896); also R. T. Young, *Biology in America* (Boston, 1922), chap. iv.

geologists found it desirable to take field lessons on this side of the Atlantic.

In no phase of science was the evolutionary doctrine of such essential importance as in biology. American botanists did much to reconstruct the older system of plant classification in accordance with the principle of descent; and in zoology interest turned strongly to embryological and morphological studies, branches in which W. K. Brooks, Edmund B. Wilson, E. L. Mark, C. S. Minot and C. O. Whitman were leading figures.[1] Biological research was greatly aided by the setting up of study centers like the Arnold Arboretum (1872) in Boston, the Marine Laboratory (1887) at Wood's Hole and the New York Aquarium (1896) on Manhattan. The chief progress, however, was made in the applied aspects of biology, especially as regards farming, for here the state and national governments lent generous support and the agricultural experiment stations were powerful allies. For the first time, systematic attempts were made to throw light on crop diseases, while scientific methods were devised to combat fungi, bacteria and other organisms which lived on food-producing plants.[2]

Equally efficacious were the means employed to protect fields and orchards from the ever present menace of injurious insects and birds.[3] When, for instance, the white scale threatened to ruin the citrus crops of California in 1889, they were saved only by the importation

---

[1] W. R. Coe, "A Century of Zoology," and G. L. Goodale, "The Development of Botany," Dana and others, *Science in America*, esp. 411-412, 453-454.

[2] The work of T. J. Burrill of the University of Illinois, W. J. Farlow of Harvard, J. C. Arthur of the Geneva (N. Y.) experiment station and B. T. Galloway of the U. S. department of agriculture was particularly important. See B. T. Galloway, "Progress in the Treatment of Plant Diseases," U. S. Dept. of Agr., *Yearbook for 1899*, 191-200.

[3] L. O. Howard, "Progress in Economic Entomology," and T. S. Palmer, "A Review of Economic Ornithology," U. S. Dept. of Agr., *Yearbook for 1899*, esp. 153-154, 259-292.

of its enemy, the Australian ladybird beetle. At the same time systematic measures were taken to conserve useful native birds whose existence was menaced by the inroads of game markets, the egg trade and the millinery business. States were induced to repeal ill-advised laws and to protect beneficial species, New Hampshire and Ohio beginning with eagles, Rhode Island with fishhawks and New York and Minnesota with owls.[1] The federal government coöperated by establishing great national parks such as Yellowstone in 1872 and Sequoia and Yosemite in 1890. There an unmatched natural scenery provided an appropriate setting for the survivors of a brute creation which had once covered most of the continent.[2] Important advances were also made in methods of plant and animal breeding and in scientific forestry.[3] Though farmers still had to gamble with the weather, which might be forecast but could not be controlled, in other respects some of their worst enemies had been routed by science.

Psychology had traditionally been an appendage of philosophy, but the rapid developments in biological science hastened the end of the ancient connection. No longer could a psychologist deem his own important self a sufficient basis for generalizations respecting all mankind; he must forsake his armchair for the laboratory. Experimental psychology—the study of mental processes

[1] Following the passage of a Pennsylvania act in 1885 placing bounties on hawks and owls, ornithologists proved by examining the stomachs of twenty-seven hundred that only six of the seventy-five varieties were harmful. By 1898 Pennsylvania was actively protecting all birds except six genuinely injurious species. Palmer, "Economic Ornithology," 265-266.

[2] John Muir gives a delightful account in *Our National Parks* (Boston, 1902).

[3] Gifford Pinchot, "Progress of Forestry," H. J. Webber and E. A. Bessey, "Progress of Plant Breeding," and John Clay, "Work of the Breeder in Improving Live Stock," U. S. Dept. of Agr., *Yearbook for 1899*, 293-306, 465-490, 627-644.

by exact, objective, experimental methods—became the
new gospel. For this trend G. Stanley Hall, a former
student of Wilhelm Wundt, and particularly William
James of Harvard, also German-trained, were largely
responsible.[1] With James the chief emphasis was on the
discovery of physiological changes in the nervous system which might explain psychic processes. His *Principles
of Psychology* (1890), clothed in an irresistible magic
of words, had a wide and deep influence, and furnished
a point of departure for the behaviorists in the next
century.[2]

Meantime philosophy itself could not remain indifferent to the scientific temper. Both here and abroad it
tentatively reconsidered its technique and concepts in
the light particularly of the Darwinian hypothesis and
the new psychology. Within these limits, however, many
winds of doctrine blew across the scene.[3] From 1879
to 1888 popular interest in the subject was keen enough
to bring together each summer at Concord, Massachusetts, a band of men and women to hear philosophical
discussions presented both by amateurs and professionals.
The long-suffering daughter of Bronson Alcott, the
picturesque genius who presided over the gatherings,
wrote of the "budding philosophers" who "roost on
our steps like hens waiting for corn." [4]

[1] G. T. Ladd of Yale contributed to the movement though in a less
important way. E. G. Boring, *A History of Experimental Psychology*
(N. Y., 1929), chap. xx; W. B. Pillsbury, *The History of Psychology*
(N. Y., 1929), chap. xiv; Josiah Royce, "The New Psychology,"
*Forum*, XXVI (1898-1899), 80-96.

[2] See P. W. Slosson, *The Great Crusade and After* (*A History of
American Life*, XII), 382-383.

[3] The main trends are considered by Woodbridge Riley, *American
Thought* (rev. edn., N. Y., 1923), chaps. vii-ix; A. K. Rogers, *English
and American Philosophy since 1800* (N. Y., 1922), 283-296, 359-
387; and M. R. Cohen, "Later Philosophy," W. P. Trent and others,
eds., *Cambridge History of American Literature* (N. Y., 1921), III,
226-265; IV, 751-760.

[4] Louisa spoke for most of her fellow countrymen when she added:

The Concord School of Philosophy provided a meeting place for many minds. Such success as it met was due largely to the organizing talent of William T. Harris, an ardent Hegelian, long editor of the *Journal of Speculative Philosophy*. His appointment as federal commissioner of education, though bringing the meetings to a close, did not end his battles for his philosophic creed, which he renewed in a series of provocative treatises. Hegelianism had its opponents, notably in James Mc-Cosh, leader of the Scottish school of common-sense realism. But the doughty president of Princeton felt obliged to give his chief attention to rendering the new evolutionary philosophy, which John Fiske had done so much to champion, harmless to the cause of religious orthodoxy.

The impact of scientific thought was best represented by Charles S. Peirce, son of the mathematician Benjamin Peirce, and a man thoroughly familiar with laboratory method by reason of his own achievements in science. While he never constructed a finished system, his restless mind was fertile in new insights of seminal importance. Not least to his credit is the deep influence he exerted upon two of the most powerful thinkers of the time, who, save for being friends and colleagues at Harvard, had otherwise little in common: Josiah Royce and William James. Royce was a full-fledged metaphysical idealist who united moral energy with wide historical learning, command of scientific method and an intense interest in logical technique. James, on the other hand, sought to humanize philosophy and, through his mastery

"Speculation seems a waste of time when there is so much real work to be done." E. D. Cheney, *Louisa May Alcott* (Boston, 1889), 321. See also T. W. Brown, *Alcott and the Concord School of Philosophy* (Concord, 1926); Austin Warren, "The Concord School of Philosophy," *New England Quar.*, II (1929), 199-233; U. S. Comr. of Educ., *Rep. for 1891-92*, II, 909-917.

of psychology, bring it to terms with everyday living. He cared less for cosmic purpose than for individual achievement and was frankly scornful of dialectical legerdemain.

Throughout these years James's mind was growing toward a theory of method which, first clearly formulated in his University of California address in 1898, was to be widely influential under the name of pragmatism. His emphasis on individualism and his concern with the immediate results of conduct brought him nearer the dominant temper of America than any of his fellow philosophers. His "philosophy of practicality" made a profound impression abroad as well. It was left, however, to his great successor, John Dewey, to show in later years that pragmatism might become an instrument for social amelioration as well as for the attainment of individual satisfactions.[1]

To the average American the beneficent effects of the scientific revolution were brought home most forcibly in the domain of medicine. The phrase, science and health, was a potent formula even for the new religious sect which rejected medicine as the science of health. For the man on the street the words implied fresh safeguards against the ravages of sickness and greater certainty of recovery. This new posture of affairs was, in large measure, the result of an epochal discovery as to the cause of communicable diseases. First worked out by the Frenchman Louis Pasteur in the 1860's and 1870's, the germ theory in the early 1880's was rapidly widened in its application to human ills by the German Robert Koch's invention of improved methods and his isolation of the microbes of tuberculosis and Asiatic cholera. Then in 1884 G. T. A. Gaffsky introduced a better knowledge of the typhoid bacillus and Friedrich Loeffler discovered

---

[1] See Faulkner, *Quest for Social Justice*, 189, 245.

the diphtheria bacillus.[1] Americans also made primary contributions to medical bacteriology, notably in the work of Theobald Smith and F. L. Kilborne on Texas fever, a plague which was decimating Western cattle herds.[2] With the development of the serum treatment of infectious diseases, so strikingly exemplified by the use of antitoxin in diphtheria, the healing art attained possibilities undreamed of a few years before. Medical practice in the United States was profoundly affected as respects both the diagnosis and treatment of sickness and also, as we shall see, as regards the science of epidemiology.[3]

America's original contributions to medical science were perhaps better represented by the attention given to the nervous ailments which tightened their hold on the people as the social order became more urban and complex. In this field George M. Beard of New York, who coined the term, neurasthenia, was a pioneer.[4] His researches, however, were less influential than those of S. Weir Mitchell of Philadelphia, who originated the familiar "rest cure," and of William A. Hammond in New York City. At the same time the practice of psychiatry was enriched by the work of Shobal V. Clevenger in Illinois, his treatise *Spinal Concussion* (1889) gaining international repute. The new science

[1] Other significant contributors to medical bacteriology were Roux, Strauss, Metchnikoff and Bouchard of Paris, Fränkel, Behring and Klebs in Germany, and Kitasato of Japan.

[2] D. E. Salmon, "Some Examples of the Development of Knowledge Concerning Animal Diseases," U. S. Dept. of Agr., *Yearbook for 1899*, esp. 124-134; Paul de Kruif, *Microbe Hunters* (N. Y., 1926), chap. viii.

[3] G. F. Shrady, "Recent Triumphs in Medicine and Surgery," *Forum*, XXIII (1897), 33-41. Dr. Henry Gradle of Chicago, a former student of Koch, published in 1883 *Bacteria and the Germ Theory of Disease*, the first book in the English language on the subject.

[4] See his readable volume, *American Nervousness* (N. Y., 1881), with its provocative sociological explanation of the disorder.

of laryngology was similarly advanced by the efforts of
F. H. Bosworth of New York and J. Solis Cohen of
Philadelphia, whose publications on throat and nose
diseases also had a deep influence abroad. In a related
field A. H. Buck's *Diagnosis and Treatment of Ear
Diseases* (1880) was for many years the *vade-mecum*
of otologists.

Among general practitioners and the public at large
medical sects continued to thrive. Besides "regulars,"
homeopaths and eclectics, there was a profusion of magnetic healers, physiomedicalists (who prescribed only
botanical remedies), vitapaths, hydropaths, electropaths,
sun curists and the like. Some states explicitly banned
nonmedical healing, but others, like Illinois and most of
the New England states, were on much the same footing as the Cherokee Nation in Indian Territory which
permitted "enchantments in any form." Of the new sects
osteopathy, whose principles were first formulated in
1874 by Dr. Andrew T. Still of Baldwin, Kansas, possessed the greatest vitality. By the close of the century
its practice had express legal sanction in the Dakotas,
Iowa, Missouri, Michigan, Tennessee and Vermont.[1]

Many people preferred self-dosing in the form of pills,
tablets and liquids, obtained as proprietary medicines
from drug stores.[2] While some of these nostrums were
harmless, others were habit-forming opiates or thinly
disguised alcoholic stimulants. The enormous demand
for "cures" for "lost manhood" and alleged remedies
for venereal diseases sheds an interesting, if somewhat
puzzling, light on the moral conditions of the time. The
use of patent medicines, stimulated, as we have seen, by

[1] J. R. Parsons, "Professional Education," Butler, *Education*, II,
513-515.
[2] Anthony Comstock, *Frauds Exposed* (N. Y., 1880), chap. xix;
G. P. Rowell, *Forty Years an Advertising Agent* (N. Y., 1906), chaps.
xlv-xlvi.

high-pressure advertising,[1] was also assisted, especially in rural towns, by traveling medicine shows. These reached their greatest vogue in the 1880's and 1890's. Gathered about the medicine wagon in a circle dimly lighted by a flickering kerosene torch, the gaping crowd listened approvingly to the banjoist's vocal rendition of such ditties as "The Animal Fair," and then, as the long-haired, self-styled doctor harrowed their feelings with tales of the fatal results of certain symptoms common to all, showered the boards with coins for his famous "Indian" remedy.[2] The addiction of untold numbers to fantastic "cures" forms a splendid testimonial to the basic robustness of the American stock.

As in medical science, so in surgery the germ theory wrought a transformation, largely through the efforts of the Englishman Joseph Lister, a follower of Pasteur, who about 1865 established the principle of cleanliness in wound treatment. By opening up new opportunities for operative skill, antiseptic surgery, as it was called, gave American practitioners for the first time ample scope for their manual dexterity.[3] Intestinal operations had seldom been attempted earlier because even accidental wounds of internal tissues might cause destructive inflammations; but now the whole domain of abdominal

---

[1] See earlier, 196-198.

[2] The Kickapoo Indian Medicine Company, organized in 1881, for a time hired about a thousand Indians as "atmosphere" for its wagon shows. N. T. Oliver (Nevada Ned) and Wesley Stout, "Med Show," *Sat. Eve. Post*, CCII, 12 ff. (Sept. 14, 1929). T. J. Le Blanc, "The Medicine Show," *Am. Mercury*, V (1925), 232-237, is a veracious sketch. Both James Whitcomb Riley and Paul Dresser, future composer of "On the Banks of the Wabash," traveled with such shows in the 1870's. Marcus Dickey, *The Youth of James Whitcomb Riley* (Indianapolis, 1919), chap. v, and Theodore Dreiser, *The Songs of Paul Dresser* (N. Y., 1927), v.

[3] Shrady, "Recent Triumphs in Medicine and Surgery," 28-33; same author, "American Achievements in Surgery," *Forum*, XVII (1894), 167-178; Frederick Peterson, "Recent Progress in Medicine and Surgery," *Journ. of Social Sci.*, XXXI (1894), 1-lx.

surgery was explored and conquered, in large part by Americans. Appendicitis was robbed of most of its terrors, and the removal of the appendix reduced to almost a minor operation, as a result of the researches of Reginald H. Fitz at Harvard.[1] Great advances were also made in the surgery of eye, ear and brain.

At one critical turn in the history of these years the surgeon's hand proved more effective than the statesman's in holding to a steady course the ship of state. In July, 1893, at the crest of the financial panic, the knife of Dr. J. D. Bryant of New York saved President Cleveland's life from a malignant growth (sarcoma) of the upper left jaw. The principal operation occurred on a yacht in New York Harbor and, because of the precarious state of public affairs, all knowledge of the president's desperate plight as well as of his convalescence was withheld from Congress and the nation.[2] When the closing years of the period brought to America Roentgen's discovery of the X-ray, satisfaction at this new boon to surgery was alloyed only by the reflection that, had the knowledge been possessed twenty years before, the assassin's bullet in Garfield's body would have been correctly located and the life of another president probably saved.

The germ theory registered its greatest triumph in the new direction given to community efforts for health conservation. Recurrent epidemics had caused most of the large cities and fifteen of the states to set up boards of health prior to 1878.[3] In 1878-1879 yellow fever swept

[1] In his classic paper, "Perforating Inflammation of the Vermiform Appendix; with Special Reference to Its Early Diagnosis and Treatment," published in the first volume of the *Transactions* of the Association of American Physicians in 1886, he named the disease appendicitis, traced its origin to the appendix and, in defiance of existing practice, advocated radical surgical intervention for its cure.

[2] W. W. Keen, *The Surgical Operations on President Cleveland in 1893* (Phila., 1928), chap. i.

[3] See Nevins, *Emergence of Modern America*, 322-323.

through the Gulf states, Tennessee and, in some measure, Kentucky and Missouri, exacting a toll of sixteen thousand lives out of about seventy-four thousand afflicted.[1] At Memphis, where the scourge raged most fiercely, over five thousand died while twenty thousand others, fleeing in terror before an effective quarantine could be established, helped spread the plague to other communities. Although the transmitting cause of the disease continued to elude scientists, Memphis hastened to repair its criminal neglect of the past by laying out many miles of sewers and drainage tiles; and the nation-wide horror was reflected in the prompt creation of additional state boards of health. Twelve commonwealths acted before 1882 and fifteen others followed by the close of 1898.[2]

To the service of public-health agencies medical bacteriology brought a rational or scientific knowledge of disease prevention in place of the older empirical methods.[3] Early and definite diagnosis of infectious ailments became possible; new and effective systems of control were devised. Quarantine was extended to other ills than the traditional ones of smallpox and yellow fever, and port cities were barred against the admission of dangerous imported plagues like cholera and typhus. Progress was made also in providing special hospitals for the isolation and treatment of infectious cases. Equally important was the fact that, through a well-sustained publicity, the average citizen came to accept

[1] *Appletons' Annual Cyclopaedia*, XVIII (1878), 315-322; XIX (1879), 359-364.

[2] A national board was also created in 1879, but unfortunately was allowed to lapse four years later. In addition, the new interest led to the holding of an international sanitary conference at Washington in 1881. S. W. Abbott, *The Past and Present Condition of Public Hygiene and State Medicine in the United States* (H. B. Adams, ed., *Monographs on American Social Economics*, XIX, Boston, 1900), 11, 14-16.

[3] F. P. Gorham, "Bacteriology and Its Relation to Public Health Work," M. P. Ravenel, ed., *A Half Century of Public Health* (N. Y., 1921), 76-90.

personal cleanliness as an ally of health as well as of godliness. Smooth-shaven jowls began to emerge from behind the unhygienic whiskers of Civil War times; and the constant drive against tuberculosis led to a steady banishment of the national vice of spitting, noted by foreign travelers since colonial times.

Such efforts, it will be recalled, were supplemented by the enterprise of municipalities in constructing water and drainage systems, inspecting milk supplies, undertaking pure-food measures, and the like.[1] Sanitary engineering, though it had its own reasons for being, was an indispensable arm of the public-health movement. The war against disease, of course, was hampered by the limited knowledge of the age, especially in regard to methods of immunization, and sometimes also by the interference of time-serving politicians. Yet, despite these handicaps and the further difficulty presented by the herding of immigrants in the worst quarters of the cities, the mortality rate in the United States fell nearly ten per cent from 1890 to 1900, and the average age at death rose from thirty-one years to thirty-five.[2] This gain was due largely to the lessening mortality from tuberculosis, diphtheria and children's diseases. The benefits of public-health efforts fell chiefly to the cities where, of course, the need was greatest. It was a fortunate conjunction of circumstances for America that, when the age of large cities arrived, medical science made it possible to protect the dense population centers from the terrible scourges which for so many centuries had ravaged Europe.

[1] See earlier, 102-105, 110-111, 133-134.
[2] In the absence of reliable vital statistics for most of the country, these figures, strictly interpreted, apply only to the registration area. See *U. S. Twelfth Census* (1900), III, lvii, lxxxvi-lxxxvii, and *Supplementary Analysis and Derivative Tables* (U. S. Twelfth Census, *Special Rep.*), 495, 504-507.

# CHAPTER VIII

## The Renaissance in Letters and Arts

SUPERFICIALLY, America presented such an appearance of bustle and clatter that Bryce did not understand how anyone could "withdraw his mind from the endless variety of external impressions" long enough for the "repose and meditation which art and philosophy need." "The noise of living drowns the celestial harmonies," agreed a French visitor.[1] Yet, just as American life was being channeled by science and scholarship, so amidst the turmoil of everyday living significant changes were occurring in literature and the fine arts. Noise need not drown celestial harmonies if one's ear be attuned to stiller voices. Specialization of sense function seemed, indeed, a price of survival in the strange new complexity of life.

In the great cities writers and artists were quickly drawn into comradeship with persons like themselves, while in the nearness of publishers, art dealers and wealthy patrons they possessed a potential market for their wares. Hearkening to the siren call of Boston in the early 1880's, Hamlin Garland, having mortgaged his newly won Dakota homestead for the purpose, spent a bleak but glorious winter living in an attic room on Boylston Place. "My mental diaphragm creaked with the pressure of inrushing ideas," he wrote in later years. Shortly he discovered himself freely communing with

---

[1] James Bryce, *The American Commonwealth* (London, 1888), III, 559; S. C. de Soissons, *A Parisian in America* (Boston, 1896), 182.

fellow craftsmen like Mary E. Wilkins (Freeman) and Sylvester Baxter and even with the great Mr. Howells himself.[1] About the same time the youthful James L. Ford in New York found intellectual oases on every hand—in newspaper rooms and magazine offices, in the convivial gatherings at cheap *table d'hôte* restaurants, in the homes of established literary friends.[2] The early 1890's saw the first migration of artists and writers to Greenwich Village in the heart of lower Manhattan. There, in old dwellings reclaimed from wretchedly poor tenants, they would in time evolve a colorful life somewhat like that of the Latin Quarter in Paris. While no Western city could rival the older cultural centers, yet Cincinnati, St. Louis, San Francisco and notably Chicago had their own colonies of literary and artistic folk, which did for their localities what New York and, in lesser degree, Boston and Philadelphia did for the nation.

Many influences help account for the character and variety of literary production. In greater or less measure both author and publisher must bow to "the tyranny exercised by the taste of the common-schooled millions who have been taught to read, but have never learned to discriminate."[3] The republic of letters had reached its period of Jacksonian democracy. But if the number of undiscriminating readers had never before been so large, the same was also true of the number of cultivated readers. "The conscientious publisher," wrote Charles Dudley Warner, "asks two questions: Is the book good? and Will it sell? The publisher without a conscience asks

[1] Hamlin Garland, *A Son of the Middle Border* (N. Y., 1917), chaps. xxv-xxix.

[2] J. L. Ford, *Forty-Odd Years in the Literary Shop* (N. Y., 1921), *passim*.

[3] Paul Shorey, "Present Conditions of Literary Production," *Atlantic Mo.*, LXXVIII (1896), 156. See also James Bryce, *Studies in History and Jurisprudence* (N. Y., 1901), I, 200.

only one question: Will the book sell?"[1] The author, too, had to make his choice, though compunctions of conscience probably played a lesser part with him than financial need or his particular literary flair.

A special characteristic of the enlarged reading public was the arbitrament exercised by women. Apart from newspaper humorists, who might safely cater to crude masculine tastes, no writer of fiction could hope to get far without the favor of that sex which, generally speaking, had both greater leisure and liking for literary cultivation.[2] And women were stalwart upholders of the genteel tradition, being averse to vulgarity or frank discussion of sex, and partial to sentiment, especially moral and domestic sentiment. To a literary rebel like H. H. Boyesen the woman reader was "the Iron Madonna who strangles in her fond embrace the American novelist."[3] It seems likely that the feminine influence had much to do with preventing the local-color school from achieving the stark realism of Continental European portraiture. Besides, women themselves were prolific and successful as fictionists, especially in New England and the South, and thus, by direct intervention, helped buttress that attitude toward literature which Gilder of the *Century* called "good taste."

To meet the increased demand for books publishing houses grew in number and size. The *Dial*, which contained notices of just ten firms in its first issue in 1880, twenty years later carried advertisements of nearly a

[1] C. D. Warner, "The Novel and the Common School" (1890), reprinted in *The Relation of Literature to Life* (N. Y., 1897), 272.

[2] W. D. Howells, *Literature and Life* (N. Y., 1902), 21-22; Bryce, *American Commonwealth*, III, 521-522; R. W. Gilder, "Certain Tendencies in Current Literature," *New Princeton Rev.*, IV (1887), 7-10; O. B. Bunce, "Literature for Women," *Critic*, n.s., XII (1889), 67-68.

[3] H. H. Boyesen, "Why We Have No Great Novelists," *Forum*, II (1886-1887), esp. 619.

hundred.[1] Publishing houses sprang up in New York like mushrooms after a spring rain. Besides important new concerns like the Century Company, the Frederick A. Stokes Company and the Macmillan Company, a migration of publishers set in from other cities. Yet Boston, Philadelphia and other places continued to be centers of consequence.[2] Chicagoans were not slow to point out that in sheer volume of output their city outranked even New York, their presses emitting tons of German and Scandinavian Bibles for the farmhouses of the Northwest and enormous quantities of school-books, not to mention unnumbered cheap editions of trashy novels and "pirated" works.[3]

So keen was the popular appetite for books that the publishers' annual lists contained an ever increasing number of new titles in nearly every department of reading matter. While fiction consistently led every other class, at no time did it represent more than a minority of the total. In the first few years religious works and children's stories contended for second position, but both were presently outstripped by legal publications.

[1] F. F. Browne, "American Publishing and Publishers," *Dial,* XXVIII (1900), 340-343. The total number of publishers was actually much larger, for in 1894 Harper listed 617, of which 187 were in New York, 60 in Philadelphia, 52 in Boston, 51 in Chicago and 12 in San Francisco. Most of these, however, published only a few books annually. J. W. Harper, "American Publishing," C. M. Depew, ed., *One Hundred Years of American Commerce* (N. Y., 1895), I, 309.

[2] In Boston the historic firm of Houghton, Osgood & Company split into Houghton Mifflin & Company and J. R. Osgood & Company. Similarly, Ginn, Heath & Company divided into Ginn & Company and D. C. Heath & Company.

[3] H. B. Fuller, "The Upward Movement in Chicago," *Atlantic Mo.,* LXXX (1897), esp. 544. Because of the character of much of this output E. W. Bok denominated Chicago "something akin to a literary sewer," but others thought it no worse than other great cities. *Publishers' Wkly.,* XLVII, 460-461, 537 (March 16, 30, 1895). Of course, Chicago possessed firms like A. C. McClurg & Company and the Fleming H. Revell Company which vied with those of the East in the quality of their publications.

During the economic unrest of the mid-nineties books on history, government and social questions forged into second place, with works on law and religion ranking third and fourth.[1]

In fiction the interest of readers is more clearly indicated by library-circulation figures. These show a strong persistence of past preferences with but a cautious adoption of new ones. Judged by a canvass of leading libraries in 1893, *David Copperfield* was the most popular novel, then *Ivanhoe*, followed by *The Scarlet Letter, Uncle Tom's Cabin, Ben Hur, Adam Bede, Vanity Fair, Jane Eyre* and *The Last Days of Pompeii*.[2] Dickens was the most widely read novelist, with Louisa May Alcott, Walter Scott, E. P. Roe, James Fenimore Cooper, George Eliot, Nathaniel Hawthorne, O. W. Holmes, Bulwer Lytton and Thackeray as his chief rivals— evidence a-plenty of the existence, not of one but of a gradation of reading publics. Mark Twain, F. Marion Crawford, Frank R. Stockton and W. D. Howells appeared respectively as thirteenth, fifteenth, eighteenth and twenty-sixth on the list. Their relatively low ranking, together with the absence of the leaders of the American local-color school, probably indicates merely that the public was content as yet to read them in the current magazines. On the other hand, the omission of the younger English novelists like Hardy, Meredith and Stevenson and of contemporary Russian and French fictionists suggests the restricted horizon of the average reader.

For both publisher and author, the chaos resulting

[1] Classified data appear in annual summaries published in the *Publishers' Wkly.*, starting in Jan., 1880; and the totals of copyrighted works may be found in the annual reports of the Librarian of Congress. The discrepancies between the two sets of figures are too great to justify any but the most general conclusions.

[2] H. W. Mabie, "The Most Popular Novels in America," *Forum*, XVI (1893-1894), 508-516.

from the lack of international copyright arrangements was fast becoming intolerable. It would be difficult to exaggerate the hampering effect which this anomalous situation had had for many years on the growth of an autochthonous literature.[1] So long as publishers and magazine editors could reprint, or pirate, popular English authors without payment of royalty, and so long as readers could buy such volumes far cheaper than books written by Americans, native authorship remained at a marked disadvantage.[2] As early as 1837 petitions signed by prominent authors on both sides of the Atlantic had been presented to Congress on behalf of an international copyright; but to this and later appeals that body had remained uniformly cold. Publishers, for the most part, were satisfied with the existing situation, while many other persons, lacking a selfish motive, deemed low-priced books essential for a rapid diffusion of culture among the mass of the people. Even Mark Twain wrote Howells in 1880:

> My notions have mightily changed lately. I can buy *Macaulay's History*, three vols., bound, for $1.25; *Chambers's Cyclopaedia*, ten vols., cloth, for $7.25 (we paid $60), and other English copyrights in proportion; I can buy a lot of the great copyright classics, in paper, at from three to thirty cents apiece. These things must find their way into the very kitchens and hovels of the country.[3]

[1] For the consequences in an earlier period, see C. R. Fish, *The Rise of the Common Man* (*A History of American Life*, VI), 248-249.

[2] "A volume of Carlyle," said the *Hour* (N. Y.), April 21, 1883, "may be bought at the price of a glass of whiskey, but a volume of Emerson . . . is as costly as a pint bottle of champagne."

[3] A. B. Paine, *Mark Twain* (N. Y., 1912), II, 687. In another and soberer mood he pointed out that the "cheap alien books" contained "an ounce of wholesome literature to a hundred tons of noxious." G. H. Putnam, comp., *The Question of Copyright* (N. Y., 1891), 343; "Mark Twain on Copyright," *Publishers' Wkly.*, XXXIII, 77 (Jan. 21, 1888).

This attitude, which Twain swiftly repented, ignored, of course, other aspects of the matter, notably the question of common honesty involved in the international theft of literary property.

Among the better publishers a "courtesy of the trade" had gradually developed whereby, if one of them bought the advance sheets or made other payment to a foreign author or publisher, the rest refrained from issuing reprints. But the practice collapsed with the crowding in of many new book concerns in the 1870's and 1880's and the sharp competition offered by their endless "libraries" of cheap paper-back reprints. Disreputable piracy was ruining the business of respectable piracy. At the same time American publishers discovered that their own books were being increasingly pirated abroad. By 1878 one in every ten works issued in England was an American reprint.[1] Longfellow ruefully admitted having twenty-two unsought publishers there. By a process perhaps more appropriately called kidnaping than piracy, John Habberton's *Helen's Babies* appeared in nine British editions besides four in the colonies. The serial publication of his next book precipitated such a scramble that one British firm issued it without the final chapter and another with the conclusion furnished by an English hand.[2] The prime recipients of the dubious compliment, however, were Hawthorne, Mrs. Stowe, Miss Alcott and Roe. Meanwhile, across the Canadian border, enterprising dealers not only marketed reprinted American novels locally, but sold them in the United States by mail in

---

[1] Putnam, *Question of Copyright*, 92. Brander Matthews, "American Authors and British Pirates," *New Princeton Rev.*, IV (1887), 201-212, and V (1888), 54-65, cites many specific instances of British literary piracy.

[2] G. H. Putnam, "International Copyright," *Publishers' Wkly.*, XV, 350 (March 22, 1879). James Russell Lowell's ministership to England (1880-1885) was the occasion for the unauthorized reprinting of his many writings in countless cheap "libraries."

competition with the authorized editions. Mark Twain believed that Canadian piracy cost him an average of five thousand dollars a year.[1]

As a result of these developments the more reputable American publishers became as clamorous as the united authors for an international copyright. In 1878 Harper & Brothers, long in opposition, proposed to the state department a draft treaty on the subject with Great Britain, but the slow negotiations were brought to a close by the death of President Garfield.[2] His successor, Chester A. Arthur, recommended legislative action instead. At the same time public opinion, energized by the American Copyright League, founded by leading authors and magazine editors in 1883, and the American Publishers' Copyright League (1887), exerted increasing pressure upon Congress. The chief resistance came from organizations representing typographers, binders and employing printers. When their objections were met by a provision requiring separate manufacture of the foreign book in America, the international-copyright law was finally enacted by Congress on March 4, 1891.[3]

Under this act authors belonging to foreign countries willing to make reciprocal arrangements were granted the privilege of copyright on virtually the same terms as native authors. France, Great Britain, Germany and other governments speedily made the required arrangements with the United States. While the law, particu-

[1] Paine, *Mark Twain*, II, 687.

[2] J. H. Harper, *The House of Harper* (N. Y., 1928), 425-428; R. R. Bowker, *Copyright: Its History and Its Law* (Boston, 1912), 354-356.

[3] Putnam, *Question of Copyright*, 142-185, 380-410. The law also applied to works of art and musical compositions without, however, requiring American manufacture. In the case of the latter this made possible a continuance of "song piracy," greatly to the discontent of reputable music publishers. *Publishers' Wkly.*, XL, 141-142 (July 25, 1891); LI, 997 (June 19, 1897); LIII, 489 (March 12, 1898).

larly in its manufacturing clause, fell short of the standard set by leading powers in the Berne copyright convention of 1887,[1] it had the important effect of
stabilizing the book market at home and abroad for
both publisher and author. By the same token it removed a stain from the national honor. Whether aspiring young authors found it easier thereafter to secure
publishers it would be difficult to know; but it is at
least suggestive that the year 1894 saw, for the first time,
more novels published in the United States from American pens than from European.[2]

Never before had writers been more authentically
children of their own era. Responding instinctively to
the sharpening conflict between urban and rural culture,
their sensitive artistry mirrored the varying and incon-
sistent moods evoked by the new orientation of society.
Some sought to preserve in their pages idyllic glimpses
of a civilization fast passing: a new South recalled the
old South. Some, symbolizing their own removal to
the city, viewed the traditional culture with acute dis-
taste. Others perceived in the city itself an unanticipated
source of gathering ills. And amidst this confusion of
tongues flourished still others who, turning their backs
on what they did not care to see, sounded the clarion call
to romance and forgetfulness.

Literary preoccupation with the West, so pronounced
in the 1870's,[3] was eclipsed by the new attention given
the South. The West still spoke, but with feebler voice

[1] All the signatory nations agreed, as among themselves, to treat
foreigners and citizens identically alike in the matter of copyright; there
was no manufacturing clause. Putnam, *Question of Copyright*, 297-323.

[2] *Publishers' Wkly.*, XLVII, 170 (Jan. 26, 1895). See also A. R.
Spofford, "Directions and Volume of Our Literary Activities," and
G. H. Putnam, "Results of the Copyright Law," *Forum*, XVI (1893-
1894), 602-604, 616-623.

[3] Allan Nevins, *The Emergence of Modern America* (*A History of
American Life*, VIII), 247-254; F. L. Pattee, *A History of American
Literature since 1870* (N. Y., 1915), chap. xiv.

and usually to less eager listeners. In 1878 Bret Harte left America to spend the rest of his life abroad, writing year after year new volumes of highly colored stories of California life without regaining his earlier American following. Edward Eggleston, while publishing several novels concerned with his favorite theme of primitive society in Hoosierland, gave himself by preference to magazine editing and historical research. Mark Twain, however, succeeded in adding Huckleberry Finn (1884) and Pudd'nhead Wilson (1894) to his notable gallery of Mid-Western characters, and Helen Hunt Jackson, an Easterner by birth, scored a brilliant success in *Ramona* (1884), a romance of the passing of the old Spanish order in California.

By contrast, the fictional world veritably swarmed with decayed Southern gentlemen, ladies of the old régime, Virginia darkies, Georgia crackers, Tennessee mountaineers and Louisiana Creoles, limned by brushes that blended a nice attention to dialect and local color with a mellow glow of sentiment. It was as though Dixie, long negligent of her literary riches and freed from the palsying effects of slavery, had commissioned her sons and daughters to take their rightful place in the world of letters. Virtually all the important writers, Harris being a notable exception, were children of the prewar planter aristocracy. Thomas Nelson Page and F. Hopkinson Smith portrayed with tender feeling the life of the old Virginia gentry. In finely wrought sketches George W. Cable, Grace King and Kate Chopin introduced a wondering America to the exotic orange-scented atmosphere of Creole life among the Louisiana bayous. Charles Egbert Craddock's *In the Tennessee Mountains* (1884) and many later volumes wove tales about the humble folk living amid the grandeur of the interior highlands, while James Lane Allen wrote with careful artistry of human passion and conflict against a Kentucky background.

None of these literary creations, however, seems so certain of lasting fame as the folk stories retold by a young Georgia reporter writing against time to fill up space in his newspaper, the *Atlanta Constitution*. When Joel Chandler Harris in 1880 published his first volume of Uncle Remus tales, he at once gained a wide audience —among lovers of humor, among children, among students of folklore—which he was never to relinquish. Quite apart from their literary charm, these Negro animal legends, recounted so faithfully by Harris through Uncle Remus, are of interest to the social historian, for they are an unconscious revelation of the soul of a people —their wisdom, their fun, their pathos. Br'er Rabbit, most timid of forest creatures, was none other than the black race itself. Br'er Rabbit's versatile use of roguery and deceit to outwit Br'er Fox and Br'er Wolf betokened a helpless people's sole defense against major force and vested oppression.

While New England also had its sectional spokesmen, they wrote not of a glamorous past but of the gray realities of the present. How had the drift to the cities affected the inner life of the men and women who continued to dwell in the stagnant villages and on the deserted countryside? Their pages abound in acute but sympathetic portrayals of narrow, repressed, introspective lives. Authors like Sarah Orne Jewett, Mary E. Wilkins and Rose Terry Cooke made themselves authentic chroniclers of New England's rural decline.

In general, the local colorists of all sections erred upon the side of *genre* painting, their art failing to make vital and convincing the part their regional characters played in the situations in which Fate had entangled them. The

limits of realistic treatment were so sharply marked
among the new Southern school that in 1879 Cable
changed his residence to Northampton, Massachusetts,
in order to be able to write without constraint on Southern themes, particularly the Negro question. Likewise
Walter Hines Page, thwarted in his ardent efforts as a
North Carolina newspaper editor to lay those foes of
progress, "the Ghost of the Confederate dead, the Ghost
of religious orthodoxy, the Ghost of Negro domination,"
removed in 1885 to the North, where his literary abilities
soon won him recognition, first as staff writer on the
*New York Evening Post,* and then as editor successively
of the *Forum* and of the *Atlantic.*[1]

The local colorists, for the most part, wrote in in-
nocence of the school of mordant realism which had its
exemplars in Europe in such masters as Flaubert,
Maupassant, Zola, Tolstoy, Gogol, Turgeniev, Dostoi-
evski and Björnson.[2] For traces of this powerful movement one must look, rather, to the writings of William
Dean Howells and Henry James who worked more consciously in the world stream of literature. Their realism,
however, was less of the sordid and ugly aspects of life
than a faithful reporting of the foibles and trials of
middle-class folk living on the same general plane of
existence as themselves. As a wit phrased it, "the present
realism in fiction is in France a discovery of the un-
clean, and in America a discovery of the unimportant."[3]
Howells was a Middle Westerner who had deserted his
native heath for the cultured atmosphere of Boston;
James an Easterner who, sensitive to the crudenesses of

---

[1] B. J. Hendrick, *The Life and Letters of Walter H. Page* (Garden
City, 1921), I, 42-63, 72-83; W. H. Page (Nicholas Worth, *pseud.*),
*The Southerner* (N. Y., 1909), chaps. xi-xxxi.

[2] The great activity in publishing translations from the Russian began
in 1886. *Publishers' Wkly.,* XXXIII, 319 (Feb. 11, 1888).

[3] Quoted by Gilder, "Certain Tendencies in Current Literature," 2.

even literary Boston, fled American shores for the older, riper civilization of Europe.

Both were expert craftsmen; but Howells tempered his acute observation of everyday mankind with kindly and tolerant understanding, while James, impaling his human creatures as an entomologist his insects, subjected them to a relentless dissection which made his pages more minutely psychological than those of his brother William, the professional psychologist. Howells dealt characteristically with American life and American materials, and never perhaps rose to greater artistic heights than in *A Modern Instance* (1882) and *The Rise of Silas Lapham* (1884), both unforgettable transcripts of Boston life. James displayed his unique powers to best advantage in tales like *Daisy Miller* (1878), *An International Episode* (1879) and *The Portrait of a Lady* (1881), dealing with the clash of Old World culture upon Americans abroad. Along with the local colorists, these men did much to mold the short story into a finished work of art, a form characterized by compactness and singleness of impression.

The grimmer realism lacking in Howells and James found expression in a younger group of writers. Their work, however, reflected less the current European mode than it did a sharp dissent from the romantic notions of pioneer life prevalent among Easterners. To Western youths ambitious of the intellectual opportunities afforded by the city, the rural life of the 1880's seemed, by contrast, a barren, drear, soul-starving existence. They were less impressed by the pleasures of communing with nature than by "the grime and the mud and the sweat"; "the working farmer . . . must pitch manure as well as clover."[1]

The note of disillusionment was first powerfully

[1] Garland, *Son of the Middle Border*, 377. See also earlier, 60-61.

sounded in E. W. Howe's *The Story of a Country Town* (1884), a morbid, strongly etched tale of the constricted life of Atchison, Kansas, written by a local newspaper editor.[1] Two years later Joseph Kirkland added to the indictment *Zury; the Meanest Man in Spring County,* and Harold Frederic wrote *Seth's Brother's Wife.* Then in 1891 Hamlin Garland published his first of a series of harsh, acrid sketches dealing with Mid-Western rural life. For it the author sardonically chose the title *Main-Travelled Roads* because, as he explained in a foreword, in a farming region the main road "is long and wearyful and has a dull town at one end and a home of toil at the other." [2]

Other fictionists, however, were discovering that even the city was not all sweetness and light; that it had drab and sordid aspects, its way of thwarting human hopes; that the industrial system upon which it fed was a prolific womb of man's inhumanity to man. Such writers as John Hay, the anonymous author of *The Bread-Winners* (1883), and Robert Barr in *The Mutable Many* (1896) dealt trenchantly with the labor problem. In *The Mammon of Unrighteousness* (1891) Boyesen exposed the brutalizing effects of ill-gotten wealth. Paul Leicester Ford's *The Honorable Peter Stirling* (1894) presented a striking study of ward politics in New York with Grover Cleveland supposedly as its central figure. The youthful Stephen Crane, after the manner of Zola,

[1] A reviewer thought it "not true to Western life, which is the most cheerful and rollicking life in the world; but it is true to Mr. Howe's disgust for its limitations, its lack of sympathy with art, its rawness, and its uninspiring air of mere bigness." "Contributors' Club," *Atlantic Mo.,* LVI (1885), 715.

[2] Garland was execrated in the West as "a bird willing to foul his own nest." Statistics were discovered to show "that pianos and Brussels carpets adorned almost every Iowa farmhouse." Garland, *Son of the Middle Border,* esp. 415. *Prairie Folks* (Chicago, 1892) and *A Little Norsk* (N. Y., 1892) repeated the essential qualities of the first book. He set forth his literary creed in *Crumbling Idols* (Chicago, 1894).

contributed a somber picture of slum degeneracy in
*Maggie, a Girl of the Streets* (1892).[1]

Even Howells, confronted by "the hideousness of a
competitive metropolis" when he removed to New York
in the late eighties, and deeply disquieted by the Hay-
market riot and other portents of threatening class war,
turned his deft pen to criticism of the existing social
order.[2] "What I object to," he makes Basil March say in
*A Hazard of New Fortunes,*

> is this economic chance-world in which we live. . . .
> It ought to be law as inflexible in human affairs as
> the order of day and night in the physical world, that
> if a man will work he shall both rest and eat, and shall
> not be harassed with any question as to how his repose
> and provision shall come.[3]

What "ought to be law" was magically made law by
a group of novelists who dreamed worlds in which chaos
and self-seeking were replaced by a society of millennial
perfection. Under different circumstances America might
have experienced another epidemic of socialistic communities like those of the thirties and forties.[4] But with
desirable cheap lands difficult to get and the growing
disrepute of rural life, the heat vented itself through the
exhaust pipe of fiction. Over two score writers indulged

[1] In his best-known work *The Red Badge of Courage* (N. Y., 1895)
Crane recreated out of his imagination a story of the Civil War, stocked
with repulsive details of army life and the battle-field.

[2] The quoted phrase is taken from a striking passage attributed to
a character in *The World of Chance* (N. Y., 1893), 297. Howells's
recent discovery of Tolstoy undoubtedly facilitated the transition. See
D. G. Cooke, *William Dean Howells* (N. Y., 1922), chap. vii; W. F.
Taylor, "On the Origin of Howells' Interest in Economic Reform,"
*Am. Literature*, II, 3-14; and A. L. Bass, "The Social Consciousness
of William Dean Howells," *New Republic*, XXVI (1921), 192-194.

[3] W. D. Howells, *A Hazard of New Fortunes* (N. Y., 1889), II,
252. See also his *Annie Kilburn* (N. Y., 1888), *The Quality of Mercy*
(N. Y., 1892) and *The World of Chance.*

[4] See Fish, *Rise of the Common Man*, 189-190, 252-253.

themselves in such fine-spun fancies; and while few of their efforts ranked high as *belles-lettres,* there can be no doubt that they ministered to an inarticulate yearning of the public.[1]

The most widely read, though not the earliest, of these homespun utopias was Edward Bellamy's *Looking Backward, 2000-1887,* published in 1888. The author visioned a society in which the mighty trust development of the 1880's had fruited in one great all-embracing trust, owned and operated by the people in their own interest. Everyone was obliged to work, hence everyone had leisure. Poverty and its attendant evil, crime, were unknown; hospitals served in the place of prisons; and the creative energies of humanity were released for an unparalleled intellectual and technological advance. With minor variations the same theme recurred in most of the other novels. Howells made his contribution in *A Traveller from Altruria* (1894), while in the Middle West the Populist *littérateur* Ignatius Donnelly, skillfully reversing the formula in *Caesar's Column* (1890), pictured the climax of current economic tendencies in a stupendous social cataclysm. More than any of its competitors, Bellamy's fantasy captured the popular imagination, nearly four hundred thousand copies being sold in ten years in the United States alone. His system of "Nationalism" seemed so far from visionary that it led to a short-lived organized movement in its support.[2]

Romance, however, did not need to be flavored with purpose in order to win a large audience. Lew Wallace's

---

[1] A. B. Forbes, "The Literary Quest for Utopia, 1880-1900," *Social Forces,* VI, 179-189, includes a list of these writings. The absence of the terms, socialism and communism, from these volumes suggests that the authors' inspiration came wholly, or chiefly, from their American environment.

[2] See later, 426. While writing the book Bellamy became so convinced of its early practicability that he shifted the date of his commonwealth from the year 3000 to 2000. *Nationalist* (Boston), I (1889), 1-4.

*Ben Hur,* published in 1880, was probably more widely read than any other American novel of equal merit produced during these years. The most brilliant romancer of the era, however, and a much more fecund author, was F. Marion Crawford, son of the sculptor Thomas Crawford, whose long residence abroad fitted him in an unusual degree to deal with Old World themes. To read him gave the public a sense of cosmopolitan breadth and an intimate familiarity with aristocratic society in many lands. Beginning with *Mr. Isaacs* (1882)—which anticipated Kipling by five years in its Indian *locale*— nearly every year saw one or more volumes from his pen. By the close of 1896 his American sales alone totaled nearly half a million copies.[1] Mark Twain also entered the lists but with tongue in cheek. His *The Prince and the Pauper* (1881) and *A Connecticut Yankee in King Arthur's Court* (1889), designed to rob the past of its spurious claims to high romance, were vastly enjoyed by countless readers.

For the semiliterate masses nothing less would suffice than the sentimental unrealities of writers like Mary J. Holmes, Bertha M. Clay and Laura Jean Libbey.[2] Such novels as *Parted at the Altar* and *Fancy Free Yet Linked for Life* injected a welcome glow of romance into drab lives and enabled factory girls and kitchen maids to see themselves as beautiful, suffering heroines courted by knightly and quite impossible heroes. The death of the Reverend E. P. Roe in 1888 revealed the fact that his

[1] *Publishers' Wkly.,* LI, 83 (Jan. 23, 1897). His Italian cycle: *Saracinesca, Sant' Ilario, Don Orsino* and *Corleone* (1887-1896), reveal his work at its best. For the outburst of historical romances at the end of the nineties, see H. U. Faulkner, *The Quest for Social Justice* (*A History of American Life*, XI), 261-262.

[2] Bertha M. Clay was the pen name at various times of Frederick Van Rensselaer Dey and J. R. Coryell who were also expert dime novelists. Miss Libbey was known to her acquaintances as Mrs. Van Mater Stilwell, the prosperous wife of a Brooklyn lawyer. J. E. Pember, "Laura Jean Libbey's 'Happy Endings,'" *Boston Herald,* Nov. 2, 1924.

unnumbered moralistic tales had been earning him an annual royalty of fifteen thousand dollars.[1]

No department of fiction showed more varied currents or, on the whole, greater progress than that for children. Where parental rule was firm and watchful, the older type of didactic story was apt to prevail— tales of saintly candidates for early graves. This persistence of goody-goody literature, for example, brought almost yearly additions to the *Elsie* series, in which the author, Martha F. Finley, painstakingly followed the career of her exemplary heroine, Elsie Dinsmore, from infancy to old age. Where parents were less vigilant the dime novel made its inroads. Youthful imagination, sated with "moral sugar-plums," [2] was naturally attracted by legendary feats of valor on the Western plains and the exciting exploits of criminal bands in the great cities. "Stories for children," remarked a newspaper humorist, "used to begin, 'Once upon a time there lived —.' Now they begin, 'Vengeance, blood, sdeath, shouted Rattlesnake Jim,' or words to that effect." [3] Among the favorite characters were Deadwood Dick, Mustang Sam, Denver Dan and the superdetectives, Old Cap Collier and Old Sleuth, all heroes of a succession of gory and breathless adventures illustrated by luridly colored paper covers.

Harlan P. Halsey, author of the *Old Sleuth* series, wrote nearly six hundred and fifty dime novels before his death in 1898 and is said to have amassed nearly half a million dollars from his trade.[4] Like his fellow crafts-

---

[1] *Publishers' Wkly.*, XXXIV, 140 (July 28, 1888). See also Matthew Arnold, *Civilization in the United States* (Boston, 1888), 184.

[2] Julian Hawthorne's characterization in *Confessions and Criticisms* (Boston, 1886), 125.

[3] "Phunnygraphs," *Exeter* (N. H.) *News-Letter*, May 5, 1882.

[4] *Publishers' Wkly.*, LIV, 1137 (Dec. 24, 1898); anon., "Harlan Page Halsey," *Current Literature*, XXV (1899), 114-115; Edmund Pearson, *Dime Novels* (Boston, 1929), 191-197.

# Old Sleuth Library

### OLD IRONSIDES IN NEW YORK; OR, THE DAUGHTER OF THE G. A. R.
#### By OLD SLEUTH.

A SERIES OF THE MOST THRILLING DETECTIVE STORIES EVER PUBLISHED.

| No. 54. | SINGLE NUMBER. | GEORGE MUNRO'S SONS, PUBLISHERS, 17 to 27 Vandewater St., New York | PRICE 5 CENTS. | Vol. III. |

Old Sleuth Library, Issued Quarterly.—By Subscription, 25 cents per Annum.
Entered at the Post Office at New York at Second Class Rates.—September 26, 1891.
Copyrighted in 1886, by George Munro.

# Old Ironsides in New York;

OR,

# The Daughter of the G. A. R.

### BY OLD SLEUTH.

NEW YORK: GEORGE MUNRO'S SONS, PUBLISHERS, 17 TO 27 VANDEWATER STREET.

A "Dime Novel"

men he could dash off a book in a single day. George Munro, his publisher, engaged in a series of law suits to restrain rival firms from using the word, sleuth, which Halsey had coined as a synonym for detective; but in the end the New York supreme court decided against him and a new word, or at least a word with a new meaning, found its way into the American language.[1] Halsey served for ten years as a member of the New York board of education, much to the consternation of those who regarded his literary effusions as " 'hurrah-for-hades' publications" and incitements to juvenile criminality.[2] As a matter of fact, dime novels, though crudely written and replete with sensational incidents, pictured a world of immaculate morality in which villains always met their just deserts and virtue ever triumphed.

Of a somewhat higher degree of respectability were the boys' books written by Horatio Alger, Jr., and William T. Adams (Oliver Optic). Avoiding blood-and-thunder plots, these men wrote volume after volume to glorify the theme of worldly success, telling with mild variations of the poor but honest lad who, through pluck and perseverance, battled his way against seemingly impossible obstacles to fame and fortune. But even these books were banned by most librarians as presenting a false picture of life.

Luckily, children possessed the thumb-worn volumes of an earlier day: *Robinson Crusoe, Gulliver's Travels, The Swiss Family Robinson, Hans Brinker* and the

[1] *Publishers' Wkly.*, XXXV, 24-25 (Jan. 12, 1889); XXXVII, 253-254, 718 (Feb. 8, May 31, 1890).
[2] For stern disapproval of such "boy and girl devil-traps" and instances of their alleged responsibility for juvenile crime, see Anthony Comstock, *Traps for the Young* (N. Y., 1883), chap. iii, and *Library Journal* (N. Y.), VIII (1883), 36-37. For a more sympathetic attitude, read W. H. Bishop, "Story-Paper Literature," *Atlantic Mo.*, XLIV (1879), 383-389, and Pearson, *Dime Novels*, 90-103.

delightful girls' stories of Miss Alcott.[1] Luckily, too, their stock of reading was greatly enriched during these years by some of the most eminent writers of the time. Unwilling to leave the field to catch-penny sensationalists, such authors wrote books which combined honesty, virility and an understanding of American youth with good literary style. Two editors of the *Atlantic*— Howells and H. E. Scudder—entered the lists, Mark Twain, Harris and Stockton appealed to the spirit of youth in readers of all ages, while J. O. Kaler (James Otis) scored a merited success with his child classic of circus life, *Toby Tyler* (1881).

Soon young America was busily discovering new treasures in a stream of books flowing from the pens of Kaler, Kirk Munroe, Howard Pyle, Kate Douglas Wiggin, Hezekiah Butterworth and C. C. Coffin.[2] At the same time the very little ones found delight in Palmer Cox's drawings and stories of the inimitable "Brownies" —the Brownie Wheelman, the Brownie Policeman and other roly-poly reflections of the life of grown-ups. Much of the new juvenile fiction was purveyed through the pages of *St. Nicholas,* founded in 1873 with Mary Mapes Dodge as editor, its enterprise being rivaled by that of *Harper's Young People,* begun in 1879, and by a change of policy on the part of the older *Youth's Companion.* Two books by American authors scored sensational successes. One, Frances Hodgson Burnett's *Little Lord Fauntleroy* (1886), pictured the model child which every mother in her secret heart wants her boy to be; the other, *Peck's Bad Boy and His Pa*

[1] C. B. Tillinghast, "Books and Readers in Public Libraries," *Forum,* XVI (1893-1894), 64-65; Constance C. Harrison, "Some Favorites, Old and New," *Critic,* n.s., IV (1885), 253-254.

[2] Almost as popular were the pseudoscientific romances of the Frenchman Jules Verne, the historical novels of Anglo-Saxon valor written by the Englishman G. A. Henty, and Robert Louis Stevenson's tales of high adventure.

(1883) by George W. Peck, narrated the pranks of the kind of child every normal boy aspires to be. Though classed by most parents with dime novels, *Peck's Bad Boy* had already sold half a million copies by 1885.[1]

Every branch of literature was pervaded by humor— from Henry James's keen-edged satire and James Whitcomb Riley's wistful poems of childhood to the droll exaggerations of Bill Nye and Mark Twain.[2] Country folk had never· before seemed so funny, particularly when they ventured out of their rustic environment. The experiences of the bucolic up-state New Yorker Samantha Allen at Saratoga, the Chicago World's Fair and elsewhere, as told by Marietta Holley, kept the nation in gales of laughter. The polyglot city had its own ludicrous characters. Charles Follen Adams wrote in rhyme of *Leedle Yawcob Strauss* (1877), while E. W. Townsend brought the slangy Bowery youth *Chimmie Fadden* (1895) to national attention. If misspelled words no longer seemed amusing for their own sake, dialect differences continued to delight a public rapidly becoming standardized in speech.

The typical humorists were trained in newspaper offices and, under pressure of the daily grind, their writings tended to be crisp, racy and ephemeral. Newspaper wags like the *"Danbury News* Man" (J. M. Bailey) and "M. Quad" (C. B. Lewis) commanded a delighted following, and prepared the way for the coming of Eugene Field and his many successors of a later day.[3]

[1] *Publishers' Wkly.*, XXVIII, 919-920 (Dec. 12, 1885).

[2] Although Mark Twain's humor marked an advance over that of his Western predecessors, it is unlikely that he would ever have become the force he was in American letters if Mrs. Clemens, Howells and other friendly critics had not helped turn him from the hoaxes and rollicking burlesque of his earlier work to the fields where his real talents lay. He seemed particularly lacking in the faculty of self-criticism.

[3] See P. W. Slosson, *The Great Crusade and After* (*A History of American Life*, XII), 355-356.

Perhaps the greatest of all "colyumists," Field from 1883 until his death in 1895 contributed a daily column of "Sharps and Flats" to the *Chicago News*. His personal life was a ceaseless round of hoaxes and practical jokes, and into his column he distilled the essence of a brilliant and incorrigible wit.[1] If most American humor lacked delicacy, composure and literary charm, the balance was in some measure redressed by the prolific writings of Frank R. Stockton. *Rudder Grange* (1879) and *The Casting Away of Mrs. Lecks and Mrs. Aleshine* (1886) illustrate his calmly ingenious manner of entangling matter-of-fact people in absurdly whimsical situations. One of his short stories, "The Lady or the Tiger?" (1884), though somewhat less characteristic of his drollery, divided the reading public into two factions in a vain attempt to answer the question which the author had artfully refrained from solving.

In poetry this generation fared less well. The great masters of mid-century—Emerson, Whittier, Whitman and the rest—dropped quietly from the scene burdened with years, their places being taken by lesser figures. R. H. Stoddard, T. B. Aldrich, E. C. Stedman, R. W. Gilder, Richard Hovey, Madison Cawein—men like these wrote with neatness, delicacy and faultless technique, but they were essentially romantic, seldom, if ever, coming to grips with the throbbing life of their times. Emily Dickinson, "small like the wren" and living secluded in her Berkshire village, composed brief breathless poems which stabbed and startled by their deftness of thought and phrase.[2] One of her fellow

---

[1] Cullings from his column were given book form in *A Little Book of Western Verse* (N. Y., 1889), *A Little Book of Profitable Tales* (N. Y., 1889) and other volumes.

[2] The first volume of her poems appeared in 1890. four years after her death. For a critical appraisal of her work, see Conrad Aiken, ed., *Selected Poems of Emily Dickinson* (London, 1929), 5-22.

bards, Joaquin Miller, more bird of paradise than wren, sang the beauties of the mountain ranges from Alaska to Nicaragua—the poet preëminent of the untamed West. It was left, however, to two versifiers of lesser merit, both Middle Westerners, to tune their lyres to the heart of average humanity. Riley wrote wistfully tender dialect poems about rustic life—about "home," "old times," the "old swimmin' hole." His rival in popular favor, Will Carleton, had anticipated him with *Farm Ballads* (1873) and *Farm Legends* (1875); then, joining the trek to the city, discovered new play for his talents in *City Ballads* (1885), *City Legends* (1889) and *City Festivals* (1892).

While essayists addressed a more limited circle, these years showed that the number of such writers might be legion. None, however, displayed so rich or undisciplined a genius as Lafcadio Hearn.[1] The nature essay won increasing favor as outdoor life receded before the advance of the city. Thoreau, neglected earlier, came finally into his own, and the prose form which he did so much to perfect was further developed by John Burroughs and John Muir. Literary criticism flourished in the pages of the *Nation,* the *Dial* and the *Critic;* and never before in America had the art of book reviewing reached so high a plane. Yet professional criticism did less to mold literature than the standards imposed by publishers and editors intent on sales' possibilities and by the popular aversion to plain talk about the physical aspects of sex.[2]

When Mark Twain wrote his *Fireside Conversation in the Time of Queen Elizabeth,* a Rabelaisian effusion,

[1] Half Greek, half Celt, a wanderer in many lands, Hearn stands out of relation to his American environment—exotic, intensely individualistic, yet a dealer in fragments of imperishable beauty.

[2] As Gilder remarked in "Certain Tendencies in Current Literature," 8, "There are many who believe that America has the purest society in the world. Is not this purity worth paying for with a little prudery?"

it was hotly rejected by a magazine editor and, though privately printed by John Hay, its circulation was carefully restricted to a few friends.[1] When the Chicago merchant prince John Crerar in 1889 bequeathed two and a half million dollars for founding the great library which bears his name, he expressly excluded from the proposed collection "dirty French novels" and "works of questionable moral tone."[2] To nearly everyone Gallic frankness was a thorn in the flesh. Funk & Wagnalls wrathily declined to publish Daudet's *Sappho*, and when another firm issued Zola's *La Terre*, two booksellers in Nashville were fined for selling it.[3] The *American Medico-Surgical Journal* in 1895, after descanting on the moral poison administered by such works, added sarcastically, "As yet there exists no novel of the ear, no drama of the digestive organs, no romance of the kidneys, no pastels of the intestines."[4]

Victorian reticence found sanction in a federal law of 1873, which had been passed at the instigation of Anthony Comstock, a reformer whose nature embodied the passionate propriety of a long line of Puritan ancestors. As amended in 1876, the act inflicted heavy penalties for sending through the mails printed material or pictures of "an indecent character," the indecency to be adjudged by a federal court and jury. Although its repeal was demanded in 1878 by a two-thousand-foot petition containing fifty thousand names, the law not only remained on the statute books but was supplemented by state legislation as well. Moreover, Com-

---

[1] The pamphlet was retitled *1601*. Paine, *Mark Twain*, II, 580-581.

[2] J. D. Wade, "John Crerar," *Dict. of Am. Biog.*, IV, 537.

[3] *N. Y. Eve. Post*, July 10, 1884; *Publishers' Wkly.*, XXXIV, 184 (Aug. 11, 1888). For further evidence of a similar attitude, see Herbert Edwards, "Zola and the American Critics," *Am. Literature*, IV, 114-129.

[4] Quoted by *Publishers' Wkly.*, XLVII, 630 (April 13, 1895).

stock's Society for the Suppression of Vice in New York and similar groups in Boston, Cincinnati, Chicago, St. Louis and elsewhere undertook energetic enforcement. Thus, from 1873 to 1882, Comstock confiscated fourteen tons of books and sheet stock and a million and a half obscene circulars, poems and pictures.[1] While his efforts lessened improper newspaper advertising and reduced the amount of erotic matter in circulation among school youth, he unfortunately failed to distinguish between pornography on the one hand and literary classics and medical treatises on the other. His square, stocky figure, bald head and ginger-tinted side whiskers became for many the symbol of a licensed bigotry destructive of much that was choice in art and letters.

Despite deterrent influences these years stand forth as a new creative epoch in American letters, backed by a popular appreciation and support without earlier parallel in the country's history.[2] The true distinction of the eighties, however, appears in the fact that the renaissance in *belles-lettres* was attended by an equally significant renaissance in the arts of line, color and form. Aesthetic appreciation had been greatly stimulated by the Centennial Exhibition of 1876. Not only was the general taste in domestic decoration raised, not only did American workmanship in glass, tableware, pottery and fabric designing improve, but courses in art appreciation began to creep into the universities.[3] Meanwhile new mechani-

[1] He also waged war against gambling, dishonest advertising, birth control and nudity in art. Heywood Broun and Margaret Leech, *Anthony Comstock* (N. Y., 1927), chaps. ix-xv, is a balanced treatment. Comstock defended his militant course in *Frauds Exposed* (N. Y., 1880) and *Traps for the Young* (N. Y., 1883).

[2] "The decade 1880-1890 produced more good novels than any other American decade," says Carl Van Doren, *The American Novel* (N. Y., 1921), 221, citing an amplitude of evidence.

[3] For the rising interest in art, see S. G. W. Benjamin, "American Art since the Centennial," *New Princeton Rev.*, IV (1887), 14-30; E. A. Barber, "Recent Advances in the Pottery Industry," *Pop. Sci.*

cal processes, by simplifying the reproduction of art works in magazines and books, helped further to familiarize the public with better standards.[1] The new interest effloresced in a trebling of the number of art training schools and, at the same time, the spread of art schools, art societies and galleries to inland cities like Chicago, St. Louis, Detroit, Milwaukee and Minneapolis.[2] Frank Duveneck, who earlier had taught a notable group of younger painters at his studios in Munich and Florence, was content to spend the years after 1888 in Cincinnati, where for the next quarter of a century he continued to exert a fruitful influence on American art as dean of the Cincinnati Academy.[3]

Among the painters themselves there appeared a so-called New School.[4] In the late 1870's the first of a throng of young artists returned to New York after study in Munich and particularly in Paris. Trained in the careful draftsmanship of European studios, they were scornful of older American traditions. The "Younger Men," though sometimes affecting eccentric mannerisms, sought in general to render nature naturally rather than in accordance with certain arbitrary principles. Their advent was like a fresh breeze on a sultry day. "There are new ideas afloat,—dash, breadth, free-

*Mo.*, XL (1891-1892), 289-322; Ford, *Forty-Odd Years*, 75-77; I. E. Clarke, "Art and Industrial Education," N. M. Butler, ed., *Education in the United States* (Albany, 1900), II, 707-767.

[1] Illustrations which once cost $100 and a month's labor could, by means of photoengraving, be reproduced for one tenth the price and sometimes in a single day. T. L. De Vinne, "American Printing," Depew, *American Commerce*, I, 318-319.

[2] Anon., "The Field of Art," *Scribner's Mag.*, XX (1896), 649-652.

[3] Norbert Heermann, *Frank Duveneck* (Boston, 1918), chap. vi.

[4] Sadikichi Hartmann, *A History of American Art* (Boston, 1901), I, chap. iv; Samuel Isham, *The History of American Painting* (N. Y., 1905), chaps. xix-xx; C. H. Caffin, *The Story of American Painting* (N. Y., 1907), chaps. ix-xi; Suzanne La Follette, *Art in America* (N. Y., 1929), chaps. vi-vii.

dom, originality," wrote a contemporary.[1] Snubbed by the leaders of the National Academy of Design, they founded in 1877 their own Society of American Artists, drawing into their ranks some of the more progressive older artists like John La Farge and W. M. Chase. The leaders of the new body included such men of later distinction as J. Alden Weir, A. H. Thayer, E. H. Blashfield, Kenyon Cox and F. D. Millet. The clash of the old and new schools and the rivalry excited by their annual exhibitions had a healthful effect on both, and ushered in a period of American art which in quantity and quality surpassed any earlier era.

From such an embarrassment of riches it is difficult to make a selection, a difficulty increased by the fact that most artists displayed versatile talents, trying all things from landscape to miniature, from mural decoration to illustration, from etching to water color. Professor Münsterberg, reporting to his German compatriots on the state of American art shortly after the close of the period, rated James A. McNeill Whistler and John S. Sargent as the most noted painters. Though, as we know, neither had yet reached the summit of his powers, Sargent was already well established as a brilliant portraitist of "elegant ladies, prosperous men, and interesting children," while Whistler, like Henry James in a kindred field, "reproduced his human victims with positively uncanny perspicacity."[2] One of the latter's early masterpieces, "Portrait of the Artist's Mother," a study in rich twilight tones, was bought in 1891 by the French government after failing of a purchaser in America at an absurdly low price.

As Münsterberg was well aware, however, portraiture

[1] Raymond Westbrook, "Open Letters from New York," *Atlantic Mo.*, XLI (1878), 95. See also W. C. Brownell, "The Younger Painters of America," *Scribner's Mo.*, XX (1880), 1-15, 321-335.

[2] Hugo Münsterberg, *The Americans* (N. Y., 1904), 480-483.

was less characteristic of American effort than landscape painting. The increasing popularity of photography, especially after the improvements introduced by George Eastman in the 1880's, undermined portrait painting as a profession. The photograph supplied every commemorative need of the average household, and only the very wealthy continued to indulge in the luxury of oil likenesses. On the other hand, landscape painting reflected the revived interest in nature which pervaded much American poetry and essay writing. Among the productions in this mode Münsterberg particularly noted those of George Inness, "who has seen American landscapes more individually than anyone else," the bold seascapes of Winslow Homer, Childe Hassam's street scenes, the autumn forests of J. J. Enneking, the blossoming apple trees of J. Appleton Brown and the delicate landscapes of Weir and D. W. Tryon. The temptation to add to this list indicates the richness and variety of the work which the generation produced.[1]

Though less significant than other phases, mural art became for the first time an important branch of American painting, thanks to the opportunities afforded by imposing public edifices and pretentious private dwellings and to a technical proficiency hitherto lacking among native artists. In 1878 William Morris Hunt decorated the vaulted ceiling of the new Albany capitol, and later years saw R. F. Blum's panels for Mendelssohn Hall in New York, the wall paintings of Blashfield and W. H. Low in the Waldorf-Astoria ballroom and the notable murals of the Library of Congress by John W. Alexander, H. O. Walker, Elihu Vedder and others. La Farge, besides his memorable decorations of Trinity

---

[1] Thus, a recent critic esteems Thomas Eakins and A. P. Ryder superior to any of the painters mentioned above. See Lewis Mumford, *The Brown Decades* (N. Y., 1931), 210-231.

Church in Boston, added to the richness of artistic interiors by his invention of opalescent for stained glass in decorated windows. The new windows, distinguished by subtlety of color, recalled the ancient glories of medieval glass work.

Some of the painters, discouraged by slow recognition at home, followed the example of Whistler, Sargent and Mary Cassatt by pursuing their careers amidst more congenial surroundings in London or Paris. Others from lack of sufficient patronage were obliged to devote their chief energies to art instruction rather than to creative work. Still others found a useful and profitable outlet for their talents in illustration.[1] While most artists did occasional work in this medium, with some it was their principal claim to fame. At a time when magazine and book illustration was reaching untold numbers of people, men like Howard Pyle, E. A. Abbey and Joseph Pennell lifted the art to a dignity and distinction never before attained in America. Pyle was at his best in picturing the life of pirates and buccaneers, the traffic at colonial waterfronts, the fanciful world of Sherwood Forest. Perhaps more characteristic were the illustrators who spoke the idiom of their own times: M. A. Woolf and W. A. Rogers when they portrayed immigrant types and ragged slum youngsters, A. B. Frost in his humorous delineations of rustic life, E. W. Kemble in his sprightly pictures of Negroes and Frederic Remington in his spirited sketches of cowboy and Indian.

Meanwhile political caricature throve as never before.[2]

[1] Frank Weitenkampf, *American Graphic Art* (rev. edn., N. Y., 1912), chaps. xi, xiii; Hartmann, *American Art*, II, chap. ii.

[2] J. A. Mitchell, "Contemporary American Caricature," *Scribner's Mag.*, VI (1889), 728-745; anon., "Historical Campaign Caricature," *World's Work*, I (1900), 73-77; La T. Hancock, "American Caricature and Comic Art," *Bookman*, XVI (1902-1903), 120-131, 263-274; R. R. Wilson, "Caricature in America," *New England Mag.*, n.s., XXXI (1904-1905), 95-104; and esp. A. B. Maurice and F. T.

Thomas Nast's assaults on the Tweed Ring in the early 1870's had taught politicians the power of the cartoon as a partisan weapon; and, with the restoration of genuine party rivalry after the Hayes-Tilden contest, two weeklies devoted exclusively to humor were founded: *Puck* (1877), representing the Democratic point of view, and *Judge* (1881), representing the Republican.[1] Bernhard Gillam's forceful series in *Puck* in 1884, presenting James G. Blaine as the "Tattooed Man," did much to convince the voters that the Republican candidate had too checkered a political past to warrant their support.

The leading cartoonists, like Gillam himself, were of European birth and worked in the tradition of the *Fliegende Blätter*. From these weeklies the cruder form of comic art which became general in the newspapers of the 1890's was a logical development.[2] Of a somewhat different cast was *Life,* founded in 1883. Though Democratic in bias, it devoted its energies chiefly to social caricature, for which the growing urbanization, the life of the summer resorts and the manifold discomforts involved in being fashionable gave ample scope. One of its artists, Charles Dana Gibson, developed such skill in portraying the smart set that in the 1890's his black-and-white drawings of the "Gibson girl" and the "Gibson man," immaculately groomed and exultantly self-reliant, excited emulation among the younger generation throughout the land.

In sculpture, too, new forces were astir. Vulgar taste was typified by the civic monuments which began to dot

Cooper, *The History of the Nineteenth Century in Caricature* (N. Y., 1904), chaps. xxvi-xxxi.

[1] *Puck,* founded by the Austrian-American Joseph Keppler in 1876 as a German-language weekly, became English the next year. For Nast's cartoons of the Tweed Ring, see Nevins, *Emergence of Modern America,* 184, 311 and plate vii.

[2] See earlier, 188-190.

American towns in the late 1870's—statuary pieces of a pronounced foundry type intended to commemorate the heroic achievements of the late war.[1] Washington, commented an observer in 1884, is "in the military phase. Its statues represent warriors on horseback and on foot, some of them—most of them, in fact—wonderful to behold."[2] Except for Joseph Henry in front of the Smithsonian Institution no image of a scientist or artist or humanitarian was to be found anywhere in the nation's capital. Nor does the history of the times record the instance of a single general who, like Cato, preferred to have posterity ask why there was no statue of him rather than why there was. In the average household the acme of taste was represented by the plaster statuettes of John Rogers, illustrating such themes as "The Slave Auction," "One More Shot" and "The Emancipation Proclamation."

To stem this flood of mediocrity a high order of creative talent was needful; and fortunately this generation was able to supply it. Returning from Paris in the 1870's were sculptors as well as painters—young men bored with the cold neoclassicism of the Italian school which had hitherto dominated American sculpture, and skilled in the superior technique and greater naturalism of the French school. They endeavored to translate form into fresh and spirited compositions, often of a pictorial tendency, and they succeeded in stamping their art with an individuality which made it something more than derivative.[3]

[1] Factories were said to keep on hand a stock of military statues, complete in every detail except the number of the regiment, which was riveted on to suit the requirements. C. H. Caffin, *American Masters of Sculpture* (N. Y., 1903), 136.

[2] O. B. Frothingham, "Washington as It Should Be," *Atlantic Mo.*, LIII (1884), 841.

[3] Lorado Taft, *The History of American Sculpture* (J. C. Van Dyke, ed., *The History of American Art*, I, N. Y., 1903), pt. iii;

When the statue of Admiral Farragut was unveiled in 1881 in Madison Square, New York, its young author Augustus Saint-Gaudens at once took his place at the forefront of the new group. Of Irish birth, he had been identified with his adopted country since infancy, and his conception of Farragut, as well as his Lincoln Park statue of Lincoln (1887) in Chicago, revealed him as an accurate and forceful interpreter of the American spirit. His "Peace of God" (1891), erected at the grave of Mrs. Henry Adams in Rock Creek Cemetery, Washington, is generally accounted the greatest sculpture America has yet produced. A shrouded figure, the proud face expressing the majesty of despair, is made to symbolize the universality of grief while posing the eternal question: to what end? In these and other compositions his influence was profound. More than anyone else, he demonstrated the value of dignity and repose in sculptured figures and taught the importance of a proper setting.

To say that Saint-Gaudens stood first need not obscure the merits of his fellow artists. Less prolific than some, Olin L. Warner displayed an almost Greek sensitiveness to form, while Saint-Gaudens's pupil F. W. MacMonnies did his most distinctive work in the rendering of exuberant movement. One of MacMonnies's masterpieces, the bronze "Bacchante" (1894), became a moral issue in Puritan Boston. Rejected for the court of the public library, the "nude, drunken woman" was obliged to find sanctuary in the Metropolitan Museum of Art in New York.[1] Daniel Chester French, though almost wholly without foreign training, revealed equally

Hartmann, *American Art*, II, chap. i; La Follette, *Art in America*, 221-239; P. W. Bartlett, "American Sculpture and French Influence on Its Development," *N. Y. Times*, Feb. 9, 1913.

[1] In 1910 a replica was admitted to a rear hallway of the Museum of Fine Arts in Boston.

strongly the effects of transatlantic influence. His statue of John Harvard (1884), with its thoughtful face and sensitive hands, and his bronze allegory, "Death Staying the Hand of the Sculptor" (1892), in the Forest Hills Cemetery, Boston, were among the notable productions of the age.

A fuller and more unconventional talent found expression in the work of George Grey Barnard. Of Mid-Western rearing, Barnard's natural robustness of temper was accentuated by his studies with Rodin in Paris. Scorning mere decorative beauty, he devoted himself to subjects of crude and elemental strength. This is evidenced by one of his early symbolic pieces, "Brotherly Love" (1887), a strangely moving sculpture composed of a massive rough-hewn block in which two powerful nude figures are shown with groping hands, their faces half submerged in the marble. Though nothing less than an earthquake could have cleared away the monumental excrescences of American cities, yet the increasing public patronage accorded the newer sculptors and the excellence and variety of their work evinced a marked improvement in general taste. Their acceptance prefigured an epoch of even greater achievement in the years just ahead.[1]

While civic pride provided new opportunities for sculpture, the sheer growth of cities afforded new possibilities for architecture. Unfortunately the architectural traditions and practices inherited from the mid-century were unsafe guides.[2] Unfortunately, too, the ease with which factories could turn out iron ornaments and jig-saw wood into fantastic shapes proved a constant temptation to a people just learning to distinguish between pretentiousness and art. When city streets did not dis-

---

[1] See Faulkner, *Quest for Social Justice*, 274-276.
[2] See Nevins, *Emergence of Modern America*, 203-205.

play a monotonous regularity, they were apt to present an array of shrieking, discordant individualities which Bill Nye called the "mental hallucination and morbid delirium tremens peculiar to recent architecture."[1]

Yet already in 1878 this vernacular style showed signs of yielding to better standards.[2] Henry Hobson Richardson, fresh from his triumph of Trinity Church in Boston, trained in the best methods of the École des Beaux Arts, proceeded in the short years left him to sow Eastern cities with public and private structures in the Romanesque style of southern France. These sturdily built stone or brick edifices, marked by short massive columns, low arches, wide-spreading gables and heavy balconies, were imitated by architects and builders throughout the land. A recent critic has said that Richardson's houses were not defensible except in a military sense; but their very ruggedness and large simplicity was a needful object lesson to a nation which had run architecturally amuck. His deeper influence was reflected in the work of craftsmen who realized that the vigor of his treatment was independent of the detail he employed or of his style.

Like Richardson, most of the leading architects had had the benefit of Parisian training. In the 1880's Richard Morris Hunt, his senior in years, built the magnificent mansions of W. K. Vanderbilt and John Jacob Astor on Fifth Avenue in New York as well as summer "cottages" of equal splendor at Newport and elsewhere. Two of Richardson's pupils, C. F. McKim and Stanford White, associated in the New York firm of McKim, Mead and White, made their chief contributions in the

[1] Quoted in anon., "Crazy Quilt Architecture," *Scientific Am.*, LIII (1885), 49.

[2] For the new era in architecture, see T. E. Tallmadge, *The Story of Architecture in America* (N. Y., 1927), chaps. vii-x; Fiske Kimball, *American Architecture* (Indianapolis, 1928), chaps. x-xiii; G. H. Edgell, *The American Architecture of To-day* (N. Y., 1928), *passim*; La Follette, *Art in America*, 262-272.

classical style or some of its Renaissance derivatives, among their more notable edifices being the new buildings of Columbia University on Morningside Heights and the Boston Public Library.

Such architectural achievements denoted the growing acceptance of sound canons of design and construction, the substitution of harmony and beauty for eclecticism and ostentation. Nor were the improved standards confined to a few great cities or to the Atlantic Seaboard. "Some of the new residential streets of places as recent as Chicago or St. Paul," attested the editor of the American *Baedeker*, "more than hold their own . . . with any contemporaneous thoroughfares of their own class in Europe." [1] While the average abode continued to be contrived by carpenter or contractor, even at this level improvement appeared as a result of the better taste fostered by widely read magazines like *Scribner's*, *Harper's Bazar* and the *Ladies' Home Journal*. Domestic architecture, however, refused to be regimented. One of the features of these years was the unceasing warfare of styles: Romanesque, Queen Anne, Eastlake, Colonial, Victorian Gothic and nondescript blends of each and all of them.

The advances in domestic and public architecture were less distinctive of the age than the efforts to solve the problems created by the concentration of business in the down-town districts of cities. The need to economize ground area, coupled with the invention of the hydraulic (and later the electric) elevator, suggested great perpendicular buildings as the answer. If built of masonry, however, the supporting piers would be so huge as to devour the space in the lower floors most desirable for office use; Richardson's tallest structure, the Marshall Field Wholesale Building in Chicago, rose but seven

[1] J. F. Muirhead, *The Land of Contrasts* (Boston, 1898), 192.

stories from the street. Moreover, unlike the greatly admired builders of medieval times, the architect had to cope with countless difficulties as a result of modern systems of heating, lighting, plumbing and ventilation.[1]

Less bound by tradition than Boston or even New York, it was Chicago, only recently risen from its ashes, which discovered the solution. This was the use of iron or steel for the support of floors and walls, thus reducing the masonry to a mere veneer resting on a vast metal framework solidly riveted together and braced to resist stresses and strains. The first of all skyscrapers was the Home Insurance Building in Chicago in 1885, contrived by William LeB. Jenney and rising ten stories.[2] Soon, with constant structural improvements, followed the twelve-story Rookery Building, designed by the firm of Burnham & Root, the fourteen-story Tacoma Building, by Holabird & Roche, and in 1891 the Masonic Temple, one of Burnham's creations, which soared skyward for twenty-one stories. The challenging opportunities afforded by this marriage of art and engineering brought to the fore a trio of great leaders: Daniel Burnham, John W. Root and, most individual of the three, Louis Sullivan, who "had the analytical mind of a scientist, the soul of a dreamer and artist."[3] A skyscraper, said Mait-

[1] Henry Van Brunt, "On the Present Condition and Prospects of Architecture," *Atlantic Mo.*, LVII (1886), esp. 381-382, and his "Architecture in the West," same mag., LXIV (1889), esp. 778.

[2] W. A. Starrett, *Skyscrapers and the Men Who Build Them* (N. Y., 1928), chaps. i-iii; Francisco Mujica, *History of the Skyscraper* (Paris, 1929), chaps. i-ii. The credit for designing, rather than building, the first example of the new structural form has been claimed for the Minneapolis architect, L. S. Buffington, who finished the plans for a twenty-eight-story structure in 1883. H. W. Corbett, "America's Great Gift to Architecture," *N. Y. Times Mag.*, March 18, 1928; Starrett, *Skyscrapers*, 27-28.

[3] Kimball, *American Architecture*, 153. The Wainwright Building (1890) in St. Louis and the Transportation Building at the Chicago World's Fair, the latter of course not a skyscraper, were in Sullivan's best vein.

land's *American Slang Dictionary* (1891) in the earliest known definition, is "a very tall building such as now are being built in Chicago."

But New York was already entering the race and, spurred by her narrow insular limits, her office structures soon began to overtop those of Chicago. Her loftiest achievement came in the final year of the period with the completion of the twenty-nine-story Ivins Syndicate Building. The soar and sweep of the great vertical structures stirred the imagination of the average man. They emphasized the new elements in modern life rather than its continuity with the past. As one contemporary said, "I admire the daring, wisdom, and genius of the men who designed and erected them without reference—in the jargon of politics—to any other nation on earth." [1] Many æsthetic critics, however, seeing in the skyscraper only an elongated boxlike structure, perceived in it neither beauty nor the possibilities of beauty.

All the aspiring artistic tendencies of the period reached a brilliant climax in the World's Columbian Exposition, held at Chicago from May 1 to October 26, 1893.[2] As early as 1889 New York, Washington, St. Louis and Chicago had begun to urge upon Congress their respective claims as the appropriate place for celebrating the four-hundredth anniversary of the discovery of America. But the great midland metropolis, conscious of her waxing power, eager for notice, heady with ambition, was not to be denied. When the matter came up for decision in the spring of 1890, she carried Con-

[1] O. L. Triggs, "Democratic Art," *Forum*, XXVI (1898-1899), 75. See also A. L. A. Himmelwright, "High Buildings," *N. Am. Rev.*, CLXIII (1896), 580-586.

[2] The exposition was a year late in being held. *History of the World's Fair* (n.p., 1893), by B. C. Truman and others prominently connected with the exposition, recites the main facts.

gress by storm. At once a national commission was appointed, particularly for intercourse with foreign nations, and a local corporation was formed for planning and conducting the enterprise.

A skeptical East, blind to the recent cultural progress of the Middle West, visioned a colossal but tasteless display of the nation's economic resources as the outcome. Chicago's answer was decisive. America's most noted landscape architect, F. L. Olmsted, was called into consultation, and with him were associated the principal architects, sculptors, painters and engineers of the nation under Burnham's general supervision. "Look here," cried Saint-Gaudens as the leaders gathered to consider their tentative plans, "do you realize that this is the greatest meeting of artists since the fifteenth century!" [1] Coming from many different parts of the country, representing many different points of view, these men worked with a zeal and concert of purpose which made their finished product a landmark in the history of American artistic achievement.[2] The classical rather than the Romanesque style was adopted as the prevailing architectural mode.

On the shore of Lake Michigan a rough, tangled stretch of bog and dune was transformed into a dream of loveliness. No one who set foot within the Court of Honor, the crowning glory of the whole, could fail to be thrilled by the beauty of the spectacle—the splashing fountains, the snowy colonnades, the graceful arches, the gleaming domes, the clustered sculptures, all set off with greenery and interlaced by lagoons of tranquil water. Within, the principal buildings were decorated

[1] Charles Moore, *Daniel H. Burnham* (Boston, 1921), I, 47.
[2] Edgell, *American Architecture of To-day*, 42-49, 68; Tallmadge, *Story of Architecture*, chap. viii; Moore, *Burnham*, I, chaps. iv-vi; Henry Van Brunt, "The Columbian Exposition and American Civilization," *Atlantic Mo.*, LXXI (1893), 577-588.

*The World's Columbian Exposition*

by the foremost mural painters of the nation, while in the regal Palace of Fine Arts there was spread before the visitor an array of the products of pen, brush and chisel in which American artists easily held their own with their European contemporaries. Like other international expositions, the fair was also a mammoth ledger on which were recorded the nation's material achievements. Foreign countries, too, displayed their distinctive wares; and the Midway Plaisance, with its great Ferris Wheel, its Streets of Cairo and other exotic attractions, provided a playground for the twelve million visitors.[1] The event, moreover, was made the occasion for holding important congresses of scientists, scholars and students of affairs.

But it was the sheer splendor of the ensemble, rather than any special feature, that made the "White City" so significant in its impress on American civilization. The bad business conditions resulting from the Panic of 1893 seemed to have little effect upon attendance. The exposition was visited, in great part, by average men and women, particularly from the Middle West, whose lives had hitherto been colorless and narrow, many of whom indeed had never before seen a large city. "Sell the cook stove if necessary and come," wrote Hamlin Garland to his aged parents on their Dakota farm. "You *must* see this fair."[2] They came, saw and, like countless other rural folk, were moved to tears by the compelling power of its beauty. Even sophisticated Easterners like Charles Eliot Norton and Henry Adams were poignantly stirred.[3]

Only seventeen years had elapsed since the Centennial

[1] This is the official estimate. The admissions totaled 27,500,000. Truman and others, *World's Fair*, 609.

[2] Garland, *Son of the Middle Border*, 458-461.

[3] Norton was moved to say to William James that if he were a younger man he would like to cast his lot with a city like Chicago. Moore, *Burnham*, I, 78-79; Henry Adams, *The Education of Henry Adams* (Boston, 1918), 339-343.

Exposition in Philadelphia but, in terms of artistic accomplishment, a whole age had passed. Just as the earlier event had awakened the nation somewhat from its preoccupation with commercial gain, so the World's Fair quickened and strengthened all the new forces making for æsthetic appreciation in American life. While Chicago and Middle America were most directly affected, no part of the country remained untouched.[1] If rural families began to demand better taste in their surroundings, it was no less true that creative artists everywhere worked with renewed inspiration, and that municipal authorities for the first time began seriously to plan cities made beautiful with boulevards and wooded stretches and vistas. The Chicago exposition was both the visual evidence and the promise of a new stage in American civilization.

[1] Alice F. Palmer, "Some Lasting Results of the World's Fair," *Forum*, XVI (1893-1894), 517-523; M. C. Robbins, "The Art of Public Improvement," *Atlantic Mo.*, LXXVIII (1896), esp. 751; H. B. Fuller, "The Upward Movement in Chicago," *Atlantic Mo.*, LXXX (1897), esp. 534.

# CHAPTER IX

## THE PURSUIT OF HAPPINESS

JAMES A. GARFIELD, pausing at Lake Chautauqua for a nonpartisan address during his presidential campaign in 1880, declared: "We may divide the whole struggle of the human race into two chapters; first, the fight to get leisure; and then the second fight of civilization—what shall we do with our leisure when we get it." [1] There can be no doubt that the closing decades of the century marked a great advance on the part of the American people in gaining freedom from bread-winning toil. Nearly all classes were affected: the extremely rich whose idle wives and children knew so well how to "make amusement into a business"; [2] the wage-earners who benefited from the gradual shortening of the workday; the salaried workers who were coming to consider a two weeks' summer vacation part of the normal conditions of employment. Only the tillers of the soil continued to live very much as of yore. To the farmers, more toil, rather than less, seemed necessary to pull them out of their slough; and constant contrast with the frivolous aspects of urban life deepened the conviction of the older generation that leisure was a polite name for laziness.

It was, indeed, in the city that the people were squarely engaged in "the second fight of civilization." With more leisure at their command than so large a

[1] J. L. Hurlbut, *The Story of Chautauqua* (N. Y., 1921), 184.

[2] James Bryce's phrase in *The American Commonwealth* (London, 1888), III, 559. See earlier, 151-154.

body of mankind had ever before enjoyed, their use or abuse of its opportunities would give at least a provisional answer to the question as to the capacity of the masses to achieve the arts and graces of living. Certainly the new freedom caught many methodically ordered lives in a state of dishabille. Life under American conditions had taught them how to work but not how to relax.[1] They were inclined to pursue their avocations with the same feverish intensity that had won success in their other undertakings. As Matthew Arnold remarked in 1883 while in New York, "Old Froissart, who said of the English of his day, that 'they take their pleasures sadly, after their fashion,' would, doubtless, if he lived now, say of the Americans, that they take their pleasures hurriedly, after their fashion." [2]

For the average person no use of leisure so well suited his taste as that afforded by the ubiquitous fraternal orders which sprang up during the last quarter of the century. Earlier organizations of this character had been few in number and usually imported from abroad.[3] Now Americans turned with furious zeal to the creation of secret societies cut to their own pattern. In the large cities some form of organized social commingling seemed called for to replace the spontaneous friendliness of small rural towns. Liberty and equality this generation was willing to take for granted, but fraternity filled a compelling human need. Moreover, the romantic opportunity to posture before a mystic brotherhood in

[1] For a contemporaneous appreciation of this fact, see C. D. Warner, "Aspects of American Life," *Atlantic Mo.*, XLIII (1879), 1-9.

[2] Quoted by W. G. Moody, *Land and Labor in the United States* (N. Y., 1883), 279.

[3] Such as the Freemasons (1730) and the Odd Fellows (1819), introduced from England, the Ancient Order of Hibernians (1836) from Ireland, the German Turnerbund (1850) and the Bohemian Sokol (1865). For the earlier antagonism to secret societies, see C. R. Fish, *The Rise of the Common Man* (*A History of American Life*, VI), 39-40.

all the glory of robe, plume and sword restored a sense of self-importance bruised by the anonymity of life amidst great crowds.[1] If further inducement were needed, it was supplied by the provision made by most lodges for sickness and death benefits for their members.[2]

Though some important indigenous orders like the Knights of Pythias and the Elks had appeared in the sixties, in the two decades after 1880 their number became legion. At least one hundred and twenty-four new secret societies were founded between 1880 and 1890, one hundred and thirty-six between 1890 and 1895, and two hundred and thirty more by 1901.[3] The nomenclature of fraternalism will doubtless some day offer interesting material for the student of suppressed desires and wishful thinking, but to one of less imaginative endowment there seems little enough in common among such names as the Knights and Ladies of the Golden Rule, the Royal Society of Good Fellows, the Modern Woodmen of America, the American Order of Druids, the Owls, the Prudent Patricians of Pompeii and the Concatenated Order of Hoo-Hoo.

As was to be expected, membership was greatest in the urbanized sections of the country notwithstanding the energy with which the Negroes of the South aped their white brethren and the increasing interest of Western farmers in lodge activities. By the end of the period there were over six million names on the rosters of

[1] H. C. Merwin, "A National Vice," *Atlantic Mo.*, LXXI (1893), esp. 769; W. B. Hill, "The Great American Safety-Valve," *Century*, XLIV (1892), 383-384.

[2] Walter Basye, *History and Operation of Fraternal Insurance* (Rochester, 1919), chaps. i, iv-v.

[3] These data are taken from H. B. Meyer, "Fraternal Beneficiary Societies in the United States," *Am. Journ. of Sociology*, VI, 655-656. According to this enumeration, which seems more reliable than the somewhat different estimates in A. C. Stevens, comp., *Cyclopaedia of Fraternities* (N. Y., 1899), only seventy-eight fraternal orders antedated 1880.

fraternal bodies.[1] America possessed more secret societies and a larger number of "joiners" than all other nations. The "big four" were the Odd Fellows, the Freemasons, the Knights of Pythias and the Ancient Order of United Workmen which collectively embraced more than one third of the entire lodge membership. Nor did students of religion fail to note that in all the large cities the lodges outnumbered the churches, Brooklyn and Boston each having twice and St. Louis and Chicago three times as many.[2]

The great increase of city dwellers also provided wider patronage for the theater. As the nation's metropolis New York was the chief producing center; its supremacy in matters histrionic was unquestioned.[3] There money could be found for new theatrical ventures, there actors' reputations were won or lost, there aspiring playwrights flocked to offer their wares. There, too, in the field of the polite drama, were to be found the three greatest producing managers of the 1880's: J. Lester Wallack, Augustin Daly and A. M. Palmer. At their theaters they maintained stock companies which gave the best performances of the era and included such finished players as Fanny Davenport, Ada Rehan, Stuart Robson, Charles Coghlan, James O'Neil and Annie Russell.

Throughout the decade, however, the resident stock-company type of production was losing ground to the

---

[1] Stevens, *Cyclopaedia*, v, 114; W. S. Harwood, "Secret Societies in the United States," *N. Am. Rev.*, CLXIV (1897), 617-624; J. M. Foster, "Secret Societies and the State," *Arena*, XIX (1898), 229-239.

[2] Josiah Strong, *The New Era* (N. Y., 1893), 128 n.

[3] Anon., "New York Theatres," *Atlantic Mo.*, XLIII (1879), 452-455. For general treatments of the drama during the period, see L. C. Strang, *Players and Plays of the Last Quarter Century* (Boston, 1902), II; M. J. Moses, *The American Dramatist* (Boston, 1926), chaps. v-xi; Arthur Hornblow, *A History of the Theatre in America* (Phila., 1919), chaps. xxiii-xxix; Mary C. Crawford, *The Romance of the American Theatre* (Boston, 1913), chaps. xii-xiv; A. H. Quinn, *A History of the American Drama from the Civil War* (N. Y., 1927), I.

traveling company and the "star" system.[1] Easier and cheaper means of transportation led newer producers to reach out for the patronage that awaited in the cities of the hinterland. With this in view it was more profitable to employ a featured actor, supported by nonentities, than to maintain the standards of performance which a sophisticated New York audience expected at a place like Daly's or Palmer's Madison Square Theatre. The new system also benefited local managers by relieving them of the greater financial risks of a stock company.

As road companies multiplied, the supply of actor talent could not keep up with the demand.[2] Some of the pathetic or ludicrous mishaps which befell the roving Thespians were less attributable to the arrested mental development of their audiences than to their own histrionic deficiencies. A performance of a perennially popular play was dismissed by a Minnesota paper in the 1890's with the laconic comment: "Thompson's Uncle Tom's Cabin company appeared at the opera house last night. The dogs were poorly supported."[3] A favorite subject with cartoonists in *Puck* and *Judge* was the hollow-cheeked actor attired in a mangy fur-collared overcoat and straw hat, indulging in delusions of grandeur before a group of his fellow artists similarly arrayed. "We notice of late," said the *New York Dramatic News* of March 29, 1884, "that professionals

---

[1] The *N. Y. Dramatic Mirror* in 1879 listed the routes of forty-nine traveling companies; twenty years later the list was nearly ten times as great.

[2] Difficulties of booking also increased, leading by gradual stages to the formation of a theatrical syndicate or trust in 1896. See M. B. Leavitt, *Fifty Years in Theatrical Management* (N. Y., 1912), 265-272; J. L. Ford, *Forty-Odd Years in the Literary Shop* (N. Y., 1921), chap. xii; Norman Hapgood, *The Stage in America, 1897-1900* (N. Y., 1901), chap. i; and H. U. Faulkner, *The Quest for Social Justice* (*A History of American Life*, XI), 300.

[3] Cited by W. W. Stout, "Little Eva Is Seventy-Five," *Sat. Eve. Post*, CC, 10 ff. (Oct. 8, 1927).

returning by rail to New York after the company has 'busted up' have got past complaining of this mode of travel. . . . They admit, however, that it is exceedingly annoying to have to get off the track so often to allow the trains to pass up and down." Yet so great was the lure of the footlights that between 1880 and 1900 the number of actors increased from less than five thousand to nearly fifteen thousand.[1]

To satisfy the miscellaneous public which now went to plays, the theater had to spread a fare pleasing to many palates and all pocketbooks. While some persons attended, or imagined they did, to enjoy the drama as a form of art, the vast majority frankly sought amusement, forgetfulness or the thrill of vicarious romance or adventure. Yet the serious drama has perhaps never been better presented in America than in the 1880's and 1890's. To see Edwin Booth or John McCullough as Hamlet; Mary Anderson portray Galatea or Juliet; Lawrence Barrett, Cassius; or Clara Morris, Camille, was an experience no theatergoer was ever likely to forget.

One of the versatile and successful actresses of the time was Louisa Lane Drew whose theatrical career went back to her first stage appearance in 1827. During her seventy years before the footlights she played with nearly every noted actor from Edwin Forrest to Joseph Jefferson. What was of even greater consequence was the fact that she was the founder of America's most famous actor family.[2] In the 1870's two of her children, John and Georgiana, began to establish themselves as players in their own right, the former as an accomplished member

---

[1] These figures include performers in musical plays as well as the legitimate drama. *U. S. Tenth Census* (1880), I, 744; *U. S. Twelfth Census* (1900), II, cxliv.

[2] M. J. Moses, *Famous Actor-Families in America* (N. Y., 1906), chap. vii.

of Augustin Daly's troupe. In 1876 Georgiana Drew, then in "The Princess Royal," married a fellow performer, a handsome young Oxford graduate named Maurice Barrymore. In 1878-1879 a road company, headed by the Barrymores and John Drew, started on tour, and subsequent years often found two or more of the Drew-Barrymore connection acting together. The three Barrymore children, Lionel, Ethel and John, could hardly escape their destiny. Lionel made his début in 1893 in "The Rivals," in which his grandmother, Louisa Lane Drew, was playing the part of Mrs. Malaprop; three years later Ethel began her stage career as a member of her uncle John Drew's company.

Native performers, however, had to look to their laurels as the promise of unusual profits attracted to American shores the foremost artists of the European stage. Players like Sarah Bernhardt, Tommaso Salvini, Henry Irving, Helena Modjeska, Adelaide Ristori and Eleanora Duse could always count on an enthusiastic welcome.[1] On the other hand, American actors—Booth, Barrett, Ada Rehan and others—met with a cordial response in England and on the Continent when they betook themselves thence.

Just as the reading public demanded fictional treatments of American life, so theatergoers were increasingly eager to see plays about themselves—plays depicting American types, American backgrounds, and humorous or exciting situations compatible with American conditions.[2] Departing from the custom of older producers like Daly and Wallack, venturesome young managers—

[1] Ford, *Forty-Odd Years*, 137-143, 249-251; Crawford, *Romance of American Theatre*, chap. xii; Leavitt, *Fifty Years*, 488-502; H. A. Clapp, *Reminiscences of a Dramatic Critic* (Boston, 1902), chaps. xvi-xvii, xx.

[2] Strang, *Players and Plays*, II, chap. vii. The lack of an international copyright provision until 1891 was a discouragement to the native playwright as well as to the native *littérateur*. See earlier, 252-255.

David Belasco, Charles and Daniel Frohman and others —perceived the box-office possibilities of the native drama and used it as a means of climbing to a position of financial stability and eventual theatrical dominance. Though some of the plays like "Pudd'nhead Wilson" and "Editha's Burglar" were dramatizations of popular novels, every year saw a greater number prepared in first instance for the stage. "Hazel Kirke," written by Steele MacKaye, had a New York run of four hundred and eighty-six nights, beginning on February 4, 1880. This record was exceeded only by another play of native authorship, Charles Hoyt's "A Trip to Chinatown," which started its career of six hundred and fifty nights on November 9, 1891. The successive offerings of Bronson Howard, the foremost American dramatist of the time, were also usually certain of a cordial reception. "The Young Mrs. Winthrop," produced in 1882, continued uninterruptedly in New York for more than one hundred and fifty nights, while three years later "One of Our Girls" held the boards for two hundred nights. "The Henrietta," produced in 1887, ran for sixty-eight weeks, earning admission receipts of nearly half a million dollars.

Though MacKaye's greatest success and some of Howard's pieces had a European setting, native playwrights turned more and more to purely American themes and materials. Like the local-color novel, the drama of rural life made a special appeal to nostalgic city dwellers desirous of renewing their childhood memories. A prime favorite was "Joshua Whitcomb" (later renamed "The Old Homestead") which toured the country almost continuously with Denman Thompson, who had helped write it, in the title rôle of the simple, lovable old farmer. Two other popular hits were "The County Fair," by Charles Barnard and Neil Burgess, first staged

in 1889, and Lottie Blair Parker's "Way Down East,"
produced early in 1898, each of which enjoyed an
initial New York run of more than a year. Thickly but-
tered with sentimentality and rural heroics, such offerings suffered artistically beside James A. Herne's "Shore
Acres," first performed in Chicago in 1892. Herne was
an apostle of realism in the drama in much the same
sense that his friends, Howells and Garland, were of
realism in literature.[1] "Shore Acres," though largely
devoid of theatricalism and dealing primarily with the
fundamentals of human character, was nevertheless long
in demand.

In general, however, the public did not care to see
real life on the stage. One could hardly have guessed
from the serious drama, as he might from the serious
fiction, that industrialism and the growth of cities were
thrusting forward acute problems to plague society. For
purposes of stage presentation all such matters had to
be given a comic turn. By exploiting humorous possibilities of immigrant life, Edward Harrigan succeeded in
writing a series of hilarious comedies about the relations
of the embattled Mulligans with their friendly enemies,
the Lochmüllers—pieces which incidentally shed much
light on the feudal character of New York machine politics.[2] Other aspects of the passing scene were caricatured
by Charles Hoyt who turned off a succession of rapid-
fire farces which reached their climax in "A Texas Steer"
(1890) and "A Trip to Chinatown" (1891), already

---

[1] His more important play "Margaret Fleming," produced in 1890,
proved quite too bold in its realism, according to the standards of the
time, to win public favor. Herne's confession of faith, "Art for Truth's
Sake in the Drama," *Arena*, XVII (1897), 361-370, is a significant
document in the history of the American drama.

[2] Among Harrigan's chief comedies were "The Mulligan Guard Ball"
(1879), "The Mulligan Guard Nominee" (1880) and "Cordelia's
Aspirations" (1883). Harrigan also acted in the plays; and the team
name of Harrigan and Hart was considered by theatergoers a guarantee
of an evening of unmitigated fun.

mentioned. Profiting by his experience as paragrapher on the *Boston Post*, he paraded before his delighted audiences all the stock characters of comic journalism: the temperance crank, the mannish feminist, the social climber, the chronic joiner, the spiritualist, the baseball hero and their like.

The comedy of contemporary manners was also cultivated with notable facility by Howard, Belasco and, starting in the 1890's, by the youthful Clyde Fitch. But as the generation which had fought the Civil War died off, such dramatists turned to romantic plays based on the sectional struggle and its outcome. William Gillette's "Held by the Enemy" (1886), Howard's "Shenandoah" (1888), Augustus Thomas's "Alabama" (1891) and Belasco's "The Heart of Maryland" (1895) proved to be among the most popular offerings of the closing years.

A great many playgoers, however, demanded stronger meat than the polite drama offered. Nourished on the dime novel and the yellow press, they saw life in terms of startling contrasts and swift sensational action. "Uncle Tom's Cabin," greatest of all native melodramas, retained its accustomed following only by introducing novel features.[1] A half-dozen or more troupes, in the eighties and later, gave performances featured by two Toms, two Evas, two Topsys and two Simon Legrees. In the nineties the colored pugilist, Peter Jackson, played Uncle Tom in one company, sparring three friendly rounds with Joe Choynski who played George Shelby. A rival company presented John L. Sullivan in the part of Simon Legree. Meantime "East Lynne" retained its earlier vogue; and "The Two Orphans," a French adaptation first produced in 1874 with Kate

---

[1] J. F. Davis, "Tom Shows," *Scribner's Mag.*, LXXVII (1925), 350-360.

Claxton as the blind orphan, reached its twenty-five-hundredth performance at Dayton, Ohio, on May 6, 1884.[1]

More distinctive of the changing national scene were the gun-and-gore dramas of Western life in which, it will be remembered, Buffalo Bill and other actual frontier Bills strode the boards.[2] These presently gave way to a plethora of melodramas depicting the dangers and wickedness of metropolitan life, endless variants of the theme of honest Nell and the city slicker. Although the better dramatists occasionally indulged, such pieces were ordinarily concocted by specialists in the *genre* like Charles Gayler, C. H. Foster and Bartley Campbell. Foster was responsible for more than seventy-five thrillers, including "Bertha, the Sewing-Machine Girl," "The Gunmaker's Bride" and "The Turf Digger's Doom." Campbell, before he went insane in 1886, produced "The Galley Slave," "The White Slave" and other smashing hits, besides composing the deathless line, "Rags are royal raiment when worn for virtue's sake."[3] On Campbell's letterhead were displayed portraits of himself and Shakespeare with the legend, "A friendly rivalry." Any lack of plausibility in such effusions was compensated for by the scenic effects: snowstorms, raging fires, shipwrecks, the thundering approach of the fast mail. The standard admission price was ten, twenty and thirty cents, and the plays proved quite as popular in the great cities as in the country villages where they were often presented, with nightly changes, under canvas.

The principal attraction in the rural towns, however, was the circus, which reached the zenith of its popular-

---

[1] *N. Y. Dramatic Mirror*, XLI, no. 1043, 40 (Dec. 24, 1898).
[2] See earlier, 51.
[3] Quinn, *American Drama from the Civil War*, I, 118-124.

ity in the last quarter of the century with nearly forty organizations annually on tour.[1] Traveling by train or wagon during the warm seasons, the human freaks and exotic animals were exhibited in the ubiquitous dime museums during the winter while the acrobats dispersed into the vaudeville circuits. When the two principal circus magnates, P. T. Barnum and J. A. Bailey, combined their shows in 1881, they set a new pace for their competitors, signalized further by acquisition of the elephant Jumbo from the Royal Zoological Gardens, a piece of Yankee enterprise loudly resented by the London populace. Intense rivalry with the Adam Forepaugh circus led in 1882 to a short-lived agreement for a division of routes between them and later to the purchase of the Forepaugh outfit. American circuses, notably Barnum & Bailey's, also met with great favor abroad, and one, W. W. Cole's Colossal Circus, in 1880-1881 made a thirty-thousand-mile tour to Australia and New Zealand.

While circuses grew bigger, it is doubtful whether the Toby Tylers of the time thought they grew better, for the increasing size of the "big top" diminished the importance of the clowns whose fun making under the new conditions was reduced mainly to broad pantomime and slapstick acrobatics. The chief new development in tent entertainment was the advent of Buffalo Bill's Wild West Show in 1883, a truly autochthonous circus exhibiting to the descendants of pioneers stirring glimpses of vanishing frontier life, including real cowboys, Indian attacks, bronco busting and stagecoach holdups.[2]

[1] Leavitt, *Fifty Years*, chaps. x-xi; M. R. Werner, *Barnum* (N. Y., 1923), chap. xiii.

[2] In the second season Sitting Bull and other Sioux who had participated in the Custer massacre joined the company. W. F. Cody (Buffalo Bill, *pseud.*), *Story of the Wild West and Camp Fire Chats* (Chicago, 1902), 693-700, and Leavitt, *Fifty Years*, esp. 143.

*Horsemanship Delights All Classes*

When Buffalo Bill took his show to England in 1887, the tour netted seven hundred thousand dollars and it is said that Gladstone witnessed the performance no less than six times.

It was the production of the Gilbert and Sullivan operas in America, beginning with "Pinafore" in 1878, that brought music into general favor as a form of light entertainment. The delightful nonsense of these two British masters of the art not only set a high standard, but also helped break down a popular disapproval based on the supposed naughtiness of musical shows of the "Black Crook" type.[1] A veritable "Pinafore" craze ensued, with amateur productions galore, an endless number of hastily assembled road companies and at one time, in 1881, five simultaneous New York presentations. The chief home of comic opera was the New York Casino, opened in 1882 under the direction of Rudolph Aronson.[2] His presentation in 1886 of "Erminie," an English operetta with Pauline Hall and Francis Wilson in the leading rôles, enjoyed a phenomenal run of twelve hundred and fifty-six performances. It was the Casino stage which established the reputation of such favorites as Lillian Russell, Fay Templeton, De Wolf Hopper and David Warfield, making it possible for them in time to go forth as stars heading their own companies.

In Boston the best standards of light opera were maintained by a company first known as the Boston Ideals and then the Bostonians. H. C. Barnabee, Marie Stone,

---

[1] See Allan Nevins, *The Emergence of Modern America* (*A History of American Life*, VIII), 93. The staid *Philadelphia Public Ledger* editorially gave "Pinafore" a clean bill of health and invited the attendance of the pure-minded. J. P. Sousa, *Marching Along* (Boston, 1928), 62.

[2] T. A. Brown, *A History of the New York Stage* (N. Y., 1903), III, 485-506; Rudolph Aronson, *Theatrical and Musical Memoirs* (N. Y., 1913), chaps. iv-viii; same author, "Most Successful Operetta Ever Heard Here," *Theatre*, XVIII (1913), 17 ff.

Eugene Cowles and Jessie Bartlett Davis were their bright particular stars. In 1890 they presented in Chicago Reginald de Koven's "Robin Hood," one of the most melodious and certainly the most popular American operetta ever written.[1] This striking success led to almost yearly scores from De Koven's pen and made easier the path of other composers such as John Philip Sousa and the Irish American, Victor Herbert. Among the most successful operas of the closing years were Sousa's "El Capitan" and Herbert's "The Wizard of the Nile."

Musical extravaganza after the English fashion also enjoyed wide popularity. One of the most famous, "Evangeline," first presented in 1875, was frequently revived, being played over five thousand times.[2] At its vulgarest, musical entertainment took the form of burlesque—performances patronized by males who were more intent on nature's lines than on the author's and in which music served as a pretext for suggestive posing.[3] Meantime the old-fashioned black-face minstrel show, confronted with competition on every hand, became constantly bigger and more pretentious, but thereby lost

[1] H. B. Smith, *First Nights and First Editions* (Boston, 1931), esp. chap. xviii; C. B. Palmer, "As the Bostonians Caroled a Half Century Ago," *Boston Transcript*, Dec. 27, 1930; H. C. Barnabee, *Reminiscences* (Boston, 1913), chaps. xxvii-xxxvii.

[2] "Adonis" (1884) in which Henry E. Dixey starred and "1492," first produced in Chicago during the World's Fair, were other successes of a similar kind under E. E. Rice's direction. Leavitt, *Fifty Years*, 315-316; L. C. Strang, *Celebrated Comedians of Light Opera and Musical Comedy* (Boston, 1901), 195-202.

[3] M. J. O'Neill, *How He Does It. Sam T. Jack* (Chicago, 1895), is a highly colored, press agent's account of the "King of Burlesque," who at the date of publication was proprietor of Lilly Clay's Colossal Gaiety Company, the Ada Richmond Folly Company, the Creole Burlesque Company, the Big Burlesque Company, the Big Brazilian Company, the Mazeppa Company and other similar troupes which were advertised by such descriptions as: "50—Pairs of Rounded Limbs, Ruby Lips, Tantalizing Torsos—50." Everyone, of course, understood that the "limbs" and "torsos" would be clothed in tights, usually of cotton.

its distinctive flavor and eventually its grip on the public.[1] The thirty-odd touring minstrel companies of the early 1880's dwindled to perhaps ten in the late nineties.

In place of the minstrel show there sprang up a type of theatrical *mélange* better adapted to the restlessness of city life and the urban dwellers' craving for novelty.[2] Like megalopolis itself, vaudeville was of hybrid origin, tracing its paternity variously to the dime museum (in which the youthful Weber and Fields got their start), the cheap variety hall with its rude stage and loose women, the circus and the minstrel show. Following the Civil War Tony Pastor in New York strove valiantly to purvey variety without vulgarity, but it was not until the early 1880's that modern "refined vaudeville" really established itself.[3] When B. F. Keith in 1885 introduced into Boston the continuous performance, he added a feature so popular that it was presently adopted by his rivals.[4] Keith, F. F. Proctor, J. W. Considine and other managers vigorously exploited the new field, acquiring more theaters, developing circuits and improving the quality of their offerings. Legitimate actors were tempted by fancy salaries to try the "con-

[1] Carl Wittke, *Tambo and Bones* (Durham, 1930), esp. chap. iii.

[2] "The vaudeville theatre belongs to the era of the department store and the short story," wrote E. M. Royle in "The Vaudeville Theatre," *Scribner's Mag.*, XXVI (1899), 495.

[3] Leavitt claims he was the first to adopt the word, vaudeville, for a variety show, in 1880. *Fifty Years*, 189, 382. But C. P. Sawyer, "Mirrors of Variety," *Boston Transcript*, Oct. 2, 1926, found the term used in America as early as 1852; and a handbill in the Boston Public Library shows that in 1840 there was a "Vaudeville Saloon" in Boston which presented variety. On the rise of modern vaudeville, see anon., "Twenty Years of Vaudeville," *N. Y. Dramatic Mirror*, XLI, 90-95 (Dec. 24, 1898); and W. J. Kingsley, "Thirty Years of Vaudeville," same mag., LXX, 4-5 (Nov. 26, 1913).

[4] B. F. Keith, "The Origin of Continuous Vaudeville," *N. Y. Dramatic Mirror*, XLI, 95-96 (Dec. 24, 1898). Proctor introduced the innovation into New York in 1893. Keith two years later showed the first motion pictures in connection with vaudeville. Leavitt, *Fifty Years*, 205-206.

tinuous" from time to time, and the vaudeville stage in
turn proved a training ground for musical-comedy talent. Vaudeville accounted for the attendance of perhaps
half the theatergoers in the 1890's. Keith's circuit alone,
though embracing but four theaters and not showing on
Sundays, entertained over five million annually.[1]

People living or visiting in the cities could hardly
escape the contagion of the latest popular tune. If they
avoided the theater and the amusement park, the strains
assailed their ears from the Italian organ grinder or the
roving German street band. Each year, too, saw improvements in the phonograph, first put upon the market by Edison in 1877-1878. The original instrument,
consisting of a tin-foil cylinder record turned by a hand
crank, emitted loud, scarcely recognizable sounds; but
further experimentation by Edison, C. A. Bell, C. S.
Tainter, Emile Berliner and others led to the use of flat
waxlike disks operated by spring or battery motors and
resulting in much clearer tone reproduction.[2] How many
of these contrivances invaded American homes in the
1880's and 1890's it is impossible to say, but in the
single year 1900 over one hundred and fifty thousand
machines and nearly three million records were sold.

The rage for popular music was without precedent
in the earlier history of America. Chosen by a spontaneous universal suffrage, these melodies were subject to
the proverbial fickleness of democracy. Most of them
were composed by self-made bards who did not venture
beyond the average person's singing range of eight notes
or less. However trivial or trite the words, they are of
continuing interest to the student of American life as
current memoranda of manners, emotions, morals and

[1] Royle, "Vaudeville Theatre," 485.
[2] U. S. Twelfth Census, X, 181-184; P. G. Hubert, "The New
Talking Machines," Atlantic Mo., LXIII (1889), 256-261.

absurdities. The same thick vein of sentimentality
mined by the yellow press and the writers of sentimental romances and melodrama found musical outlet
in an endless succession of moralistic ballads, characterized by such "hits" as Jennie Lindsay's "Always Take
Mother's Advice" (1884) —

> To you in this world she is dearest,
> At your downfall her grief is severest;

Charles Graham's "The Picture That Is Turned to the
Wall" (1891) —the story of why one girl left home;
Charles K. Harris's "After the Ball" (1892) —

> Many a heart is aching,
>    If you could read them all;
> Many the hopes that have vanish'd
>    After the ball;

Gussie L. Davis's "The Fatal Wedding" (1893) —
"Just another fatal wedding, Just another broken
heart"; James Thornton's "She May Have Seen Better
Days" (1894) ; Joe Stern's "My Mother Was a Lady"
(1896) —

> I've come to this great city
>    To find a brother dear,
> And you wouldn't dare insult me, Sir,
>    If Jack were only here;

and Paul Dresser's "On the Banks of the Wabash"
(1896).[1] Few of such songs, however, attained the
musical distinction of De Koven's "O Promise Me"
which, popularized by Jessie Bartlett Davis in "Robin

---

[1] In every case above the composer's name is given. Many popular
songs of the period have been reprinted by Sigmund Spaeth in *Read
'Em and Weep* (Garden City, 1926) and *Weep Some More, My Lady*
(Garden City, 1927). See also E. C. May, "Words with Music," *Sat.
Eve. Post*, CXCVII, 11 ff. (Oct. 18, 1924), and Isaac Goldberg, *Tin
Pan Alley* (N. Y., 1930), chaps. v-vi.

Hood," soon became a melodic accompaniment of every well-conducted American wedding.

Hardly less popular than the theme of misplaced affections was the spirited balladry which centered about life in the city tenements—such songs as "The Mulligan Braves" (1879) and "The Widow Nolan's Goat" (1881), from the Harrigan and Hart comedies; J. J. Sullivan's "Where Did You Get That Hat?" (1888); Joseph Flynn's "Down Went McGinty" (1889); Frank Harding's "Throw Him Down, McCloskey" (1890)—

And future generations, with wonder and delight,
Will read on hist'ry's pages of this great McCloskey fight;

and C. B. Lawler's "The Sidewalks of New York" (1894). While the Negro continued to be a subject of the white man's compositions, the slow-paced, wistful melodies of the plantation type gave way to the sprightly "coon song," written in syncopated time to suit the quicker tempo of urban life and designed to stir people's feet instead of their hearts. The first genuine "ragtime" pieces were Barney Fagan's "My Gal Is a High-Born Lady" and C. E. Trevathan's "The Bully," both written in 1896. Their appeal was so great that they set a fashion which lasted into the second decade of the next century.

It remains an open question whether music of the lighter and more ephemeral sort debases the public taste or whether it breeds an appreciation of the nobler forms. The relationship between the two in the eighties and nineties may have been wholly fortuitous, but there can be no doubt that the craze for popular songs was attended by a remarkable growth of interest in serious music. The public schools helped by imparting a knowledge of the rudiments of music; by 1885 seven out of every eight pupils were being taught singing and the ability to read notation.[1] Private teachers also abounded in almost every locality; and piano playing was an ordeal which fond parents customarily imposed upon their offspring, musical and unmusical alike. "There is no country where there are so many pianos and players on them," commented Soissons with not entire approval.[2] A traveler observed a Chickering piano in a miner's tent at Leadville, Colorado, in 1878,[3] and no self-respecting home in the more settled sections was without an instrument of some make or other.

In nearly every important city one or more conservatories of music were to be found. The largest and most distinguished, the New England Conservatory, established at Boston in 1867, closely approached the best European schools in the excellence of its curriculum. After 1896 it was under the direction of George W. Chadwick who had long been a member of its faculty. The Cincinnati College of Music, dating from 1878, maintained artistic standards that leavened the musical culture of the entire West. From the start most women's colleges had special instruction, while men's institutions began to follow in 1875 when Harvard made music a regular part of the curriculum with John Knowles Paine in charge.[4] Though the older musicians had felt obliged

[1] U. S. Bureau of Education, *Circular of Information for 1886*, no. 1.

[2] S. C. de Soissons, · *A Parisian in America* (Boston, 1896), 186. From 1880 to 1900 the number of establishments making pianos and materials increased from 174 to 263, their products from more than twelve million dollars to well over thirty-five. While before 1866 nearly all the pianos made were square pianos, by 1900 nearly all of them were uprights, an indication perhaps of the more crowded conditions of living. *U. S. Twelfth Census*, X, 448, 454.

[3] L. P. Brockett, *Our Western Empire* (Phila., 1882), 198-199.

[4] Yale and Columbia established chairs in 1894 and 1896 with Horatio Parker and Edward A. MacDowell respectively as the incumbents. L. C. Elson, *The History of American Music* (J. C. Van Dyke, ed., *The History of American Art*, II, N. Y., 1904), 339-358.

to get their training in Germany, the younger men were finding it increasingly possible to secure adequate instruction without leaving American shores.

In the matter of artists' concerts the leading cities could be sure of hearing some of the best native performers every season, as well as distinguished European visitors like Adelina Patti, Ignace Jan Paderewski and Fritz Kreisler. Where the German element was strong, choral societies also flourished. The May musical festivals at Cincinnati, beginning in 1873 and long directed by Theodore Thomas, had a chorus of nearly a thousand, drawn in part from the singing societies of near-by cities. In addition, almost every town possessed a brass band, usually made up of self-taught players. A few bands, notably Patrick S. Gilmore's in New York and John Philip Sousa's United States Marine Band, commanded a nation-wide reputation. When Sousa organized his own troupe in 1892, he went on to new and greater triumphs. Besides being a conductor, he was a composer of merit, and his stirring martial airs—"The Washington Post," "The Liberty Bell," "The Stars and Stripes Forever" and others—quickly won him the title of the "March King." "The Washington Post" (1889) was probably the best-known instrumental piece in the world at the time, and in America its lively rhythm established the vogue of the two-step as successor to the old-time waltz.[1]

Similarly, orchestral music finally became naturalized in America during this period. The year 1878 saw the founding of the New York Symphony Orchestra, conducted at first by Leopold Damrosch and from 1885 by his son Walter. Meantime, in 1881, the Boston Symphony Orchestra was established with a guarantee of

[1] In England and Germany the new dance was known generically as the "Washington Post." See Sousa, *Marching Along*, chaps. iv-ix.

financial independence provided by the public-spirited banker Henry Lee Higginson. Along with the older New York Philharmonic and Theodore Thomas's Chicago Orchestra (1891), these orchestras presented to American audiences in many parts of the country musical masterpieces with something akin to European technique and ensemble. The conductors and most of the performers, however, were of European birth and training, a condition which also held true of grand opera.[1]

Though remaining an exotic, grand opera was placed upon a firmer footing with the opening in New York in 1883 of the Metropolitan Opera House, an edifice costing nearly two million dollars. The most eminent singers from all over the world were attracted to its stage and, under the conductorships of the elder Damrosch and Anton Seidl (1884-1892), Wagnerian and other German opera won favor with audiences hitherto habituated to the Italian school.[2] But, apart from New Orleans where good French troupes had long held forth, no other American city felt able to indulge in the luxury of a resident company.

If the record of these years is mainly one of the growth of musical appreciation, yet America began in a modest way to repay a part of its debt for the rich stores of melody which it had derived from Europe.[3] Paine, Chadwick and Horatio Parker all achieved a transatlantic reputation for their orchestral and choral scores, setting a high standard for the next generation to emulate. Similarly, the compositions of Dudley Buck

[1] America in this period, however, contributed to the grand-opera stage two prima donnas in Emma Eames and Lillian Nordica.

[2] H. E. Krehbiel, *Chapters of Opera* (N. Y., 1908), chaps. viii-xix.

[3] For the composers mentioned in the text and others, see J. T. Howard, *Our American Music* (N. Y., 1931), 315-403, and Rupert Hughes, *Contemporary American Composers* (Boston, 1900), chaps. ii-v.

exerted a profound influence for good on American choir music. Ethelbert Nevin and Edward A. MacDowell, on the other hand, devoted their talents to art-songs and piano selections. The latter was the most original composer America had yet produced. He had a genius for catching the moods of forest, field and ocean and expressing them in a musical idiom exquisitely his own. "To a Wild Rose" and "To a Water Lily," published in 1896 as a part of his *Woodland Sketches,* quickly became a precious folk possession of America.

While music and the drama were extending their dominion over men's leisure time, open-air recreations attained a new and stronger hold upon the public. "The disappearance of the backwoods and the growth of large centres of population have created the demand for an artificial outlet," wrote a contemporary, "and the games are the natural successors of the youthful activities of a pioneer period."[1] Indeed, with an increasing proportion of mankind cooped up for long hours in factory and office, working a single set of muscles or benumbing their minds with columns of figures, some form of outdoor diversion was indispensable. But the pioneer inheritance unfortunately did not ordinarily include pioneer biceps. Most people were therefore content to take their more strenuous forms of exercise by proxy, a tendency zealously stimulated by sport promoters who coveted the gate receipts which gladiatorial contests made possible. The audience habit, cultivated by the theater, thus came to infect sport lovers as well.

Much of this new play life reflected the athletic revival which had been taking place in England since the

---

[1] I. N. Hollis, "Intercollegiate Athletics," *Atlantic Mo.,* XC (1902), esp. 534. See also D. A. Sargent, "The Physical State of the American People," N. S. Shaler, ed., *The United States of America* (N. Y., 1894), III, 1135-1136.

middle of the century. In the United States, however, the new games were not deemed a special perquisite of the upper classes but rather a boon to be enjoyed by all. Nor did the Americans hesitate to modify the rules when it suited their pleasure so to do. In only one instance did they invent a sport of their own; yet that effort was conspicuously successful. Basketball, an indoor game devised by James Naismith in 1891 at the Y. M. C. A. Training College in Springfield, Massachusetts, quickly spread to other countries.[1]

Of the older sports thoroughbred racing enjoyed an era of unparalleled prosperity.[2] Capital was lavishly invested in new club houses and courses, faster tracks were built at the county and state fairs, stakes were increased in size and the great stables sent horses to meets in all parts of the country. In 1876 the record for the mile was set by Ten Broeck at one minute thirty-nine and three-quarters seconds, where it remained until Salvator in 1890 brought the crowd to their feet at Long Branch by clipping the time by four and a quarter seconds. One of the noted racing horses, Hanover, sired by Hindoo, also a great racer of the 1880's, won thirty-two events and finished second thirteen times, earning for his owners, Philip and Michael Dwyer, over one hundred and twenty thousand dollars in a four years' turf career. Despite its wide popularity, however, racing failed of universal favor because of the evils of betting and fraud which ordinarily attended it and which neither the true friends of the sport nor the enactments of legislatures could suppress.

[1] By 1894 it had encircled the globe and had ardent advocates in such extremes as Paris and Melbourne. J. P. Paret, "Basketball," *Outing*, XXXI (1897), 224.

[2] S. C. Hildreth and J. R. Crowell, *The Spell of the Turf* (Phila., 1926), chaps. ii-vii. On all phases of sport, J. A. Krout, *Annals of American Sport* (R. H. Gabriel, ed., *The Pageant of America*, New Haven, 1926-1929, XIV), is valuable.

Even more was professional pugilism viewed askance by the respectable elements. Generally banned by law, the fighting was usually with bare fists, the bouts often lasting forty or fifty rounds. In 1882 John L. Sullivan, a slugging fighter of great power, won the heavyweight championship from Paddy Ryan in a battle marked by hitting, wrestling, scratching and biting. Five years later, while fighting Patsy Cardiff at Minneapolis, he broke his right arm in the third round, but continued to a six-round draw. In 1889,

> Nigh New Orleans
> Upon an emerald plain
> John L. Sullivan
> The strong boy
> Of Boston
> Fought seventy-five red rounds with Jake Kilrain,

winning twenty thousand dollars and a diamond belt offered by the *Police Gazette*.[1] His admirers now talked of running him for Congress; but he undertook a boxing tour to Australia instead, coming back only to lose his title in a twenty-one-round bout to the young Californian, James J. Corbett. "Gentleman Jim's" victory in 1892 marked a turning point in the sport, for it demonstrated the superiority of scientific boxing over sheer brute strength. His reign, however, was ended in 1897 when, in the fourteenth round of a match with "Bob" Fitzsimmons at Carson City, his Cornish opponent in less than three seconds "accomplished three epochal feats: he had knocked out an Irishman on Saint Patrick's Day, he had won the heavyweight champion-

---

[1] This was the last bare-knuckle championship fight. The quotation is from Vachel Lindsay's rhythmic commemoration of the event in *Collected Poems* (N. Y., 1925), 93-95. For pugilistic development in general, see Alexander Johnston, *Ten—and Out* (N. Y., 1927), chaps. vi-xi.

ship of the world, and he had invented the terrible 'solar plexus punch' " that is always associated with his name.[1]

Baseball reached far larger numbers of people than either racing or pugilism. Though everywhere a vacant-lots sport, it was in its professionalized aspects that it took on the dimensions of "the national game." [2] Alert to stamp out gambling and dishonesty, the National League, formed in 1876 by teams representing four Eastern and four Western cities, made professional baseball respectable at the same time that it offered the most expert playing that could be witnessed anywhere in the country. Minor or "bush" leagues also existed in profusion and in 1882 a rival to the National League appeared in the American Association.

As competition between nines and leagues grew keener, constant modifications of the rules gave greater scope for both individual skill and team play. Following 1875 the umpire was given power to call strikes and balls, three of the former and four of the latter being made the limit for the batsman. The removal in 1884 of all restrictions on pitching led to the rapid development of the outcurve, incurve, drop and fadeaway, aspects of the game of which J. B. Clarkson of Chicago and Boston and Timothy Keefe of New York were the particular masters. Protective equipment was also adopted such as the catcher's mask, breastpad and mitt. In demonstrating the possibilities of team strategy and coördinated play no nine equaled the Baltimore Orioles which, under Ned Hanlon's leadership, won the

---

[1] R. F. Dibble, "Robert Prometheus Fitzsimmons," *Dict. of Am. Biog.*, VI, 443.

[2] A. G. Spalding, *America's National Game* (N. Y., 1911), chaps. xiv-xx, xxxiv; G. L. Moreland, *Balldom* (N. Y., 1914), 16-133; Bozeman Bulger, "What Made Great Ball Players Great," *Des Moines Register*, March 14-April 11, 1924, *passim*.

National League pennant for three successive years after 1893.

Rivalry between the major leagues led in 1884 to the inauguration of postseason battles between the pennant-winning teams, an annual event which continued until the collapse of the American Association in 1891.[1] Beginning with Providence's triumph over the New York Metropolitans, victory in the World Series, as it was called, usually rested with the National League. That the world whose championship was yearly at stake might actually learn of America's premier sport, A. G. Spalding in 1888 arranged a series of exhibition matches around the globe between "Pop" (A. C.) Anson's Chicago White Sox and an all-American team. At Kensington Oval grounds the Prince of Wales (later Edward VII) was an excited, if somewhat uncomprehending, spectator, while in Egypt a game was played on the desert close enough to one of the pyramids for it to serve as a backstop. At home ever greater throngs found the baseball season the most zestful period of the year. The unprecedented number of forty thousand paid admission to the four games between New York and Chicago in 1885 at the Chicago Club grounds. The World Series in 1887 between Detroit and St. Louis had a total attendance of over fifty-one thousand.

In the closing years of the period another sport threatened the supremacy of the national game. As long as bicycling was confined to gymnasts whose courage was not daunted by an occasional header from the lofty perch over the high front wheel, it tended to remain in the hands of professionals.[2] Nevertheless, as early as 1880, the League of American Wheelmen was formed

[1] The World Series was revived in 1903 between the winners of the National League and the newly formed American League.
[2] See Nevins, *Emergence of Modern America*, 223-224, for the earlier form of bicycle.

with a steadily enlarging membership, and in 1883 a California amateur, Thomas Stevens, undertook a four-year cycling tour of the globe.[1] The real vogue of the sport, however, began a few years later with the introduction of the "safety" bicycle—possessing low wheels of equal size—and the substitution of pneumatic tires for solid rubber ones. At the same time a drop frame was designed for the sake of the gentler sex who could, if they wished, reassure themselves further by attaching a folded screen to the front of the bicycle "to protect the feet and ankles from view when mounting or riding." [2]

By 1893 a million bicycles were in use.[3] It seemed as though all America had taken to wheels. Frances E. Willard, the temperance leader, fell prey to the craze, announcing her conversion in a book *A Wheel within a Wheel: How I Learned to Ride the Bicycle* (1895). By physicians the therapeutic benefits were declared to be beyond compare, while dress reformers welcomed cycling as an aid to more rational fashions.[4] The new means of locomotion carried people to and from their work; it sped mail carriers and physicians on their rounds; for countless thousands it renewed the forgotten pleasures of open road and countryside. The historian Claude H. Van Tyne, while an undergraduate at the University of Michigan, made a thirty-five-hundred-

[1] Thomas Stevens, *Around the World on a Bicycle* (N. Y., 1887-1888).

[2] Anon., "Skirt Protecting Screen for Bicycles," *Scientific Am.*, LXXIV (1896), 261.

[3] In the single year 1895, over half a million were manufactured; in 1900, well over a million. A. A. Pope, "The Bicycle Industry," C. M. Depew, ed., *One Hundred Years of American Commerce* (N. Y., 1895), II, 551; *U. S. Twelfth Census*, X, 328.

[4] Not only skirts of short walking length, but even bloomers, it was urged, might be worn without offense to "feminine dignity and modesty." L. H. Porter, *Cycling for Health and Pleasure* (N. Y., 1895), 3-22, 106-117, 177-195.

mile trip from Ann Arbor over the Rockies in 1894. Meantime, bicycle clubs were formed which pedaled together in a body for pleasure, or conducted meets in which professional riders strove to set new records for speed or endurance.

From the outset the League of American Wheelmen carried on a vigorous propaganda for good roads, which finally bore fruit in the nineties. Starting with New Jersey in 1891, the last decade saw new and improved highway legislation in over half the states.[1] "It is safe to say," declared an expert of the census bureau in 1900, "that few articles ever used by man have created so great a revolution in social conditions as the bicycle."[2] Only a person of fevered imagination could have guessed that the noisy, puffing "horseless carriages," which now and then ventured forth upon the roads, would within a few years spell the doom of the universally popular "bike."[3]

Other forms of physical recreation, while attracting fewer devotees, resembled cycling in their essentially amateur character. Roller skating was an epidemic which raged intermittently and affected all ages; in 1885 skating rinks represented an investment of over twenty million dollars. Croquet made a wide appeal by reason of its simplicity and leisurely pace, though it was objected to by some because of the opportunity it afforded for flirtation.[4] With the hope of converting the game into an exhibition of skill the National Croquet Association was formed in 1882 and held annual tournaments. Lawn tennis, introduced from England in 1875, was

---

[1] M. O. Eldridge, "Progress of Road Building," U. S. Dept. of Agr., *Yearbook for 1899*, 377-380; N. S. Shaler, *American Highways* (N. Y., 1896), chap. vi.

[2] *U. S. Twelfth Census*, X, 329. See also J. B. Bishop, "Social and Economic Influence of the Bicycle," *Forum*, XXI (1896), 680-689.

[3] See Faulkner, *Quest for Social Justice*, 132-133.

[4] G. B. Bartlett, "The Recreations of the People," *Journ. of Social Sci.*, XII (1880), 141.

at first also regarded merely as a pleasant pastime; but with the formation of a national association six years later, uniform rules were adopted and the annual tournaments at Newport and elsewhere quickly brought to the fore such masters of the racquet as R. D. Sears, James Dwight and H. W. Slocum. Meanwhile the formation of the American Canoe Association in 1880 popularized this water sport. Within a dozen years there were some sixty canoe clubs in the East with over five thousand members.[1] Skiing was a contribution of Norwegian Americans, who organized the first ski club at Red Wing, Minnesota, in 1883, and held the first tournament the following year.[2]

Rifle shooting also had its addicts, and since 1874 international matches had been held with picked teams from Ireland, England, Australia and other lands. Fishing and hunting, which belonged to the older American tradition, had now to be carried on with due regard to the laws for preserving wild life.[3] In the last quarter of the century anglers' associations and sportsmen's clubs appeared everywhere; in the East the members were usually city dwellers who journeyed long distances to find their pleasure. To discourage the indiscriminate slaughter of game birds George B. Grinnell brought about the formation in 1886 of the Audubon Society, which soon had fifty thousand members; and the following year Theodore Roosevelt, an expert hunter, helped organize the Boone and Crockett Club for the protection of big game. Though less adventurous, trap shooting also enjoyed considerable vogue, the first national tournament being held in 1886 at New Orleans.

Certain sports—trap shooting, archery, polo, golf—

[1] J. H. Mandigo, "Outdoor Sports," *Chautauquan*, XIX (1894), 393.

[2] *Daily Eagle* (Red Wing, Minn.), Feb. 2, 1928.

[3] See earlier, 237.

were largely monopolized by the fashionable few.[1] This
was notably true, of course, of international yacht racing
in which vessels sponsored by the New York Yacht
Club continued successfully to defend the *America's* cup
against all challengers.[2] It was the wealthy, too, who
fostered the growth of country clubs where, amidst the
lovely verdure of hill and dale, such pleasures as polo
and golf might be pursued under the best obtainable
conditions.[3] In the nineties country clubs could be
found in well-to-do communities from Palm Beach to
Puget Sound.

The new gospel of physical well-being led everywhere
also to an extension of indoor facilities for exercise.
Gymnasiums were proliferated by the Y. M. C. A. and
Y. W. C. A., while the rapid spread of city athletic
clubs provided additional opportunities, especially for
track sports.[4] Beginning in cities like Milwaukee (1877)
and Kansas City (1885), where the German Turner
influence was strong, physical training was also introduced into the schools.[5] At the university level the erection of the Hemenway Gymnasium at Harvard in 1878
and the effective work of its director, Dr. D. A. Sargent,
set new standards which other colleges quickly followed.

[1] The growth of interest in such games is indicated by the formation
of the National Archery Association in 1879, the United States Polo
Association in 1890, and the United States Golf Association in 1894.
Polo had been introduced from Great Britain in 1873 or 1874, golf
in 1878.

[2] Against a Canadian sloop in 1881, and British cutters in 1885,
1886, 1887, 1893 and 1895.

[3] The Brookline Country Club, founded in 1882 near Boston, was
apparently the first. Caspar Whitney, "Evolution of the Country Club,"
*Harper's Mag.*, XC (1894), 16-33; Robert Dunn, "The Country Club:
A National Expression," *Outing*, XLVII (1905), 160-174.

[4] Samuel Crowther and Arthur Ruhl, *Rowing and Track Athletics*
(Caspar Whitney, ed., *The American Sportsman's Library*; N. Y.,
1905), pt. ii, chap. iii.

[5] U. S. Commissioner of Education, *Report for 1891-92*, I, 518-521;
*for 1897-98*, I, 549-557; C. F. Thwing, *A History of Education in
the United States since the Civil War* (Boston, 1910), chap. x.

Yet, despite the interest lent indoor exercise by the new apparatus which Sargent and his disciples introduced, college youths continued to find greater zest in open-air contests.[1] Few of these did they wholly neglect, and there was one, football, in which they admittedly excelled. As played in the late seventies the sport still bore a strong family resemblance to the English game of Rugby; but under the influence of innovators, notably Walter Camp at Yale, constant changes were made until the game became thoroughly Americanized.[2] The number of players was reduced from fifteen to eleven; the free-for-all scramble for the ball was replaced by having one side put it in play; the quarterback, thus promoted to a key position, introduced numerical signals; and new rules were adopted as regards downs, tackling and interference. For many years the best teams were in the East and, when Walter Camp selected his first "All-American" eleven in 1889, he did not need to look beyond the "Big Three": Yale, Harvard and Princeton. The appointment of A. A. Stagg as coach at the University of Chicago in 1892 began a new era for the sport in the Middle West. Most institutions, however, could not afford to employ regular coaches. At Connecticut Wesleyan Professor Woodrow Wilson, in his hours away from the classroom, helped train a team that in 1889 defeated Pennsylvania, Amherst, Williams, Rutgers and Trinity.

The intensity of intercollegiate rivalry aroused sharp criticism of the game both on and off the campus in the early 1890's. The absorbing interest of undergraduates

[1] A. M. F. Davis, "College Athletics," *Atlantic Mo.*, LI (1883), 677-684; N. S. Shaler, "The Athletic Problem in Education," same mag., LXIII (1889), 79-88; A. B. Hart, "Status of Athletics in American Colleges," same mag., LXVI (1890), 63-71.

[2] Walter Camp and L. F. Deland, *Football* (Boston, 1896), chap. vii; P. H. Davis, *Football* (N. Y., 1911), 65-105; A. M. Weyand, *American Football* (N. Y., 1926), chaps. i-ii.

made one college president fear lest the degree of B.A. would come to stand for "Bachelor of Athletics." [1] As mass tactics and momentum plays became the common practice under the new regulations, parents grew increasingly alarmed at the annual toll of injuries. [2] Moreover, the contests, constantly more expensive and elaborate, took on the aspect of shows conducted primarily for the pleasure of alumni and the general public. Over fifty thousand watched the annual Yale-Princeton game on Thanksgiving Day, 1893, while telegraphic bulletins acquainted the country with the fortunes of the battle. Some light is shed on the prevalent laxness of standards by the fact that seven members of the University of Michigan squad in 1893 were not even enrolled as students. From time to time the Eastern colleges took measures to improve conditions, while the Western Conference of seven leading institutions was formed in 1896 for a similar purpose. But the problem was far from solved when the period closed.

The athletic awakening of the 1880's and 1890's added a new dimension to American life. Though primarily of concern to men, outdoor play increasingly enlisted the interest of the gentler sex, and in sports like tennis and archery they established excellent records for skill. Sometimes it seemed as if the mass of people could take a serious interest in nothing else. F. B. Opper, the *Puck* cartoonist, drew a phrenological chart, dividing Uncle Sam's cranium among such interests as football, bicycling, tennis and golf with the biggest bump of all assigned to baseball. [3] That Uncle Sam did have sport

[1] U. S. Comr. of Educ., *Rep. for 1896-97*, I, 705. The chief objections to football are summarized in H. D. Sheldon, *Student Life and Customs* (W. T. Harris, ed., *International Education Series*, LI, N. Y., 1901), 235-245.

[2] E. G. Dexter, "Accidents from College Football," *Educational Rev.*, XXV (1903), 415-428.

[3] *Puck*, XXI, 236 (June 1, 1887).

on the brain seemed conclusive to the English visitor who found that, of two events occurring on September 7, 1892, his American newspaper gave one column to the death of John Greenleaf Whittier and nearly a dozen to the Corbett-Sullivan prize fight.[1]

If the generation did not solve the problem of leisure, it at least succeeded in dodging it. The "second battle of civilization," as Garfield called it, found the average citizen in an attitude of nonresistance toward the forces that rushed in on him from every side. He did as others did and hence discovered himself without leisure. The pursuit of happiness tended to become a breathless chase, the provision of recreation an organized traffic. Yet such is not the whole story. Human beings, even when regimented for purposes of historians' generalizations, have a way of remaining annoyingly individualistic and self-willed. It is important to recall that the deeper values of leisure were also explored and by an ever larger number of people. Only in this way can one understand some of the most striking developments of the time: the longer years spent in school and university, the phenomenal growth of the reading habit, the increased enjoyment of good music, the deepened interest in works of mercy, the growth of transatlantic travel, the wider appreciation of the rôle of art and beauty in life. And these were enduring gains of which any age might be proud.

[1] J. F. Muirhead, *The Land of Contrasts* (Boston, 1898), 158.

# CHAPTER X

## THE CHANGING CHURCH

DESPITE the multiplying demands on their leisure hours a majority of the people, at least in the rural sections, continued to find time to go to church each Sunday and many of them also to mid-week prayer meeting. Judging not only from this habit but also from other indications—the sale of theological works, the general respect paid to Christian precepts and ministers, the lively interest in doctrinal questions, the religious coloration of so much philanthropic effort— Bryce considered the influence of the church deeper and stronger than in any European nation.[1] Most professed Christians accepted unhesitatingly what the Reformation had handed down, provided it bore a Protestant label, whether the Nicene doctrine of the Trinity, the Augustinian theory of man's fall, Calvin's insistence upon God's arbitrary will, or less exacting modern variants of these traditional dogmas. With over one hundred and fifty denominations from which to choose, no country in the world so well exemplified Frederick the Great's principle that everyone should be allowed to go to heaven in his own way. Save in rural neighborhoods and particularly in the South, differences within Protestantdom, however, had lost their ancient fierceness. Religious attendance and church work were often hardly more than "a kind of sacred amusement," a social rather

[1] James Bryce, *The American Commonwealth* (London, 1888), III, 483.

than a spiritual fellowship.[1] In the new communities of the Great West the dearth of churches eased the passage from one denomination into another, a trait characteristic also of the great cities.

A disposition to distinguish sharply between the sacred and the secular tended to divorce religion from everyday thought and conduct. So far as the mass of churchgoers were concerned, this made possible the survival, into a critical and scientific age, of theological ideas which the more progressive clerics were questioning or had already rejected. After the feverish labors of the week Americans generally displayed a "docile acquiescence" in any teachings which freed them from mental disturbance and satisfied their emotional need of belief.[2] The theological cosmos of the average man is probably mirrored in a census of the religious opinions of a thousand California children in the early 1890's.[3] God was generally conceived as an old man with a long beard and flowing white garments, benevolent rather than stern of mien, but possessing power to "have an earthquake at any time." Heaven, suspended "in the clouds," had houses and streets of gold where angels flew about and strummed on harps. For Satan the conventional figure in *Faust* was the prototype, though two pupils derived their impressions more immediately from the labels on deviled-ham cans. If such views show little change from those of colonial times, they were, for the godly at least, an anchor of faith and the source of abiding comfort.

Yet above these quiet depths the winds of contro-

---

[1] [J. B. Harrison], *Certain Dangerous Tendencies in American Life* (Boston, 1880), 10-11.

[2] See comments of the French psychologist Gabriel Compayré, quoted in U. S. Commissioner of Education, *Report for 1895-96*, II, 1165.

[3] Earl Barnes, "Theological Life of a California Child," *Pedagogical Seminary*, II, 442-448, which summarizes the views expressed by 1091 school children of from six to twenty years of age. Nine different religious groups, including the Catholic, were represented.

versy were chopping the theological seas and affrighting conservatives as to the eventual survival of revealed religion. The new findings of science and scholarship impelled intellectual people to reconsider their traditional attitude toward the Bible, while the devout were driven to blind resistance or a new apologetics. Religion, in other words, was engaged in one of those recurrent conflicts between orthodoxy and heterodoxy, between fundamentalism and modernism, which have formed a law of its growth. In the eyes of stalwart believers the foundations of faith were imperiled by three grave heresies: the doctrine of Darwinism, the science of Biblical criticism, and the new interest in comparative religion.

The religious controversy over biological evolution reached its most critical stage in the 1880's, for by that time American scientists stood a solid phalanx in its support and many of the thoughtful public had been won over by the persuasive writings of Spencer, Huxley and Fiske.[1] It no longer sufficed for theological disputants to castigate Darwinism with such epithets as materialistic and atheistic. If evolution was the "bestial hypothesis" of man's origin, it was only too easy to retort in kind that the Biblical account was the "mudman theory" of creation. Reason must be appealed to as well as inherited belief.[2] An analysis of the turbid flood of argument which poured from the press during the decade reveals a steady advance—or retreat—from a position of pure emotional obscurantism to one of concession and accommodation. Some found the way out

[1] See earlier, 231. Allan Nevins, *The Emergence of Modern America* (*A History of American Life*, VIII), 286-289, treats the initial stages of the dispute.

[2] The antievolutionists made the most of the internal strife among naturalists, which, however, did not question the fact of evolution but rather the particular mode set forth by Darwin. See *Nation* (N. Y.), XLIV, 121-123 (Feb. 10, 1887), and LX, 31 (Jan. 10, 1895).

by asserting that religion and science belonged to mutually exclusive spheres; that the Bible was a rule of conduct and a guide to faith, not a scientific cyclopedia.[1] Others held that the account in Genesis, when allegorically construed, really anticipated and supported Darwin's thesis.[2] Still others contended that genuine religion remained unaffected by what was, at most, a conflict between science and theology.[3]

Gradually, an increasing number of ministers, influenced by the example of Henry Ward Beecher in his Brooklyn pulpit and by Lyman Abbott's sermons and writings in the *Christian Union* and elsewhere, came to embrace evolution as a new and grander revelation of the mysterious way God moves his wonders to perform.[4] Mark Twain's facetious proposal, early in the eighties, of a monument to Adam before that great progenitor of mankind should be wholly supplanted by Darwin's simian, was decidedly premature. But unmistakable evidence of a sweeping change of sentiment among thoughtful religionists appeared when, after another decade of discussion, the great New York Chautauqua gave over its platform in 1893 to a series of lectures by the well-known Scotch evolutionist Henry Drummond. "It is a sign of the times which no observer can neglect," commented the *Nation*.[5]

Like the doctrine of natural selection, textual criti-

[1] Henry Calderwood, *The Relations of Science and Religion* (N. Y., 1881), esp. 298, 308; C. B. Warring, *Miracle, Law and Evolution* (N. Y., 1887), esp. 8; review of Arnold Guyot's *Creation, Am. Catholic Quar.*, IX (1884), 374.

[2] S. B. Goodenow, "Primeval Man," *Bibliotheca Sacra*, LI (1894), esp. 159.

[3] T. T. Munger, "Religion's Gain from Science," *Forum*, VI (1888), 45-54.

[4] Beecher introduced evolution into his sermons as early as 1880. Lyman Abbott, *Henry Ward Beecher* (Boston, 1903), 317-324.

[5] A. B. Paine, *Mark Twain* (N. Y., 1912), II, 707-709; edit., *Nation*, LVII, 21 (July 13, 1893).

cism of the Bible also called into question the infallibility of the Scriptures. Imported from German
university centers, the higher criticism, as it was
known, subjected the Holy Writ to rigorous historical
analysis. According to the new findings, the sixty-six
books, far from being all of one piece and inspired
throughout, comprised a storehouse of history, folklore, discourses, poetry and prophecy brought together
over a period of a thousand years.[1] Acceptance of the
new point of view was somewhat facilitated by the
appearance of a revised version of the King James Bible
in 1881 and 1885, a laborious enterprise carried through
by a group of English and American scholars.[2] So great
was the public interest that two hundred thousand
copies of the New Testament were sold in New York
alone within less than a week, and the *Chicago Times*
and the *Chicago Tribune* printed the text entire.

While ministers and churchgoers accustomed themselves to changed readings and often changed meanings
of treasured passages, liberal theologians wrote books
and articles to disseminate the teachings of the higher
critics. President Orello Cone of Buchtel College, for
example, published in 1891 his *Gospel Criticism and
Historical Christianity,* the ablest work in its field from
an American pen. All was not smooth sailing, of course.
Dwight L. Moody, the famous evangelist, venting contempt on those who found inconsistencies and contradictions in the Scriptures, shouted to vast audiences with

[1] George Harris, *A Century's Change in Religion* (Boston, 1914),
chap. iv; C. A. Briggs, *Whither?* (N. Y., 1889), 277-285; A. D.
White, *A History of the Warfare of Science with Theology in Christendom* (N. Y., 1896), II, chap. xx.

[2] The first installment, in 1881, consisted of the New Testament.
Philip Schaff was chairman of the American revisers. D. S. Schaff,
*The Life of Philip Schaff* (N. Y., 1897), 354-363, 382-388; anon.,
"The New and Old Versions," *Nation,* XXXII, 401-402 (June 9,
1881).

all the force of his two hundred and eighty pounds: "The Bible was not made to understand." [1] Professor W. H. Green of Princeton Seminary stoutly defended the orthodox position in a notable debate with President Harper of Chicago, and many a household and congregation continued to find solace in an unquestioning acceptance of the King James version. Yet the reception accorded Washington Gladden's *Who Wrote the Bible?*, published in 1891, indicates the broad appeal of the more advanced attitude. A summary and popularization of the newer studies, it not only enjoyed the largest sale of any of his widely read books, but became a manual for Bible classes and Young Men's Christian Associations.[2] Sober reflection was convincing even many of the earlier objectors that, if critical analysis stripped the Bible of its vesture of infallibility, it revealed it as a work of literary, spiritual and ethical power, a veritable book among books.[3]

The crumbling of orthodoxy was furthered by certain by-products of American missionary enterprise in the Orient. Thousands of Christian workers, brought into contact with the great faiths of Asia, learned that Christianity and religion were not coextensive, that all good was not monopolized by their own system of belief. At the same time the work of secular scholars in the realms of mythology, folklore, psychology and anthropology suggested points of departure for an understanding of religious phenomena. James Freeman Clarke's sympathetic portrayal of *Ten Great Religions* made such an impression upon the public that in the

[1] E. J. Goodspeed, *A Full History of the Wonderful Career of Moody and Sankey in Great Britain and America* (Ashland, Ohio, 1877), 315.

[2] Washington Gladden, *Recollections* (Boston, 1909), 320-321.

[3] Lyman Abbott, *Reminiscences* (Boston, 1915), 460-462; C. W. Shields, "Does the Bible Contain Scientific Errors?," *Century*, XLV (1892-1893), 126-134; C. A. Briggs, "Works of the Imagination in the Old Testament," *N. Am. Rev.*, CLXIV (1897), 356-373.

fifteen years after 1871 it passed through twenty-one
editions. Comparative religion became not only a preoccupation of scholars but a new measuring rod for
Christianity. As dramatic evidence of the widened horizon, a World's Parliament of Religions, the first of its
kind, was convened during the Columbian Exposition
of 1893. More than one hundred and fifty thousand
people attended. While all was not harmony, the animating spirit of the great assemblage was expressed in
the words of Malachi, which served as its motto: "Have
we not all one Father? hath not one God created us?" [1]
In the light of fuller knowledge the old misunderstanding and intolerance once accorded non-Christian faiths
was beginning to wane.

If these new intellectual currents little touched the
average mind, they deeply affected the thinking of the
more intelligent. In 1881 the American Institute of
Christian Philosophy was formed in New York state
for the purpose of producing and distributing literature
upon the relations of science and the Bible. Magazines,
both religious and secular, gave generous space to appraisals of the new learning. Even more significant was
the discussion of theological issues in certain notable
works of fiction. The best sellers of the year 1888 were
Margaret Deland's *John Ward, Preacher,* described by
a contemporary as "a profound outcry against the intolerance of the creeds," and Mrs. Humphry Ward's
*Robert Elsmere,* an English novel of similar import
which sold more copies in America than in the author's
own country.[2] Here and there theological schools intro-

---

[1] F. H. Stead, "The Story of the World's Parliament of Religions,"
*Am. Rev. of Revs.,* IX (1894), 299-310.
[2] Anon., "The Books of 1888," *Publishers' Wkly.,* XXXV, 205,
208 (Feb. 9, 1889); anon., "The Influence of the Religious Novel,"
*Nation,* XLVII, 329-330 (Oct. 25, 1888). Sarah B. Elliott's novel
*The Felmeres,* published in 1879, was of the same *genre,* as was also

duced courses dealing with the relations of science and religion and with the study of comparative religion.[1]

Traditionalism, however, maintained a stubborn front where it could. In 1878 the geologist Alexander Winchell was dismissed from the Methodist-controlled Vanderbilt University, with the exultant pronouncement of the Tennessee Methodist conference—anticipating the state of mind behind the Dayton "monkey trial" of 1925—that "our university alone has had the courage to lay its young but vigorous hand upon the mane of untamed Speculation and say, 'We will have no more of this.' " [2] Not to be outdone in good works, the Southern Baptist Seminary at Louisville followed Vanderbilt's example within a year by forcing Professor C. H. Toy's resignation because of his attempts to interpret the Old Testament from the viewpoint of modern science. Five years later Dr. James Woodrow was driven from his post in the Presbyterian Theological Seminary at Columbia, South Carolina, for avowing the truth of evolution, and in 1891 W. J. Alexander was dropped from the chair of philosophy at the state university because of unorthodox views regarding the divinity of Christ.[3]

Such bigotry, however, was not confined to the South or to three denominations. In 1882 Dr. E. P. Gould was obliged to resign from Newton Theological Insti-

the widely discussed *The Damnation of Theron Ware* (1896) by Harold Frederic.

[1] U. S. Comr. of Educ., *Rep. for 1889-90*, II, 942-943.

[2] White, *Warfare of Science with Theology*, I, 313-316. Winchell's views are set forth in *The Doctrine of Evolution* (N. Y., 1874) and *Adamites and Pre-Adamites* (Syracuse, 1878). For the Dayton trial, see P. W. Slosson, *The Great Crusade and After* (*A History of American Life*, XII), 431-432.

[3] G. F. Moore, "An Appreciation of Professor Toy," *Am. Journ. of Semitic Languages and Literatures*, XXXVI, 3-5; White, *Warfare of Science with Theology*, I, 316-318; F. B. Simkins, *The Tillman Movement in South Carolina* (Duke Univ., *Publs.*; Durham, 1926), 142, 144.

tution (Baptist) in Massachusetts as a result of doctrinal differences with the president.[1] The next year the Reverend R. Heber Newton of All Souls' Protestant Episcopal Church, New York City, was charged with heresy at the instance of Bishop H. C. Potter and other divines, the case later being allowed to drop.[2] In 1886 a fire that for several years had been smoldering at Andover Theological Seminary (Congregational) in Massachusetts burst into flame when the board of visitors tried five professors for theological liberalism and declared one of them guilty.[3]

Even more rancorous than the "Andover controversy" was the storm that rose in 1891 within Presbyterian ranks over the transfer of Professor Charles A. Briggs, a distinguished exponent of the higher criticism and long an ornament of Union Theological Seminary, to the new chair of Biblical theology. More than seventy presbyteries protested the appointment. Although the New York Presbytery recommended that in the interests of "the peace . . . of the Church" no action be taken, the General Assembly in 1893 suspended Briggs from the ministry for heresy. The peace of the church was indeed involved. In Albany a clergyman resigned because of the decision, while Professor H. P. Smith was suspended from Lane Theological Seminary in Cincinnati for supporting Briggs's views.[4]

[1] Edit., *Nation*, XXXV, 279 (Oct. 5, 1882).

[2] Edit., *Nation*, XXXVIII, 179 (Feb. 28, 1884).

[3] The professors were J. W. Churchill, George Harris, E. Y. Hincks, W. J. Tucker and E. C. Smyth, the last for some reason being the only one adjudged guilty. The case was taken before the state supreme court and in 1893 a decision handed down against the board. W. J. Tucker, *My Generation* (Boston, 1919), chap. vii.

[4] The incident caused Union Seminary to sever its affiliation with the General Assembly and Briggs continued in his professorship, subsequently becoming an Episcopal clergyman. Philip Schaff, "Other Heresy Trials and the Briggs Case," *Forum*, XII (1891-1892), 621-633; *Nation*, LVI, 412, 414-415 (June 8, 1893).

The harm to the cause of religion inflicted by such incidents was greater than that to the cause of science and learning. Yet the wayward religious tendencies of the times help explain the fears of the pious that, once old moorings were cut, the people would drift into uncharted seas. Untold thousands listened receptively to the eloquent and pungent discourses of Robert G. Ingersoll, the "notorious infidel"; many a village Jaques won his reputation for bold speculation by filching the doughty Colonel's iconoclastic shafts. Himself a minister's son in lifelong revolt against his father's extreme Calvinism, Ingersoll was an agnostic, not an atheist: "I do not deny. I do not know—but I do not believe." [1] A relentless foe of dogmatism and illiberalism, he inveighed against Old Testament terrors and New Testament miracles, finding good in all the great religious systems and extolling science as "the only true religion, . . . the only Savior of the world." Starting from much the same position, Dr. Felix Adler, like Ingersoll a clergyman's son though of the Jewish faith, rejected Ingersoll's negative attitude and sought to erect ethical purpose as the vital principle of living without reference to any kind of theological doctrine.[2] With this as his aim he founded in 1876 the Society for Ethical Culture, which presently attracted small bands of intellectuals, usually of Hebrew extraction, in the great cities of the East and Middle West.

Whatever Ethical Culture lacked in mysticism was supplied in full measure by another sect which sought disciples during these years. Originated by Helena P. Blavatsky, an obese Russian woman of somewhat un-

---

[1] For a summary of his views, see R. G. Ingersoll, "Why Am I an Agnostic?," *N. Am. Rev.*, CXLIX (1889), 741-749; CL (1890), 330-338.

[2] His work *Creed and Deed* (N. Y., 1877) sets forth his view that the essence of religion is "fervent devotion to the highest moral ends."

savory antecedents, Theosophy was a curious blend of spiritualism and certain occult doctrines derived from the Brahmanic and Vedic literatures of India.[1] The Theosophical Society, formed in New York in 1875, was to be the spearhead of the new movement, but, converts remaining few, Madame Blavatsky three years later transferred her colorful activities to India and Europe. Meantime the cult managed to maintain a tenuous existence in America and was temporarily stirred to a flurry of activity in the 1890's by the arrival of numerous swamis at the time of the World's Fair.

If these new systems lacked warmth of appeal, their plight was shared to some extent by the older, Protestant sects whose ministers, immersed in intellectual controversy, often failed to satisfy deeper spiritual needs.[2] Even more harmful was the failure of the church to adjust itself to the unprecedented conditions created by rapid urban and industrial growth.[3] American Protestantism, the product of a rural, middle-class society, faced a range of problems for which it had neither experience nor aptitude. In the cities the building of church edifices lagged behind the advance of population, while the shifting of residential districts left once pros-

---

[1] For her exposition of the tenets of Theosophy, see *Isis Unveiled* (N. Y., 1877) and *The Secret Doctrine* (London, 1888).

[2] [Harrison], *Certain Dangerous Tendencies*, 206-213; F. H. Hedge, *The Church in Modern Society* (n.p., 1882), 266-267; C. F. Thwing, "Young Men and the Preaching They Want," *Century*, XLIX (1894-1895), 637-639.

[3] Awareness of this failure is expressed in books like Washington Gladden, *Applied Christianity* (Boston, 1886), 146-179; S. L. Loomis, *Modern Cities and Their Religious Problems* (N. Y., 1887), esp. chap. iii; Josiah Strong, *The New Era* (N. Y., 1893), chap. x; and W. T. Stead, *If Christ Came to Chicago!* (Chicago, 1894), 389-405; as well as in an abundant periodical literature, including O. F. Adams, "Aristocratic Drift of American Protestantism," *N. Am. Rev.*, CXLII (1886), 194-199; C. M. Morse, "The Church and the Working Man," *Forum*, VI (1888), 653-661; T. B. Wakeman, "Our Unchurched Millions," *Arena*, II (1890), 604-613; and C. A. Briggs, "The Alienation of Church and People," *Forum*, XVI (1893-1894), esp. 375-377.

perous houses of worship stranded and abandoned on the bleak shores of factory and slum neighborhoods. In the twenty years preceding 1888 seventeen Protestant churches moved out of the district below Fourteenth Street, New York, though two hundred thousand more people crowded into it.[1] In the decade after 1878 twenty-two thousand residents in the thirteenth ward of Boston were without a single Protestant church, and it was said that in the heart of Chicago sixty thousand people had no church either Protestant or Catholic. It was generally true of large cities that those parts which needed most religious attention got least.

When better accommodations existed, the working class commonly regarded the church—with its fine upholstery, stained-glass windows and expensive choirs—as an institution where ill-clad worshipers were unwelcome and the Nazarene himself would have been rebuffed. As someone has observed, in religion nothing fails like success. The pulpit, increasingly beholden to contributions from the rich, ordinarily ignored or condoned the terrible injustices from which the wage-earning multitude were suffering. In one instance, reported by Professor Ely, when the bakers' union petitioned five hundred clergymen of New York and Brooklyn to preach sermons against compulsory Sunday labor, all but half a dozen ignored the appeal.[2] Even popular sects like the Baptists abandoned their contempt for wealth. In 1890 the Indiana state Baptist convention "thankfully recognized the rich blessing of the Great

[1] Data in regard to the distribution of churches in urban centers are summarized in Loomis, *Modern Cities*, 7-9, 88-89, and Strong, *New Era*, 197-201.
[2] R. T. Ely, *Social Aspects of Christianity* (rev. edn., N. Y., 1889), 44-45. In at least one case on record, that of a Lutheran congregation in Oshkosh, Wis., in Feb., 1894, trade unionists were excluded from the church on the ground that membership in a labor organization violated the law of God. Stead, *If Christ Came to Chicago*, 394-395 n.

Head of the Church in the recent gift of Brother John D. Rockefeller to the Baptist Seminary in Chicago." [1] To laborites religion seemed a sort of capitalistic soothing-syrup. Samuel Gompers bluntly charged that the intellect and talent of the ministry had been suborned by the plutocratic oppressors of the poor.[2]

While few religious bodies, like Trinity Church in New York City, actually owned slum properties, too many congregations imbibed their Sabbath teachings at the hands of preachers such as the one Kipling heard in Chicago in 1891.[3] "With a voice of silver and imagery borrowed from the auction-room," the minister exultantly portrayed

> a heaven on the lines of the Palmer House (but with all the gilding real gold, and all the plate-glass diamond), and set in the centre of it a loud-voiced, argumentative, very shrewd creation that he called God. One sentence . . . caught my delighted ear. It was apropos of some question of the Judgment, and ran:— "No! I tell you God doesn't do business that way."

"Go into an ordinary church on Sunday morning," declared a Protestant clergyman in 1887, "and you see lawyers, physicians, merchants, and business men with their families . . . but the workingman and his household are not there." [4] Of the older faiths the Roman Catholic and the Jewish alone knew how to attract and hold the laborer and the immigrant newcomer. Evan-

---

[1] R. H. Johnson, "American Baptists in the Age of Big Business," *Journ. of Religion*, XI, esp. 72.

[2] H. F. Perry, "The Workingman's Alienation from the Church," *Am. Journ. of Sociology*, IV (1898-1899), esp. 622.

[3] Rudyard Kipling, *American Notes* (Boston, 1899), 97-98. For the public exposure of Trinity's connection with slum properties, see H. U. Faulkner, *The Quest for Social Justice* (*A History of American Life*, XI), 221-222.

[4] Loomis, *Modern Cities*, 82.

gelistic endeavors might temporarily bridge the chasm in the case of Protestants; but even such ardent harvesters of souls as Dwight L. Moody and Ira D. Sankey found their chief work among laggard members of existing congregations and did little to reach the unchurched masses.[1] The Catholic Church, on the other hand, reared its edifices where humanity was densest and thronged its pews three or four times each Sunday with worshipers whose hands and clothing plainly betrayed their humble station.

Another token of alienation from the church appeared in the growing secularization of the Sabbath. This, too, was largely a city phenomenon, for in rural communities, and notably in the South, the people continued to regard the day as one set aside for religious observance and rest.[2] In urban centers, on the other hand, the pressure of life turned the toiling masses to thoughts of pleasure on their one free day while, to satisfy their desire, thousands of their fellows needs must operate trains and street cars and provide the means of recreation.[3] The altered attitude owed much to the practices of immigrant groups unfamiliar with the strait-laced American Lord's Day—the Germans with their Continental Sabbath, the Irish and other aliens with their Catholic Sunday and the Jews who observed Saturday as their holy day. "Where is the city in which the Sabbath day is not losing ground?" asked one sad voice. "To the mass of the workingmen Sunday . . . is a

---

[1] Gamaliel Bradford, *D. L. Moody* (Garden City, 1927), 115-118.

[2] W. R. Crafts, "Impressions of a Transcontinental Tour," *Our Day* (Boston), IV (1889), 543; Bryce, *American Commonwealth*, III, 488; B. J. Ramage, "Sunday Legislation," *Sewanee Rev.*, IV (1895), 121.

[3] J. H. Ward, "The New Sunday," *Atlantic Mo.*, XLVII (1881), 526-538; C. W. Clark, "The Day of Rest," *Atlantic Mo.*, LXIV (1889), 366-375. For the Catholic attitude, see anon., "The Catholic Sunday and the Puritan Sabbath," *Catholic World*, XXIII (1876), 550-565.

day for labor meetings, for excursions, for saloons, beer-
gardens, base-ball games and carousals." [1]

The change in Sabbath habits had little relation to
Sabbath legislation. Such laws existed in almost every
state and were usually very strict, forbidding all labor
except works of necessity and charity and, in many
cases, banning also travel and nearly every kind of
amusement.[2] As late as 1885 Vermont and South Carolina required church attendance on Sunday and in Pennsylvania the stay-at-home was liable to the penalty of
sitting in the stocks. But if rural majorities in the legislatures insisted on retaining the laws, they seemed
strangely indifferent to lax law enforcement in the
cities. Indeed, certain strongly urban states like New
York (1883) and Massachusetts (1887) markedly
relaxed their statutes; and in California in 1883, after
a thorough public discussion of the issue, the legislature
repealed all the Sabbath blue laws.[3] The running of
passenger trains was a particular affront to sabbatarians
who, however, saw each year an increasing number on
the tracks.

The portentous spread of Sabbath desecration
brought a revival of militant efforts to restore its sanctity. In 1884 the W. C. T. U. established a department
of Sabbath observance, and four years later the American Sabbath Union, formed by several evangelical
churches, began organizing local branches to arouse
opinion. In addition, the International Sabbath Association and the Sunday League of America were in the
field. But even such bodies reflected a changed attitude

[1] Loomis, *Modern Cities*, 104.

[2] Bryce, *American Commonwealth*, III, 488-489; W. F. Crafts, *The
Sabbath for Man* (N. Y., 1885), 111; J. G. Woerner, "Sunday and
Sunday Laws," *Am. Law Rev.*, XVIII (1884), 778-800.

[3] *Laws of New York for 1883*, chap. ccclviii; *Acts and Resolves of
Massachusetts for 1887*, chap. cccxci; W. A. Blakely, ed., *American State
Papers Bearing on Sunday Legislation* (N. Y., 1891), 275 n.

on the subject. Their main plea was less a religious than a humanitarian one: Sabbath breaking was condemned not so much as an offense against God as against man.[1] In other words, a rational regard for a secular day of rest was supplanting the old idea of a day exclusively for religious consecration. For this reason their efforts often won support from powerful labor groups like the Knights of Labor, the Brotherhood of Locomotive Engineers and the American Federation of Labor.

It was a union of these forces which bombarded Congress from 1887 to 1889 with memorials, said to represent fourteen million people, for a cessation of dispensable Sunday labor in interstate commerce and the postal and military services and also in the territories and the District of Columbia. The desired measure was introduced by Senator H. W. Blair on May 21, 1888; hearings were held, but the bill mysteriously never came to a vote.[2] On the matter of Sabbath recreation, however, laborites parted company with the professional sabbatarians. The question of opening the World's Fair on Sunday proved the occasion for a pitched battle. The management vacillated and, when finally it opened the gates but with incomplete exhibits, the attendance was so poor that after a few weeks it shut them again.[3]

Whether or not a more vibrant religious message would have kept more people within bounds on the

[1] See, for example, W. R. Crafts, "Valid Grounds for Sabbath Observance," Our Day, II (1888), 262-275.

[2] "Sunday Observance," 50 Cong., 1 sess., Miscel. Senate Doc., no. 108; "Sunday Rest Bill," 50 Cong., 2 sess., Miscel. Senate Doc., no. 43; Our Day, III (1889), 51-53, 192, 310.

[3] W. R. Crafts, "Sunday Closing of the Columbian World's Fair," Our Day, VIII (1891), 259-267; edit., "Jesus, the Church, and the World's Fair," Arena, VI (1892), 250-260; Elizabeth C. Stanton, "Sunday at the World's Fair," N. Am. Rev., CLIV (1892), 254-256; J. W. Chadwick, "Why the Fair Must Be Open on Sunday," Forum, XIV (1892-1893), 541-550; edit., Nation, LVII, 39 (July 20, 1893).

Lord's Day, the older Protestant churches, as we have seen, were not prepared to give it. To help the common man rekindle the altar fires of his faith two new religions, however, made their appearance. One was a British importation, the other an authentic American creation. The Salvation Army had been organized in London by William Booth in an effort to adapt the Methodist revivalistic technique to the needs of the city wilderness. Extended to America in 1879, it grew by leaps and bounds in the next two decades.[1] Its uniformed bands, parading the down-town districts with bass drum and trombone, gathered knots of the curious at the street corners and preached to "rumdom, slumdom and bumdom" the exciting gospel of repentance and reform. After 1889 the Army added social service to its evangelism. By means of its employment bureaus, "slum brigades" to work with tenement families, cheap lodgings for vagrants and rescue homes for fallen women, it carried on an essential work of Christian service.[2]

The rise of Christian Science is inseparably bound up with the life and personality of its founder, Mrs. Mary Baker Glover Patterson Eddy.[3] Of New England Puritan descent and a prey from childhood to ill health and recurrent hysteria, she had dabbled in mesmerism, spiritualism and hydropathy until she found relief from a distressing spinal malady at the hands of P. P. Quimby, a mental healer of Portland, Maine. Upon his

[1] F. W. Farrar, "The Salvation Army," *Harper's Mag.*, LXXXII (1891), 897-906; C. A. Briggs, "The Salvation Army," *N. Am. Rev.*, CLIX (1894), 697-710.

[2] A schism within the ranks led in 1896 to the establishment of the Volunteers of America which had less military autocracy in its form of organization but was otherwise devoted to a similar mission. Anon., "Ballington Booth and the Salvation Army," *Public Opinion*, XX (1896), 304-305.

[3] Two recent biographies are E. F. Dakin, *Mrs. Eddy* (rev. edn., N. Y., 1930), a critical study, and L. P. Powell, *Mary Baker Eddy* (N. Y., 1930), a work commended by Mrs. Eddy's followers.

death in 1866 she presently set up as a practitioner in her own right. At first an avowed Quimbyite, using one of his manuscripts as the fount of her teachings, she gradually evolved a system which she came to regard as wholly her own and which she put into print in 1875 under the title of *Science and Health*.[1] "Disease is caused by mind alone" and matter is an illusion—this was the essence of the newly proclaimed Christian Science. "You can prevent or cure scrofula, hereditary disease, etc., in just the ratio you expel from mind a belief in the transmission of disease" by working in harmony with the Eternal Mind as revealed through Jesus Christ.[2]

The founder gathered about her a small band of adherents in Lynn, Massachusetts, consisting mostly of factory workers and other artisans, "their hands stained with the leather and tools of the day's occupation."[3] She also provided for the training of healers by setting up the Massachusetts Metaphysical College in 1881, with herself as the faculty. Converts coming too slowly to suit her, she next changed her base of operations to Boston eight miles away. Though the period of struggle was not yet over, the removal to a large population center proved the turning point. Attacked by foes both within and without the church and harried by delusions

[1] There were many later editions and revisions. Though in retrospect Mrs. Eddy denied any indebtedness to Quimby, Powell in *Mary Baker Eddy*, 103, admits he played an important part in shaping her thinking. Incidentally, the exact term, Christian Science, had occasionally been used by Quimby. P. P. Quimby, *The Quimby Manuscripts* (H. W. Dresser, ed., 2d edn., N. Y., 1921), 388. Unadulterated Quimbyism became the basis of the New Thought movement which began to emerge toward the end of the century. See Faulkner, *Quest for Social Justice*, 215.

[2] Moreover, "Healing the sick through mind instead of matter, enables us to heal the absent as well as the present." Edn. of 1875, 334, 348, 398. Conversely, vindictive persons, through malicious animal magnetism ("M.A.M."), can produce disease or misfortune in others—a doctrine which first appeared in the edition of 1878.

[3] Sibyl Wilbur (O'Brien), *The Life of Mary Baker Eddy* (N. Y., 1907), 198.

of persecution, this frail, spectacled, ill-educated woman, already past sixty, proceeded to build up a solid support in Boston and to spread her doctrines afar. As a philosophy Christian Science would probably have had little appeal, but as a system of therapeutics it assured nerve-racked urban dwellers of the immediate cure of their bodies as well as the ultimate cure of their souls.

By 1890 there were over two hundred Christian Science groups with nearly nine thousand members, a majority of them in the larger cities of the Middle West. The number of local bodies doubled in the next decade while the membership perhaps quadrupled.[1] Meanwhile, as Mrs. Eddy became increasingly well-to-do and many of her practitioners acquired economic security, the cult sloughed off its working-class origins, directing its chief appeal to members of other denominations at higher income levels. This transition to a religion of the comfortable may be said to have been completed in 1895 when the First Church of Christ, Scientist, built at a cost of two hundred thousand dollars, opened in Boston as the "Mother Church" of the faith.[2]

Unlike the Salvation Army, the Christian Scientists did not develop social work as one of their interests, since poverty, like disease, was regarded as an illusion of mortal mind. Meantime, however, leaders in some of the older Protestant sects were awakening to a sense of responsibility for the world about them. Those most active in the effort to liberalize religious thought were

---

[1] *U. S. Eleventh Census* (1890), XVI, 297-298; *Christian Science Journal*, XVIII (1900), 202. From a scrutiny of the advertisements in the *Journal* it appears that the number of practitioners rose from fourteen in April, 1883, to two hundred in April, 1890, and to nine hundred and sixty-three in April, 1896.

[2] *Christian Science Journal*, XII (1894), 90-93, 451-454; *Boston Herald*, Jan. 7, 1895. Edward Eggleston's novel *The Faith Doctor* (N. Y., 1891) satirized the growing enthusiasm for Christian Science among the socially ambitious of New York.

usually also at the forefront of the effort to socialize religious practice. Notable among them were Lyman Abbott, Beecher's successor at the Plymouth Church in 1888; his neighbor on Manhattan, R. Heber Newton; and Francis G. Peabody, who from 1886 occupied the chair of Christian morals at the Harvard Divinity School. Particularly influential were Josiah Strong, general secretary of the Evangelical Alliance from 1886, and author of an eloquent book on social religion, *Our Country* (1885), which sold a half-million copies in twenty years; and Washington Gladden, Congregational minister in Columbus, Ohio, whose voice and example made him perhaps the great outstanding leader.[1] The more liberal theological schools responded by introducing courses in economics and sociology and even in some cases, as at Andover Seminary and the Chicago Theological Seminary, encouraging their students to get practical experience in social work. In the last years of the century it was possible to say that the "theological seminary of today . . . is a totally different institution from that of a generation ago."[2]

At the same time efforts began to be made by Protestant bodies to minister to the religious and practical needs of immigrants when they landed in the great Atlantic ports. In 1883 the interdenominational American Home Missionary Society organized German, Scandinavian and Slavic departments for this purpose. Of single sects the Lutherans in particular vied with the Catholics and the Jews in watching over the alien newcomer.[3] More significant was the steady tendency of

[1] Professor R. T. Ely, though not a cleric, also wielded great influence, especially through his volume *Social Aspects of Christianity.*

[2] John Tunis, "Social Science in the Theological Seminaries," *Lend-a-Hand*, XVI (1896), 3-10; anon., "Sociology and the Church," *Nation*, LIII, 114 (Aug. 13, 1891).

[3] Helen M. Sweeney, "Handling the Immigrant," *Catholic World*, LXIII (1896), 497-508. Early in the eighties Jewish charitable agen-

Protestant churches in down-town districts to develop "institutional" features, that is, conduct organized philanthropic and educational work among the poor and unchurched.[1]

Thus, St. George's Episcopal Church in New York, the People's Temple (Congregational) in Denver and Russell H. Conwell's Baptist Temple in Philadelphia began in the eighties to provide reading rooms, gymnasiums, social clubs, day nurseries, sewing classes and manual-training courses which, along with religious instruction, were available throughout the week to all comers. By 1894 the number of institutional churches was sufficiently large to justify the organization of an Open and Institutional Church League on an intercity and interdenominational basis. The success of the new methods was attested by phenomenal increases in religious membership.[2] St. George's Episcopal Church, which had but seventy-five communicants in 1882 when it started institutional work, numbered over four thousand in 1897; Berkeley Temple (Congregational) in Boston grew in seven years from three hundred to eleven hundred; and the Ninth Street Baptist Church of Cincinnati added nearly nine hundred members in four years. It was reported in 1900 that over a period of six years Congregational churches employing institutional methods had increased six times as fast as those which did not.

cies began to look after the needs of their Russian coreligionists; Baron de Hirsch in 1890 established a fund of $2,400,000 for this and allied uses. E. J. James and others, *The Immigrant Jew in America* (N. Y., 1906), 64-66, 79, 84-85.

[1] C. S. Mills, "The Institutional Church," *Bibliotheca Sacra,* XLIX (1892), 453-470; G. W. Cooke, "The Institutional Church," *New England Mag.,* n.s., XIV (1896), 645-660; Josiah Strong, *Religious Movements for Social Betterment* (H. B. Adams, ed., *Monographs on American Social Economics,* XIV, N. Y., 1900), 15-34.

[2] G. W. Mead, *Modern Methods of Church Work* (N. Y., 1897), 337-339; Strong, *New Era,* 245, and *Religious Movements,* 31-33.

*Moody*

*Sankey*

*Though still flanked by "old-time religion," the
institutional church was emerging.*

## Protestant Christianity.

To give the new social tendencies a wider backing various organizations were formed, one of the most influential being the Church Organization for the Advancement of the Interests of Labor in 1887 among the Episcopal clergy. Two years later some of the more radical religionists of Boston, following an English example and inspired by the Reverend W. D. P. Bliss of Grace Church (Episcopal), founded the Society of Christian Socialists in order "to awaken members of the Christian churches to the fact that the teachings of Jesus Christ lead directly to some specific form or forms of Socialism." [1] Though the movement did not prosper widely, the Congregationalists and Baptists in the early nineties formed national agencies to direct attention to social and economic problems, and two interdenominational societies, the Christian Social Union in 1891 and the American Institute of Christian Sociology in 1894, gave further impetus to the cause. In the latter year, too, the Evangelical Alliance of the United States, largely as a result of Josiah Strong's efforts, turned definitely to a social program. [2]

These attempts to socialize Christian thought and practice, of course, represented the efforts of energetic minorities. "We were few and we shouted in the wilderness," a pioneer of the social gospel later wrote of this time. [3] Yet that a rich harvest awaited beyond the turn of the century was plainly indicated by the extraordinary interest excited among the lay public by the ap-

[1] *The Dawn* (Boston), I (1889), no. 1, 3. R. Heber Newton became president of the New York branch.

[2] As further evidence of the socializing trend, the United Society of Christian Endeavor, composed of young people, began to take an active interest in civic and social reform after 1893. J. W. Baer, "The Work of Christian Endeavor Societies in Behalf of Better Citizenship," Natl. Conf. for Good City Government, *Proceeds. for 1895*, 517-523.

[3] Walter Rauschenbusch, *Christianizing the Social Order* (N. Y., 1912), 9.

pearance of *In His Steps,* a book written by the Reverend
C. M. Sheldon of Topeka in 1896. It told the story of
a congregation which resolved to live for a year, regardless of consequences, in accordance with the teachings of Jesus. Its wider message was inescapable: "If
the church members were all doing as Jesus would do,
could it remain true that armies of men would walk the
streets for jobs, and hundreds of them curse the church,
and thousands of them find in the saloon their best
friend?" [1] Within a year sixteen different publishers
were issuing the book to meet a demand that showed no
sign of appeasement.

Since early colonial times clergymen had often lifted
their voices at critical public junctures, but never before
had religious ethics been so sharply challenged by the
practices of the business order or the ministry so apparently helpless before the economic masters of society.
Yet, despite Gompers's sweeping denunciation of church-
men, individuals stood forth who, not content with
"making faces at the devil from behind the pulpit" or
with treating symptoms rather than the disease itself,
strove to cope with the deeper forces responsible for the
conditions. Few went so far as Bliss when he became a
Master Workman of the Knights of Labor and candidate
for lieutenant governor of Massachusetts on the Labor
ticket; nor were many willing to risk the obloquy which
befell the Methodist pastor, W. H. Cawardine of Pullman, Illinois, when he flayed the Pullman corporation
for precipitating the strike of 1894.

Washington Gladden, on the other hand, showed how
actively a minister might concern himself with indus-

[1] Edn. of 1899 (Street & Smith, N. Y.), 261. In 1925 it was estimated that over eight million copies had been sold in the United States
and twelve million more in the British Empire. The author received
little financial return because of a defective copyright. C. M. Sheldon,
*His Life Story* (N. Y., 1925), chap. iv.

trial relations without forfeiting the confidence of even a well-to-do congregation. During the Hocking Valley coal strike of 1884 he preached the "right and necessity of labor organizations" to a congregation which included high officers of the corporation involved. Two years later, while a fierce street-car strike raged in Cleveland, he journeyed thither from Columbus and spoke to a great meeting of employers and employees on "Is It Peace or War?" again declaring the right of wage-earners to organize. A little later he headed a committee of Ohio Congregationalists to investigate employment conditions in the state in an effort to promote better understanding between capital and labor. He visioned the solution of the difficulties in an "industrial partnership" in which the toilers would receive "a fixed share of the profits of production."[1]

The attitude of the Roman Catholic clergy toward the labor problem was greatly influenced by the course of Cardinal Gibbons of Baltimore. Thoroughly American in outlook and deeply sympathetic with the workingmen who composed the great bulk of his church, he made an eloquent plea to Rome in 1886 which saved the Knights of Labor from papal condemnation and ultimately secured the reversal of an edict against the organization in Canada.[2] He also resisted the recommendation of Archbishop Corrigan of New York that Henry George's *Progress and Poverty* be put upon the Index, again winning his point in Rome.[3] Of other

[1] Gladden, *Recollections*, 291-293, 300-305; same author, *Applied Christianity*, 1-37, 102-145. For the Reverend C. H. Parkhurst's effective battle against Tammany and organized vice, see earlier, 115-116.

[2] A. S. Will, *Life of Cardinal Gibbons* (N. Y., 1922), I, chaps. xviii-xx.

[3] In 1887 Archbishop Corrigan removed Father Edward McGlynn from his pastorate in New York City because of activity on behalf of Henry George's candidacy for mayor. When Dr. McGlynn declined to go to Rome to make submission to the pope, he was excommunicated. He was, however, reinstated as a priest in 1892. There was the closely

Catholic ecclesiastics Archbishop Ireland of St. Paul was notable for the pacificatory part he took in two great railway strikes in 1894 in the Northwest.[1] Catholic liberalism received high sanction in 1891 from the encyclical *Rerum Novarum* in which the pope, while denouncing socialism, defended the dignity of labor and declared that the problem could be solved only through the application of religious ethics.

Despite the many difficulties, theological and practical, which beset the path of religion, the last two decades of the century witnessed a substantial gain in church membership. Protestant communicants increased from ten million to nearly eighteen; the Roman Catholic population from well over six million to more than ten; the number of Jews from less than a quarter million to approximately a million. It was a striking testimonial to the vitality of organized religion that the growth was proportionately greater than the general advance of population, though, as was to be expected, less than the rate of increase of the urban wage-earning class.[2] Of the Protestant communicants the Methodist bodies repre-

similar case of Father R. L. Burtsell, also a follower of George. F. J. Zwierlein, *The Life and Letters of Bishop McQuaid* (Rochester, 1927), III, chap. xxix; Will, *Cardinal Gibbons*, I, chap. xxi; J. R. Commons and others, *History of Labour in the United States* (N. Y., 1918), II, 453-461.

[1] *Appletons' Annual Cyclopaedia*, XXXIV (1894), 699.

[2] The religious statistics of the period, unhappily, have to be used with great caution. The statements in the text must therefore be regarded as only rough approximations. The principal sources of information are Philip Schaff, "Progress of Christianity in the United States," *Princeton Rev.*, LV (1879), esp. 217-219; Bryce, *American Commonwealth*, III, 476, giving figures for 1887; H. K. Carroll, *Report on Statistics of Churches* (*U. S. Eleventh Census*, XVI); same author, *The Religious Forces of the United States* (Philip Schaff and others, eds., *The American Church History Series*, I, N. Y., 1893); Daniel Dorchester, *Christianity in the United States* (rev. edn., N. Y., 1895), pt. iii; David Sulzberger, "Growth of Jewish Population in the United States," Am. Jewish Hist. Soc., *Publs.*, no. 6 (1897), 144-145, 149; Daniel Dorchester, "The Evangelical Churches at the Close of the Nineteenth Century," *Christian Advocate*, LXXVI, 52-53 (Jan. 10, 1901).

sented a third of the total throughout the period, followed in order by the Baptists, Presbyterians, Lutherans
and Congregationalists. At all times, however, the
Catholics greatly outnumbered any Protestant group.

The geographic distribution of the sects remained
substantially as before. The East continued to be the
seat of Catholicism, Congregationalism and Episcopa-
lianism with a strong infusion of Presbyterianism, while
the Methodists and Baptists, numerous everywhere,
dominated the religious life of the South. In the Middle
West all faiths flourished—Chicago was the most
Catholic of American cities—and in that section, too,
the Lutherans had their principal stronghold. The most
conspicuous religious feature of the Great West was the
Mormon community in Utah.[1] As might be expected,
the great Scandinavian influx swelled the number of
Lutherans, while it was the anti-Semitic persecutions in
Russia, Austria-Hungary and Roumania that made the
Jewish faith for the first time important in America.[2]

Roman Catholicism, however, garnered the richest
harvest from among the immigrant newcomers, notably
those from Ireland, Germany, Austria-Hungary, Italy,
Poland and French Canada.[3] The heightened importance
of the American Church was signally recognized not
only, as we have seen, by the creation of a pontifical university, but also by the appointment of an American
cardinal and, in 1893, the sending of an apostolic dele-
gate to Washington.[4] On the other hand, many Americans, particularly in the Middle West,/ viewed with

[1] See earlier, 44-46.
[2] Samuel Joseph, *Jewish Immigration to the United States* (Columbia
Univ., *Studies*, LIX, no. 4), pt. i, chap. iv; pt. ii.
[3] Gerald Shaughnessy, *Has the Immigrant Kept the Faith?* (N. Y.,
1925), 162-172.
[4] See earlier, 213. The first American cardinal, John McCloskey, was
appointed in 1875; James Gibbons, his successor, was elevated in 1886.

mounting alarm the rapid accretion of Catholic power. They took amiss the agitation to secure public funds for parochial schools and regarded even the labor encyclical of 1891 as a sinister move by the Vatican to gain American working-class support.

As in the 1830's and 1840's, the fear and misunderstanding took the form of organized bigotry, embodied this time principally in the American Protective Association, a secret oath-bound order founded in 1887 by H. F. Bowers, a sixty-year-old lawyer of Clinton, Iowa.[1] Cradled in the heart of agricultural America, the anti-Catholic animus was vaguely mingled with the long-standing rural antagonism toward the great cities where, of course, the citadels of Romanism were to be found. The A. P. A. gained adherents slowly at first, having only seventy thousand members in 1893. Then, spurred by fear of immigrant competition for jobs during the hard times and a sudden flaming resentment on the part of urban dwellers against Irish machine politicians, the movement had a mushroom growth in the cities, probably commanding a million members in 1896.[2]

All the familiar phenomena of the earlier Know-Nothing movement were reproduced. The members of the order swore not to vote for or employ Catholics. "Escaped nuns" and "converted priests" told their harrowing tales to any who would listen. Forged documents

[1] H. J. Desmond, *The A. P. A. Movement* (Wash., 1912). For the earlier anti-Catholic movement, see C. R. Fish, *The Rise of the Common Man* (*A History of American Life*, VI), 115.

[2] In Chicago in 1894 the mayor, chief of police, fire chief, city attorney, a number of judges, forty-five aldermen, nine out of ten policemen, four fifths of the fire department and two thirds of the school teachers were said to be Catholics. Stead, *If Christ Came to Chicago*, 265. It was alleged that the municipal offices of New York, St. Louis, New Orleans, San Francisco and other important cities were also largely under Catholic control. W. H. J. Traynor, "The Aims and Methods of the A. P. A.," *N. Am. Rev.*, CLIX (1894), 69. Traynor, the national president, claimed a membership of two and a half million for the A. P. A.

were circulated to expose the designs of Rome against free America, one of them, an alleged papal encyclical, ordering the faithful to "exterminate all heretics" at the time of the feast of Ignatius Loyola (July 31) in 1893.[1] In a similar spirit stories were whispered of the gathering of arms in the basements of Catholic churches; and in at least one instance, that of the Toledo council of the A. P. A., a quantity of Winchester rifles was purchased as a measure of self-defense—a fact revealed by the dealer's suit for nonpayment.[2] At Dallas, Keokuk and elsewhere mob outrages occurred, the riot in East Boston on July 4, 1895, causing the death of one man and the injury of forty others.

As the movement turned to political action, its stronghold was shown to be a zone extending through northern Ohio, eastern Michigan and northern and central Illinois into the southern half of Iowa, northern Missouri and eastern Kansas and Nebraska, an area originally peopled largely by religionists of New England Puritan background.[3] The anti-Catholic groups held the balance of power in many local elections, controlled the Ohio legislature and helped pile up a triumphant majority for William McKinley in 1893 when he ran for governor.[4] By 1896, however, free silver and Bryanism made the Catholic menace seem the veriest specter. Both major

[1] Washington Gladden, "The Anti-Catholic Crusade," *Century*, XLVII (1893-1894), 789-795; T. J. Jenkins, "The A. P. A. Conspirators," *Catholic World*, LVII (1893), 685-693.

[2] Anon., "The Purchase of Guns by the A. P. A.," *Public Opinion*, XVI (1893-1894), 621.

[3] The movement also possessed strength in Massachusetts and Rhode Island and in parts of the remoter West. Desmond, *A. P. A. Movement*, chaps. iii, vii.

[4] McKinley kept his peace while his Democratic opponent denounced the A. P. A. As late as October, 1894, Governor McKinley, when asked by a heckler, "What is the matter with the A. P. A.?" replied blandly, "The question with us is: What is the matter with the country?" "The A. P. A. in Politics," *Public Opinion*, XVII (1894-1895), 615; Desmond, *A. P. A. Movement*, 34.

parties snubbed the A. P. A., and the movement withered as suddenly as it had grown. By bringing to the defense of Catholicism and fair play such respected figures as Gladden, Roosevelt and Senator Hoar, the church issued from the conflict in a stronger position before the public than when the attack began.[1] Within a few years it could be written, "Old feuds between Protestant and Catholic have ceased to be as important as their united battles against moral decay."[2] Organized religion had made great strides in the two decades, not the least of which was an enhanced appreciation of the common spiritual ideals for which all faiths stood.

[1] Gladden, *Recollections*, 359-365; Theodore Roosevelt, "What Americanism Means," *Forum*, XVII (1894), 196; G. F. Hoar, *Autobiography of Seventy Years* (N. Y., 1903), II, 278-293.

[2] H. D. Sedgwick, jr., "The United States and Rome," *Atlantic Mo.*, LXXXIV (1899), 445-458.

# CHAPTER XI

## Society's Wards

IF the church as such was slow to engage in works of social amelioration, the humanitarian leaders of the day were deeply imbued with the Christian spirit and most of them were loyal church members. The zeal to serve afflicted humanity, receiving impetus from the prolonged depression following 1873, was intensified by the hardship and misery which, even in normal times, befell the lot of many city dwellers. To Professor Sumner, the uncompromising individualist, there seemed "an unlimited supply of reformers, philanthropists, humanitarians, and would-be managers-in-general of society." Bryce with kindlier intent opined that no other country equaled the United States either in the sums spent or the personal effort devoted to beneficence.[1] Megalopolis, having crushed the human spirit with its million iron hoofs, became suddenly sorry, wept from its innumerable eyes and strove ardently to make up for its carelessness and greed. The driving force behind much of this effort came from women and the personnel which carried on the work was drawn increasingly from them.[2]

America in 1878 did not so much lack agencies of social welfare as a knowledge of how most wisely to use them. For many years the state and even some local governments had provided almshouses, orphanages, hos-

[1] W. G. Sumner, *What Social Classes Owe to Each Other* (N. Y., 1883), 112; James Bryce, *The American Commonwealth* (London, 1888), III, 498.
[2] Annie N. Meyer, ed., *Woman's Work in America* (N. Y., 1891), chaps. xii-xv, xvii-xviii.

pitals, homes for inebriates, insane asylums and institutions for the deaf, the dumb and the blind; but their administration was often marred by incompetent or wasteful methods. Such instrumentalities were supplemented by the work of church societies, individual charity and philanthropic organizations of widely diverse origins. In the single city of Philadelphia in 1878 there were more than eight hundred agencies engaged in aiding the poor and unfortunate.[1] It was typical of the situation generally that these bodies, lacking knowledge of each other's activities, often worked at cross purposes, duplicating almsgiving and thus indirectly encouraging duplicity and chronic improvidence on the part of applicants.

Because of the need to bring order out of the chaos, the example of Massachusetts in 1864 in setting up a state board of charities prompted other commonwealths to do likewise, until by 1893 nineteen states had established central boards to oversee and coördinate their tax-supported relief institutions.[2] The highly individualistic field of private philanthropy presented a more difficult problem; yet the Reverend S. H. Gurteen, an English migrant who had been active in a similar body in London, pointed the way to a solution when he brought about the establishment of the Charity Organization Society at Buffalo in 1877.[3] Its purpose was to serve as a clearing house for all existing agencies, public as well as private, and through concerted action to curtail the

[1] D. O. Kellogg, "On the Organization of Charity in Philadelphia," *Penn Mo.*, IX (1878), 707-723.

[2] Allan Nevins, *The Emergence of Modern America* (*A History of American Life*, VIII), 329-330; A. G. Warner, *American Charities* (R. T. Ely, ed., *Library of Economics and Politics*, IV, N. Y., 1894), chap. xviii.

[3] Earlier attempts of a somewhat similar but more limited character had been made in a Philadelphia ward (1873), New York City (1873) and Boston (1876). F. D. Watson, *The Charity Organization Movement in the United States* (N. Y., 1922), chaps. vi-vii.

abuses of indiscriminate charity while at the same time fostering constructive methods of dealing with poverty. The new ideal was the use of temporary aid to help the needy help themselves. By 1880 New Haven, Philadelphia, Brooklyn, Syracuse, Newport, Boston, Indianapolis, Cincinnati and Detroit had formed similar bodies under various names, and by the close of the century a total of one hundred and thirty-eight cities had followed their example. Though handicapped by a dearth of trained workers and often by jealousy among the associated charities, the plan richly justified itself by the results.

The newer trend was even more strikingly exemplified by the migration of resident colonies of social workers to the worst quarters of the larger cities. Anticipated in part by the institutional church, the social settlement was more immediately indebted to the example of Toynbee Hall in East London, which many American pioneer workers knew at first hand.[1] The initial settlement to open its doors was the Neighborhood Guild, started in New York in 1886 by Dr. Stanton Coit, an Amherst graduate, but the most famous one was Hull House, founded three years later in Chicago by Jane Addams and her coworker Ellen G. Starr.[2] Reared under Quaker influences, Miss Addams while yet a student at Rockford College had evinced an ardent interest in social questions. A trip to Europe during which she was irresistibly drawn to Toynbee Hall deepened her concern

---

[1] Among the more noted settlement workers who visited for a time at Toynbee Hall, besides Jane Addams, were Stanton Coit, Ellen G. Starr, Charles Zueblin and Robert A. Woods.

[2] Jane Addams, *Twenty Years at Hull House* (N. Y., 1910), chaps. iv-xi; Dorothea Moore, "A Day at Hull House," *Am. Journ. of Sociology*, II (1897), 629-642; Thérèse Blanc, *The Condition of Woman in the United States* (Abby L. Alger, tr., Boston, 1895), 67-87; Jane Addams and others, *Philanthropy and Social Progress* (N. Y., 1893), chap. ii.

for the plight of the poor and made her resolve to set up a similar institution in the metropolis of her native state.

Hull House was planted on South Halsted Street amidst a factory and tenement district swarming with Russian and Polish Jews, Italians, Bohemians, Germans and Irish, and containing nine churches and missions along with two hundred and fifty-five saloons. At first the founders contented themselves with inviting the street waifs and strays to take part in clubs and kindergartens. But as relations of mutual confidence were established they branched out into myriad activities such as men's clubs, a day nursery for working mothers, courses in arts and crafts, a gymnasium, a penny savings bank, an employment bureau and an orchestra.

Though only four settlements were established before 1890, they increased rapidly in the years thereafter, particularly in the train of the Panic of 1893. By 1895 over fifty were to be found in the principal Northern and Western cities and by the close of the century their number had perhaps doubled.[1] Not every one of these, of course, was equipped to perform the varied services of a Hull House or a South End House (Boston), but all of them, within the limits of their resources and opportunities, gave convincing demonstration of the truth of the adage that a fence at the top of a precipice is better than an ambulance at the bottom. The settlement movement appealed strongly to the idealism of young college men and women. Everywhere they were active in the work. The New York College Settlement on Rivington Street, begun the same year as Hull House, was initiated by Smith College students, while enterprises

---

[1] A chronological table of the more important ones is given in C. R. Henderson, *Social Settlements* (N. Y., 1899), 43-46; a complete list in R. A. Woods and A. J. Kennedy, eds., *Handbook of Settlements* (N. Y., 1911).

*Recruiting poor children among city tenements to be sent for outings on "Fresh Air" farms.*

## The Social Worker

under similar auspices were launched in Boston, Philadelphia and Chicago.

Whether engaged in putting up fences or providing ambulances, humanitarian workers could not avoid seeing that the social maladjustments with which they dealt were often conditioned by forces and influences of which the individual was a hapless victim. Their aggressive altruism thus caused them to support all movements for uplift—better working conditions, abolition of child labor, sanitary housing, public-health reform, penal reform, campaigns against municipal corruption.[1] In particular, they perceived in the ubiquitous saloon a relentless foe; and without caring whether poverty caused intemperance or intemperance poverty, they coöperated with those groups in American society which had long been battling against the evil.

The mainspring of the temperance movement had always been rural sentiment.[2] When the period opened it was four rural states—Maine, New Hampshire, Vermont and Kansas—which had state-wide prohibition. Likewise, it was the churches most deeply rooted in the farming regions—the Methodist, Baptist and Presbyterian—that furnished the shock troops for the "dry" assault. Most important of all was the Women's Christian Temperance Union, founded in 1874 by women dwelling mainly in country towns. When Frances E. Willard became president in 1879, she changed its emphasis from moral suasion to an insistence upon outright legal proscription. The W. C. T. U. under

---

[1] See, for example, Addams, *Twenty Years*, chaps. vii, ix-x, xiii-xiv; Eleanor H. Woods, *Robert A. Woods* (Boston, 1929), chaps. xi, xiii; R. A. Woods and A. J. Kennedy, *The Settlement Horizon* (N. Y., 1922), chaps. xvi-xvii; Julia C. Lathrop and others, "Social Settlements and the Labor Question," Natl. Conf. of Charities and Correction, *Proceeds. for 1896*, pt. iii.

[2] On this point, see J. R. Elliott, *American Farms* (*Questions of the Day Series*, LXII, 2d edn., N. Y., 1890), 236-239.

her energetic direction became the leading force in the antiliquor movement.[1] Soon no community in the land was without its corps of "white ribboners," ready at a moment's notice to join battle for the cause.

Shrewder than any other reform group of the time, the W. C. T. U. seized upon the public schools as a means of attaining in the future what might not be accomplished at once. Systematic pressure caused state after state to require "scientific temperance instruction" as part of the school curriculum. With Vermont leading the way in 1882, within five years thirty-one states and territories had followed suit, and by 1898 only two states held off. The textbooks used, according to two well-qualified medical authorities, "fairly bristle with statements of a character to work upon the fears of the reader, and remind one in this respect of patent medicine advertisements." After analyzing a number of the books they concluded that such teaching was "neither scientific, nor temperate, nor instructive."[2] But that it was effective as propaganda the future was to disclose.

The principal battlements of the "wet" interests were in the cities. There the strains and stresses of existence made the ordinary man seek solace in the flowing cup after a hard workday. There the immigrant horde found no reason to surrender cherished folk customs in a land of freedom. There the saloon with its free lunch and rough sociability took the place which the lodge and the club filled in the lives of those higher up in the social

[1] Frances E. Willard, *Glimpses of Fifty Years* (Boston, 1889), 368-478.

[2] H. P. Bowditch and C. F. Hodge, "Report," W. O. Atwater and others, eds., *Physiological Aspects of the Liquor Problem* (Boston, 1903), I, 33, 44. The main facts concerning temperance instruction may be found in the same vol., 21-45, 95-136; U. S. Commissioner of Education, *Report for 1889-90*, II, 695-742; edit., "Temperance Text-Books," *Outlook*, LXVI (1900), 706-709, 974-975, with a reply by the W. C. T. U., 996-999.

scale.[1] New York in 1890 possessed seventy-five hundred saloons, or one to every two hundred people. Chicago was proportionately well supplied, while smaller places like Albany, San Francisco and Cincinnati had an even greater relative number.[2] In the cities, too, the liquor industry was firmly intrenched, representing millions of capital and employing countless persons not only in the retail traffic but at every stage of manufacture and distribution. Besides, the liquor interests had their state and national organizations, formidable by reason of their funds. With the formation of the National Protective Association in 1886 these forces were enabled to present a united front to the common enemy.

Yet some counteracting influences were at work in the cities. As the trade unions waxed in strength, their policy opposed the abuse, if not the use, of alcoholic beverages.[3] A few, like the Order of Railroad Conductors and the Brotherhood of Locomotive Firemen, refused membership to persons connected with the sale of intoxicants. The International Typographical Union in 1894 even demanded "the state and national destruction of the liquor traffic." Had the Knights of Labor, instead of their rival, the American Federation of Labor, inherited the kingdom, the labor movement might have become a militant force for temperance. The Knights in 1878 denied admission to liquor employees; and in 1886, the year that marked the crest of their strength, Terence V. Powderly, head of the order, secured a hun-

[1] S. L. Loomis, *Modern Cities and Their Religious Problems* (N. Y., 1887), 101-102; Raymond Calkins, *Substitutes for the Saloon* (Boston, 1901), chap. i; John Koren, *Economic Aspects of the Liquor Problem* (Boston, 1899), chap. viii.

[2] J. S. Billings, comp., *Report on the Social Statistics of Cities* (*U. S. Eleventh Census*, 1890), 109-117.

[3] Koren, *Economic Aspects of Liquor Problem*, 35-37; Calkins, *Substitutes for Saloon*, 303-313; T. V. Powderly, *Thirty Years of Labor* (Columbus, 1889), 580-626; *Cyclopaedia of Temperance and Prohibition* (N. Y., 1891), 264-266.

dred thousand signatures to a five-year teetotal pledge.
Business leaders here and there also began to sense
the advantages of a sober working force. George Pullman in establishing his model industrial town in 1880
banned the drink traffic through his control of the title
deeds to the land. Before the decade ended, the Philadelphia and Reading, the Lake Erie and Western, the
Northern Pacific and the Missouri Pacific railways had
forbidden the use of intoxicants by men on duty. An
inquiry by the federal commissioner of labor in 1897
disclosed that fifty-three hundred employers out of seven
thousand customarily inquired into the bibulous habits
of job seekers, while eighteen hundred "prohibited, more
or less strictly, drinking."[1]

Most urban Protestant churches maintained total-
abstinence societies. To the efforts of the Catholic Total
Abstinence Union were added the weighty words of the
third plenary council of Baltimore in 1884-1885, in-
structing priests to induce all Catholic liquor dealers to
"choose a more honorable way of making a living."[2]
Though the sentiment for legal prohibition was not the
same as that for self-abstinence, the drys received aid
and comfort from such sources, as well as from persons
who favored prohibition for others if not for themselves.
They could also count ordinarily upon the support of
good citizens outraged by the lawlessness of the saloon
power and its evident relationship to corruption, vice
and crime.[3]

[1] Koren, *Economic Aspects of Liquor Problem*, 37-38; *Economic
Aspects of the Liquor Problem* (U. S. Comr. of Labor, *Ann. Rep. for
1897*), chap. vii.

[2] *Cyclopaedia of Temperance and Prohibition*, 536, 597-600, 632 *n.*
Bishop John A. Watterson of Columbus, Ohio, in 1894 went so far
as to deny liquor dealers the right of joining any Catholic society in
the diocese. *Nation* (N. Y.), LIX, 73, 113 (Aug. 2, 16, 1894).

[3] G. F. Parsons, "The Saloon in Politics," *Atlantic Mo.*, LVIII
(1886), 404-414; Josiah Strong, *Our Country* (rev. edn., N. Y.,

As the record of accomplishment shows, the embattled drys were able to wrest few lasting gains from the forces arrayed against them. The question of state-wide prohibition was submitted to popular vote in eighteen states between 1878 and 1898, but only one commonwealth, North Dakota from 1889, continued long with the four which had already taken that stand.[1] The restrictionists, however, had other strings to their bow. For a time they saw in high-license laws—imposing annual fees of perhaps five hundred or a thousand dollars for the saloon privilege—a means of lessening in wet states the number of liquor resorts and hence of reducing liquor consumption. Though, following the example of Nebraska in 1881, thirty-two states and territories had gone over to this system by 1889, high-license laws unexpectedly resulted everywhere in handsomer and more commodious saloons, many of them maintained as retail establishments of great breweries and distilleries.[2]

The drys therefore turned with redoubled zeal to that method of divide-and-conquer known as local option—local prohibitory enactments by popular vote. Centering their efforts first upon rural counties and villages, they pressed forward a policy of encirclement of

1891), 131-137; H. M. Boies, *Prisoners and Paupers* (N. Y., 1893), chap. xi; H. G. Wadlin, "Relation of the Liquor Traffic to Pauperism, Crime and Insanity," Mass. Bur. of Labor Stat., *Twenty-Sixth Ann. Rep.* (1895), pt. i; D. L. Colvin, *Prohibition in the United States* (N. Y., 1926), 209-211, 216-217, 555-574.

[1] Rhode Island from 1886 to 1889, and South Dakota from 1889 to 1896, had prohibition by constitutional amendment. Kansas in 1880, Maine in 1884 and North Dakota in 1889 made prohibition a constitutional requirement. E. H. Cherrington, *The Evolution of Prohibition in the United States* (Westerville, 1920), 202-266; Colvin, *Prohibition*, 137-144, 177-183, 202-216.

[2] *Cyclopaedia of Temperance and Prohibition*, 207-220; E. L. Fanshawe, *Liquor Legislation in the United States and Canada* (London, 1893), chap. v; J. G. Woolley and W. E. Johnson, *Temperance Progress of the Century* (Justin McCarthy, ed., *The Nineteenth Century Series;* Toronto, 1903), chap. x.

the larger towns and cities. But beyond this point they were seldom able to get. From year to year the saloon-less area expanded or shrank as the fortunes of battle veered. The most notable progress under local option was made in the South and the Middle West. Sometimes it seemed as though communities changed merely for change's sake, but even in such cases the recurrent public discussions kept voters primed as to the merits of the issue.[1]

The chief difficulties of enforcing liquor restrictions occurred in places where public sentiment was hostile or sharply divided. Local prohibition was often tolerated merely because of the accessibility of near-by city dram-shops. In states dry by state-wide enactment it was constantly necessary to make the enforcement provisions more drastic. Maine, the vaunted Eden of prohibitionists, found it impossible to keep applejack produced in local cider mills away from rural tipplers. In Portland, her chief city, "blind tigers" and "pocket peddlers" (boot-leggers) plied a brisk trade alongside of saloons, hotel bars, apothecary shops and bottling establishments where, as a result of collusion with the police, "customers lounged about, smoking and drinking, with an apparent sense of freedom and security." In 1893 no less than one hundred and sixty-one dealers paid federal liquor taxes in that city.[2]

[1] Fanshawe, *Liquor Legislation*, chap. iv. As a variant from the usual methods of dealing with the liquor problem, South Carolina in 1893, under prod of Governor Tillman, set up exclusive government dispensaries, a system which remained in force until 1907. Its dual purpose was to garner larger revenues for the state and reduce the private-profit motive in the sale of drinks. Though modeled upon a municipal system in Athens, Ga., the plan gained no favor elsewhere; for once prohibitionists and private saloonists saw eye to eye. F. H. Wines and John Koren, *The Liquor Problem in Its Legislative Aspects* (2d edn., Boston, 1898), 141-180 *b;* F. B. Simkins, *The Tillman Movement in South Carolina* (Duke Univ., *Publs.;* Durham, 1926), chap. viii; Gallus Thomann, *The South Carolina Dispensary* (N. Y., 1905).

[2] This view of the situation is based upon evidence presented in Wines

The ever present problem of alcoholic shipments into dry territory directed attention to the need for federal action. Since 1876 proposals for a national prohibition amendment had vainly been offered in Congress. The two great parties refrained from committing themselves on the question, fearing either the disruptive effects of a new and uncertain issue or the loss of campaign contributions from the liquor magnates. Nor did the Prohibition party, despite temporary gains in the elections of 1888 and 1892, succeed in winning an electoral vote. Nevertheless Congress in 1890, in order to offset certain adverse judicial decisions, provided that liquor shipments into any state or territory should, upon arrival, be subject to the laws there in effect. The Supreme Court interpreted the law to mean, however, that importations for private consumption were not affected.[1] In response to the need for more vigorous action upon all fronts the Anti-Saloon League of America was born in 1895. It frowned upon the third-party effort and used its energies to bore from within both major parties. Of great future significance, it was still operating chiefly in local politics when the period closed.[2]

To the observer in 1898 the temperance forces appeared to have been fighting a losing battle. The growth of cities and the increasing tension of living constantly raised up new adherents of the doctrine of "personal liberty." Moreover, though both the W. C. T. U. and the Prohibition party favored woman suffrage, none of

and Koren, *Liquor Problem*, 22-95, and Fanshawe, *Liquor Legislation*, chap. vii. These authors also review enforcement difficulties in Massachusetts, New York, Pennsylvania, Ohio, Indiana, Iowa, Missouri, South Carolina and elsewhere.

[1] *U. S. Statutes at Large*, XXVI, 313; Fanshawe, *Liquor Legislation*, 21-24; Wines and Koren, *Liquor Problem*, 119-122, 180.

[2] E. H. Cherrington, *History of the Anti-Saloon League* (Westerville, 1906), chaps. i-ii; H. U. Faulkner, *The Quest for Social Justice* (*A History of American Life*, XI), 225-226.

the equal-suffrage states took the dry side. The two decades saw an enormous increase in alcoholic consumption, from three hundred and eighty-six million gallons in 1878 to one and a quarter billion in 1898. The annual consumption per capita rose from a little over eight gallons to more than seventeen.[1] Since there was also probably a larger proportion of teetotalers at the end than at the beginning of the period, it is clear that the habit of drinking to excess had greatly increased. Yet, in spite of the dark outlook, Miss Willard spoke truly when she said, "While the enemy has brewed beer, they [the drys] have brewed public opinion."[2]

If the efforts of temperance reformers and humanitarian workers were designed in part to check the impulse to crime, others made it their main concern to look after the welfare of those who had run afoul of the law. The condition of jails and prisons in the late seventies remained as bad as in the years immediately following the Civil War.[3] The structures were generally antiquated and unsanitary, the officials in charge politicians ignorant of penal science, and the discipline stupid or brutal. Of the Kentucky state prison Governor L. P. Blackburn asserted, "The Black Hole of Calcutta, so abhorred in history, was not much worse than this."[4] Through the South generally the practice prevailed of leasing convicts,

---

[1] If ten-per-cent reduction be allowed for use in manufactures and the arts, the increase in personal consumption still remains startling. The capital investment in liquor grew from $118,000,000 to $458,-000,000. *U. S. Statistical Abstract for 1906*, 687; *U. S. Twelfth Census* (1900), IX, 599, 612, 624.

[2] Meyer, *Woman's Work in America*, 404.

[3] See Nevins, *Emergence of Modern America*, 330-331.

[4] *Appletons' Annual Cyclopaedia*, XIX (1879), 539-540. As for lesser prisons, according to a leading penal authority, "the American jails of today are, with here and there an exception, substantially what Howard in the eighteenth century found jails to be." Z. R. Brockway, "Needed Reforms in Prison Management," *N. Am. Rev.*, CXXXVII (1883), esp. 40.

usually Negroes, to railways, lumber camps and mines
where they were subjected to conditions often worse
than those of prewar slavery.[1] Counties and even states
operated their own chain gangs for road construction
and repair.

The progress of prison reform owed much to the
activities of the state boards of charities and correction,
much also to the work of educating public opinion
carried on by leaders of the National Prison Association,
notably the Reverend E. C. Wines, Dr. Theodore
Dwight, Franklin B. Sanborn and Zebulon R. Brockway. In line with the best European penological thought
these men stressed reformation, rather than retribution,
as the prime object of imprisonment as well as the best
guarantee of future law observance. Make the convict
good, they said, and make him good for something.
Such ideas, while too far in advance of the times in
respect to habitual criminals, appealed strongly as a
means of reclaiming juvenile offenders of twenty years
or younger, a class which in 1880 formed over a fifth
of the prison population.

The new program was first put into effect with the
opening of the New York State Reformatory at Elmira
in 1877 under Brockway's superintendency.[2] Young men
of from fifteen to thirty years of age who had been
convicted of a first offense were admitted under indeter-

[1] G. W. Cable gives a harrowing account of the system in *The Silent
South* (N. Y., 1885), 111-180. In *The American Siberia* (Phila.,
1891) J. C. Powell describes vividly his fourteen years as manager of
a Florida convict camp.

[2] The Elmira plan was drawn very largely from the Irish prison
system established by Sir Walter Crofton in the middle of the century.
For the Elmira system in operation, see Alexander Winter, *The New
York State Reformatory at Elmira* (London, 1891); F. H. Wines,
*Punishment and Reformation* (Crowell's Library of Economics and Poli-
tics, VI, N. Y., 1895), chap. x; Z. R. Brockway, *Fifty Years of Prison
Service* (N. Y., 1912), pt. ii; and F. B. Sanborn, "The Elmira Re-
formatory," S. J. Barrows, ed., *The Reformatory System in the United
States* (Wash., 1900), 28-47.

minate sentence. There, free from association with hardened criminals, the length of their stay (up to the maximum period set by the statute) depended largely upon their good conduct and their earnest application to means of self-improvement. When released they were sent to places of employment previously arranged, and continued under parole until their discharge was made absolute. It was claimed after ten years' trial that four out of every five Elmira graduates showed complete reformation.[1] The merits of the system commended themselves so strongly that before 1898 it was adopted, in more or less modified form, by Massachusetts, Pennsylvania, Ohio, Michigan, Illinois, Minnesota, Kansas, South Dakota and Indiana. Reformatories for girls apart from older women developed less rapidly, New York again leading the way with the Western House of Refuge at Albion in 1893.

Improvement, though less radical, was also introduced into the treatment of older criminals. Beginning in the 1870's Massachusetts experimented with the plan of placing reformable offenders, immediately upon conviction, on probation without physical confinement.[2] The parole system, another form of conditional liberation, spread to Ohio's prisons in 1884 and by 1898 was in effect in twenty-five states.[3] New and larger prisons were constructed, most of them upon approved sanitary principles, while Massachusetts and other states made a trial of state farms worked by convict labor. In the South the benighted situation showed signs of abate-

[1] *Appletons' Annual Cyclopaedia*, XXVII (1887), 703; Brockway, *Fifty Years*, 325.

[2] First tried out in Suffolk County, the scheme was made permissive for the entire state in 1891. No state followed Massachusetts till Rhode Island acted in 1899. L. N. Robinson, *Penology in the United States* (Phila., 1921), 194-196.

[3] E. H. Sutherland, *Criminology* (E. C. Hayes, ed., Lippincott Sociological Series; Phila., 1924), 525.

ment when Mississippi in 1890 abolished the lease system.

Agitation against the death penalty added but one state, Colorado in 1897, to the four—Michigan, Rhode Island, Wisconsin and Maine—which had abolished it before the period opened.[1] The worst conditions obtained within the United States civil jurisdiction in which eighteen crimes were capital, in Georgia where ten offenses were so classified, and in Alabama, Louisiana and Maryland which specified seven each. In 1892, however, the number of capital crimes in the federal code was reduced to three (murder, rape and treason). In a spirit of reform New York in 1888 first provided for electrocution in place of hanging, and two years later this new mode of death was inflicted upon the murderer William Kemmler.

In other respects the situation was less encouraging. Glaring contrasts in the sentences inflicted for the same offense in different states, or in the same state in different courts, or in the same court on different days, rendered the administration of justice chaotic.[2] Political pull determined the appointment of too many judges and prison officials. Moreover, plans for the self-support of inmates were badly disorganized by the success of trade unions in securing laws against prison contract labor. Finally, the county jails and city lock-ups, ill planned and worse managed, jumbled together young and old in such a fashion as to make these minor prisons a veritable "public school of crime."[3] Progress had been made dur-

---

[1] Maine, which had acted in 1876, restored the death penalty in 1883 only to abolish it again in 1887. In Colorado it was restored in 1901. S. J. Barrows, "Legislative Tendencies as to Capital Punishment," Am. Acad. of Polit. and Social Sci., *Annals*, XXIX, 619-620; "Capital Crimes," 54 Cong., 1 sess., *House Rep.*, no. 108, 4-7.

[2] Wines, *Punishment and Reformation*, 212-213; *U. S. Eleventh Census*, XXII, 373-411.

[3] W. F. Spalding, "The Progress of Prison Reform," Natl. Conf. of

ing the two decades, however, and the foundations laid for the notable advances which impended in the years ahead.[1]

One class of unfortunates, the temporary sufferers from public disasters, lacked regular provision for relief until the formation of the American Red Cross Society in 1881. This event was due largely to the persistent efforts of Clara Barton of Massachusetts, who, from comparing her experiences as nurse in the Civil War with those in the Franco-Prussian War, was strongly convinced of the superior advantages of the Red Cross type of organization in caring for the sick and wounded. Haunted by the specter of entangling alliances, the United States delayed ratifying the Geneva international pact until 1882, being then the thirty-second nation (in Miss Barton's phrase) to take itself "out of the roll of barbarians." [2] From the first the American leaders thought primarily in terms of disaster relief, for in their far-flung country recurrent public calamities were unavoidable while war seemed a remote and odious contingency. Even before the official ratification, the preliminary Red Cross organization carried succor to refugees from the Michigan forest fires of 1881. Miss Barton succeeded three years later in having the Geneva pact amended to provide for similar humanitarian activities in all the signatory nations.

From 1881 to 1898 the American Red Cross dispensed relief to fifteen scenes of fire, cyclone, flood and pestilence,

Charities and Correction, *Proceeds. for 1896*, esp. 409; J. F. Willard (Josiah Flynt, *pseud.*), *Notes of an Itinerant Policeman* (Boston, 1900), 86-92; Wines, *Punishment and Reformation*, 313-315.

[1] See Faulkner, *Quest for Social Justice*, 182-183, and P. W. Slosson, *The Great Crusade and After* (*A History of American Life*, XII), 103-104, 357-358.

[2] Helen H. S. Thompson, "The Red Cross," *Atlantic Mo.*, LX (1887), 646-654; W. E. Barton, *The Life of Clara Barton* (Boston, 1922), II, chaps. i-x.

three of them in lands across the sea. Nearly one million dollars in money and supplies were handled at a total cost of less than two per cent.[1] One of the worst catastrophes was the memorable flood at Johnstown, Pennsylvania, in 1889.[2] On Friday afternoon, May 31, an enormous wall of water released from a broken mountain dam roared down the narrow Conemaugh Valley, catching the inhabitants as unready as the people of Pompeii. With incredible swiftness the swirling torrent uprooted a city of twenty-eight thousand inhabitants, snuffed out several thousand lives and jammed a huge fantastic mass of blazing wreckage against the stone railroad bridge below the town. Red Cross workers arrived by the first train from the east and for five weary months labored amid scenes of want and woe. Over twenty thousand persons were reached by their ministrations.

While the Red Cross strove to mitigate the horrors of peace, other humanitarians busied themselves with plans to preclude the possibility of future war. Discredited by the Civil War and outrivaled by the veterans' organizations, the once promising pacifist movement had much lost ground to regain. The old American Peace Society, however, found fresh allies in the Universal Peace Union, arrayed since 1866 against defensive as well as offensive war, the National Arbitration League (1881), and various bodies representing religious groups, such as the Peace Association of the Friends (1869), the Christian Arbitration and Peace Society (1886) and the Peace Department of the W. C. T. U. (1887). Ceaselessly active, these bodies diversified their attack from opposition to the use of toy soldiers and the erection of military statues, to the sending of a protest of

[1] Clara Barton, *The Red Cross* (Wash., 1898), 101, 104-358.
[2] *N. Y. Tribune*, June 1, 1889, and later; *Appletons' Annual Cyclopaedia*, XXIX (1889), 476-482; Barton, *Red Cross*, 155-171; W. F. Johnson, *History of the Johnstown Flood* (Edgewood, 1889).

five hundred thousand women to Washington at the time of the Chilean crisis in 1891.[1] Their main purpose, however, was to secure the negotiation of arbitration treaties and, beyond that, the establishment of a permanent arbitral court.

So far as arbitration was concerned, they were investing in a rising market.[2] In the afterglow of the settlement of the *Alabama* claims the House and Senate adopted resolutions in 1874 indorsing the plan. Moreover, the state department repeatedly used its good offices to quiet the turbid waters of Latin-American international relations, and the Pan-American Congress, which the United States called into being at Washington in 1889, drew up a thoroughgoing scheme of arbitration for submission to the several governments. Two years earlier some two hundred members of the British House of Commons had memorialized the president and Congress in behalf of a general arbitration treaty between the two English-speaking powers. Congress in 1890 responded with a unanimous reaffirmation of its attachment to the principle, and in 1892 the government agreed with Great Britain to arbitrate the Bering Sea controversy.

Three years later, however, this structure of good will was imperiled by President Cleveland's blunt threat to go to war in defense of the Monroe Doctrine if Britain declined to arbitrate her boundary differences with Venezuela. Important elements of public opinion

[1] B. F. Trueblood, "History and Work of Peace Societies in America," *Am. Advocate of Peace*, LV (1893), 219-222; Frances E. Willard, "Peace and International Arbitration," *Am. Advocate of Peace*, LVI (1894), 271; Devere Allen, *The Fight for Peace* (N. Y., 1930), 465-497; H. L. Boyle, *History of Peace* (Grand Rapids, 1902), chap. viii.

[2] *Arbitration and the United States* (World Peace Found., *Pamphlets*, ıX, nos. 6-7), 463-467, 492-513; E. L. Whitney, *The American Peace Society* (Wash., 1928), chaps. xx-xxvi; A. C. F. Beales, *The History of Peace* (N. Y., 1931), chaps. viii-ix.

in both countries recoiled in horror; but Congress accorded the executive unanimous support, while Roosevelt, bespeaking still a different point of view, wrote privately to his friend Senator Lodge, "The clamor of the peace faction has convinced me that this country needs a war."[1] Fortunately the British government, for its own reasons, gracefully yielded the point. Events in 1897 and 1898 showed further how little the will to peace had penetrated responsible government circles. In the former year the Senate refused to ratify a general arbitration treaty which had been negotiated with Great Britain. In the latter, the same president who in his inaugural address had declared that "peace is preferable to war in almost every contingency" was rushed into war with Spain by the sound and fury of the sensational press joined to the vociferations of the jingoes in Congress.[2] Even the churches, hitherto the mainstay of the organized peace movement, promptly set their seal of approval upon this war "for humanity's sake."

The operations in Cuba gave the Red Cross its first opportunity to mobilize for war service. A few months before the American intervention Miss Barton and a staff had gone to Havana to carry on work among the sick and starving *reconcentrados*. After the declaration of war on April 25 their activities expanded to all parts of Cuba as well as to the mobilization camps in southern United States and eventually to the Philippines and Porto Rico.[3] Local branches to the number of two thousand

[1] *Selections from the Correspondence of Theodore Roosevelt and Henry Cabot Lodge* (N. Y., 1925), I, 205.

[2] The experienced diplomat John W. Foster wrote in 1910 that if McKinley had kept his head "the war might have been averted." Cleveland shared this opinion during the event and later. J. F. Rhodes, *The McKinley and Roosevelt Administrations* (N. Y., 1922), 63-64; Robert McElroy, *Grover Cleveland* (N. Y., 1923), II, 271-274.

[3] Margherita A. Hamm, "The Red Cross in the Spanish War," *Am. Rev. of Revs.*, XIX (1899), 56-59; Barton, *Red Cross*, 359-665; American National Red Cross Relief Committee, *Report* (N. Y., 1899).

were formed throughout the nation to collect money
and provide supplies. The Pacific states alone raised
over one hundred thousand dollars and the grand total
exceeded half a million. The camps and hospitals served
by the Red Cross in the field were often located in places
accessible only by difficult mountain passes or long sea
voyages, but the organization proved equal to every
emergency. Though the soldiers were repeatedly subject
to an almost criminal mismanagement, the responsibility
fell solely upon the war department, not on this volunteer army of humanitarians whose initial proffer of
coöperation had been rebuffed by army officials.

The Red Cross issued from its first baptism of fire
with fresh claims upon the gratitude of the American
people. To the peace leaders, on the other hand, it seemed
that the labors of a generation had gone for naught.[1]
Little could they guess in their hour of gloom that forces
already at work in European chancelleries were paving
the way for the speedy attainment of their cherished
objective, the establishment of a permanent international arbitration tribunal.[2]

Not all the social questions confronting this generation stemmed from the maladjustments of city living
or the perversity of nature or nations. Two far-reaching
problems, heritages from America's rural past, were
localized in the two great agricultural sections of the
country. One concerned the civilizing of the American
aborigine, the other the assimilation of the ex-slave to
conditions of freedom. By 1878 Indian outbreaks had
become the exception rather than the rule. The fierce
Apache in the Southwest fought desperately from 1882
to 1886 to resist being penned up in reservations; in
1889-1890 the unregenerate Sitting Bull, conqueror of

[1] Whitney, *American Peace Society*, chap. xxvii.
[2] See Faulkner, *Quest for Social Justice*, 327-328.

General Custer, helped propagate the Messiah craze among the Dakota Sioux, culminating in the battle of Wounded Knee and a loss of over five hundred lives; and as late as 1898 a Chippewa band in Minnesota were stung to warlike reprisals.[1] But every mile of Western railroad enhanced the military effectiveness of the United States, while the spreading zone of settlement reduced the savage's chances of living solely by the chase. The typical red man of the 1880's was a pensioner of the government, living a tribal life within the narrow limits of a reservation, his health impaired by the white man's contagious diseases and his self-reliance sapped by annuities and rations provided by the Great White Father.

At the beginning of the eighties there were a quarter of a million Indians in the United States, the vast majority west of the Mississippi, dwelling on one hundred and twenty different reservations aggregating an area as large as Texas. Many of the government agents to whose care they were confided were deplorably inefficient when not outright corrupt, and the savages were further victimized by unscrupulous licensed traders who grossly overcharged or otherwise duped them. The remnants of about thirty tribes had been herded in Indian Territory, often by methods violating every dictate of humanity. The removal thence of the peaceable Cheyenne of the Upper Missouri is a story of the ill-deserved sufferings of a band taken from an invigorating northern climate to a fever-infested district where the rascality of the agent exposed them to slow starvation. When in the fall of 1878 three hundred of the Indians, men, women and children, escaped in an at-

[1] Flora W. Seymour, *The Story of the Red Man* (N. Y., 1929), chap. xvii; L. H. Roddis, "The Last Indian Uprising in the United States," *Minn. History*, III, 273-290.

tempted flight to their old home, the fugitives after a desperate resistance surrendered upon condition of being restored to their former reservation. Confined in midwinter in a Nebraska fort without food or fuel, they broke prison only to be shot down by the troops until but sixty remained.[1]

Equally shocking was the treatment accorded the Ponca whose story, told to audiences throughout the East in 1879 by Standing Bear and an educated girl Bright Eyes, appalled the humane.[2] Their pathetic recountal prompted Helen Hunt Jackson to write her widely influential *A Century of Dishonor* (1881), a passionate indictment of long-continued Indian mistreatment based upon a study of official records. Shortly afterward Eastern humanitarians formed two organizations—the Indian Rights Association in 1882 and the annual Lake Mohonk Conference of Friends of the Indians in 1883—to influence public opinion and official action for reform. In the next few years the legislatures of Maine, Connecticut, New York, Pennsylvania, Delaware and Michigan memorialized Congress on behalf of a peaceable and constructive solution.[3]

In reality, the government had not been wholly remiss in its duty to the red man, but its efforts had been halfhearted, vacillating and of limited application. For many years it had aided missionary schools, and in 1878 four thousand Indian children were attending schools which the government itself had provided. Something had been

[1] "The Report of the Senate Committee on the Removal of the Northern Cheyennes to Indian Territory," 46 Cong., 2 sess., *Senate Rep.*, no. 708 (June 8, 1880).

[2] The Ponca episode is described in "The Report of the Senate Committee on the Removal of the Poncas to Indian Territory," 46 Cong., 2 sess., *Senate Rep.*, no. 670 (May 31, 1880).

[3] Women's National Indian Association, *Report for 1885*, 26. This body, formed in 1879 under Protestant auspices, had seventy branches in leading centers in 1886.

done also to encourage the use of domestic animals and farm implements. By special treaties and other enactments certain tribes had even been authorized to abandon the communal system of land ownership (though few did so), and at least three thousand individuals before 1887 had attained citizenship status.[1] Congress, however, had resisted the repeated recommendations of presidents, secretaries of the interior and Indian commissioners, over a long space of years, to provide a normal and general means by which capable individuals wherever found might attain to the white man's way of life. All students of the question, in the government and out, were agreed that no amount of education, or even the gift of citizenship, would civilize the red man so long as he remained enmeshed in tribal and reservation life. Nor could he be expected to turn earnestly to farming when, like the Ponca, he might at any time be robbed of his improved lands. Indian sloth and improvidence, in the opinion of thoughtful agents on the spot, were the fruits of a system for which the government, not the savage, was to blame.[2]

President Cleveland, whose sympathies had been deeply stirred by Mrs. Jackson's volume, actively interested himself in the problem.[3] Moreover, the philanthropic incentive to reform was now reënforced by a growing Western demand for the break-up of reservations in order to open virgin tracts for white occupancy.[4]

[1] *Congressional Record*, XI, pt. ii, 1060-1061; Commissioner of Indian Affairs, *Report for 1891*, I, 21.

[2] See, for example, Comr. of Indian Affairs, *Rep. for 1877*, 114, 119, 165; *for 1878*, vii, 5, 31, 84, 128, 140.

[3] G. F. Parker, "Grover Cleveland's First Administration," *Sat. Eve. Post*, CLXCV, esp. 52, 54 (April 7, 1923). Cleveland's private papers reveal that he also received much unsolicited advice from the spirit world through the Indian "controls" of self-avowed mediums. McElroy, *Cleveland*, I, 226.

[4] Secretary of Interior, *Rep. for 1879*, 4; *for 1884*, xi; Mohonk Conference, *Proceeds. for 1886*, 34; *for 1887*, 68.

The humanitarians sought rights for the Indians, the Westerners lands for themselves. This combination of forces resulted on February 8, 1887, in the adoption of a general allotment law, sponsored by Henry L. Dawes of Massachusetts, Charles Sumner's successor in the Senate and a leading spirit in the Mohonk Conference. By its provisions the president was authorized, whenever time and circumstances seemed ripe, to end the tribal government and parcel out the lands of any reservation among individual owners according to certain fixed amounts.[1] The private owners were thereupon to become American citizens though, in order to protect them from white avarice, they were denied the right to sell or mortgage their holdings for twenty-five years. The land remaining undivided might be bought by the government for sale to actual settlers, the money to be held as a trust fund for educating and civilizing the Indians concerned. Although the Five Civilized Tribes in Indian Territory preferred to remain outside the scope of the statute, systematic pressure was exerted to get them to accept its underlying principles, an end finally attained in 1898.[2]

As the benefits of the Dawes law were extended to an increasing number of tribes, the results attested the wisdom of the policy. An official inquiry five years after

[1] One hundred and sixty acres for each head of family, smaller allotments for others, the amounts to be doubled in the case of grazing lands. *U. S. Statutes at Large*, XXIV, 388-391. Because of the discrimination against the younger and more educable tribesmen a supplementary act of 1891 provided for tracts of eighty acres share and share alike. *U. S. Statutes at Large*, XXVI, 794-796. Eleven tribes were, for various reasons, exempted from the operation of these laws.

[2] *U. S. Statutes at Large*, XXX, 495-519. This antagonistic attitude was due to many causes, chiefly perhaps to the position of power and profit held in the semiautonomous Indian states by mixed bloods and to the influence of cattle magnates who were benefiting from a cheap rental of the rich pasture lands. In 1901 the Five Tribes were brought specifically under the terms of the Dawes law. *U. S. Statutes at Large*, XXXI, 848, 861.

its passage showed that a large proportion of the favored Indians were tilling the soil or raising stock.[1] While the older generation often clung tenaciously to tribal traditions and customs, the younger men tended to break away from the chief's influence and adopt civilized ways. This tendency grew markedly with the extension of educational facilities.[2] Some of the children attended neighborhood day schools, but the majority were taken from home influences and placed in reservation boarding schools, or in training schools outside the reservation as at Carlisle, Pennsylvania, or at Haskell Institute in Lawrence, Kansas. Everywhere stress was placed upon vocational training and an appreciation of the values of civilization. The young buck who graduated from Carlisle was not likely to return to the blanket of his forefathers or prefer a squalid tepee to a livable frame house.

Though school accommodations lagged behind the need, nearly twenty thousand youths were enrolled as pupils in 1898. Between 1878 and that year the annual government appropriations rose from thirty thousand dollars to well over two and a half million. Meantime the break-up of the reservations had been proceeding apace. Between 1887 and 1906, when important changes were made in the Dawes act, seventy-five million acres, or nearly three fifths of the total, were disposed of. About seven million acres were allotted to fifty-eight thousand Indians, and over fifty million were acquired by the government for sale to white settlers.[3] In addi-

---

[1] Comr. of Indian Affairs, *Rep. for 1892*, 185-195.

[2] W. N. Hailmann, "Education of the Indian," N. M. Butler, ed., *Education in the United States* (Albany, 1900), II, 941-972; H. L. Dawes, "Have We Failed with the Indian?," *Atlantic Mo.*, LXXXIV (1899), 280-283.

[3] The government reserved relatively small tracts for religious and educational purposes and as timber preserves. Detailed figures as regards allotments may be found in Esther F. Cooper, The Genesis and Application

tion, before 1906 ninety-two thousand members of the Five Civilized Tribes received allotments aggregating fourteen and a half million acres.

Despite this gratifying progress certain evils attended the application of the law. Allotments were sometimes made before the red men were ready for the responsibility. In other instances, capable and self-reliant individuals chafed at the inflexible twenty-five-year restriction. Cases were also numerous in which well-meaning Indians were induced to enter illegal leasing arrangements with powerful cattle interests.[1] As voters, moreover, the adult males were preyed upon by unscrupulous politicians who taught too many of them to regard the franchise as a "merchantable article to be disposed of in the best market."[2]

From their new status as citizens came also the right to buy liquor at will. The startling increase in drunkenness, resulting often in immorality and crime, caused Congress somewhat belatedly, in 1897, to ban the traffic among Indians during the probationary period.[3] The reversal of this law by the Supreme Court in 1905, as a denial of the equal rights of citizens, would hasten the passage of the Burke act (1906), designed to cure this as well as other defects in the original statute.[4] Even without these remedial provisions no one doubted that this oldest of American race problems was in a fair way to solution. The "Emancipation Act of the Indians,"

of the Dawes Act (M.A. thesis, Univ. of Iowa, 1924), 111-112, and app. C. See also Dawes, "Have We Failed with the Indian?," 283.

[1] The original statute was amended from time to time to permit leasing but under strict conditions. *U. S. Statutes at Large*, XXVI, 794; XXVIII, 305; XXX, 85.

[2] Comr. of Indian Affairs, *Rep. for 1892*, 139, 186, 192; *for 1893*, 335.

[3] *U. S. Statutes at Large*, XXIX, 506; Koren, *Economic Aspects of Liquor Problem*, chap. vii.

[4] U. S. *v.* Heff, 197 U. S., 488; Faulkner, *Quest for Social Justice*, 13-14.

as the Dawes law was called, may be rated as perhaps the generation's most notable humanitarian venture. Without any regard to consistency, the Americans of the eighties and nineties were resolved that the Negro question was one for the South to solve, not for the politicians in Washington.[1] President Hayes's recall of the last garrisons in 1877, after a decade of ceaseless governmental activity on behalf of Negro equality, was a tacit admission of the South's right to manage its own race relations, as well as a symbol of the North's increasing absorption in the exigent problems arising from its new industrial order. When a belated flare-up of Radical fervor in 1890 secured from the House of Representatives the passage of a "force bill" for facilitating federal intervention in congressional elections, party leaders in the Senate quietly quashed the measure mainly because of their greater concern for the enactment of a new tariff law.[2]

Partly in response to the Republican party's desertion of their cause, a mass movement of Negroes set in toward the North and West in the spring and summer of 1879, directed chiefly toward Kansas.[3] For several years Benjamin ("Pap") Singleton, a Tennessee ex-slave, and Henry Adams of Louisiana, a colored veteran of the late war, had been sowing seeds of unrest, and the agents of

[1] See, for example, edit., "Political Rights of Negroes," *Andover Rev.*, XIII (1890), 305; R. P. Hollowell, *The Southern Question Past and Present* (Boston, 1890), 21-26. The policy of noninterference was facilitated by the fact that until 1889 the Republicans were at no time in effective control of both the presidency and the two houses of Congress.

[2] J. F. Rhodes, *History of the United States from Hayes to McKinley* (N. Y., 1919), 358-364.

[3] W. L. Fleming, " 'Pap' Singleton, the Moses of the Colored Exodus," *Am. Journ. of Sociology*, XV, 61-82; J. C. Hartzell, "The Negro Exodus," *Methodist Quar. Rev.*, LXI (1879), 722-748; F. R. Guernsey, "The Negro Exodus," *International Rev.*, VII (1879), 373-390; J. B. Runnion, "The Negro Exodus," *Atlantic Mo.*, XLIV (1879), 222-230; *Appletons' Annual Cyclopaedia*, XIX (1879), 354-358; XX (1880), 417.

Western railway and land companies, for their own reasons, vigorously seconded their efforts. Crop failures and low cotton prices in 1879, added to the usurious credit system and increasing election brutalities, brought matters to a head. By the thousands Negroes, ill clad and often penniless, threw down their hoes in Louisiana, Mississippi, Tennessee, Texas and elsewhere, crowded toward the river wharves and, by hook or crook, made their way to the new Canaan. Some of them were turned back at St. Louis or Kansas City; others, upon arrival at their destination, were saved only by the exertions of emergency relief societies.

But the great majority, perhaps twenty or twenty-five thousand in all, remained in Kansas, winning the respect of their white neighbors by their diligence and self-denial.[1] Meantime the Southern planting interests, fearful of losing their principal labor supply, sought by argument and force to stay the exodus. A biracial convention at Vicksburg on May 6 discussed ways and means of improving the lot of the Negro in the South.[2] In many localities would-be migrants were dealt with by violence, defrauded of their money or jailed on false charges. But the movement ended mainly for other reasons, chiefly, perhaps, a better understanding by the credulous blacks of the difficulties and hardships which the northward trek involved.

For the remainder of the century the bulk of Afro-Americans stayed in Dixie, content to work out their destiny in the land where slavery had originally planted

---

[1] Successful examples of Negro colonies were Nicodemus, Baxter Springs, Morton City and Singleton. F. H. Fletcher, *Negro Exodus* (n.p., 1879) ; Henry King, "A Year of the Exodus in Kansas," *Scribner's Mo.*, XX (1880), 211-218; anon., "The Administration of Governor John P. St. John," Kan. Hist. Soc., *Colls.*, IX, 378-395.

[2] "The Proceedings of a Migration Convention and Congressional Action Respecting the Exodus of 1879," *Journ. of Negro History*, IV, 41-92.

them. Migration, however, occurred within the area, notably a steady southwesterly trend from the old border states into the Gulf region, where their dense numbers along the river courses and in the rich alluvial plains made the black belt still blacker. While the vast majority clung to the rural districts, local centripetal movements resulted in straggling colonies in the alley ways and poorer quarters of the cities. The total colored population of the ex-slave states advanced from six million in 1880 to eight in 1900, a rate of growth which should not have caused (though it did) fears of impending Africanization, for the whites meantime increased from eleven million to nearly twenty.[1] Though the Negro birth rate was higher than the Caucasian, it was greatly offset by excessive infant mortality and the inroads of diseases from which the paternalistic life of the plantation had in large degree protected the race in slavery.[2] In 1880 they made up a third of all the people of the section and at no time did they form less than a quarter of the total. In certain states of the Lower South—Georgia, Alabama and Florida—the two races were about evenly divided, while in South Carolina, Mississippi and Louisiana the Negroes actually outnumbered the whites.

While Pap Singleton was still exhorting tumultuous crowds to flee the land of their oppressor, Frederick Douglass, the Nestor of his race, sounded a solemn note of warning. "The exodus the colored people want," he affirmed, "is the exodus from ignorance, vice and lack of thrift." [3] The history of the years that fol-

[1] *Negroes in the United States* (Bur. of the Census, *Bull.*, no. 129, 1915), 12-13, 57-58.

[2] F. L. Hoffman, *Race Traits and Tendencies of the American Negro* (N. Y., 1896), chaps. i-ii; T. N. Chase, ed., *Mortality among Negroes in Cities* (Atlanta Univ., *Publs.*, no. 1), *passim*.

[3] *Appletons' Annual Cyclopaedia*, XX (1880), 585. See also Frederick Douglass, "The Negro Exodus," *Journ. of Social Sci.*, IX (1880), esp. 12-21.

lowed is an impressive commentary on his words. For the Negro it was a time of painful awakening from the fool's paradise of Reconstruction days—of sordid, unremitting struggle with ignorance and poverty. The statesman of this new emancipation was Booker T. Washington, an ex-slave who, as a result of youthful schooling at Hampton Institute, Virginia, was inspired, as he later said, to go into the Lower South and "give my life to providing the same kind of opportunity for self-reliance and self-awakening that I had found provided for me at Hampton." [1] Starting at Tuskegee, Alabama, in 1881 with one teacher, thirty students and a borrowed log shanty, he succeeded, with state aid and Northern benefactions, in building up his Normal and Industrial Institute until by 1898 it had about ninety instructors, nearly a thousand students, twenty-three hundred acres of land, and forty buildings erected largely by student labor.

Believing that his people must begin at the bottom and that it was to their best interest to perfect the mechanical skills which they had been taught in slavery, he provided training in all the trades and occupations necessary for securing a footing in Southern economic life. Along this path too, he maintained, lay the best hope for the recovery of legal equality, for "No race that has anything to contribute to the markets of the world is long in any degree ostracized." His reply to those who beat their breasts for immediate recognition of Negro rights was: "The opportunity to earn a dollar in a factory just now is worth infinitely more than the opportunity to spend a dollar in an opera-house." [2]

[1] B. T. Washington, "The Awakening of the Negro," *Atlantic Mo.*, LXXVIII (1896), esp. 322. See also same author, *Up from Slavery* (N. Y., 1901), chaps. vii-xii, and M. B. Thrasher, *Tuskegee* (Boston, 1900).

[2] The quotations are taken from his noted speech in 1895 at the

The scarcely perceptible emphasis on the words, "just now," was missed by Southern whites who, thinking it his purpose to breed a race of robots, acclaimed his wisdom and leadership.

Washington's teachings, backed by the visible success of the work carried on at Hampton and Tuskegee and the ever widening influence of their graduates, made a deep impress on Negro education everywhere.[1] As we have already seen, the South was too poor to provide enough schools for the scattered inhabitants of the great rural areas and especially so under the policy of separate instruction for the two races.[2] This, perhaps more than white indifference or antagonism, impeded the development of adequate instructional facilities.[3]

Fortunately Northern philanthropy did something to relieve the situation. A small part of the Peabody Fund was used for training colored teachers, while two new benefactions exclusively for Negroes—the John F. Slater Fund of a million dollars in 1882 and Daniel Hand's gift of one and a half million to the American Missionary Association in 1888—stimulated educational effort in every department. Though about half the Afro-American children had no schools of any kind to attend,

opening of the Atlanta Exposition, reprinted in *Up from Slavery*, 218-225, and elsewhere.

[1] U. S. Comr. of Educ., *Reps.*, 1878-1901, *passim;* esp. J. L. M. Curry, "The Slater Fund and the Education of the Negro," *Rep. for 1894-95*, II, 1367-1424; Kelley Miller, "The Education of the Negro," *Rep. for 1900-01*, I, 731-859; and A. D. Mayo, "The Work of Certain Northern Churches in the Education of the Freedmen, 1861-1900," *Rep. for 1901-02*, I, 285-314.

[2] See earlier, 163-166.

[3] Miller estimates that the per-capita school expenditure in the ex-slave states was in 1878-1879 $2.60 for whites and $1.00 for blacks, the comparable figures for 1897-1898 being $4.25 and $2.27. "Education of the Negro," 753. If his estimates are accurate, it is probable that the disparity may be, in considerable degree, accounted for by the difference in the per-capita expenditure on education in the cities, where Negroes were few, and in the rural districts where the vast bulk of them dwelt.

the total number of those who did attend rose from six hundred and eighty-five thousand in 1878 to a million and a half in 1898.[1] A serious lack was the dearth of secondary schools in which more intensive instruction in manual training and industrial education could be given. The score or more of Negro colleges and universities, however, were of hardly better than high-school rank and they usually stressed courses of the vocational type. Howard University at Washington was about the only one whose standards of admission approximated those of the better Northern colleges.

As farmers the race continued to be handicapped, on the one hand, by the shiftless habits learned in slavery and, on the other, by the vicious crop-lien system.[2] All through the black belt they lived in wretched single-room cabins, tilling "one-mule" cotton farms of from twenty-five to thirty acres, and managing to pay their rent and buy supplies only by mortgaging their unharvested crops at exorbitant interest rates. For many it was an economic serfdom from which there was no release. Their diet rarely included much more than hominy, corn bread, rank fat "sidemeat" and coffee, while half their clothing was begged from the whites. In Tennessee, Kentucky and Virginia the situation was somewhat more hopeful, and a higher proportion of tenants were emerging into the class of farm owners and householders.

In 1890 six out of every ten Negroes gainfully em-

[1] U. S. Comr. of Educ., *Rep. for 1898-99*, II, 2202. The rural school term usually lasted about two months, and Negro parents were not able to lengthen it by voluntary contributions as was often done by the whites for their own schools.

[2] S. J. Barrows, "What the Southern Negro Is Doing for Himself," *Atlantic Mo.*, LXVII (1891), 805-815; P. A. Bruce, *The Plantation Negro as a Freeman* (*Questions of the Day Series*, LVII, N. Y., 1889), chaps. xiii-xiv; L. J. Greene and C. J. Woodson, *The Negro Wage Earner* (Wash., 1930), chap. ii.

ployed were husbandmen, while three out of the remaining four were in domestic and personal service, mostly in the towns.[1] Cartmen and porters were ordinarily Negroes, and many were doing well as carpenters, barbers, bricklayers, blacksmiths and mechanics. There were individual cases of conspicuous affluence. Several Negroes in Baltimore were reputed to be worth fifteen thousand dollars, and three or four from forty to sixty thousand. A few doctors and lawyers were also to be found in the larger Southern cities, though their livelihood suffered because of the preference of their own race for white men in the same lines. Of the older professions the ministry was the only one in which an Afro-American could count upon an enthusiastic following of his own color, but success here depended less upon training than upon a sonorous eloquence.

Race antipathy hampered economic progress only when blacks competed with poor whites for the same jobs, particularly in the skilled trades. Although both the Knights of Labor and the American Federation of Labor were willing to have them as members, and white employers valued them as a docile labor force, local working-class sentiment often managed to block their employment.[2] The antagonism sometimes took the form of strikes; yet in thirty-nine recorded instances from 1882 to 1898 only seven strikes had the desired outcome of excluding Negro workers.

The color line was most rigidly drawn at points where the association of the two peoples might suggest social equality. While white persons might cheerfully work side by side with colored employees or be attended in public places by their ebon-hued nurse maids, they

[1] Barrows, "What the Southern Negro Is Doing," 807, 810; C. H. Wesley, *Negro Labor in the United States* (N. Y., 1927), 226-235; Greene and Woodson, *Negro Wage Earner*, chap. iii.

[2] Wesley, *Negro Labor*, 236-237, 254-263.

did not voluntarily tolerate such proximity when the Negroes were not in a menial relationship.[1] Blacks and whites even worshiped their common God in different churches. Though the law throughout the South prohibited intermarriage, few states expressly forbade irregular sex relations. Yet Philip A. Bruce, a Virginian of the former master class, writing in 1888, deemed it a "remarkable evidence of the social antipathy of the white people" that since abolition "illicit sexual commerce between the two races has diminished so far as to have almost ceased, outside the cities and towns." The reason, he believed, was that since the woman was no longer a slave the relationship implied a kind of temporary social recognition.[2]

While the census reveals a growing proportion of mixed strains in the South, it is possible that the enumeration was inaccurate or that the increase derived from the intermarriage of mulattoes with others having more or less Negro blood. At any rate, the figures for 1890 indicate that the greatest admixture existed outside the ex-slave states and that within that section the race grew generally blacker as it approached the Gulf.[3] A single drop of Negro blood, if it could be detected, everywhere stigmatized the individual as a "person of color." Nothing more strikingly evinced the difference in the Caucasian's attitude toward the two major race problems of the time than that men of the standing of

[1] Bruce, *Plantation Negro*, 48-53; G. W. Cable, *The Negro Question* (N. Y., 1890), 21-24.

[2] Bruce, *Plantation Negro*, 53-55, 243. See also same author, "The Negro Population of the South," *Conservative Rev.*, II (1899), 276.

[3] The percentage of mulattoes in the Negro population of the nation, as determined by the census enumerators, was 12 in 1870, 15.2 in 1890 and 20.9 in 1910. No data are available for the intermediate census years. In Bruce's own state of Virginia the official count reveals a growth from 14.1 per cent in 1870 to 33.2 per cent in 1910. *Negroes in United States*, 15, 60. See also E. B. Reuter, *The Mulatto in the United States* (Boston, 1918), esp. 118-126.

Senator Matthew S. Quay took pride in the Indian blood in their veins.[1] Apart from the denial of intermarriage and the provision for separate schools, Southern legislatures moved cautiously in applying the color test to race relations. As early as 1881 Tennessee passed a "Jim Crow" law requiring different coaches or compartments on trains, but it was not until the Supreme Court two years later emasculated the federal civil-rights act of 1875 that her sister commonwealths generally followed her example.[2] On the other hand, Negroes could at no time and in no place secure accommodations in hotels, restaurants and amusement places conducted by whites, though such discrimination seldom had statutory sanction. Opinions differed as to whether colored citizens received equal treatment before the courts, but their treatment at the hands of self-appointed enforcers of the law was a reproach to Anglo-Saxon ideas of justice. In the period 1882-1898 over sixteen hundred recorded lynchings, mainly of blacks, took place in the former slave states, the most tragic years falling in the early nineties.[3] Though these outrages were supposed to represent a species of degenerate chivalry, the victims suspected of rape or attempted rape formed but a minority of the whole number murdered.

In the matter of voting the South allowed the guarantees in the Reconstruction state constitutions to stand for a time. Meanwhile, however, the dominant race actually disfranchised most Afro-Americans by "bull-dozing" and other terroristic methods, by fantastic gerry-

[1] Theodore Roosevelt, *An Autobiography* (N. Y., 1919), 156.

[2] 109 U. S. (1883), 1; Franklin Johnson, *The Development of State Legislation Concerning the Negro* (N. Y., 1919), 14-19, and *passim*.

[3] Nearly four fifths of the victims were Negroes. J. E. Cutler, *Lynch-Law* (N. Y., 1905), chap. vi; Ida B. Wells, *A Red Record* (Chicago, ca. 1895); Walter White, *Rope and Faggot* (N. Y., 1929), app.

mandering arrangements and by unfair manipulation of electoral regulations.[1] In South Carolina after 1882, for instance, the voter must deposit each of his various ballots correctly in the eight or more boxes before him, a test which the untutored darky seldom found it possible to meet. When the rising agrarianism of the late eighties split the white electorate into two fairly balanced parties, however, deep-grained prejudices against the Negro in politics temporarily disappeared, particularly when victory depended upon which side could poll the colored vote. Thoughtful Southerners, fearing the remoter consequences of such tactics, believed the time had come to disfranchise the race by constitutional mandate provided, of course, that the step could be taken without infringing the letter of the Fifteenth Amendment.

The three states in which Negroes outnumbered the whites were the first to act. Mississippi in 1890 pointed the way by limiting the ballot to paid-up male taxpayers who were able to read a passage from the state constitution or understand it when read to them or give "a reasonable interpretation thereof." The flexible clause was confessedly designed to enable election officials to reject illiterate blacks without rejecting illiterate whites. Five years later South Carolina followed with a somewhat similar provision and then, in 1898, Louisiana found a means of exempting whites from the property and educational tests by placing on the voting list all male applicants whose fathers or grandfathers had been eligible to vote prior to 1867. Other states were presently to devise ingenious variants of these restrictions. Thus the postwar political importance of the Negro

[1] S. B. Weeks, "History of Negro Suffrage," *Polit. Sci. Quar.*, IX, 671-703; W. A. Dunning, *Essays on the Civil War and Reconstruction* (N. Y., 1904), 363-385; W. C. Hamm, "The Three Phases of Colored Suffrage," *N. Am. Rev.*, CLXVIII (1899), 285-296; Paul Lewinson, *Race, Class, & Party* (London, 1932), chaps. iv-v.

vanished almost as quickly as it had come. He became
once more a negligible factor in Southern public life.
Notwithstanding these many onerous restrictions,
even George W. Cable conceded that the Afro-American
enjoyed "a larger share of private, public, religious and
political liberty than falls to the lot of any but a few
peoples . . . ." [1] The most salient rights of all—to
accumulate property, establish a home and acquire some
measure of schooling—remained unobstructed by legal
barriers. Nor could any disinterested observer deny that
the race had taken excellent advantage of its opportunities. By 1900 one Negro in every five owned his home,
and the total value of the farms they operated reached
nearly half a billion dollars. About two hundred thousand owned their farms while over half a million more
worked as tenants.[2] Fifty-six per cent were literate as
compared with thirty per cent twenty years before, and
with the advance of education had gone a slow but
steady improvement in morals and family relations.
One-room cabins were everywhere beginning to give
way to two or even three-room houses, with an occasional parlor organ and some attention to the decencies
and comforts of living. If one test of racial capacity is
the ability to breed leaders, the Negroes could evidence
not only Booker T. Washington, but also Paul Laurence
Dunbar, the lyric poet, Henry O. Tanner whose painting "The Raising of Lazarus" was bought by the French
government, the novelist C. W. Chesnutt, the electrical
inventor Granville T. Woods, as well as others equally
distinguished in their fields.[3] We may agree with the

[1] Cable, *Negro Question*, 66.
[2] *Negroes in United States*, 29, 158-160.
[3] C. G. Woodson, *The Negro in Our History* (Wash., 1922), 291-
304. Four of the five named above were of hybrid descent. Reuter,
*Mulatto in United States*, chap. viii, presents long lists of names which
show, at least at this transitional stage of the race's development, that
mixed bloods greatly predominated among the more gifted individu-

contemporary judgment of a young Negro intellectual that thirty years of struggle and privation had "changed the child of emancipation to the youth with dawning self-consciousness, self-realization, self-respect." [1]

als. Benjamin Brawley, himself a mulatto, briefly denies the advantage of an infusion of white blood in *A Social History of the American Negro* (N. Y., 1921), 330-332.

[1] W. E. B. Du Bois, "Strivings of the Negro People," *Atlantic Mo.*, LXXX (1897), 196.

# CHAPTER XII

## POLITICAL FACTORS AND FORCES

THE average American in the 1880's accepted democracy as he accepted the telephone, sanitary plumbing and the electric light, expecting someone to furnish him with as much of them as he needed, or could afford, and keep them in good running order. Though the party managers usually succeeded in getting him to the polls on election day, he saved himself the vexation of thinking about candidates and issues by voting the straight party ticket. Nor did the epoch possess its due proportion of political leaders of the first rank. Henry Adams declared in retrospect: "No period so thoroughly ordinary had been known in American politics since Christopher Columbus first disturbed the balance of American society." [1] Apparently the men of creative vision and constructive ability were attracted into fresher and more challenging fields. Bryce was impressed, for example, by the "splendid practical capacity" of the great railway builders, whose scope of activities required "administrative rulers, generals, diplomatists, financiers, of the finest gifts," talents which in the Old World would have gone into parliamentary management and civil administration. [2]

Surprisingly enough, the extraordinary educational opportunities which the generation boasted did little to increase the participation of the "better classes" in poli-

[1] Henry Adams, *The Education of Henry Adams* (Boston, 1918), 355.

[2] James Bryce, *The American Commonwealth* (London, 1888), II, 407.

387

tics. To be sure, Henry Cabot Lodge, one of Harvard's first Ph.D.'s, deserted teaching for public life, but as early as 1883 it was observed that he was "the gentleman and scholar in politics without the guilelessness and squeamishness of the said gentleman and scholar."[1] When Roosevelt fresh from Harvard in 1881 decided to run for the New York legislature, his lawyer and business friends sought to dissuade him from a career which, they pointed out, was controlled not by "gentlemen" but by "saloon-keepers, horse-car conductors, and the like."[2]

The opinion that "politics were low," so forcibly conveyed to young Roosevelt, caused most men of cultivation and scholarly training, including such gifted students of public affairs as Woodrow Wilson and F. J. Goodnow, to prefer the rôle of observer and critic. A few like George W. Curtis and Dorman B. Eaton, whose emotions were too strong to permit inactivity, compromised by indulging in that form of nonpartisan organized effort which it is now fashionable to call "pressure politics." As a result, political management, like other phases of man's activities, fell increasingly into the hands of specialists, of professional practitioners, known to the public as bosses and machine politicians. Roosevelt quickly discovered that his district in New York City was run by Jake Hess and "his captains of tens and of

[1] Clement's weekly Boston letter to the *N. Y. Tribune,* quoted by S. E. Morison, "Memoir of Edward Henry Clement," Mass. Hist. Soc., *Proceeds.,* LVI, 64.

[2] Theodore Roosevelt, *An Autobiography* (N. Y., 1919), 56. Henry Adams wrote Lodge, rather sourly, the same year: "I have never known a young man go into politics who was not the worse for it . . . from my two brothers, John and Brooks, down to Willy Astor, Ham Fish, and Robert Ray Hamilton." Henry Adams, *Letters (1858-1891)* (W. C. Ford, ed., Boston, 1930), 331. English travelers were naturally much struck by "the divorce between politics and . . . the higher culture." See, for example, E. A. Freeman, *Some Impressions of the United States* (N. Y., 1883), 202-204, and Emily Faithfull, *Three Visits to America* (Edinburgh, 1884), 10-12.

hundreds"; but Jake himself was but a tiny cog in a well-integrated Republican organization which reached upward through the state into all parts of the nation. At no point was the political mettle of the generation so sorely tried as in the government of cities. From long experience Americans had learned how to rule populations scattered over large areas, but they had had little or no training in the management of densely packed urban centers. Yet every year a larger proportion of the people hived in cities, rendering all human relations more complex, creating new social maladjustments and requiring governmental services and safeguards unknown to the earlier and simpler days of the republic.[1] If conscientious municipal officials floundered in the effort to administer their unruly charges, all too frequently those in the seats of power were not actuated by upright motives. Lax enforcement of the law commanded a price which the liquor interests and the purveyors of commercialized vice were ever ready to pay. Even more serious was the corruption and fraud involved in the letting of municipal contracts and in the sale of the social values created by the rapid growth of population.

Some of the shrewdest and most unscrupulous men of the time specialized in the exploitation of municipal utilities (water, fuel, light and rapid transit), their activities often embracing a network of cities.[2] One group of six capitalists—C. T. Yerkes, W. L. Elkins, P. A. B. Widener, W. C. Whitney, T. F. Ryan and Thomas Dolan—combined the street railways of New York City, Philadelphia, Chicago, Pittsburgh and at

[1] G. W. Julian, "The Pending Ordeals of Democracy," *International Rev.*, V (1878), 737-738; W. R. Martin, "Cities as Units in Our Polity," *N. Am. Rev.*, CXXVIII (1879), esp. 21; Josiah Strong, *The Twentieth Century City* (N. Y., 1898), 60-61.

[2] B. J. Hendrick, *The Age of Big Business* (Allen Johnson, ed., *The Chronicles of America Series*, New Haven, 1918-1921, XXXIX), chap. v.

least a hundred other places in New England, Pennsylvania, Ohio and Indiana. Either jointly or severally they also controlled the gas and electric-light facilities of eighty-some communities as far apart as Philadelphia, St. Augustine, Vicksburg, Kansas City, Minneapolis and Syracuse. A single corporation developed most of the trolley and lighting companies of the cities of New Jersey; another managed similar utilities in San Francisco and other places on the Pacific Coast.

The full story of the graft and dishonor involved in the traffic in franchises will never be known. From indirect evidence as well as from occasional court testimony it seems clear that there was a cesspool under nearly every city hall, dug secretly by politicians in the pay of respectable, or at least respected, business men. Hazen S. Pingree of Detroit, one of the few reform mayors, was offered a bribe of fifty thousand dollars by one company and a trip around the world by another if he would refrain from vetoing certain franchises.[1] "Keep the newspapers on your staff" as well as the city officials, advised a speaker before the Ohio Gas-Light Association in 1896, and proceeded to explain how a friendly press could be nurtured by a judicious distribution of stock.[2] Moreover, if the public-utility interests failed to take the initiative, they were likely to be held up by venal aldermen with the threat of ordinances —"strike bills"—hostile to them. In Pingree's opinion, "Good municipal government is an impossibility while valuable franchises are to be had and can be obtained by corrupt use of money in bribing public servants."[3]

<hr>

[1] E. W. Bemis, ed., *Municipal Monopolies* (R. T. Ely, ed., *Library of Economics and Politics;* 4th edn., N. Y., 1904), 657.

[2] Just a month before, court testimony had disclosed the secret financial control of the *Minneapolis Tribune* by the president of the street railways of the Twin Cities. Bemis, *Municipal Monopolies*, 658-660.

[3] Quoted in Bemis, *Municipal Monopolies*, 658.

The evil fruit of this unholy alliance of big business and bad politics was the worst city government the country had ever known. The voters themselves were in part responsible because of their habit, in municipal as well as national elections, of dividing along national party lines. Wrongdoers also found many advantages in the cumbersome form of government which, in faulty analogy to the state government, ordinarily consisted of a mayor and a two-chambered council. In New York the Tammany organization, recovering quickly from the shock of the Tweed Ring exposure, resumed its career of systematic looting of the city's wealth.[1] After an investigation in 1884 three aldermen were sentenced to prison, six fled to Canada, three turned state's evidence and ten others were indicted but not brought to trial. According to the *New York Evening Post*, April 3, 1890, the Tammany executive committee at that time consisted of twenty-seven "professional politicians," including

> convicted murderer, 1; acquitted of murder, 1; convicted of felonious assault, 1; professional gamblers, 4; former dive-keepers, 5; liquor dealers, 4; former liquor dealers, 5; sons of liquor dealers, 3; former pugilists, 3; former toughs, 4; members of Tweed gang, 6; office-holders, 17.

Richard Croker, Irish immigrant, former prize fighter and gang leader, who had reigned as boss since 1886, had already justified his early training under Tweed by becoming the possessor of untold wealth.

But New York City did not stand alone. The "gas ring" in Philadelphia, the "real-estate ring" in the

[1] Allan Nevins, *The Evening Post* (N. Y., 1922), chap. xxii; Gustavus Myers, *The History of Tammany Hall* (rev. edn., N. Y., 1917), chaps. xxvii-xxix; Lothrop Stoddard, *Master of Manhattan: The Life of Richard Croker* (N. Y., 1931).

nation's capital, George B. Cox's strangle hold on
Cincinnati's political life, Colonel "Ed" Butler's organized traffic in the franchises and contracts of St. Louis,
the malodorous Ames régime in Minneapolis, the systematic exploitation of San Francisco by "Blind Boss"
(Christopher A.) Buckley—these provided hardly less
glaring instances of what Bryce called "the one conspicuous failure" of American democracy.[1] Echoing
Bryce's sentiment, Andrew D. White asserted that,
"with very few exceptions, the city governments of the
United States are the worst in Christendom—the most
expensive, the most inefficient, and the most corrupt."[2]
Audiences might more profitably have been stirred to
wrath instead of laughter by a famous sally in one of
the Harrigan and Hart comedies. When the municipal
fathers fell asleep at the Mulligan home from too much
entertainment, "Will I wake them?" asked Mrs. Mulligan. "Lave thim be," replied her spouse. "While they
sleep the city's safe."[3] The immigrant was often blamed
for the sorry condition of affairs, but outside New York
City the bosses and grafting politicians were usually of
native stock. Moreover municipal misrule was as ram-
pant in "American" cities like Philadelphia and Portland, Oregon, as in those which had a far larger proportion of foreign-born voters.[4]

[1] Bryce considered these cities along with Chicago, Brooklyn, Baltimore and New Orleans as the places where "Ring-and-bossdom" throve
most luxuriantly. Bryce, *American Commonwealth*, II, 281, 468-473.
[2] A. D. White, "The Government of American Cities," *Forum*, X
(1890-1891), 357.
[3] J. L. Ford, *Forty-Odd Years in the Literary Shop* (N. Y., 1921),
98.
[4] C. W. Eliot, "One Remedy for Municipal Misgovernment," *Forum*,
XII (1891-1892), 153-168; C. R. Woodruff, "Cleveland Conference
for Good City Government," *Am. Mag. of Civics*, VII (1895), 169;
T. N. Strong, "Municipal Condition of Portland," Natl. Conf. for
Good City Government, *Proceeds. for 1895*, 432-438; edit., "Redemption of our Cities," *Nation* (N. Y.), LXIII, 359-360 (Nov. 12, 1896).

The commanding position of the city in cultural life made its failure as a political organism all the more tragic. From time to time the citizens, stung beyond endurance, banded together to "turn the rascals out." Sometimes they were betrayed by their own officials; more often they were so spent by their exertion of virtue that at the next election the machine romped back into power. Philadelphia chose a reform mayor against the gas-ring candidate in 1881, only to sink back into its shame two years later. Buffalo similarly secured a respite in 1881 by electing Grover Cleveland who, by his defiance of a corrupt council, quickly won the name of "the veto mayor." The famous revolt against Tammany in 1894, of which the preacher Parkhurst was the particular hero, was followed three years later by the triumph of the Tammany henchman Robert A. Van Wyck.

Few cities, unfortunately, emulated the example of Detroit which, from 1889 to his elevation seven years later to the governorship, continued to reëlect the militant reformer Pingree as mayor. During his lease of power Pingree exposed grafting members of the council, wrung important concessions from the street-railway and gas companies and, against the most ruthless opposition, secured the establishment of a municipal electric-lighting plant.[1] He was the forerunner of a series of local executives who in the early years of the next century were to bring about a civic renaissance.[2]

For the most part, reform interludes left few enduring gains. More significant was the improvement which came from state legislation requiring secret, uniform and officially printed ballots. Until Kentucky in February,

[1] G. B. Catlin, The Story of Detroit (Detroit, 1923), chaps. ci-cvi.
[2] See H. U. Faulkner, The Quest for Social Justice (A History of American Life, XI), 93-104.

1888, imposed this plan upon the city of Louisville, it had everywhere been the practice of party organizations to print and distribute their own lists to voters who, with or without help, marked them before going to deposit them in the plain view of any who cared to see. Massachusetts, acting the same year as Kentucky, gave the system state-wide application.[1] So keenly was the need for reform felt that within a decade the new plan, in complete or partial form, prevailed throughout the country save in Georgia, the two Carolinas and New Mexico. Though the results were not miraculous, vote buyers thereafter were obliged to take a sporting chance, intimidation and rioting at the polls tended to disappear, and municipal politics was freed from one of the most blatant aspects of public disregard of the citizens' rights.

Less successful were the efforts to better the method of appointing city officeholders. The National Civil Service Reform League, formed in 1881, from the start included municipal offices as a part of its program. In 1883 and 1884 the New York and Massachusetts legislatures prescribed the merit system for the larger cities, though local politicians often managed to circumvent it in practice. By 1898 laws providing for the new method were also operative in Philadelphia, Chicago, New Orleans and elsewhere.[2] While ballot and civil-service laws im-

---

[1] The original proponents of the influential Massachusetts statute were in touch with English experience, but did not learn until at a later stage of the Australian law, which antedated the English one and which provided the popular tag for the reform in America. R. H. Dana, "Sir William Vernon Harcourt and the Australian Ballot Law," Mass. Hist. Soc., *Proceeds.*, LVIII, 401-418. For the quick spread of the reform, see J. B. Bishop, "The Secret Ballot in Thirty-Three States," *Forum*, XII (1891-1892), 589-598.

[2] F. M. Stewart, *The National Civil Service Reform League: History, Activities, and Problems* (Austin, 1929), 34-37; T. C. Devlin, *Municipal Reform in the United States* (Questions of the Day Series, XC, N. Y., 1896), 89, 99.

proved the municipal system at certain points, few of the reformers saw as clearly as Seth Low and Andrew D. White that a more drastic reconstruction was required—that American cities with their vastly expanded functions were "not so much little states as large corporations." [1] The bitter lessons learned during these years, however, did much to clear the way for that experimentation in new governmental forms which was to signalize the opening decades of the next century.

Because of the close control wielded by legislatures over cities, municipal bosses and their henchmen took up their residence in the state capital when the law makers were in session. Particularly in urbanized states like New York and Pennsylvania, ways could be found of inducing the legislature to oblige the city to buy property, undertake costly construction and create lucrative municipal offices.[2] The chief threat to legislative purity, apart from this fecund source of infection, came from privilege-seeking corporations. By 1890, however, so many states had enacted statutes against conspiracies and agreements in restraint of trade that corporation lobbyists centered their efforts chiefly on maintaining the lax laws effective in a few places like New Jersey, Delaware and West Virginia. From any one of these as a base, big business could, under a guarantee in the federal Constitution, trade unmolested across state lines.

Laws were also enacted in an attempt to regulate the expenditure of money in elections. Beginning with New

---

[1] Seth Low, "An American View of Municipal Government," Bryce, *American Commonwealth*, II, esp. 303; White, "Government of American Cities," 368-369.

[2] In the 1880's the New York legislature passed 390 acts amending the laws governing New York City and 189 relating to Brooklyn. Bryce in 1888 rated the New York and Pennsylvania legislatures as lowest in political morality while accounting those of Massachusetts, Vermont and several Mid-Western states as substantially "pure." *American Commonwealth*, II, 191, 519.

York in 1890, seventeen states adopted corrupt-practices acts before the close of the century, and in 1897 three states—Nebraska, Tennessee and Florida—expressly prohibited contributions by corporations.[1] When all is said and done, legislative corruption was the exception rather than the rule. In the country as a whole, and notably in the new South, the political life of the states had risen high above the moral ebb tide of postwar years. The outpouring of legislation for educational and humanitarian welfare attested a reassuring devotion on the part of law makers to the public weal.

Even more so than the states, the national government had purged itself of the bribery and wrongdoing which had come with the moral backwash of the Civil War.[2] Though United States senators were still occasionally elected with a taint of corruption, as in the case of Henry B. Payne of Ohio in 1884, the only major scandal involving high federal officials was the belated exposé of the Star Route frauds in the post-office department, dating from the Grant era. These cases, involving among others the Republican ex-Senator S. W. Dorsey of Arkansas, dragged through the courts from 1881 to 1884. While the principal rascals in some mysterious way escaped prison, in Attorney-General B. H. Brewster's opinion they might better have taken their punishment than face an aroused public opinion, the "objects of scorn and aversion."[3]

The sharpened insistence upon public probity in the nation's rulers was dramatically exemplified in the presi-

---

[1] Four states—Kansas, Nevada, Michigan and Ohio—quickly repealed their laws. G. L. Fox, "Corrupt Practices and Election Laws in the United States since 1890," Am. Polit. Sci. Assoc., *Proceeds.*, II, 171-172.

[2] See Allan Nevins, *The Emergence of Modern America* (*A History of American Life*, VIII), chap. vii.

[3] E. P. Oberholtzer, *A History of the United States since the Civil War* (N. Y., 1917, in progress), IV, 115-119, 132-140.

dential election of 1884.[1] The Republican candidate, James G. Blaine, nominated over the protests of the progressive members of his party, had a congressional record scarred by such dubious relations with privilege-seeking railway corporations that even his rare personal magnetism had not erased the memory of them. The Democrats, on the other hand, chose as their leader Grover Cleveland who, since leaving the mayoralty of Buffalo, had shown the same stubborn devotion to reform as governor of the state. By the precedents of earlier campaigns (that of 1876 excepted), the Democrats, still popularly tainted with Copperheadism and rebellion, had small chance for success. Party loyalty was a religion; and even Roosevelt and Lodge, who in the convention had fought Blaine's nomination to the last ditch, yielded him their support, though Roosevelt only after sulking for a time on his Dakota ranch.

Nevertheless an influential group of so-called Independents bolted the ticket and began an electioneering campaign which eventually covered most of the Northern states. The name of Cleveland, they declared in a public pronunciamento, "is the synonym of political courage and honesty and of administrative reform," while Blaine was "a representative of men, methods, and conduct which the public conscience condemns." [2] Stigmatized by the regulars as "Mugwumps," "dudes" and "assistant Democrats," the group included such high-minded publicists as Carl Schurz, George W. Curtis, Francis A. Walker, E. L. Godkin and T. W. Higginson, and attracted the support of Republican newspapers in

[1] H. C. Thomas, *The Return of the Democratic Party to Power in 1884* (Columbia Univ., *Studies*, LXXXIX, no. 2), chaps. vi-x; Oberholtzer, *United States*, IV, 159-212; A. A. Lawrence, jr., Aspects of the Whispering Campaign of 1884 (unpublished seminar report, Harvard Univ.).

[2] *N. Y. Times*, July 23, 1884.

many of the leading cities. The Democrats, on their part, made their campaign slogan: "Public office is a public trust"—a precept which gained fresh cogency from the disclosure of additional letters bearing upon Blaine's tortuous financial dealings while speaker of the House.

Alarmed by such tactics, the Republican managers tried desperately to divert attention to other matters. Party orators resorted to the customary emotional appeal of "waving the bloody shirt." Meantime, efforts made to draw Irish Catholics from their Democratic allegiance—Cleveland being, it was said, a "Presbyterian bigot" while Blaine's mother was a Romanist—succeeded at least to the point of winning the fiery support of the *Irish World,* American organ of the Irish Land League.[1] "Agonize more and more on the tariff," Blaine implored his campaign associates, regardless of the fact that not on this or any other concrete policy did the opposing platforms present real differences.[2]

In their dilemma the Republicans gladly seized upon the whispers concerning Cleveland's personal character, which began to circulate shortly after his nomination. These rumors were first categorically spread before the public by the *Buffalo Evening Telegraph* on July 21. On the authority of the Reverend G. H. Ball, a Baptist minister of that city, Cleveland was charged with the "grossest licentiousness" and specifically with being the father of a seven-year-old bastard son whose mother he had tried vainly to keep locked up in an insane asylum. The friends of reform were struck with consternation. A group of Independent Republicans in Buffalo, after an investigation, admitted the fact of the liaison stripped of the embellishments of seduction and abduction, but

[1] Blaine was also supposed to have been notably active as secretary of state in safeguarding the interests of Irish Americans imprisoned in England.

[2] Royal Cortissoz, *The Life of Whitelaw Reid* (N. Y., 1921), II, 83.

repudiated the general charges of libertinism and drunkenness.[1] The Buffalo Association of Ministers divided, some asserting and others denying that the circumstances evinced Cleveland's unfitness for the presidency. The candidate himself, importuned by anxious friends, replied tersely, "Whatever you say, tell the truth." [2]

By this unexpected turn of events the conscientious citizen was confronted with a perplexing choice. The ultra-Republican *New York Tribune* felt confident the voters were not yet "so degraded" as to "care nothing for home, nothing for the attractiveness of domestic life, nothing for the offenses which the religious press so strongly censures." [3] So sure was the pious P. T. Barnum that no decent man could now vote for Cleveland that he offered a high price for the *rara avis* "provided I could make the people believe that the monster was real flesh and blood and not another humbug." [4] Under the impact of the "sickening disclosures" the *Independent*, a magazine under denominational auspices, hastily repented of its earlier advocacy, though later, in good conscience, it felt obliged to demand the withdrawal of both candidates. The religious press generally joined in the hue and cry against Cleveland while clergymen in all parts of the North ardently carried the "moral issue" into the pulpit. Even so staunch a Mugwump as Henry

[1] Committee of Independent Republicans of Buffalo, *The Charges Swept Away* (n.p., 1884). The Reverend Kinsley Twining of New York, quoted in the same pamphlet, commended Cleveland for "showing no attempt to evade responsibility, and doing all he could to meet the duties involved, of which marriage was certainly not one."

[2] There are grounds for believing that Cleveland's reply was more cryptic than candid. The child was apparently of doubtful paternity; it may or may not be significant that he was given the name of one of Cleveland's close friends, a married man. See edit., "What We Think About It Now," *Nation*, XXXIX, 106 (Aug. 7, 1884); Oberholtzer, *United States*, IV, 191, and citations; H. T. Peck, *Twenty Years of the Republic* (N. Y., 1906), 36.

[3] *Semi-Weekly Tribune*, Aug. 26, 1884.

[4] *Springfield Republican*, Aug. 7, 1884.

Ward Beecher wavered for a time, made wary perhaps by alleged sexual irregularities in his own past.[1] With redoubled zeal the pro-Cleveland hosts insisted that the issue remained unchanged; that the test of public, not private, morality should be applied to the candidates. Asked why it was backing the Democrat, the *New York World* replied: "(1) He is an honest man. (2) He is an honest man. (3) He is an honest man. (4) He is an honest man . . . ."[2] The outcome of the election was very close. Cleveland carried the ordinarily doubtful states of Connecticut, New Jersey and Indiana by a few thousand votes each, and the pivotal state of New York by but 1149 out of a total of over a million votes. If he had lost New York, or if he had lost New Jersey and either of the other two states, Blaine would have won a majority in the electoral college and hence the presidency.

Many factors helped tip the scale for Cleveland: the current business depression, the lukewarmness of the old Republican Stalwart faction toward Blaine, the deflection of Republican votes into the Prohibition party, the estrangement of Irish Catholics by the "Rum, Romanism and Rebellion" remark made at an important Blaine rally.[3] But, in last analysis, the chief credit belongs to the reform hosts whose strength was greatest in those

[1] See Nevins, *Emergence of Modern America*, 227; Carl Schurz, *Speeches, Correspondence and Public Papers* (Frederic Bancroft, ed., N. Y., 1913), IV, 222; *Boston Transcript*, Aug. 6, 7, 1884. Washington Gladden and Felix Adler could not bring themselves to vote for either candidate. Gladden, *Recollections* (Boston, 1909), 316, 378; Adler, *The Ethics of the Political Situation* (n.p., 1884).

[2] *N. Y. World*, Sept. 22, 1884. The text of sexual morality, Godkin believed, "would have prevented Washington, Franklin, Jefferson, Hamilton, not to go any further, from taking any prominent part in the foundation of the American Republic." *Nation*, XXXIX, 106 (Aug. 7, 1884).

[3] This characterization of the Democracy was uttered by a Presbyterian clergyman in introducing Blaine. W. C. Hudson, *Random Recollections of an Old Political Reporter* (N. Y., 1911), 205-212; F. W. Mack,

states where the Republicans could least afford to lose support. Through their persistent campaign of education they had clarified the "moral issue" and induced a sufficient number of voters, as one of their leaders said, to "elect Mr. Cleveland to the public office which he is so admirably qualified to fill and remand Mr. Blaine to the private life which he is so eminently fitted to adorn." [1] The lesson of 1884 was not learned in vain. At no election later in the period did the leading parties present presidential candidates whose official rectitude was open to question.

Meantime the sentiment for governmental purity was waging war against another form of political vice, one which long-continued practice had endowed with a certain halo of respectability: the federal spoils system. In the course of time the spoils system had come to exhibit two glaring evils: first, the prostitution of the civil service to purely party ends and, second, the systematic exploitation of officeholders for campaign funds. Flagrant instances of incompetence and dishonesty in the public service since the Civil War, together with the high-pressure methods of Republican managers in raising a hundred thousand dollars from federal employees in 1878 and again in 1880, would in themselves have been enough to alarm the friends of good government. In addition, the assumption by the federal departments of a wide variety of new scientific and technical work emphasized the importance of safeguards such as had

"Rum, Romanism and Rebellion," *Harper's Wkly.*, XLVIII, 1140-1142 (July 23, 1904).

[1] Quoted in M. A. DeW. Howe, *Portrait of an Independent: Moorfield Storey* (Boston, 1932), 151. When the voters of Nebraska in the gubernatorial election of 1891 were presented with a somewhat similar option, they too elected the candidate of reform leanings, though his opponents had revealed his paternity of an illegitimate child. J. D. Barnhart, The History of the Farmers' Alliance and of the People's Party in Nebraska (unpublished Ph.D. thesis, Harvard Univ., 1930), 282-285.

recently been introduced so successfully into the English civil service.

The half-hearted attempts of Grant and the zealous devotion of President Hayes had done little to improve the situation, thanks to the bitter hostility of the professional politicians in Congress. Starting in 1877, civil-service-reform societies sprang up in many cities. *Harper's Weekly* and the *Nation* helped keep the issue alive, and the National Civil Service Reform League came into existence with George W. Curtis as president. But it was the assassination of President Garfield by a disappointed office seeker that shocked the public into an awareness of the real gravity of the evil.[1]

The new president, Chester A. Arthur, himself a notorious spoilsman before entering office, promptly championed the reform and Congress acceded in 1883 with the passage of the Pendleton act. Drafted by Dorman B. Eaton of the Civil Service Reform League, this law provided for the creation of a bipartisan commission which should set up and administer a system of competitive examinations as a test of fitness for appointment to office. The new plan applied at once only to the executive departments in Washington, the customhouses and the larger post offices, and there only in the case of future vacancies. But the president was given discretion to extend the "classified list," as it was called, to other groups of federal employees.[2]

Because of this elastic provision the act has rightly been termed the "Magna Charta of civil-service reform." When Arthur left the presidency nearly 16,000 offices out of a total of about 110,000 had been transferred to

[1] C. R. Fish, *The Civil Service and the Patronage* (*Harvard Historical Studies*, XI), chap. x; W. D. Foulke, *Fighting the Spoilsmen* (N. Y., 1919), chaps. iii-ix; Stewart, *National Civil Service Reform League*, 8-64.

[2] *U. S. Statutes at Large*, XXII, 403-407.

the classified list; and, influenced by the example of Washington, the New York and Massachusetts legislatures had adopted the plan for state positions. The accession of the job-hungry Democrats put an enormous pressure upon Cleveland to take a backward step. While appeasing "the d——d everlasting clatter for offices" mainly from the unclassified service, he quietly extended the merit system to nearly twelve thousand more places.[1] Later presidents followed more or less falteringly in his footsteps.[2] As a member of the civil-service commission from 1889 to 1895 Roosevelt kept alive public interest in the cause and made his name a source of real terror to the politicians of both parties. Curiously enough, the alternating party control of the presidency during these years had the effect of helping rather than hurting the reform since an outgoing administration might, through an eleventh-hour enlargement of the classified list, hope to continue its followers longer in office. This practice gave coinage to the saying, "To the vanquished belong the spoils."

The Pendleton act also sought to scotch the evil of campaign assessments. Federal officeholders were forbidden to solicit or receive, directly or indirectly, political contributions or assessments from one another, or to make such payments to other federal employees. Though an improvement over an earlier statute of 1876, the provision still contained too many loopholes to do away with the practice entirely and, of course, the prohibitions did not extend to state and local officeholders, whose salaries continued to furnish the main source of

[1] Robert McElroy, *Grover Cleveland* (N. Y., 1923), esp. I, 149; Thomas, *Return of Democratic Party*, 237-246.

[2] According to D. M. Matteson's figures in J. F. Rhodes, *History of the United States from Hayes to McKinley* (N. Y., 1919), 166 *n.*, Harrison added 10,535 places, Cleveland in his second term 38,961, and McKinley 3261.

funds in the lesser elections. But political requisitions in
national politics after 1883 had to be managed in a
manner not to offend public opinion, and the yield
therefore was doubtless proportionately less.[1] Definite
figures unfortunately are not available.

One untoward result of the statutory limitation upon
assessments was the increasing dependence of the major
parties upon business and banking interests for financial
support.[2] This might have come about in any case, however, thanks to the high cost of reaching an electorate
which was rapidly expanding in numbers and geographic extent. Moreover, the waning effectiveness of
bloody-shirt tactics convinced Republican managers that
a more elaborate presentation of issues must be undertaken, while the injection of economic questions into
national politics suggested the sources from which the
golden stream might be made to gush. Already well
established as the party of conservative business, the
Republicans took prompt advantage of the opening
afforded by President Cleveland's message of 1887 in
which he squarely committed his hitherto wabbling
party to a low-tariff system.

In the ensuing presidential canvass, while spellbinders
vaunted the "American system of protection" from
every stump, the Philadelphia merchant John Wanamaker, who had had wide experience in raising money
for the Y. M. C. A., quietly bestirred himself on behalf

[1] Yet, almost a quarter-century after the Pendleton law, the Civil
Service Reform League asserted that during the campaign of 1904 "there
is no possible doubt but that assessments have been levied on federal
employees all over the country." John Carr, "Campaign Funds and
Campaign Scandals," *Outlook*, LXXXI, 549 (Nov. 4, 1905).

[2] The size of the campaign funds in the successive elections is given
in anon., "Cost of National Campaigns," *World's Work*, I (1900-
1901), 77-80, and in the *World Almanac for 1925*, 185, citing the
*Wall Street Journal*. The two lists differ in vital respects and, in view
of the secrecy which cloaked such transactions, neither list may be
correct.

of the party to collect the sinews of war from leading industrialists. "If you were confronted," he asked each of them, "with from one to three years of general depression by a change in our revenue and protective methods . . . , what would you pay to be insured for a better year?" [1] Funds rolled in to an amount variously estimated at from over $200,000 to $1,350,000. Though most of the money was doubtless devoted to legitimate campaign uses, the corruption of voters in Indiana, Connecticut, West Virginia and certain other close states was so bold and undisguised as to make the campaign of 1888 probably the most venal in American history.[2] Wanamaker himself was rewarded for his services with an office in President Harrison's cabinet.

While the Australian ballot system, adopted in most states before the next presidential contest, placed a curb upon direct bribery, the size of party war chests steadily grew as elections continued to turn upon questions of vital economic policy. Adult education directed by political schoolmasters, though expensive, proved increasingly important. As Republican manager in the free-silver campaign of 1896, the Ohio capitalist Marcus A. Hanna secured contributions of unprecedented size from business corporations, insurance companies and men of wealth and actually levied an assessment of one fourth of one per cent on the capital and surplus of leading banks.[3] The audited account shows that the national committee collected no less than $3,500,000, thus making the election of William McKinley the costliest yet

[1] Herbert Welsh, "Publicity as a Cure for Corruption," *Forum,* XIV (1892-1893), 29-30.

[2] F. A. Ogg, "The Dollars behind the Ballots," *World To-Day,* XV (1908), 947-948. Harrison was "the first American President who has obtained his office by open venality," declared a *Nation* editorial, LV, 252 (Oct. 6, 1892).

[3] Herbert Croly, *Marcus Alonzo Hanna* (N. Y., 1912), 218-221; *Congressional Record,* XL, pt. vi, 5366 ff.

held. Oddly enough, the efforts of Bryan to destroy the gold standard brought the Democratic party capitalistic support also, in the form of several hundred thousand contributed by silver-mining interests.[1] Though, as we have seen, the states were beginning to regulate expenditures in their own elections, similar action by Congress had to await the prod of the progressive movement early in the next century.[2]

While these years are generally envisaged as years of Republican supremacy, a glance beneath the surface discloses how slender was that party's hold upon the electorate. Not only did the Republicans after 1880 fail to occupy the White House for longer than a single term at a stretch, but neither they nor the Democrats controlled both the presidency and the two legislative branches for more than two years at a time. Harrison in 1888, under the curious workings of the electoral-college system, attained victory with a smaller popular support than that accorded Cleveland. Of all the successful aspirants, Republican or Democratic, McKinley alone, in the last election of the period, commanded a clear majority of the popular ballots.

The restoration of the two-party system, foreshadowed by the contest of 1876, was due partly to the growing up of a new generation of voters in the North, partly also to the unwavering support given the Democrats by the ex-Confederate states after the restoration of white supremacy. The "Solid South" in the election of 1880, for instance, cast a bloc of ninety-five electoral votes out of a total of three hundred and sixty-nine. To this irreducible minimum might ordinarily be added the

[1] According to the *N. Y. Herald*, Sept. 7, Oct. 21, 1896, Moffat of Denver gave $100,000, Straton of Helena $50,000, and Clark of Montana $70,000.

[2] See acts of 1907, 1910 and 1911. *U. S. Statutes at Large*, XXXV, 1103-1104; XXXVI, 822-824; XXXVII, 25-29.

electoral votes of the former border slave states—Missouri, Kentucky, Maryland and Delaware—amounting in that year to thirty-five.

The nice poise of parties explains both the strategic importance of the Independent movement in the eighties and the spleen of faithful party men against its leaders. The Mugwumps were, even to Roosevelt, "perverse lunatics," while Godkin of the *Nation*, their most distinguished spokesman, was nothing less than a "malignant and dishonest liar." [1] This situation, too, proved a constant spur to the formation of minor parties which, if they could not hope to sweep the nation, might at least aspire to seize the balance of power. No presidential canvass occurred without at least three of them in the field. In 1892 the People's party, by uniting the malcontents of countryside and city, actually cast a large enough vote to frighten the Democratic convention into vital concessions in the next campaign.

In the hectic scramble for votes Republican spellbinders fought the Civil War over in election after election, exhorting their Northern audiences to vote as they had shot. Every presidential candidate of the party was a war veteran except Blaine, and Blaine's running mate possessed the requisite qualification. What was even more to the point, when in power they dispensed pensions with lordly extravagance and thus consolidated the old-soldier vote of the North in their support.

While the Democrats could not hope to equal this aspect of the Republican record and Cleveland's many pension vetoes counted heavily against them, they enjoyed a decided advantage in dealing with the naturalized voters, particularly the Irish who were traditionally of their fold and politically effective in the great urban

[1] *Selections from the Correspondence of Theodore Roosevelt and Henry Cabot Lodge* (N. Y., 1925), I, 39, 74.

centers.[1] Blaine's efforts to break this alliance, though a
failure in 1884, caused Republican managers as the
years passed to give less attention to "waving the bloody
shirt" and more to "twisting the lion's tail," the latter
a sure bid for Hibernian favor. In the next two campaigns the Republicans disparaged the Democrats as
"British free traders," and in 1888 gave wide publicity
to a letter, which the British minister at Washington had
been tricked into writing, advising a supposed former
fellow countryman to vote for Cleveland as the better
president for Great Britain.[2] In both campaigns the two
parties blithely disregarded the three-mile limit by
adopting platform declarations for home rule for Ireland. Nor were more recent racial accessions overlooked,
as is indicated by the planks in 1892 condemning anti-
Semitic persecution in Russia.

With the parties so evenly matched, political managers left no stone unturned to poll their full voting
strength. Much of the increased campaign expenditures
went into providing meetings, bands, parades, picnics,
barbecues and other means of rekindling old party
loyalties. Particularly in the rural regions, politics accordingly took the place of "the opera-house, the theatre, the club, . . . the foreign tour, the summer sport,
the dinner-party, the institute, and one may almost say
the church."[3] In the poorer quarters of the great cities
a similar method was employed by machine politicians
to solidify their following. Among Alfred E. Smith's
most cherished youthful memories were the holiday
parades, the prize shooting contests and summer out-

[1] Anon., "Power of the Irish in American Cities," *Littell's Living
Age*, CLXXI (1886), 382-384; Patrick Ford, "The Irish Vote in
the Presidential Election," *N. Am. Rev.*, CXLVII (1888), 185-190;
H. C. Merwin, "The Irish in American Life," *Atlantic Mo.*, LXXVII
(1896), esp. 296-298.

[2] *Appletons' Annual Cyclopaedia*, XXVIII (1888), 269.

[3] Anon., "Two Journalists," *Atlantic Mo.*, LII (1883), 415.

ings provided for East Side families by "Big Tim" Sullivan and other Tammany henchmen.[1]

Thanks to the hot competition for electoral support, four out of every five eligible voters cast their ballots in each presidential election of the period, and this in spite of the steady decline of the Negro vote in the South.[2] Never since has so large a proportion of the electorate taken part. European visitors were constantly surprised at the good-natured acquiescence in the outcome of fiercely fought contests. Muirhead believed that the American sense of humor provided the necessary safety valve.[3] Even more ingenious was the suggestion that the passion for competitive sport was teaching the people to be good losers and to abide by the rules of the game.[4] But probably much more influential was a deep-rooted habit reaching back to the beginnings of the republic and violated but once—in 1860—then to the irreparable injury of all concerned.

The most striking political phenomenon of the times, the exaltation of national at the expense of state power, had little relation to the fortunes of party. It was due, rather, to a new sentiment of national unity which began to tide through American life as soon as Lee's surrender determined that the United States was to remain a geographic entity. Its force was increased by the notable growth of business and capital across state borders and the multiplying contacts resulting from im-

[1] A. E. Smith, *Up to Now* (N. Y., 1929), 29-33. See also H. C. Brown, *New York in the Elegant Eighties* (*Valentine's Manual of Old New York*, XI, Hastings-on-Hudson, 1926), 243-249; same author, *In the Golden Nineties* (same ser., XII, Hastings-on-Hudson, 1927), 300-305.

[2] A. M. Schlesinger and E. M. Eriksson, "The Vanishing Voter," *New Republic*, XL, 162-167 (Oct. 15, 1924).

[3] J. F. Muirhead, *The Land of Contrasts* (Boston, 1898), 140-141.

[4] L. S. Bryce, "A Plea for Sport," *N. Am. Rev.*, CXXVIII (1879), esp. 523-524. See also W. J. Shepard, "The Psychology of the Bi-Party System," *Social Forces*, IV, 795-804.

proved means of travel and communication.[1] By the 1880's it was rushing at full torrent through all the channels of American thought and action. One of the most impressive spontaneous manifestations of the new spirit was the Vesuvian energy which went into the formation of voluntary nation-wide bodies, not only of trade unionists and business men but also, as we have seen, of scholars, scientists, artists, professional men, social and political reformers, sport lovers and members of secret fraternal orders. Nothing equaling it had been known before in America or anywhere else in the world. In a quite different way the fading of local loyalties led in 1883 to the adoption of a scheme of standard time for the entire country. Without awaiting action by the general government the railways took the initiative and local communities and states fell quickly into step.[2]

The heightened sense of national pride was nourished by the succession of patriotic celebrations which clustered about the opening of a second century of Independence. Beginning with the centenary of Concord and Lexington in 1875, no year passed without one or more such jubilees, until in 1889 and 1890 the inauguration of President Washington and the setting up of the Supreme Court were commemorated with due pomp and circumstance. Everybody was "centennializing himself, and looking over his shoulder to catch a glimpse of the century behind him in the mirror which he held."[3] Those who were in a position to do so sought to garner the unearned increment of ancestral reputations by banding together in patriotic-hereditary societies. Among the

[1] For contemporary comment on the new nationalism, see anon., "The Strong Government Idea," *Atlantic Mo.*, XLV (1880), 273-277; and Bryce, *American Commonwealth*, II, 188-190; III, 649-650, 652.

[2] R. E. Riegel, "Standard Time in the United States," *Am. Hist. Rev.*, XXXIII, 84-89.

[3] R. Fellow, "American History on the Stage," *Atlantic Mo.*, L (1882), 309.

more influential of such bodies, dating from the late eighties and the nineties, were the Sons of the American Revolution, the Daughters of the American Revolution, the Colonial Dames, the Society of Colonial Wars, the Society of the War of 1812, the Society of Mayflower Descendants and the Order of Indian Wars.

But no phase of the nationalizing process so clearly revealed the deep spiritual wells which fed it as the change effected in the attitude of South and North toward each other. Crushed on the battle-field, only to be subjected to the searing humiliation of Reconstruction, the Southern people were never allowed to forget their past acts either by their own partisan zealots or by Republican demagogues in the North. Yet forces beyond the politicians' ken were steadily obliterating old rancors and misunderstandings and weaving the once broken strands into a new and firmer fabric of nationality. A fresh generation was coming of age that had no memory of the Civil War. The recurrent centennial celebrations helped by focusing attention upon that remoter past when South and North had fought as brethren in a common cause. At the centenary of Bunker Hill, for example, General Fitzhugh Lee spoke from the same platform as General W. T. Sherman and both sounded the same note of patriotism and reconciliation.[1] The Yorktown celebration in 1881 called forth the eloquent plea of James Barron Hope:

> Give us back the ties of Yorktown!
> Perish all the modern hates!
> Let us stand together, brothers,
> In defiance of the Fates;
> For the safety of the Union
> Is the safety of the States![2]

[1] *Boston Transcript*, June 16-18, 1875.

[2] J. B. Hope, *Arms and the Man* (Norfolk, Va., 1882), 70. For James Whitcomb Riley's poems on the reconciliation theme, see *Com-*

In the same year veterans' organizations of both armies met together, for the first time, for the express purpose of rejoicing that they were no longer foes. Such occasions, repeated with increasing frequency, reached a happy climax in 1888 in the great spectacle commemorating the twenty-fifth anniversary of the battle of Gettysburg.[1] Three years earlier both Union and Confederate soldiers had joined at Grant's funeral in a notable tribute to their military brother.

Other circumstances conspired to the same end. As the Northern manufacturing system extended southward, fundamental economic antagonisms began to disappear, new ties of interest emerge. Atlanta, Chattanooga and Durham were the outposts of a new nationalism as well as of a new industrialism. Northern willingness to let the South manage its own race relations, another important factor in healing the breach, rested in final analysis upon the nationalization of the Southern economic order. Senator Don Cameron of Pennsylvania spoke for the dominant group of his party when he denounced the proposed force bill of 1890 as certain to disturb the "community of commercial interests" resulting from the flow of Northern capital into Dixie and the growth of manufactures there.[2] Nor did the turn of Southern agriculture toward small farming and the growth of agrarian unrest fail to create new bonds with the rest of the country. Such influences were strengthened by Northern migrants settling in the South for business or health reasons, and by the increasing number of young Southerners frequenting Northern educational institutions or finding employment in that section.[3]

*plete Works* (Indianapolis, 1913), II, 466-467; IV, 25-26.

[1] G. L. Kilmer, "A Note of Peace: Reunions of 'the Blue and the Gray,'" *Century*, XXXVI (1888), 440-442.

[2] *Public Opinion*, IX (1890), 428.

[3] Florida had so many Northern health seekers that already by 1889

Northern opinion was perhaps even more greatly mollified by the novel and somewhat romantic view of Southern character and ideals afforded by the local-color writers. To untold numbers of fiction readers Hopkinson Smith's Colonel Carter became a more credible bit of portraiture than Mrs. Stowe's Simon Legree, while even Uncle Tom was eclipsed by the loving regard accorded Uncle Remus. In the theater few plays aroused greater enthusiasm than those which, like "Shenandoah" and "The Heart of Maryland," gave dramatic form to the theme of love triumphant over sectional barriers. Of great importance, too, particularly in Dixie, was the influence exerted by certain Southern editors and publicists who, in season and out, kept exhorting their people to look forward, not backward—such men as the educator J. L. M. Curry, A. G. Haygood of Emory College, Henry Watterson of the *Louisville Courier-Journal* and Henry W. Grady of the *Atlanta Constitution*. Yet Watterson felt, after seeing Augustus Thomas's play "Alabama" in 1891, that it "had done more to reconcile the two sections . . . than his editorials had accomplished in twenty years." [1]

Southerners could not be denied the privilege of dwelling fondly upon the "lost cause," but nearly every year brought fresh evidence of their satisfaction that the cause was indeed lost. In a Thanksgiving Day address in 1880 President Haygood declared he spoke for the "vast majority of our people" in saying, "I, for one, thank

it was "scarcely a Southern State except in climate." C. D. Warner, *Studies in the South and West* (N. Y., 1889), 37. On the other hand, according to the *St. Paul Pioneer Press*, Sept. 1, 1879, Southerners were beginning again to crowd Minnesota summer resorts. In 1890-1891 nearly 700 Southern students were attending Northern colleges. U. S. Commissioner of Education, *Report for 1890-91*, II, 822-826.

[1] A. H. Quinn, *A History of the American Drama from the Civil War* (N. Y., 1927), I, 245. See also F. P. Gaines, *The Southern Plantation* (Columbia Univ., *Studies in English and Comparative Literature*; N. Y., 1924), 113-114, 117-119, 122-125.

God that there is no longer slavery in these United States!" [1] The following year Jefferson Davis, former president of the Confederacy, concluded his two-volume *apologia* with the earnest wish that "there may be written on the arch of the Union, *Esto perpetua.*" [2] The election of a president in 1884, backed by the solid vote of the South, reassured that section of its political equality in the Union, while the character of Cleveland's administration reassured the country as to the loyalty and national outlook of the former rebel party.[3]

The coming of the war with Spain drowned the last faint notes of discord in an exultant chorus of patriotism. The well-known ex-Confederate cavalry leader, General Joseph Wheeler, promptly proffered his sword, and a song bard, catching the spirit of the hour, set the nation to singing, "He laid away a suit of gray to wear the Union blue." [4] In the surge of sentiment Congress expunged from the statute books the remaining disabilities imposed upon Confederate leaders by the Fourteenth Amendment.[5] The lightning flash of war had made the people suddenly aware of the miracle that had been hap-

---

[1] A. G. Haygood, *The New South* (Oxford, Ga., 1880), 11. See also his *Our Brother in Black* (Oxford, 1881), chap. v; J. B. Gordon and C. C. Jones, jr., *The Old South. Addresses Delivered before the Confederate Survivors' Association* (Augusta, Ga., 1887), 9; Warner, *Studies*, 101; W. F. Tillett, "Southern Womanhood as Affected by the War," *Century*, XLIII (1891-1892), 13-15; J. L. M. Curry, *Address before the Association of Confederate Veterans* (Richmond, Va., 1896), 23; J. S. Wise, *The End of an Era* (Boston, 1899), 88.

[2] Jefferson Davis, *The Rise and Fall of the Confederate Government* (N. Y., 1881), II, 774.

[3] A. K. McClure, *The South: Its Industrial, Financial, and Political Condition* (Phila., 1886), 53-54; Warner, *Studies*, 3-4; B. J. Hendrick, *The Life and Letters of Walter H. Page* (Garden City, 1922), I, 41.

[4] It was rivaled by Paul Dresser's "The Blue and the Gray," first copyrighted in 1890 but not accorded popular favor until reissued in 1898 with appropriate references to the Cuban war. Brown, *Golden Nineties*, 174; J. T. Howard, *Our American Music* (N. Y., 1931), 582.

[5] *U. S. Statutes at Large*, XXX, 432.

"YANKEE DOODLE!"

*In the Spanish War President McKinley found hearty support in North and South alike.*

## The Blue and Gray United

pening under their very eyes. As one newspaper rhyme-
ster wrote,

One thing'd make this war wuth while, 'f we hed no other
reason,
An' to yer Uncle Sam, I swaow, th' fac' is mighty pleasin';
It's good ter free th' Cubans; it's good ter lick the Spanish;
It's better far ter make th' hate 'twixt North an' Saouth ter
vanish.[1]

Within the span of a single generation the foemen of
1861 had become comrades in spirit as well as in name.

New horizons, new attachments of interest, new
views, new men—these account for the strong centripetal trend in government, which shaped the policies of
both major parties. Extreme tariff protection, lavish
grants for river and harbor improvement, increasing
restrictions upon immigration and the Sherman law
against trusts were Republican contributions toward
national consolidation. Nor did the Democrats, who
when out of power liked to complain of "Cæsarism"
and "centralizationism," show by their conduct in office
any considerable regard for the once hallowed state
rights. The interstate-commerce act of 1887, which
Cleveland signed, embodied a startling assumption of
national authority. When later he defied the traditional
reading of the Constitution by sending troops to Chicago during the Pullman strike of 1894, Governor J. P.
Altgeld of Illinois felt obliged to remind him that "the
principle of local self-government is just as fundamental
in our institutions as is that of Federal supremacy."[2]

[1] C. B. Loomis, "When North and South Unite," taken from a scrapbook of the Spanish-American War compiled by F. D. Stiles of South
Hanson, Mass. Similar rhymed rejoicings may be found in S. A. Wither-
bee, comp., *Spanish-American War Songs* (Detroit, 1898), 8-9.

[2] Cleveland later alluded to Altgeld's "rather dreary discussion of the
importance of preserving the rights of the States." McElroy, *Cleveland*,
II, 158-162.

Political conflicts no longer turned upon the constitutional question as to how much authority the general government possessed, but rather upon the alternative uses to which the expanded powers should be put. If certain minor parties had had their way, centralization would have been carried to the point of the national ownership of railways and telegraphs and a national ban upon the drink habit. Indeed, sectional and class demands usually took the form of a purpose to interpose federal authority for the protection of minority rights. The judiciary mirrored the same tendency. Under a law of 1875 the volume of federal business was greatly augmented at the cost of the state courts, while, in a series of decisions qualifying the judgment in Munn *v.* Illinois (1876), the Supreme Court gradually assumed the high function of reviewing all state legislation regulating the use of property and labor.[1] As a thoughtful contemporary admitted, "the general government now exercises authority which the stoutest Federalist of 1789 would have shuddered to foresee, yet does this with the approval of all."[2]

With the enhanced nationalism at home came a corresponding change of attitude toward internationalism. Traditional taboos continued to be mouthed by statesmen, but in countless respects the old hermitlike fear of Europe began to wane. A confident sense of national strength and well-being, of national fulfillment in scholarship, art and technology, made it possible for Americans to meet the gaze of the world with steadier nerves, to speak less often in tones edged with that boastfulness which in the past had so frequently cloaked

---

[1] Felix Frankfurter and J. M. Landis, *The Business of the Supreme Court* (N. Y., 1928), chap. ii; Charles Warren, *The Supreme Court in United States History* (Boston, 1922), III, esp. 344-429.

[2] E. B. Andrews, "Money as an International Question," *Atlantic Mo.,* LXXI (1893), 543.

an inner feeling of deficiency.[1] As the United States became more urbanized, American political and social problems became more and more like those of Western Europe, and civic leaders turned increasingly to the Old World for guidance in coping with conditions unprecedented in their own experience.

The cosmopolitan spirit was most deeply implanted in the intellectual classes, for many of the foremost men in education and the arts had spent their adolescent years in European centers of study. Nevertheless all sections of society were touched with a new sense of world community if only as a backwash from the growth of missionary activities in the remoter regions of the globe.[2] When the Russian people faced a terrible famine in 1891, the farmers of Iowa and other Western states supported the efforts of the Red Cross by sending carloads of corn, and the fraternal order of the Elks defrayed a large part of the cost of transportation. Five years later Miss Barton was directing relief work in Armenia, a labor of mercy made possible by the subscription of over one hundred thousand American dollars.[3]

Meantime, the business classes were looking beyond the national borders for new openings for trade and investment. The industrial progress of the country was beginning to produce a surplus of goods and capital which, by an imperious law of business enterprise, must be made to produce more goods and more capital. With increasing frequency from the 1880's on, American consuls in far parts of the world reported the capture of new trophies by Yankee *entrepreneurs:* now the launch-

[1] The decline of the national habit of bragging was noted, among others, by Bryce, *American Commonwealth*, III, 540, 573, 659, and Muirhead, *Land of Contrasts*, 78-79.

[2] J. S. Dennis, *Centennial Survey of Foreign Missions* (N. Y., 1902), 9-16, 279-293.

[3] Corra Bacon-Foster, *Clara Barton, Humanitarian* (Wash., 1918), 37, 48.

ing of a telephone company in Rio de Janeiro; now the construction of a railroad in Colombia; now mining enterprises in Honduras; now the establishment of branch insurance agencies in New Zealand or the owner-ship of sugar plantations in Hawaii or Cuba.[1] By the close of the period the chief of the United States bureau of foreign commerce asserted: "The 'international iso-lation' of the United States so far as industry and com-merce are concerned, has, in fact, been made a thing of the past by the logic of the change in our economic requirements, and we can no longer afford to disregard international rivalries, now that we ourselves have be-come a competitor in the world-wide struggle for trade." [2]

It is not surprising therefore that the American gov-ernment found itself drawn increasingly into the world stream of affairs. The nation was officially represented in a succession of foreign expositions and, as a matter of course, coöperated in various international scientific in-quiries, such as the polar expeditions of 1882-1883 and the simultaneous observation of basic weather phenom-ena conducted during the late seventies and early eighties throughout the northern hemisphere.[3] Follow-ing the general adoption of standard time in America,

[1] *U. S. Commercial Relations for 1880-1881*, 612; for *1885-1886*, II, 1124; for *1884-1885*, II, 918; for *1882-1883*, II, 799; *Ha-waiian Almanac and Annual for 1894*, 40-41; Perfecto Lacoste, *Oppor-tunities in the Colonies and Cuba* (N. Y., 1902), 268. These citations were kindly supplied by Mr. H. R. Bartlett of the Massachusetts Insti-tute of Technology.

[2] *Review of the World's Commerce for 1896-1897*, 22. At about that date America's foreign investments totaled more than half a billion dollars, an amount considerably less, of course, than that of European investments in the United States. R. W. Dunn, *American Foreign In-vestments* (N. Y., 1926), 2.

[3] Six foreign expositions and many international scientific confer-ences, 1878-1898, are listed in *Check List of United States Documents, 1789-1909* (Wash., 1911), I, 944-953. See also J. C. Faries, *The Rise of Internationalism* (N. Y., 1915), chaps. iii-v.

the state department in 1884 called a conference of twenty-seven nations to recommend a universal prime meridian for the reckoning of both longitude and time. Upon at least four other occasions the United States initiated international conferences to consider the bimetallic standard.

Even more indicative perhaps were the commitments involved in the signing of various multilateral treaties and pacts. In the two decades eight were ratified as compared with one in all the years before. They dealt with a wide range of nonpolitical interests of growing world concern.[1] Besides accepting the Geneva convention for establishing the Red Cross, the United States agreed to common action in such matters as weights and measures, patents and trademarks, suppression of the African slave trade and the interchange of official and learned publications. Tentative ventures were also made in the troubled waters of international politics. The United States not only joined with European powers in a treaty with Morocco in 1880, but nine years later found herself somewhat unexpectedly involved with Great Britain and Germany in a tripartite protectorate over Samoa—an "entangling alliance" in whatever sense that phrase be understood.[2]

Meanwhile America's expanding interests were fruiting in the acquisition of a few score guano islands in two oceans, the modernization of the navy and the securing of strategic naval stations in the Pacific. In 1893 a revolution in Hawaii, fomented by American interests, would have resulted in prompt annexation but for the grim refusal of Cleveland, which, however, merely delayed the final outcome. Nationalism, crossed

---

[1] W. M. Malloy, comp., *Treaties, Conventions, International Acts, Protocols and Agreements* (Wash., 1910), II, 1903-2005.

[2] J. B. Henderson, *American Diplomatic Questions* (N. Y., 1901), pt. iii.

by a sort of bastard internationalism, was begetting an American counterpart of the much decried European imperialism. The Spanish war merely hastened a process already well under way. The annexation of insular dependencies was less a new departure than a consummation.[1]

In reviewing the multifarious trends in government one is impressed by the close correlation of political action with social, economic and intellectual forces. The imposing façade of party hid more realities than it disclosed. Nor is it possible to arrive at any satisfactory balance of profit and loss in the political life of the day. The leaders of the time did, indeed, succeed in curing some of the worst evils which had been visited upon them by the sins of their fathers, but they permitted others to arise which were to make their successors despair of the safety of the republic.

[1] See Faulkner, *Quest for Social Justice*, 308-314.

# CHAPTER XIII

## Fin De Siècle

THROUGHOUT the 1890's the people of the United States were deeply imbued with the feeling that the greatest of centuries was drawing to a close. Nor was this feeling confined to the American side of the Atlantic. In France the sense of destiny fulfilling itself was compacted into the phrase *fin de siècle*. Early in the nineties the expression found its way into English newspapers and, by this channel, quickly reached the United States where, as Henry Adams tells us, "during this last decade every one talked, and seemed to feel *fin-de-siècle*." [1] To the fashionable and the light-minded the phrase denoted ultramodernism—an anticipation of the latest mode in artistic decoration and personal adornment, a new orgy of extravagance in manners and social entertainment. [2] To the humanitarians and reformers in general it meant a final opportunity to cure the abuses and injustices which a heedless society had permitted to appear. To the toilers these closing years afforded fresh hope and a desperate purpose to solve the staggering problems which beset them both in factory and on farm.

[1] Henry Adams, *The Education of Henry Adams* (Boston, 1918), 331. After accounting for the origin of the phrase a contemporary writer says: "Everywhere we are treated to dissertations on fin-de-siècle literature, fin-de-siècle statesmanship, fin-de-siècle morality." "Contributors' Club," *Atlantic Mo.*, LXVII (1891), 859-860.

[2] The philosophy of fashionable boredom is amusingly depicted in Edmund Vance Cooke's poem, "Fin de Siècle," which was set to music and introduced into Hoyt's farce, "A Night in New York." E. V. Cooke, *Rimes to Be Read* (rev. edn., N. Y., 1905), 67-69.

Life in America had never before been so complex.
An introverted personality like Henry Adams's, out of
key with the times, continually sought escape by flight—
to the South Seas, Cuba, the Yellowstone, Mexico, Russia, Egypt, Normandy—only to be drawn back each
time, fascinated and repelled by a sense of new energies
astir in human fate, comparable in his own day to the
will exerted on an earlier mankind by the Virgin. "We
call ourselves the masters of machinery: are we quite
sure that machinery is not mastering us?" wondered
Josiah Strong.[1] "Our industry is a fight of every man
for himself," warned Henry Demarest Lloyd, who saw
the vaunted American gospel of equality yielding "incal-
culable power and pleasure for a few, and partial existence for the many who are the fountains of these
powers and pleasures."[2] "The huge, rushing, aggregate
life of a great city," complained another, ". . . cur-
tails man of his wholeness, specializes him, quickens
some powers, stunts others . . . ."[3] A cloistered scholar
deplored the increasing demands placed upon the educated man: "He must be familiar with magnetism as well
as mythology, with evolution as well as elegiacs, with
geology as well as genesis."[4] Once it had been easy to
be human, Professor Wilson observed, but now "haste,
anxiety, preoccupation, the need to specialize and make
machines of ourselves have transformed the once simple
world . . . ."[5] "Do you really think the 'game pays for
the candle'?" queried a publicist. "I get yearly more

[1] Josiah Strong, *Expansion under New World Conditions* (N. Y.,
1900), 72-73.
[2] H. D. Lloyd, *Wealth against Commonwealth* (N. Y., 1894), 7,
494.
[3] Woodrow Wilson, "On Being Human," *Atlantic Mo.*, LXXX
(1897), 322.
[4] J. J. Greenough, "The Basis of Our Educational System," *Atlantic
Mo.*, LXXV (1895), 530.
[5] Wilson, "On Being Human," 321.

tired of what we call civilization. It seems to me a preposterous fraud." [1]

The attrition of town on country continued with unabated force. The unbroken frontier was gone and, as Professor Turner pointed out in his memorable address of 1893, "with its going has closed the first period of American history." [2] Yet the impetus to Western settlement was not yet spent, and a seventh state now joined the six admitted to the Union in 1889 and 1890. Utah had been denied the privilege for more than a decade because of the continuance of polygamy. By 1890, however, Mormons and non-Mormons had become about equal in numbers, mutual business advantage was dissolving religious prejudices, and the nation through recent acts of Congress had announced its implacable purpose to stamp out the hated practice.[3] Making a virtue of necessity, Wilford Woodruff, head of the church, on September 30 openly pledged his personal influence in behalf of enforcing the antipolygamy statutes, while the general conference of the church a few weeks later unanimously indorsed his stand.[4]

The sincerity of this action was widely questioned; but aside from evidence showing the unwillingness of husbands to abandon family obligations already contracted, there could be no doubt that polygamy had been dealt a death blow.[5] In local politics the People's or

[1] Quoted by D. A. Wells, *Recent Economic Changes* (N. Y., 1889), 325.

[2] F. J. Turner, *The Frontier in American History* (N. Y., 1920), 38.

[3] See earlier, 46.

[4] *Latter-day Saints' Millennial Star*, LII (1890), 648, 721-725, 737-741, 744-745, 753-757.

[5] Glen Miller, "Will Polygamists Control the New State of Utah?," *Forum*, XVIII (1894-1895), 466-467; anon., "Is Polygamy Practised?," *Home Mission Mo.*, XV (1901), 279-280; W. M. Raine and A. W. Dunn, "Mormon or Patriot," *Leslie's*, LIX (1905), 537-547; Theodore Schroeder, "Polygamy and the Constitution," *Arena*, XXXVI (1906), 492-497.

Mormon party and the Liberal or Gentile party dis-
banded to reorganize along national political lines. In
1893 President Harrison granted amnesty to such vio-
lators of the Edmunds law as had since November
1, 1890, abstained from unlawful cohabitation, while
Congress restored the escheated property and funds to
the church.[1] Nothing now stood in the way of statehood but the jockeying of the politicians in Washington
for party advantage. In 1896 Utah was admitted into
the Union upon the "irrevocable" condition that "polygamy or plural marriages are forever prohibited." [2]

In another part of the West the status of Oklahoma
continued somewhat uncertain as the decade began.
Opened under spectacular circumstances to homesteaders
in 1889, the district lay entirely surrounded by Indian
country and the people remained without proper governmental provision. In 1890, however, Congress authorized the formation of the territory of Oklahoma to
include, besides the original district, No Man's Land and
such additional lands as the tribes might be induced to
part with.[3] New tracts were opened from time to time,
attended, as in 1889, by frantic rushes of settlers. By
1898 virtually all the region outside of the area held by
the Five Civilized Tribes was occupied.[4] The population
had grown meantime from sixty-two thousand in 1890
to three hundred and eleven thousand in 1898. The
achievement of statehood awaited the coming of the
new century.

[1] U. S. *Statutes at Large*, XXVII, 1058; XXVIII, 980, 1257; XXIX,
758.

[2] U. S. *Statutes at Large*, XXVIII, 107-112; XXIX, 461, 876-877.

[3] U. S. *Statutes at Large*, XXVI, 80-100. See also earlier, 47-50.

[4] S. J. Buck, "The Settlement of Oklahoma," Wis. Acad., *Trans.*,
XV, 355-366; Helen C. Candee, "Social Conditions in Our Newest
Territory," *Forum*, XXV (1898), 426-437; F. E. Sutton and A. B.
Macdonald, "Hands Up!," *Sat. Eve. Post*, CXCVIII, 32 ff. (April 24,
1926).

The West in the *fin de siècle*, however, was less concerned with attracting new settlers than with the problem of adjusting its life to a national political and social order regulated by the people of the Eastern cities. Agrarian leaders, zealous in treating symptoms, talked cheap money, lower transportation rates, the curbing of Wall Street and big business; but behind their bill of particulars lay something less tangible and often unacknowledged: a deepening sense of frustration and defeat. The men, women and children who gathered in ten thousand schoolhouses to debate the farmers' grievances in the early 1890's had only vague notions about the intricacies of the free-silver question and its relation to prices and prosperity, but they were grimly aware that mysterious new forces in American life were robbing them of their traditional rural heritage of freedom and spiritual and material well-being.

During the decade the western and central parts of Kansas, Nebraska and South Dakota declined in population, as did also eastern Colorado, a third of the state of Nevada and eleven counties of California. Similar losses occurred in northern New England and in the backward agricultural parts of New York, Pennsylvania, Ohio and Michigan.[1] The land of promise was no longer the land of performance unless one joined the backward trail toward the East, as more and more of the ambitious youth of the countryside were doing each year. As the decade proceeded, the nation grew steadily more urbanized, the number of cities with four thousand or more inhabitants advancing from less than nine thousand to nearly twelve and the proportion of urban dwellers from one third of the total to approximately two fifths.[2]

---

[1] *Supplementary Analysis and Derivative Tables* (U. S. Twelfth Census, *Special Rep.*), 44-45, 277.

[2] *U. S. Twelfth Census* (1900), I, lxxxiv-lxxxv.

In a Farmers' Alliance campaign song a rural youth pleads with his father, before it is too late, to cast his ballot for farmers' rights:

> Free land will be gone and naught else can I do
> But be to the rich man a slave.

When the father accedes the lad rejoices:

> I'll have clothes like the rich boys in town.[1]

Yet the bulk of city wage-earners were equally irked by their lot. While millionaires raised up their gaudy palaces and Ward McAllister led society into ever more extravagant revels, the masses toiled long hours in factory and office, returning at length to their frugal abodes embittered or benumbed. Industrial outbreaks occurred with increasing frequency and destructiveness. The Panic of 1893 cast a deep black shadow across their lives. Presently began the tramp of the unemployed from all parts of the country upon Washington, a veritable petition in boots whose inglorious ending did not hide the gravity of the conditions which had given it rise.[2] James Whitcomb Riley's friend, Eugene V. Debs, jailed in Chicago in 1894 for his activities during the Pullman strike, read socialist tracts in his enforced leisure and dedicated himself to the gospel of the abolition of capitalism. Meanwhile Hamlin Garland and other intellectuals pinned their faith to Henry George's panacea of the single tax. Still others, lingering fondly over Bellamy's utopian dream, banded together in so-called Nationalist Clubs.[3]

---

[1] Luna E. Kellie, "Vote for Me," *Farmers' Alliance* (Lincoln, Neb.), Sept. 6, 1890, quoted by J. D. Barnhart, History of the Farmers' Alliance and of the People's Party in Nebraska (unpublished Ph.D. thesis, Harvard Univ., 1930), 124.

[2] D. L. McMurry, *Coxey's Army* (Boston, 1929).

[3] Such societies to the number of 163 were active in 1891 from coast to coast. *Nationalist* (Boston), III (1891), 505.

The air was full of revolt against things as they were. Howells, deploring the increasing resort to violence and murder by the unprosperous, feared lest a "blood-mist" would screen the real issues from the thoughtful.[1] Even the usually mild-spoken Thomas Bailey Aldrich predicted: "We shall have bloody work in this country some of these days, when the lazy *canaille* get organized."[2] What a vision of *fin de siècle,* cried a magazine poet:

Strange vision! The land is filled full with the harvest—
　Hungry men look for the morrow with dread;
Our hearts swell with pride of our civilization—
　God! hear that piteous crying for bread![3]

The campaign of 1896 provided vent for an expression of class antagonisms such as the country had never before known. Perhaps, like the new device employed in surgical operations, the occasion gave drainage to pent-up poisons which might have prostrated the body politic. Though embattled conservatism won the election, it could never again ignore questions that vitally concerned the average man and woman or, in Populist parlance, "drown the outcries of a plundered people with the uproar of a sham battle over the tariff."[4]

Nor, as the sequel showed, were politicians and statesmen properly accountable for all the ills to which society had fallen heir. In so far as these distresses stemmed from an insufficient circulating medium, they were, as Miss Tarbell points out, soon ameliorated by the dis-

---

[1] W. D. Howells, *Life in Letters* (Mildred Howells, ed., Garden City, 1928), II, 26.

[2] Ferris Greenslet, *Life of Thomas Bailey Aldrich* (Boston, 1908), 168-169.

[3] Margaret S. Sibley, "A 'Fin-de-Siècle' Vision," *Arena,* XI (1894-1895), 99.

[4] Platform of 1892, quoted in T. H. McKee, *The National Conventions and Platforms of All Political Parties* (Balt., 1900), 281.

covery of fresh sources of gold supply together with a return of prosperity and an expansion of credit facilities. As opportunities for work multiplied, the acerbities of the industrial struggle lessened: within a few years Mark Hanna and Samuel Gompers would join hands in a constructive effort to harmonize the interests of employer, employee and consumer.[1] In the South manufactures, recovering from the blow of 1893, actually overtopped that section's agricultural yield by nearly $200,000,000 in 1898.[2] Birmingham could boast of being the third largest iron-shipping point in the world, the first in America. The farmer in West and South shared in the general well-being, facing an era of better crops and higher prices with the discipline of much needed lessons in thrift and prudent management, learned in the lean hard years that had gone before. At the same time the introduction of rural free delivery, the springing up of mutual telephone companies, the advent of interurban electric railways, the building of good roads, and better provision for schools promised for the countryside advantages which earlier had belonged only to the urban dweller.[3] Parity with the city, of course, was not attained—perhaps never could be attained—but rural inferiority was becoming less flagrant, less a source of hopelessness and despair.

In reality, the mists and shadows that gathered over America in the beginning years of the *fin de siècle* had always been streaked with light for those with eyes to

[1] See H. U. Faulkner, *The Quest for Social Justice* (*A History of American Life*, XI), 53-54.

[2] E. G. Murphy, *Problems of the Present South* (N. Y., 1904), 102.

[3] Sylvester Baxter, "The Trolley in Rural Parts," and C. M. Harger, "The New Era in the Middle West," *Harper's Mag.*, XCVII (1898), 60-69, 276-282; W. L. Anderson, *The Country Town* (N. Y., 1906), chap. xiii. For the introduction of rural free delivery in 1896 and its development, see Postmaster-General, *Report for 1899*, 16-18; for 1900, 113-146.

see. One needed only to look about him to appreciate the justice of Muirhead's characterization of the United States as the "Land of Contrasts." Howells makes a character in one of his books assert that the passion of Americans for doing things on a large scale extended even to their inconsistencies.[1] Thus, while capitalistic greed ground the faces of the poor under its iron heel, individual potentates of wealth lavished millions upon hospitals, libraries, colleges, churches, museums and art galleries for the good of all. While the Panic palsied the country's industrial energies and turned hordes of the jobless into the streets, an extraordinary outburst of philanthropic relief effort attested the essential humaneness of the American character,[2] and the Columbian Exposition on the south shore of Lake Michigan revealed to a wondering world the summit of American accomplishment in the fine arts and the graces of life.

The year 1897 not only brought the turn to prosperity, but touched American life once more with that sense of romance and adventure which had seemed forever gone.[3] In the middle of June two steamships arrived respectively at San Francisco and Seattle with prospectors from Alaska carrying with them one and a half million dollars' worth of gold dust. In this startling fashion the world learned of the fabulously rich placer deposits discovered the preceding year along Klondike Creek in the Yukon country, mostly in British territory. The

[1] W. D. Howells, *A Traveller from Altruria* (N. Y., 1894), 50.

[2] Anon., "The Relief of the Unemployed during the Winter of 1893-94," *Journ. of Social Sci.*, XXXII (1894), 1-51; C. C. Closson, jr., "The Unemployed in American Cities," *Quar. Journ. of Econ.*, VIII (1894), 168-217; F. D. Watson, *The Charity Organization Movement in the United States* (N. Y., 1922), 248-265.

[3] W. B. Haskell, *Two Years in the Klondike and Alaskan Gold-Fields* (Hartford, 1898); Tappan Adney, *The Klondike Stampede of 1897-98* (N. Y., 1899); Charmian London, *Jack London* (London, 1921), I, chaps. xv-xvi; H. W. Clark, *History of Alaska* (N. Y., 1930), 100-107.

gold fever ran through all parts of the United States and attracted adventurers from remote corners of the globe. Taxing all available means of water transport northward, the argonauts braved incredible hardships presented by a frozen and forbidding country in order to reach the new El Dorado.

Between two and three hundred thousand set forth on the journey. Many turned back or died on the way, not more than fifty thousand reaching the interior fastnesses. In the late autumn of 1897 the carcasses of nearly four thousand horses strewed the difficult White Pass Trail. The camps, picturesque and lively, were yet more orderly than those of the forty-niners in California. From 1898 to 1904 the annual yield of the Yukon territory alone was never less than ten million dollars. Meantime gold deposits were discovered on American soil along the Yukon River and even around the head of Cook Inlet and about Nome, near Bering Strait. The richest finds were made by veteran miners. The bulk of the fortune hunters had to be content with the satisfaction of novel adventures; few of them possessed young Jack London's or Rex Beach's talent for coining their experiences into authors' royalties.

The stampede might have been the greatest in history had not the Spanish war intervened to divert popular attention to other scenes of derring-do. Whatever self-interested motives may have colored the government's decision to enter the conflict, and however much credit or blame may attach to the enterprise of Hearst, Pulitzer and company, the populace answered the call to arms in the spirit of schoolboys off for a picnic.[1] "There'll Be a Hot Time in the Old Town Tonight" inevitably out-rivaled all other popular ditties that sought to capture the spirit of the moment. Thus the *fin de siècle* which

[1] Walter Millis, *The Martial Spirit* (Boston, 1931), 160-167.

had begun in a vale of gloom and foreboding had, by an unexpected turn of events, suddenly issued forth into the sunshine of prosperity, optimism and high emprise.

It was in a mellow mood that Americans in 1898 could look backward and appraise the developments of the two decades just past. Impatient young men might mutter that the deeper economic conflict had only been postponed; that a truce, not a term, had stilled the popular outcry for social justice. But their elders could reply that, while wealth and economic power had tended to concentrate at a faster rate than they would have wished, the general condition of the masses had not been materially affected for the worse. If one eighth of the families of the United States possessed seven eighths of the country's property,[1] the enormous growth in aggregate national wealth still afforded ample elbow room for the less favored classes. In support of this contention a leading statistician pointed out that the number of persons in the higher and more skilled walks of life had increased faster relatively than the population, that the laborers' workday was lessening, and that the general tendency of wages was upward and of prices downward. Admitting that the toilers had not got their due share of the enlarged aggregate wealth, he nevertheless concluded that, though the rich were growing richer, "many more people than formerly are growing rich, and the poor are better off."[2]

The improved position of the common man, however, owed far more to the multifold mechanical inventions which these years brought forth and to the enlarged

[1] C. B. Spahr, *An Essay on the Present Distribution of Wealth in the United States* (R. T. Ely, ed., *Library of Economics and Politics*, XII, N. Y., 1896), esp. 69.

[2] C. D. Wright, "Are the Rich Growing Richer and the Poor Poorer?," *Atlantic Mo.*, LXXX (1897), 300-309.

rôle of public and private agencies in fostering better living standards. Labor-saving devices in the home, improved methods of plumbing, better lighting indoors and out, the commercial development of the telephone, the advent of the safety bicycle, the new conveniences of rapid transit in city and suburbs, showered blessings upon the many as well as the few, though urban dwellers were, of course, the chief gainers. In like manner ordinary folk benefited from the energetic attention given by municipalities to water purification, sewerage, street paving, parks, fire protection and public hygiene. Both in country and city, schools showed steady progress during the twenty years and, in the *fin de siècle*, a high-school education was becoming the normal expectation of most city youths. Poverty continued to exist, but it was treated by the new profession of social workers as a malady that was functional rather than organic. Even the churches began to take a hand in the exigent work of human rehabilitation.

Laymen and physicians alike testified to the altered physical appearance of the people. While the change was most marked in those rural parts once noted for leanness, angularity and sallowness of complexion, fifty years' familiarity with the streets of New York and Boston caused a careful observer to declare that there, also, "The men are more robust and more erect, the women have greatly improved both in feature and carriage; and in the care and condition of the teeth in both sexes a surprising change has taken place." [1] During the 1880's dealers in ready-made clothing were obliged to adopt a larger scale of sizes and many more extra sizes, in width as well as in length, than had been needed ten

[1] F. J. Kingsbury, "The Tendency of Men to Live in Cities," *Journ. of Social Sci.*, XXXIII (1895), 15. See also C. D. Warner, *The Relation of Literature to Life* (N. Y., 1897), 263-264, and S. Weir Mitchell, *Wear and Tear* (5th edn., Phila., 1887), 3-4.

years before.[1] Nor did the reasons for the improvement in physique baffle the inquirer. Apart from the advances in medical science and an ampler provision of physicians, it was generally ascribed to greater leisure, a lessening anxiety by a larger number of people concerning food and shelter, the growing cult of physical exercise and, not least of all, the varied and better-prepared diet which the generation enjoyed.

On the other hand, the restless energy bottled up in the urban centers, and constantly excited by noises, jars and the rush of crowds, tended more and more to make nervousness the national disease that medical writers were prone to call it.[2] Neurasthenia (to use Dr. Beard's term) and insanity were as characteristically city phenomena as feeble-mindedness and impaired physical vigor were rural complaints.[3] In its milder effects the high strain of urban living robbed American life of much of the repose which increasing leisure should have afforded it and often betrayed artists and writers into giving the world something less than their best.

If, as was widely asserted, women were the particular victims of the national disease,[4] it was doubtless the price they paid for their steadily enlarging share in activities outside the home—in the world of fashion, clubs, industry, the professions, literature and the arts. In educa-

[1] In the case of the Southern trade the increase was fully one inch around the chest and waist. Edward Atkinson, "The American Physique," *Science*, X (1887), 239-240, 276.

[2] G. M. Beard, *American Nervousness* (N. Y., 1881), chaps. ii-v; Mitchell, *Wear and Tear*, 7-10, 22-30; Grace Peckham, "The Nervousness of Americans," *Journ. of Social Sci.*, XXII (1887), 37-49; W. B. Platt, "Certain Injurious Influences of City Life," *Journ. of Social Sci.*, XXIV (1888), 24-30; Edward Wakefield, "Nervousness: The National Disease of America," *McClure's*, II (1894), 302-307.

[3] A. F. Weber, *The Growth of Cities in the Nineteenth Century* (Columbia Univ., *Studies*, XI), 392.

[4] Mitchell, *Wear and Tear*, 30-55; edit., *Ladies' Home Journ.*, X (1893), no. 9, 14.

tion and in enterprises of social uplift they were often the mainstay. Old notions of family integrity were rudely jarred by the centrifugal forces at work in the home. Outside agencies assumed an ever greater responsibility for the welfare of city children and the nation was startled by the leap in the divorce rate. Yet no finite intelligence could know whether even such changes implied a rise or decline in general ethical standards. Though in the large cities commercialized vice flaunted itself as never before and many would have agreed that "human life is rather more secure in Arizona than in the streets of New York," it was Bryce's considered judgment that, taking the country as a whole, "the average of temperance, chastity, truthfulness, and general probity is somewhat higher than in any of the great nations of Europe." [1] Nor is it to be overlooked that organized religion, after a period of doubt and confusion, attained a numerical and relative strength in the *fin de siècle* greater than at any preceding time in the twenty-year period.

By posterity the generation will be remembered less for the way it managed the retail traffic of life than for its more permanent contributions to American civilization. While every generation is born with its hands tied by the generation which went before, the constructive work of the 1880's and 1890's was less a fulfillment of the past than a starting point for the future. Apart from the impressive feat of forging a national economic order,[2] the men and women of the time laid the firm foundations for continuing achievement in all the elements of intellectual and æsthetic culture. The spread of

[1] W. E. Smythe, "Real Utopias in the Arid West," *Atlantic Mo.*, LXXIX (1897), 609; James Bryce, *The American Commonwealth* (London, 1888), III, 54.
[2] See *A History of American Life*, IX, by Ida M. Tarbell.

graduate schools, with their goal far beyond the reach of the college, evidenced the new emphasis upon the value of pure knowledge. In an age of supposed dominant materialism a larger proportion of Americans consecrated themselves to the cause of science and learning than ever before in history and a greater number of them attained an eminence that compelled the attention of the world. Literature and the arts had an equal drawing power, with results hardly less fruitful. A Gibbs, a Newcomb, a Ward, a James, a Mark Twain, a Whistler, a MacDowell, a Saint-Gaudens, stand out not as unexpected flowers along a scrubby roadside, but as among the most perfect blossoms in a well-tended field.

Cultural achievement, moreover, was bottomed upon a broadening popular appreciation of creative effort. So diversified a population reflected a multiplicity of standards and tastes, and popular culture contained much that was transitory and cheap. But the steady leavening of the mass was revealed in the unexampled patronage accorded public libraries, art galleries and the more serious dramatic and musical performances, as well as by the multiplication of literary periodicals and the greatly increased production of books. For the first time in the national annals, creative workers might count upon a receptive public and ample financial reward at home. The few who preferred a foreign abode usually did so because their work was more European than American in spirit.

Underlying all the varied developments that made up American life was the momentous shift of the center of national equilibrium from the countryside to the city. Long foreshadowed, it had at last become an actuality. A civilization traditionally rural was obliged to learn how to come to terms with a civilization predominantly urban. The process was painful and confusing to those who clung to the older mores and even to many who joined the cityward flight. But to untold numbers of others it meant the attainment of a new Promised Land, the release of energies and ambitions which the constricted opportunities of the farm had always denied. The city had come and, it was clear to all, it had come to stay. Was its mission to be that of a new Jerusalem or of ancient Babylon? The answer to this question was the chief unfinished business of the departing generation.

# CHAPTER XIV

## CRITICAL ESSAY ON AUTHORITIES

### PHYSICAL SURVIVALS

MEMORIALS of the life of these years may be found at every hand, though time, abetted by real-estate enterprise, has done considerable damage to architectural achievements. Most of the edifices listed in chapter viii are still standing, but it is to be regretted that the first skyscraper, the Home Insurance Building (1885) in Chicago, has recently been razed. Among the many bridges that survive is the greatest of them all, Brooklyn Bridge (1883), a structure remarkable both as an engineering feat and as an artistic creation. Several monuments of national interest date from the period: the Washington Monument at the national capital, left unfinished from 1854 but completed during 1880-1884; the Statue of Liberty (1886) in New York Harbor, executed by the French sculptor F. A. Bartholdi and presented by his countrymen to the United States; and Grant's Tomb (1897) overlooking the Hudson at One Hundred and Twenty-third Street, designed by J. H. Duncan and built by popular subscription.

Samples of pictorial art can be found in any public gallery, as well as in the form of mural paintings in the Library of Congress, Bowdoin College, the Boston Public Library and elsewhere. Sculptures also abound in the larger cities (see earlier, chap. viii), while in Cornish, New Hampshire, at Saint-Gaudens's former home, are preserved the original models of many of that genius's masterpieces. As a well-rounded representation of the work of an unusually versatile artist, the Frank Duveneck collection in the Cincinnati Museum (founded in 1881), comprising about a hundred paintings besides etchings and sculptures, is unique. Good collections of "Rogers groups" of plaster statuettes are on display at the New York Historical Society, the Albany Institute, the Essex Institute, Salem, Massachusetts, and the Harrison Gray Otis House, Boston. The ebb and flow of women's fashions is illustrated by costumes in the Essex Institute, the Minnesota Historical Society and elsewhere and by a collection of dressed wax miniatures in the Chicago Historical Society.

The United States National Museum in Washington contains the original patent-office models of the more important dynamos and arc lamps and a large collection of incandescent lights illustrating chronologically the improvements of the Edison bulb from its inception. Especially interesting is a unit of the equipment installed for the incandescent-lighting system of a New York engraving establishment in 1881. Many aspects of technological development are depicted by models in the Museum of Science and Industry in New York and in the institution of the same name in Chicago. In the British Museum, London, is preserved a "dummy-and-trailer" cable car of the original Clay Street line in San Francisco.

Most significant of all for the social historian are the results already fruiting from the recent movement to preserve aspects of American culture in their appropriate context. Following the example of great European centers, America's chief metropolis formed in 1931 the Museum of the City of New York, dedicated to the object of tracing the evolution of its civic life from earliest times by means of material remains and the use of group models. Of broader scope is the Edison Institute of Technology, founded by Henry Ford on a two-hundred-acre tract next to his experimental laboratories at Dearborn, Michigan. Here, in a vast exhibition hall and in the adjoining Greenfield Village of some two hundred and fifty historic houses, may be seen many and varied evidences of general conditions of living in different periods and sections. Phonographs, hurdy-gurdies, typewriters, kerosene lamps, barber chairs, horse vehicles, along with blacksmith shops, domestic interiors and a steam manufacturing plant in the 1880's, suggest the ramifications of the collection. Included, also, are the original Edison laboratory at Menlo Park and the office in Santa Rosa, California, where Luther Burbank did his writing. A third repository of interest is maintained by the Norwegian-American Historical Society at Luther College, Decorah, Iowa. Its collection consists of exhibits and log cabins illustrative of the life of the immigrants both before their departure from Norway and during the process of their adjustment to American life. It is earnestly to be hoped that other racial groups will follow this excellent example.

The *Handbook of American Museums* (Wash., 1932), issued by the American Association of Museums, contains information in regard to about fourteen hundred institutions in the United States and Canada, including art galleries. R. C. Smith, comp., *A Bibliography of Museums and Museum Work* (Wash., 1928), lists books and articles concerned with such interests. For nearly all phases of American civilization the fine group of pictures brought together in R. H. Gabriel, ed., *The Pageant of America* (15 vols., New Haven, 1926-1929), is helpful.

## GENERAL TREATMENTS

HISTORICAL ACCOUNTS: In the bibliography that follows, no attempt is made to cite again all the sources that have been named in the footnotes. Typical examples have to suffice, a completer enumeration being precluded by limitations of space. Until recently, historians have been so preoccupied with the details of party struggles and the sensational aspects of economic strife that Edmund Wilson doubtless expressed a widely held opinion when he declared in the *New Republic,* January 2, 1924: "The eighties and nineties in America appear . . . perhaps the most provincial and uninspired moment in the history of American society." The older historical convention is upheld by E. P. Oberholtzer, *A History of the United States since the Civil War* (5 vols., N. Y.,

1917, in progress), whose fourth volume (1931) gives an encyclopedestrian treatment of political happenings during the years 1878-1888, with an occasional squint at economic events. Other general writers, however, have ventured beyond these narrow limits, with results most interesting. In C. A. and Mary R. Beard, *The Rise of American Civilization* (2 vols., N. Y., 1927), may be found a swift but brilliant characterization of varied developments. Mark Sullivan, *Our Times* (5 vols., N. Y., 1926, in progress), dipping back occasionally into the period before 1900, has all the fascination of an old newspaper file. Lewis Mumford, *The Brown Decades* (N. Y., 1931), is a suggestive essay on the state of the arts from 1865 to 1895, while Thomas Beer, *The Mauve Decade* (N. Y., 1926), gives a sparkling, impressionistic account of certain phases of life in the 1890's. Certain volumes of Allen Johnson, ed., *The Chronicles of America Series* (50 vols., New Haven, 1918-1921), also attest that man does not live by politics alone. Despite the growing number of such works, many matters important for an understanding of intellectual currents and social growth have been omitted or insufficiently considered; nor, in many cases, have such topics had adequate monographic study.[1]

CONTEMPORANEOUS AMERICAN ANALYSES: The most important descriptive works of the period seeking to summarize salient trends in American life are D. A. Wells, *Recent Economic Changes* (N. Y., 1889); N. S. Shaler, ed., *The United States of America* (3 vols., N. Y., 1894); and C. M. Depew, ed., *One Hundred Years of American Commerce* (2 vols., N. Y., 1895), the last having a wider sweep than the title suggests. Among reminiscent personal records Henry Adams, *The Education of Henry Adams* (Boston, 1918),

---

[1] In helping fill up some of these gaps and for other assistance the author of the present volume is indebted to his wife, Elizabeth Bancroft, his secretary, Elizabeth F. Hoxie, Professor E. F. Gay and Dr. E. A. Darling of Cambridge, Mr. Stewart Mitchell of the Massachusetts Historical Society, and former members of his seminar, particularly G. P. Bauer, W. J. Bender, Ruth Jones Bowersox, Frances M. Camp, H. W. Cary, N. H. Dawes, B. J. Loewenberg, R. W. Logan, B. F. McKelvey, N. O. Mason, J. L. Norris, John O'Brien, J. F. Onthank, C. W. Upton and H. F. Wilson.

belongs in a niche by itself as an aloof but highly subjective commentary by an acute observer.

The chief general source of statistical information is, of course, the successive census inquiries. The *Tenth Census* (1880), directed by Francis A. Walker after training as superintendent of the *Ninth,* is the first to be a genuine national inventory. In 1890, through the use of the electric tabulating machine, demographic data are presented with minuter statistical analysis than had before been feasible. While the *Twelfth Census* (1900) covers a narrower field than either of the two preceding, its value in other respects is enhanced by the series of special supplementary reports prepared after the decennial work was completed and often containing valuable historical introductions. In using census data students would do well first to consult C. D. Wright, "The Limitations and Difficulties of Statistics," *Yale Rev.,* III (1894-1895), 121-143.

The best guide to social and economic materials in official state publications is Adelaide R. Hasse, comp., *Index of Economic Material in Documents of the States of the United States* (Carnegie Inst., *Publs.,* no. 85, 1907-1922), covering thirteen states down to the year 1904. There is great need of a systematic study of state legislation and court decisions for the light they can shed on social history. Very little progress has been made since G. J. Bayles wrote in *Woman and the Law* (N. Y., 1901), vi, "Within these dreary-looking books . . . is written a large portion of the life history of the nation. Read into the laws the efforts and hopes of generations of earnest men and women, and the study becomes one of living organism—human society." For a guide to the most important *corpus* of unprinted sources dealing with the period, see C. W. Garrison, comp., "List of Manuscript Collections in the Library of Congress to July, 1931," Am. Hist. Assoc., *Ann. Rep. for 1930,* I, esp. 215-227.

FOREIGN VIEWS: The most complete list of the books written by British visitors to America appears in Allan Nevins, ed., *American Social History as Recorded by British Travellers* (rev. edn., N. Y., 1931), which also contains generous excerpts from the more important volumes. While such works must be used with caution, none can be safely neglected. Perhaps the most useful accounts from British pens are E. A. Freeman, *Some Impressions of the United States* (N. Y., 1883) ; Herbert Spencer, "The Americans" [1883], *Essays, Scientific, Political and Speculative* (3 vols., N. Y., 1891), III, 471-492; Emily Faithfull, *Three Visits to America* (Edinburgh, 1884) ; Matthew Arnold, *Civilization in the United States* (Boston, 1888) ; James Bryce, *The American Commonwealth* (3 vols., London, 1888), valuable for the author's insight into social and intellectual as well as political conditions; and J. F. Muirhead, *The Land of Contrasts* (N. Y., 1898). The last is of special interest not only as a penetrating analysis, but also because the writer was the principal author of *The United States* (Karl Baedeker, ed., *Handbook for Travellers;* Leipsic, 1893; 2d rev. edn., 1899), a detailed descriptive guide to cities, traveling accommodations and sight-seeing excursions.

Though travel accounts by non-British visitors are less numerous, their variety is indicated by the following: K. T. Broberg, *Iakttagelser under en Pedagogisk Resa i Nord Amerika* (Helsingfors, 1889), observations in regard to American education by a Finlander; Paul de Rousiers, *American Life* (A. J. Herbertson, tr., Paris, 1892), an acute commentary by a French artist; Friedrich Ratzel, *Politische Geographie der Vereinigten Staaten von Amerika* (2d edn., München, 1893), an anthropogeographic interpretation of American life and problems; P. A. Tverskoi, *Ocherki Severo-Amerikanskich So-edinennich Shtatov* (St. Petersburg, 1895), based on ten years' experience in America; Marie Dugard, *La Société Américaine; Moeurs et Caractère—la Famille—Rôle de la Femme—Écoles et Universités* (Paris, 1896), a work crowned by the French Academy; and Manuel de Oliveira Lima, *Nos Estados Unidos. Impressões Políticas e Sociaes* (Leipzig, 1899), a friendly critique by a Brazilian. In later sections are cited foreign appraisals of special aspects of American culture, such as temperance reform and the status of women.

## PERSONAL MATERIAL: GENERAL

While political biography is better represented than any other kind, lives of leaders in other fields of American civilization are appearing in increasing number. Of particular interest are the following series: M. A. DeW. Howe, ed., *The Beacon Biographies* (31 vols., Boston, 1899-1910), including authors, inventors and actors; C. D. Warner, ed., *American Men of Letters* (Boston, 1881-1906); W. D. Lewis, ed., *Great American Lawyers* (8 vols., Phila., 1907-1909); Carlos Martyn, ed., *American Reformers* (N. Y., 1890-1896); and Laurence Hutton, ed., *American Actor Series* (Boston, 1881-1882). Frequently, however, a better life may be found outside any of the standard series. Particular biographies are cited later in the present chapter in appropriate contexts. An invaluable aid to the social historian is the *Dictionary of American Biography* (20 vols., N. Y., 1928, in progress), edited by Allen Johnson and Dumas Malone. It covers the whole range of American culture in crisp sketches, often written by specialists, and, in addition, presents a brief, well-selected bibliography in connection with each memoir.

## GENERAL PERIODICAL SOURCES

NEWSPAPERS: The multiplicity of newspapers in the 1880's and 1890's offers an embarrassment of riches. Their vast number and distribution are indicated by N. W. Ayer & Son, comp., *American Newspaper Annual and Directory* (Phila., from 1880), and presented analytically in W. S. Rossiter, "Printing and Publishing," *U. S. Twelfth Census* (1900), IX, 1037-1119—which also includes magazines. The leading journals are characterized in chapter vi of the present volume. The latest and best general historical survey is W. G. Bleyer, *Main Currents in the History of American Journalism* (Boston, 1927). Unfortunately the only newspapers of the period to be indexed are the *New York Tribune*, Republican, for the years 1875-1906; and the *Brooklyn Daily Eagle*, Democratic, for the years 1891-1902. Summaries of editorial opinion appear, however, in *Public Opinion* (Wash., 1886-1906) and the *Literary Digest* (N. Y., from 1890).

Particular newspapers are treated historically in a rapidly swelling literature, including Elmer Davis, *History of the New York Times, 1851-1921* (N. Y., 1921); Allan Nevins, *The Evening Post* (N. Y., 1922); D. C. Seitz, *The James Gordon Bennetts; Father and Son* (Indianapolis, 1928), dealing with the *New York Herald;* F. M. O'Brien, *The Story of the Sun* (N. Y., 1918); Royal Cortissoz, *The New York Tribune* (N. Y., 1923); J. E. Chamberlin, *The Boston Transcript* (Boston, 1930); Richard Hooker, *The Story of an Independent Newspaper* (N. Y., 1924)—the *Springfield Republican;* and anon., *William Rockhill Nelson* (Cambridge, Mass., 1915), concerned with the *Kansas City Star*. The fathers of yellow journalism are dealt with in Alleyne Ireland, *An Adventure with a Genius* (N. Y., 1920), and D. C. Seitz, *Joseph Pulitzer* (N. Y., 1924)—concerned with the proprietor of the *New York World*—and J. K. Winkler, *W. R. Hearst* (N. Y., 1928). The "Fiftieth Anniversary Number" of the *St. Louis Post-Dispatch*, December 9, 1928, reviews Pulitzer's career in that city and at the same time gives a swift panorama of St. Louis social history. Progress in coöperative journalism is traced in Victor Rosewater, *History of Coöperative News-Gathering in the United States* (N. Y., 1930).

MAGAZINES: The utility of magazine literature for the social historian is perhaps amply indicated by the footnotes of the present work. Even the humorous weeklies—*Puck* (N. Y., 1877-1918), *Judge* (N. Y., from 1881) and *Life* (N. Y., from 1883)—are valuable for the indirect evidence they afford as to social customs, moral standards, manners and foibles. Winifred Gregory, comp., *Union List of Serials in Libraries of the United States and Canada* (N. Y., 1927), offers the most complete list of magazines, with place and period of issue, while *Poole's Index to Periodical Literature* (various compilers, Boston and N. Y., 1882-1907), supplies a subject guide to the contents of the more important ones. A general critique of leading magazines appears in chapter vi of the present volume. Unlike the instance of newspapers, secondary historical accounts, even of leading magazines, are almost wholly lacking. Algernon Tassin, *The Magazine in America* (N. Y., 1916), is a readable but highly notional conspectus of magazine development.

For information in regard to the conduct of the *Century Magazine* (N. Y., from 1881), which Paul Blouët called "that most successful of all magazines in the world," the following books by its editors are essential: R. W. Gilder, *Letters* (Rosamond Gilder, ed., Boston, 1916); L. F. Tooker, *The Joys and Tribulations of an Editor* (N. Y., 1924); and R. U. Johnson, *Remembered Yesterdays* (Boston, 1923). Another important periodical is sketched in M. A. DeW. Howe, *The Atlantic Monthly and Its Makers* (Boston, 1919). The *Dial* (Chicago, from 1880), XXVIII (1900), no. 333, reviews the first twenty years of its career as an organ of literary criticism. Two weekly journals of opinion are dealt with in W. H. Ward, "Fifty Years of *The Independent*," *Independent*, L (1898), 1642-1646; and in Rollo Ogden, *Life and Letters of Edwin Lawrence Godkin* (2 vols., N. Y., 1907), and Gustav Pollak, ed., *Fifty Years of American Idealism* (N. Y., 1920), the latter a reprint of *Nation* articles and editorials. An understanding of the spirit animating the *Arena* (Boston, from 1889) is afforded by B. O. Flower, *Progressive Men, Women and Movements of the Past Twenty-Five Years* (Boston, 1914). Light is shed on the new crop of low-priced periodicals by anon., "The Cosmopolitan," *Cosmopolitan*, XXIII (1897), 465-482, a ten years' retrospect; F. A. Munsey, "Getting On in Journalism," and "The Making and Marketing of Munsey's Magazine," *Munsey's*, XIX (1898), 214-224; XXII (1899), 323-343; and S. S. McClure, *My Autobiography* (N. Y., 1914). The editor of the *Ladies' Home Journal* explains its special preëminence in *The Americanization of Edward Bok* (N. Y., 1922). Magazines of a more particularized character are mentioned later in the present chapter in appropriate connections.

RURAL LIFE

GENERAL: Many articles in L. H. Bailey, ed., *Cyclopedia of American Agriculture* (4 vols., N. Y., 1907-1909), shed light on social conditions in the farming regions. E. E. Edwards, comp., *A Bibliography of the History of Agriculture in the United States* (Dept. of Agr., *Miscel. Publs.*, no. 84, 1930), touches on many phases of the subject while emphasizing economic and political developments. J. D. Hicks, *The Populist Revolt* (Minneapolis, 1931), sets forth the economic causes for agrarian unrest in South and West. Varied reasons for the cityward trend are discussed in two studies by N. H. Egleston: *Villages and Village Life* (N. Y., 1878), and *The Home and Its Surroundings* (rev. edn., N. Y., 1883). W. G. Moody, *Land and Labor in the United States* (N. Y., 1883), and J. R. Elliott, *American Farms* (*Questions of the Day Series*, LXII, 2d edn., N. Y., 1890), paint a gloomy picture of the farmers' decline, to which W. L. Anderson, *The Country Town* (N. Y., 1906), written when the rural situation had taken a turn for the better, forms a useful corrective. The plague of tramps, with particular reference to rural neighborhoods, receives first-hand study by Jack London in *The Road* (N. Y., 1907), based on his hobo wanderings from 1892 to 1897; by W. A. Wyckoff in *The Workers* (2 vols., N. Y., 1897-1898), derived from his experiences in 1891-1892; and most notably by J. F. Willard (Josiah Flynt, *pseud.*) who sets forth material collected over a period of ten years in *Tramping with Tramps* (N. Y., 1899), *Notes of an Itinerant Policeman* (Boston, 1900) and *The World of Graft* (N. Y., 1901).

THE SOUTH: General surveys covering the period include P. A. Bruce, *The Rise of the New South* (G. C. Lee and F. N. Thorpe, eds., *The History of North America*, 20 vols., Phila., 1903-1907, XVII); and J. A. C. Chandler and others, *The South in the Building of the Nation* (12 vols., Richmond, 1909-1910). L. J. Cappon, comp., *Bibliography of Virginia History since 1865* (Univ. of Va. Inst. for Research in the Social Sciences, *Monograph*, V, 1930), not only is indispensable for its own particular subject, but should serve as a beacon light for other states to follow. Contemporaneous accounts, stressing economic change, are A. K. McClure, *The South: Its Industrial, Financial, and Political Condition* (Phila., 1886) ; W. D. Kelley, *The Old South and the New* (N. Y., 1887) ; R. H. Edmonds, *The South's Redemption* (Balt., 1890), reprinted from the *Manufacturers' Record* (Balt., from 1882) of which Edmonds was editor; and same author, *Facts about the South* (Balt., 1902).

The emergence of the white masses in economic and political life has received much study in recent years, the principal articles and monographs being listed in Edwards, *Bibliography*, and Hicks, *Populist Revolt*, both cited previously. The cultural aspects of this transformation have scarcely been noted, however. The secluded mountain population has received considerable attention in such works as S. T. Wilson, *The Southern Mountaineers* (N. Y., 1906) ; Horace Kephart, *Our Southern Highlanders* (N. Y., 1913) ; and A. W. Spaulding, *The Men of the Mountains* (Nashville, 1915). The turn to manufacturing development is considered in Broadus Mitchell, *The Rise of Cotton Mills in the South* (Johns Hopkins Univ., *Studies*, XXXIX, no. 2, 1921) ; Holland Thompson, *From the Cotton Field to the Cotton Mill* (N. Y., 1906), with special reference to North Carolina; Meyer Jacobstein, *The Tobacco Industry in the United States* (Columbia Univ., *Studies*, XXVI, no. 3, 1907) ; and Ethel Armes, *The Story of Coal and Iron in Alabama* (Birmingham, 1910). For the changing fortunes of the Afro-American, see later, Race Relations.

THE WEST: Comprehensive and authoritative descriptions at the beginning of the period are L. P. Brockett, *Our Western Empire* (Phila., 1880), prepared primarily for prospective settlers; and F. V. Hayden, *The Great West* (Bloomington, 1880), written from experiences gained while a member of the geological survey. From a group of studies, most of them quite recent, emerges a vivid picture of the cattleman and his economic and social significance. Notable among such works are P. A. Rollins, *The Cowboy* (N. Y., 1922); Douglas Branch, *The Cowboy and His Interpreters* (N. Y., 1926); E. S. Osgood, *The Day of the Cattleman* (Minneapolis, 1929); E. E. Dale, *The Range Cattle Industry* (Norman, Okla., 1930); and W. P. Webb, *The Great Plains* (Boston, 1931). William French, *Some Recollections of a Western Ranchman* (N. Y., 1928), affords a graphic picture of life in the Southwest as experienced by an Englishman from 1883 to 1899. Frontier lawlessness provides the theme for Emerson Hough, *The Story of the Outlaw* (N. Y., 1907); F. J. Wilstach, *Wild Bill Hickok* (Garden City, 1926); Robertus Love, *The Rise and Fall of Jesse James* (N. Y., 1926); W. N. Burns, *The Saga of Billy the Kid* (Garden City, 1926); and Emmett Dalton and Jack Jungmeyer, *When the Daltons Rode* (Garden City, 1931). For the Indian problem, see later, Race Relations.

Agricultural conditions and methods are ably discussed by the Britisher, Finlay Dun, in *American Farming and Food* (London, 1881) from first-hand observations in 1879. While many special studies canvass the economic sources of the farmers' difficulties, insight may be gained into the much neglected subject of psychological causes in such works as E. W. Howe, *The Story of a Country Town* (N. Y., 1883), semifictional; Hamlin Garland, *A Son of the Middle Border* (N. Y., 1917); Grant Showerman, *A Country Chronicle* (N. Y., 1916); and Herbert Quick, *One Man's Life* (Indianapolis, 1925).

## URBAN LIFE

The American city has not yet been studied generically, nor do there exist any adequate social histories of particular cities. Basic data for many aspects of urban development can be gleaned from *Social Statistics of Cities: 1880* (*U. S. Tenth Census*, XVIII-XIX); J. S. Billings, comp., *Report on the Social Statistics of Cities* (*U. S. Eleventh Census*, 1890); and *Statistics of Cities Having a Population of Over 25,000: 1902 and 1903*, and *Statistics of Cities Having a*

*Population of 8,000 to 25,000: 1903* (Bur. of the Census, *Bulls.*, nos. 20, 45). A. F. Weber, *The Growth of Cities in the Nineteenth Century* (Columbia Univ., *Studies*, XI, 1899), is an excellent comparative study covering various countries, with some reference to social implications. The expansion of municipal functions in the United States and Europe is traced in J. A. Fairlie, *Municipal Administration* (N. Y., 1901). Josiah Strong, *The Twentieth Century City* (N. Y., 1898), offers a sociological analysis of the impact of the city on American life, while W. H. Tolman, *Municipal Reform Movements in the United States* (N. Y., 1897), and C. M. Robinson, "Improvement in City Life," a series of articles in the *Atlantic Mo.*, LXXXIII (1899), set forth remedial tendencies. Willard Glazier, *Peculiarities of American Cities* (Phila., 1883), discusses the principal features of thirty-nine centers. Picturesque and amusing aspects of Manhattan life are presented in something akin to scrapbook fashion by H. C. Brown in *The Last Fifty Years in New York, New York in the Elegant Eighties* and *In the Golden Nineties* (*Valentine's Manual of Old New York*, X-XII, Hastings-on-Hudson, 1925-1927). M. M. Quaife, ed., *The Development of Chicago, 1674-1914* (Chicago, 1916), comprises a series of contemporary original narratives.

The literature on living conditions of the urban poor is voluminous. New York state commissions, especially appointed for the purpose, issued elaborate reports in 1885 and 1894. The important work edited by R. W. De Forest and Lawrence Veiller, *The Tenement House Problem* (2 vols., N. Y., 1903), reviews earlier conditions and submits the findings and recommendations of the state commission of 1900. Such inquiries should be supplemented by the personal experiences of Jacob A. Riis, embodied in *How the Other Half Lives* (N. Y., 1890), *The Battle with the Slum* (N. Y., 1902), *The Children of the Poor* (N. Y., 1892) and *The Making of an American* (N. Y., 1901), his autobiography. Equally enlightening for Chicago is *Hull-House Maps and Papers* (N. Y., 1895) by the Residents of that settlement; and for Boston, R. A. Woods, ed., *The City Wilder-*

*ness* (Boston, 1898), a collaborative study by the members of South End House. The U. S. commissioner of labor submits the results of federal investigations in C. D. Wright, *The Slums of Baltimore, Chicago, New York, and Philadelphia* (*Seventh Special Rep.*, 1894), and E. R. L. Gould, *The Housing of the Working People* (*Eighth Special Rep.*, 1895).

The chief statistical study of criminality is F. H. Wines, *Report on Crime, Pauperism, and Benevolence in the United States* (2 vols., *U. S. Eleventh Census*, 1890, XXII-XXIII), which should be scrutinized in the light of R. P. Falkner's critique, *Crime and the Census* (Am. Acad. of Polit. and Social Sci., *Publs.*, no. 190, 1897). Herbert Asbury, *The Gangs of New York* (N. Y., 1928), is a lively and reliable narrative. Contemporary accounts dealing with criminal conditions in New York include A. E. Costello, *Our Police Protectors* (N. Y., 1884); T. F. Byrnes, *Professional Criminals of America* (N. Y., 1886); W. F. Howe and A. H. Hummel, *Danger! A True History of a Great City's Wiles and Temptations* (Buffalo, 1886); and G. W. Walling, *Recollections of a New York Chief of Police* (N. Y., 1887). Alexander Gardiner, *Canfield* (N. Y., 1930), tells the story of the notorious gambler whose sumptuous Saratoga Club in New York became in the 1890's the Monte Carlo of America. Sensational accounts of notorious crimes and high scandals, originally appearing in the *Police Gazette* (N. Y., from 1845), are reprinted in S. A. MacKeever, *Glimpses of Gotham and City Characters* (N. Y., 1880), and Edward Van Every, *Sins of New York as "Exposed" by the Police Gazette* (N. Y., 1931). C. H. Parkhurst recounts his experiences as a crusader against vice and crime in *Our Fight with Tammany* (N. Y., 1895), while the findings of the Lexow Committee are embodied in *Report and Proceedings of the Senate Committee Appointed to Investigate the Police Department of the City of New York* (5 vols., Albany, 1895). B. P. Eldridge and W. B. Watts, *Our Rival, the Rascal* (Boston, 1896), is an account by two Boston police officials. The leading detective agency is the subject of R. W.

Rowan, *The Pinkertons* (Boston, 1931), while L. W. Moore, *His Own Story of His Eventful Life* (Boston, 1892), presents the authentic life story of a safe blower active in divers cities. The many mechanical inventions that helped transform urban life are discussed in E. W. Byrn, *Progress of Invention in the Nineteenth Century* (N. Y., 1900); a group of articles in the "50th Anniversary Number" of the *Scientific American*, July 25, 1896; and Waldemar Kaempffert, ed., *A Popular History of American Invention* (2 vols., N. Y., 1924). More specialized treatments are T. C. Martin and S. L. Coles, *The Story of Electricity* (2 vols., N. Y., 1919-1922); Henry Schroeder, *History of Electric Light* (*Smithsonian Miscel. Colls.*, LXXVI, no. 2, 1923), a technical account; and H. N. Casson, *The History of the Telephone* (Chicago, 1910). Other aspects of urban life are touched upon in later sections of this bibliography.

THE WOMAN'S WORLD

Annie N. Meyer, ed., *Woman's Work in America* (N. Y., 1891), is a coöperative work illuminating many aspects of the sex's increasing participation in American life. C. V. C. de Varigny, *La Femme aux États-Unis* (Paris, 1893), and Thérèse Blanc, *The Condition of Woman in the United States* (Abby L. Alger, tr., Boston, 1895), attest French interest in the subject. The position of the average middle-class woman is best understood, however, from a reading of the magazines which affected and reflected her outlook, notably *Harper's Bazar* (N. Y., from 1867), the *Delineator* (N. Y., from 1873), *Ladies' Home Companion* (Springfield, Ohio, from 1873, titled *Woman's Home Companion* from 1895), *Ladies' Home Journal*, (Phila., from 1883) and *Good Housekeeping* (Holyoke and N. Y., from 1885). All aspects of the quest for women's rights are the concern of the *History of Woman Suffrage* (6 vols., N. Y. and Rochester, 1881-1922), written by Elizabeth Cady Stanton, Susan B. Anthony and others. For intimate views of these two leaders of the movement, Ida H. Harper, *The Life and Work of Susan B. Anthony* (3 vols., Indianapolis, 1898-1908), and Elizabeth Cady Stanton, *Elizabeth Cady Stanton as Revealed in Her Letters, Diary and Reminiscences* (Theodore Stanton and Harriot S. Blatch, eds., 2 vols., N. Y., 1922), are important. A suffragist of different stamp is charmingly portrayed by her daughter, Alice Stone Blackwell, in *Lucy Stone* (Boston, 1930). Material of interest also appears in E. A. Hecker, *A Short History of Women's Rights* (N. Y., 1911); Bertha A. Rembaugh, *The Political Status of Women in the United States* (N. Y., 1911); and Jennie L. Wilson, *The Legal and Political Status of Women in the United States* (N. Y., 1911).

G. E. Howard, *A History of Matrimonial Institutions* (3 vols., Chicago, 1904), includes an account of the American family, while A. W. Calhoun, *A Social History of the American Family* (3 vols., Cleveland, 1919), though somewhat resembling a notebook on the subject, is valuable as the first attempt at a comprehensive study. For cross-sectional summaries of the legal status of married women, consult J. P. Bishop, *Commentaries on the Law of Married Women* (2 vols., Boston, 1875); James Schouler, *A Treatise on the Law of Domestic Relations* (Boston, 1889); H. C. Whitney, *Marriage and Divorce* (Phila., 1894); and G. J. Bayles, *Woman and the Law* (N. Y., 1901). *Marriage and Divorce, 1867-1906* (Bur. of the Census, *Special Rep.*, 1909, 2 pts.) is an indispensable compilation of statistical and legislative data. Additional information may be gathered from the *Reports* (dating from 1885) and the numerous special *Publications* of the National Divorce Reform League (founded in 1881; name changed in 1897 to National League for the Protection of the Family).

Contemporaneous studies of family budgets exist in profusion, representing every part of the country and all classes of people. They were usually made by state bureaus of labor statistics and published in their annual reports. Besides other details these studies show the distribution of family income among such items as food, clothing, rent, fuel, furnishings, medical care, education and reading. Lucy M. Salmon, *Domestic Service* (rev. edn., N. Y., 1901), the first comprehensive inquiry into the servant problem, emphasizes conditions as found in 1889 and 1890. Standard manuals of household management in the nineties are Helen Campbell, *Household Economics* (N. Y., 1896), and *Home Economics* (N. Y., 1898) by Maria Parloa, founder of the popular Boston Cooking School.

## HUMANITARIAN STRIVING

CHARITY AND SOCIAL WORK: The growth of scientific methods in the administration of charity can be followed in Sophonisba P. Breckenridge, ed., *Public Welfare Administration in the United States, Select Documents* (Chicago, 1927); National Conference of Charities and Correction, *Proceedings for 1893*, which contains historical papers on the new methods in charity, prison reform, and the care of the insane and feeble-minded; A. G. Warner, *American Charities* (R. T. Ely, ed., *Library of Economics and Politics*, IV, N. Y., 1894; rev. 1908, 1919); and F. D. Watson, *The Charity Organization Movement in the United States* (N. Y., 1922). Such works should be supplemented by examining the *Annual Reports* of the Charities Aid Association of New York State (from 1873), of the National Conference of Charities and Correction (from 1874) and of local bodies. *Lend-a-Hand* (Boston), founded in 1886 by Edward Everett Hale, is valuable as "a record of progress and journal of organized charity"; in 1897 it was merged with the *Charities Review* (N. Y., 1891-1901).

The movement for the prevention of cruelty to animals and children is traced in R. C. McCrae, *The Humane Movement* (N. Y., 1910), and S. H. Coleman, *Humane Society Leaders in America* (Albany, 1924), with special reference to the work of the American Humane Association, formed in 1877. *The Brother of Girls* (Chicago, 1910) is the autobiography of C. N. Crittenton, founder of the Florence Crittenton Missions for fallen women, the first one, in New York City, dating from 1883. Caroline W. Montgomery, ed., *Bibliography of College, Social, University and Church Settlements* (5th edn., Chicago, 1905), is an excellent guide to the earlier literature on the subject, while R. A. Woods and A. J. Kennedy, *The Settlement Horizon* (N. Y., 1922), gives the best general account. The career of four trail blazers can be followed in Jane Addams, *Twenty Years at Hull House* (N. Y., 1910); Eleanor H. Woods, *Robert A. Woods* (Boston, 1929), dealing with the founder of South End House in Boston (1892); Lillian D. Wald, *The House on Henry Street* (N. Y., 1915), written by the organizer of the Nurses' Settlement (1893); and H. E. Wilson, *Mary Mc-Dowell, Neighbor* (Chicago, 1928), relating the history of the early years and achievements of the University of Chicago Settlement House (1894).

TEMPERANCE: The bulk of the material on the temperance question is highly explosive. For the student the most valuable volumes are the reports of the investigations carried on from 1893 to 1903 by the Committee of Fifty consisting of prominent educators, clergymen, scientists and publicists: F. H. Wines and John Koren, *The Liquor Problem in Its Legislative Aspects* (Boston, 1897; rev. edn., 1898); John Koren, *Economic Aspects of the Liquor Problem* (Boston, 1899); Raymond Calkins, *Substitutes for the Saloon* (Boston, 1901); J. S. Billings, ed., *The Physiological Aspects of the Liquor Problem* (2 vols., Boston, 1903); and J. S. Billings and others, *The Liquor Problem* (Boston, 1905), a summary of the results. Very serviceable, too, are E. L. Fanshawe, *Liquor Legislation in the United States and Canada* (London, 1893), a disinterested inquiry by a foreigner including twenty-odd American states; and *Economic Aspects of the Liquor Problem* (U. S. Comr. of Labor, *Twelfth Ann. Rep.*, 1897), the most comprehensive official investigation. Historical sketches with a temperance bias include J. G. Woolley and W. E. Johnson, *Temperance Progress of the Century* (Justin McCarthy, ed., *The Nineteenth Century Series;* Toronto, 1903); A. F. Fehlandt, *A Century of Drink Reform in the United States* (Cincinnati, 1904); E. H. Cherrington, *The Evolution of Prohibition in the United*

*States* (Westerville, 1920); and D. L. Colvin, *Prohibition in the United States* (N. Y., 1926).

PRISON REFORM: The situation is summarized at the beginning of the period in E. C. Wines, *The State of Prisons and of Child Saving Institutions* (Cambridge, Mass., 1880), and at its end by F. H. Wines, *Punishment and Reformation* (*Crowell's Library of Economics and Politics*, VI, N. Y., 1895; also later edns.), and by S. J. Barrows, ed., *The Reformatory System in the United States* (56th Cong., 1 sess., *House Doc.*, no. 459, 1900), a volume consisting of articles by officers of leading reformatories and prisons. For all phases the *Annual Reports* and *Proceedings* of the National Prison Association (from 1881) are of the utmost value, while much that is useful can also be found in C. R. Henderson, ed., *Correction and Prevention* (4 vols., N. Y., 1910), a collection of authoritative articles, historical and descriptive, on prison reform, preventive agencies and allied topics.

PEACE MOVEMENT AND RED CROSS: The best general account of the peace movement in the eighties and nineties is given by A. C. F. Beales, *The History of Peace* (N. Y., 1931), while further information of interest appears in Devere Allen, *The Fight for Peace* (N. Y., 1930), and E. L. Whitney, *The American Peace Society, A Centennial History* (Wash., 1928). Sarah E. Pickett, *The American National Red Cross* (N. Y., 1923), sketches the history of that organization. The story of its founder is related by her kinsman W. E. Barton in *The Life of Clara Barton* (2 vols., Boston, 1922).

## RACE RELATIONS

THE IMMIGRANT: There is an extensive literature in respect to immigration in general and as regards special racial groups, but, unhappily, there are few studies of immigrant acculturation in a particular community. Important exceptions are Kate H. Claghorn, "The Foreign Immigrant in New York City," U. S. Indus. Commission, *Reports* (Wash., 1900-1902), XV, 449-492; in the case of Chicago, *Hull-House Papers,* previously cited; and in the case of Boston, two volumes edited by R. A. Woods: *The City Wilderness,* mentioned earlier, and *Americans in Process* (Boston, 1902). Supplementary material for Boston appears in F. A. Bushee, *Ethnic Factors in the Population of Boston* (Am. Econ. Assoc., *Publs.,* ser. 3, IV, no. 2, 1903).

Kate H. Claghorn, "Agricultural Distribution of Immigrants," U. S. Indus. Comn., *Reports,* XV, 492-646, is extremely useful, while many Mid-Western state historical societies, and especially the Swedish Historical Society of America and the Norwegian-American Historical Association, have published noteworthy articles dealing with particular immigrant elements in the rural sections. A circumstantial account of the German-Russian colonies is given in a series of articles, based on personal observation and interviews, contributed by Richard Sallet to the *Dakota Freie Presse* (New Ulm, Minn.), 1924-1927. The historical setting of this unusual folk migration is given more fully in Sallet, *Ruszlanddeutsche Siedlungen in den Vereinigten Staaten* (reprinted from Deutsch-Amerikanischen Historischen Gesellschaft von Illinois, *Jahrbuch,* Chicago, 1931), except for the Mennonites who are separately treated in C. H. Smith, *The Coming of the Russian Mennonites* (Berne, Ind., 1927). Of the more general works G. M. Stephenson, *A History of American Immigration* (Boston, 1926), is perhaps the best attempt at an historical synthesis. In his "Select Bibliography" will be found the titles of the principal books dealing with particular nationalities; a shorter list appears in H. U. Faulkner, *The Quest for Social Justice* (*A History of American Life,* XI), 254-255.

THE NEGRO: The most comprehensive bibliography is M. N. Work, comp., *A Bibliography of the Negro in Africa and America* (N. Y., 1928). Essential statistical information in regard to the race, 1880-1900, is brought together in *Supplementary Analysis and Derivative Tables* (U. S. Twelfth Census, *Special Rep.*), 185-272. In the same volume, 511-579, appears an analytical survey of "The Negro Farmer" by W. E. B. Du Bois, while Carl Kelsey sums up conditions at the end of the century in *The Negro Farmer* (Chicago, 1903). The growing industrialization of the race is examined in C. H. Wesley, *Negro Labor in the United States* (N. Y., 1927). C. G. Woodson, *A Century of Negro Migration* (Wash., 1918), contains a valuable chapter on the exodus of 1879. The official investigation of the exodus, with majority and minority reports as to the causes therefor, may be found in Select Committee of the U. S. Senate to Investigate the Causes of the Removal of the Negroes from the Southern States to the Northern States, *Report and Testimony* (46 Cong., 2 sess., *Senate Rep.*, no. 693, 3 pts., 1880). Franklin Johnson, *The Development of State Legislation Concerning the Free Negro* (N. Y., 1919), is a pioneer attempt at an objective study of race discrimination in law. J. E. Cutler, *Lynch-Law* (N. Y., 1905), is the best study of mob murder. Paul Lewinson, *Race, Class, & Party* (London, 1932), deals with the problem of voting.

A "Bibliography of Negro Education" appears in U. S. Comr. of Educ., *Rep. for 1893-94*, I, 1038-1061. Important phases of the subject are canvassed in J. L. M. Curry, *Education of the Negroes since 1860* (John F. Slater Fund, *Occasional Papers*, no. 3, 1894) ; J. L. M. Curry and others, "The Slater Fund and the Education of the Negro," U. S. Comr. of Educ., *Rep. for 1894-95*, II, 1367-1424; Kelly Miller, "The Education of the Negro," *Rep. for 1900-01*, I, 731-859; A. D. Mayo, "The Work of Certain Northern Churches in the Education of the Freedmen, 1861-1900," *Rep. for 1901-02*, I, 285-314; and W. E. B. Du Bois, ed., *The Negro Common School* (Atlanta Univ., *Publs.*, no. 6, 1901). An enlightening symposium on "Education for the Negro," participated in by Southern colored educational and religious leaders, may be found in the *New Orleans Times-Democrat*, January 24, 1897. The Moses of his people, Booker T. Washington, has left two autobiographies: *The Story of My Life and Work* (Toronto, 1900), and *Up from Slavery* (N. Y., 1901), presenting somewhat different material. M. B. Thrasher, *Tuskegee* (Boston, 1900), is a good brief account of its subject.

THE INDIAN: Useful general sketches include W. C. Macleod, *The American Indian Frontier* (C. K. Ogden, ed., *The History of Civilization;* London, 1928); Flora W. Seymour, *The Story of the Red Man* (N. Y., 1929); and W. K. Moorehead, *The American Indian in the United States* (Andover, 1914), the last being more concerned than the others with social aspects. C. J. Kappler in *Indian Affairs. Laws and Treaties* (2 vols., Wash., 1903) has compiled the official enactments relating to Indian affairs. Of basic importance, also, are the *Annual Reports* (from 1877) of the Commissioner of Indian Affairs and a similar series (from 1877) issued by the Board of Indian Commissioners. The administration of Indian relations is surveyed historically in an able monograph *The Office of Indian Affairs* (Inst. for Government Research, *Service Monographs,* no. 48, 1927) by L. F. Schmeckebier.

The attitude of the reformers is revealed by the *Annual Reports* (Phila., from 1882) of the Indian Rights Association and the *Proceedings* (Lake Mohonk, from 1883) of the Lake Mohonk Conference of the Friends of the Indians. Among the more reliable contemporary accounts of conditions are E. S. Otis, *The Indian Question* (N. Y., 1878); J. B. Harrison, *The Latest Studies on Indian Reservations* (Phila., 1887); G. B. Grinnell, *The Indians of Today* (N. Y., 1900); and F. E. Leupp, *The Indian and His Problem* (N. Y., 1910), based upon twenty-five years' experience with the red man.

## EDUCATION

GENERAL: Of paramount importance are the *Reports* (dating from 1867) of the U. S. Commissioner of Education. An index to the bureau's publications for the years 1867-1890 is included in U. S. Comr. of Educ., *Rep. for 1888-89,* II, 1453-1551. In 1900 there were nearly three hundred periodicals of one type or another devoted primarily to educational matters. The *Addresses and Proceedings* (from 1871; title varies) of the National Educational Association contain papers by leading educators. The annual reports of state and city superintendents are a virtually unexploited source. The most valuable single secondary work is N. M. Butler, ed., *Education in the United States* (2 vols., Albany, 1900), comprising a series of monographs prepared for the Paris Exposition of 1900 and covering all phases of educational effort. E. G. Dexter, *A History of Education in the United States* (N. Y., 1904), is broadly conceived and still useful. Thomas Woody, *A History of Women's Education in the United States* (2 vols., J. M. Cattell, ed., *Science and Education*, IV, bks. i-ii, N. Y., 1929), also treats all levels of education.

COMMON SCHOOLS: R. G. Boone, *Education in the United States* (W. T. Harris, ed., *International Education Series*, XI, N. Y., 1894), and E. P. Cubberley, *Public Education in the United States* (Boston, 1919), deal briefly with elementary and secondary-school education in the period. Caroline D. Aborn and others, eds., *Pioneers of the Kindergarten in America* (N. Y., 1924), contains short biographical sketches, while S. C. Parker, *History of Modern Elementary Education* (Boston, 1912), is the standard treatise in its field. One phase of private education is carefully explored in J. A. Burns, *The Growth and Development of the Catholic School System in the United States* (N. Y., 1912).

E. W. Knight, *Public Education in the South* (Boston, 1922), gives a somewhat darker picture of educational development than that in the present volume. A. D. Mayo has made valuable contributions to the subject in various articles in U. S. Comr. of Educ., *Reports*, including "The Final Establishment of the American Common School System in West Virginia, Maryland, Virginia and Delaware, 1863-1900," *Rep. for 1903*, I, 391-462; and "The Final Establishment of the American Common School System in North Carolina, South Carolina and Georgia, 1863-1900," *Rep. for 1904*, I, 999-1090. The best systematic account of the work of the Peabody Education Fund is *A Brief Sketch of George Peabody and a History of the Public Education Fund through Thirty Years* (Cambridge, Mass., 1898) by J. L.

M. Curry, who served as general agent after the death of Dr. Barnas Sears in 1880. For Negro education, see earlier, Race Relations.

COLLEGES AND UNIVERSITIES: C. F. Thwing has helped illuminate the history of higher education in many studies, including *The American College in American Life* (N. Y., 1897); *College Administration* (N. Y., 1900), the earliest treatment of the subject; *A History of Higher Education in America* (N. Y., 1906), the only general account; *A History of Education in the United States since the Civil War* (Boston, 1910), which emphasizes university instruction; and *The American and the German University* (N. Y., 1928), showing the importance of Teutonic influences in American higher education. Historical sketches have been published of nearly every important college and university. There is also an abundant literature by and about the great university presidents, including D. C. Gilman, *The Launching of a University* (N. Y., 1906), written by the founder of Johns Hopkins; T. W. Goodspeed, *William Rainey Harper, First President of the University of Chicago* (Chicago, 1928); and Henry James, *Charles W. Eliot* (2 vols., Boston, 1930). Two able contemporaneous appraisals of higher education by foreigners are Gabriel Compayré, *L'Enseignement Supérieur aux États-Unis* (Paris, 1896), and Athanasius Zimmermann, *Die Universitäten in den Vereinigten Staaten Amerikas* (Freiburg, 1896).

H. D. Sheldon, *Student Life and Customs* (W. T. Harris, ed., *International Education Series*, LI, N. Y., 1901), is a valuable descriptive study. G. Stanley Hall offers a psychological interpretation of Sheldon's facts in "Student Customs," Am. Antiquarian Soc., *Proceeds.*, n. s., XIV, 83-124. Further information concerning undergraduate life may be gleaned from C. F. Thwing, *American Colleges: Their Students and Their Work* (N. Y., 1878); C. H. Patton and W. T. Field, *Eight O'Clock Chapel* (Boston, 1927), describing New England college life in the eighties; a series of articles by various authors on "Social Life in American Colleges" in *Lippincott's Mag.*, XXXIX-XL (1887-1888);

and a similar series entitled "Undergraduate Life in American Universities" in *Scribner's Mag.*, XXI-XXII (1897).
LIBRARIES: H. B. Adams, *Public Libraries and Popular Education* (Home Educ. Dept., Univ. of State of N. Y., *Bull.*, no. 31, 1900), contains a full bibliography. American Library Association, *Papers and Proceedings* (from 1876), and the *Library Journal* (from 1876) throw light on the progress of the movement, while S. S. Green treats the movement as a whole in *The Public Library Movement in the United States, 1853-1893* (Boston, 1913). One important influence is discussed in T. W. Koch, *A Book of Carnegie Libraries* (White Plains, 1917).

### THE ADVANCE OF KNOWLEDGE

For learned and scientific societies the chief source of information is to be found in their periodical publications and annual reports. J. D. Thompson, comp., *Handbook of Learned Societies* (Carnegie Inst., *Publs.*, no. 39, 1908), contains a brief history of each. Among longer historical sketches are F. B. Sanborn, "The Work of Twenty-Five Years," *Journ. of Social Sci.*, XXVII, xliii-xlix, reviewing the American Social Science Association to 1890; J. F. Jameson, "The American Historical Association, 1884-1909," *Am. Hist. Rev.*, XV, 1-20; R. T. Ely, "The American Economic Association, 1885-1909," Am. Econ. Assoc., *Publs.*, ser. 3, XI, 47-111; S. W. Fernberger, "The American Psychological Association," *Psychol. Bull.*, XXIX, 1-89; D. S. Martin, "The First Half Century of the American Association," *Pop. Sci. Mo.*, LIII (1898), 822-835, dealing with the American Association for the Advancement of Science; and F. R. Hutton, *A History of the American Society of Mechanical Engineers* (N. Y., 1915). G. B. Goode, *The Smithsonian Institution, 1846-1896* (Wash., 1897), treats the chief independent research agency.
L. H. Haney, *History of Economic Thought* (rev. edn., N. Y., 1920), has a chapter on American economic theory in the late nineteenth century. Two important figures in eco-

nomics are delineated in J. P. Munroe, *A Life of Francis Amasa Walker* (N. Y., 1923), and H. E. Starr, *William Graham Sumner* (N. Y., 1925). The natal years of sociology in America are explored by A. W. Small in "Fifty Years of Sociology in the United States," *Am. Journ. of Sociology,* XXI, 721-864; "Evolution of Sociological Consciousness in the United States," same mag., XXVII, 226-231; and *Origins of Sociology* (Chicago, 1924), chap. xix; while the foremost contributor is portrayed in Emily P. Cape, *Lester F. Ward* (N. Y., 1922). For a summary of the chief developments in political science, see two works by C. E. Merriam: *American Political Ideas, 1865-1917* (N. Y., 1920), and *New Aspects of Politics* (Chicago, 1925), chap. ii. In *The New History and the Social Studies* (N. Y., 1925) and other works H. E. Barnes explicates the major trends in American historiography. More particularly concerned with the eighties and nineties are W. A. Dunning, "A Generation of American Historiography," Am. Hist. Assoc., *Rep. for 1917,* 345-354; and J. A. Woodburn, "The Promotion of Historical Study in America Following the Civil War," Ill. Hist. Soc., *Trans. for 1922,* 37-50. Full-length biographies of leading historians have also been published, such as J. S. Clark, *John Fiske* (2 vols., Boston, 1917); E. S. Bradley, *Henry Charles Lea* (Phila., 1931); and M. A. DeW. Howe, *James Ford Rhodes* (N. Y., 1929).

J. E. Sandys, *A History of Classical Scholarship* (3 vols., Cambridge, Eng., 1908), summarizes the American contributions of the period, while H. N. Fowler sketches the first forty years of "The American School of Classical Studies at Athens" in *Art and Archaeology,* XIV, 171-260. American advances in philosophy are considered in A. K. Rogers, *English and American Philosophy since 1800* (N. Y., 1922), and Woodbridge Riley, *American Thought* (rev. edn., N. Y., 1923). The share of Americans in helping to develop another field is adequately set forth in E. G. Boring, *A History of Experimental Psychology* (R. M. Elliott, ed., *The Century Psychology Series;* N. Y., 1929), and Gardner Murphy, *An Historical Introduction to Modern Psychology*

(C. K. Ogden, ed., *International Library of Psychology, Philosophy and Scientific Method;* London, 1929). G. Stanley Hall, *Life and Confessions of a Psychologist* (N. Y., 1923), an important source for both the man and his subject, should be read in the light of E. D. Starbuck, "Some Notes on the Psychology of Genius," *Journ. of Philosophy,* XXI, 141-154, an interesting psychological analysis based on the above work.

L. L. Woodruff, ed., *The Development of the Sciences* (New Haven, 1923), contains brief historical sketches of six branches of science in their international development. American contributions are more particularly considered in W. J. McGee, "Fifty Years of American Science," *Atlantic Mo.,* LXXXII (1898), 307-320; D. S. Jordan, ed., *Leading American Men of Science* (W. P. Trent, ed., *Biographies of Leading Americans;* N. Y., 1910); and E. S. Dana and others, *A Century of Science in America* (New Haven, 1918), chiefly as reflected in the pages of the *American Journal of Science.* Fuller treatments of particular branches include E. F. Smith, *Chemistry in America* (N. Y., 1914); C. A. Browne, ed., *A Half-Century of Chemistry in America, 1876-1926* (Am. Chemical Soc., *Journ.,* XLVIII, no. 8A, 1926); R. H. Chittenden, *The Development of Physiological Chemistry in the United States* (Am. Chemical Soc., *Monograph Series;* N. Y., 1930); G. P. Merrill, *The First One Hundred Years of American Geology* (New Haven, 1924); and R. T. Young, *Biology in America* (Boston, 1922), which stresses zoology. Henry Crew, *The Rise of Modern Physics* (Balt., 1928), and D. E. Smith, *History of Mathematics* (2 vols., Boston, 1923), shed light upon American developments in those fields. U. S. Dept. of Agr., *Yearbook for 1899,* contains a notable series of articles showing the transformation of agriculture into a science.

The state of astronomical knowledge at the beginning and end of the period is set forth in two manuals by Simon Newcomb: *Popular Astronomy* (N. Y., 1878), and *The Stars* (J. M. Cattell and others, eds., *The Science Series;* N. Y., 1901), while the author's own intellectual rôle may be sensed from his *The Reminiscences of an Astronomer* (Boston, 1903), an engaging human record. Among biographical treatments are W. H. Dall, *Spencer Fullerton Baird* (Phila., 1915); H. F. Osborn, *Cope: Master Naturalist* (Princeton, 1931); and D. C. Gilman, *The Life of James Dwight Dana* (N. Y., 1899). For medical progress see the next section; and for mechanical invention consult earlier, Urban Life.

## MEDICAL PROGRESS

A great medical scientist is portrayed in Harvey Cushing, *The Life of Sir William Osler* (2 vols., Oxford, 1925), which devotes fourteen chapters to Osler's American career, 1884-1905. Ruth Putnam, *The Life and Letters of Mary Putnam Jacobi* (N. Y., 1925), deals with the foremost woman physician of the time. A special branch in which Americans achieved greatly is discussed in J. A. Taylor, *History of Dentistry* (Phila., 1922). Investigators of the public-hygiene movement will get valuable help from American Public Health Association, *Public Health, Reports and Papers* (1873-1895; titled thereafter *Journal*). Much of this material is utilized in M. P. Ravenel, ed., *A Half Century of Public Health* (N. Y., 1921). H. I. Bowditch, *Public Hygiene in America* (Boston, 1877), presents the lamentable state of affairs when the period began, while S. W. Abbott, *The Past and Present Condition of Public Hygiene and State Medicine in the United States* (H. B. Adams, ed., *Monographs on American Social Economics*, XIX, Boston, 1900), summarizes the situation at its close. G. C. Whipple, *State Sanitation* (3 vols., Cambridge, Mass., 1917), is an excellent historical sketch of the activities of the influential Massachusetts state board of health. The father of medical and vital statistics in America is depicted in F. H. Garrison, *John Shaw Billings* (N. Y., 1915).

## LITERARY PRODUCTION

AUTHORSHIP: Of the innumerable histories of American letters *The Cambridge History of American Literature* (4 vols., N. Y., 1917-1921), edited by W. P. Trent and others, is outstanding as a pioneer effort to envisage literature as something broader than *belles-lettres*, while V. L. Parrington's uncompleted *The Beginnings of Critical Realism in America* (*Main Currents in American Thought*, N. Y., 1927-1930, III), is equally notable as a bold and provocative attempt at an economic and social interpretation. Surveys showing unusual perspicuity include Carl Van Doren, *The American Novel* (N. Y., 1921), and F. L. Pattee, *A History of American Literature since 1870* (N. Y., 1915), which is continued and amplified in his *The New American Literature, 1890-1930* (N. Y., 1930). Constance Rourke, *American Humor* (N. Y., 1931), is by far the best work on its subject. Among contemporaneous appraisals of American letters H. C. Vedder, *American Writers of To-day* (N. Y., 1894), and Robert Ford, *American Humourists* (London, 1897), are still of interest.

No second-hand acquaintance with literature, however, can take the place of personal familiarity with the contents of the books. Thanks to the vogue of local-color writing and realistic fiction, the delver into social history will find a rich mine of hitherto neglected ore in many of the novels and short stories, or, to adopt Paul Shorey's scornful phrase, "these laborious inventories of unconcerning things." Howells, for example, in a score or so of novels gives posterity a picture of middle-class life and thought which the most relentless scrutiny of official documents will fail to disclose. An intimate insight into current literary conditions can be gained from such books as Hamlin Garland, *Roadside Meetings* (N. Y., 1930); C. D. Warner, *The Relation of Literature to Life* (N. Y., 1897); W. D. Howells, *My Literary Passions* (N. Y., 1895), and *Literature and Life* (N. Y., 1902); and Henry James, *Letters* (Percy Lubbock, ed., 2 vols., N. Y., 1920). Representative biographies of major contributors are A. B. Paine, *Mark Twain* (3 vols., N. Y., 1912); D. G. Cooke, *William Dean Howells* (N. Y., 1922); Julia C. Harris, *The Life and Letters of Joel Chandler Harris* (Boston, 1918); F. O. Matthiessen, *Sarah Orne Jewett* (Boston,

1929); and C. H. Dennis, *Eugene Field's Creative Years*
(N. Y., 1924). Two lesser figures are pictured in Mary A.
Roe, *E. P. Roe* (N. Y., 1899), and H. R. Mayes, *Alger*
(N. Y., 1928). Juvenile "thrillers" are described and sympa-
thetically assessed in Edmund Pearson, *Dime Novels* (Boston,
1929).

PUBLISHING: The *Publishers' Weekly* (N. Y., from
1872) is the principal source of information. Its last issue in
January each year contains a summary of all the important
books of the preceding year, often with critical comments.
The *Dial*, XXVIII, no. 333 (May 1, 1900), gives a
"Twenty Years' Retrospect" of publishing, book selling and
allied interests. No adequate history of an American publishing house has yet appeared, though for three firms pertinent
material can be found in J. H. Harper, *The House of Harper*
(N. Y., 1912); G. H. Putnam, *Memories of a Publisher*
(N. Y., 1915); and Henry Holt, *Garrulities of an Octoge-
narian Editor* (Boston, 1923). One knotty problem of publishers is thoroughly canvassed in G. H. Putnam, comp., *The
Question of Copyright* (N. Y., 1891), and R. R. Bowker,
*Copyright: Its History and Its Law* (Boston, 1912). For
magazine publishing, see earlier, General Periodical Sources.

### RELIGIOUS CURRENTS

S. M. Jackson, comp., "A Bibliography of American
Church History, 1820-1893," Philip Schaff and others, eds.,
*The American Church History Series* (13 vols., N. Y., 1893-
1897), XII, 441-513, is the first systematic attempt to bring
together the titles of books and pamphlets on the subject.
P. G. Mode, comp., *Source Book and Bibliographical Guide
for American Church History* (Menasha, Wis., 1921), besides printing certain key documents, gives a select list of
books and articles. H. K. Rowe, *The History of Religion in
the United States* (N. Y., 1924), is an interpretation of
religious trends, marked by insight and a full appreciation
of diverse conditioning factors. Other general surveys of religious development, of which the latest is W. W. Sweet, *The*

*Story of Religions in America* (N. Y., 1930), are sketchy and unsatisfactory for the period since Reconstruction. Much the same is true of most denominational histories, including those in the *American Church History Series* except H. K. Carroll, *The Religious Forces of the United States* (I, rev. edn., N. Y., 1912), which is valuable for statistical analyses. Daniel Dorchester, *Christianity in the United States* (N. Y., 1887; rev. edn., 1895), also contains data on church growth.

Emotional methods and experiences are discussed in F. G. Beardsley, *A History of American Revivals* (N. Y., 1912); G. C. Loud, *Evangelized America* (N. Y., 1928); and H. C. Weber, *Evangelism* (N. Y., 1929), an attempt at graphic presentation; while the foremost revivalist is understandingly portrayed in Gamaliel Bradford, *D. L. Moody* (N. Y., 1927). For the Christian Endeavor Society, founded in 1881, and other similar organizations, the best general sketch is F. O. Erb, *The Development of the Young People's Movement* (Chicago, 1917). Three useful works on foreign missionary activity are D. L. Leonard, *Missionary Annals of the Nineteenth Century* (Cleveland, 1899); J. S. Dennis, *Christian Missions and Social Progress* (3 vols., N. Y., 1897-1906); and same author, *Centennial Survey of Christian Missions* (N. Y., 1902).

Among the influential books written by those whom Walter Rauschenbusch later called the "pioneers of Christian social thought in America" are R. H. Newton, *Social Studies* (N. Y., 1886); S. L. Loomis, *Modern Cities and Their Religious Problems* (N. Y., 1887); Josiah Strong, *Our Country* (N. Y., 1885; rev. edn., 1891), and *The New Era* (N. Y., 1893); R. T. Ely, *Social Aspects of Christianity* (N. Y., 1889); Lyman Abbott, *Christianity and Social Problems* (Boston, 1896); and Washington Gladden's volumes: *Workingmen and Their Employers* (Boston, 1876), *Applied Christianity* (Boston, 1886), *Tools and the Man* (Boston, 1893) and *Social Salvation* (Boston, 1902). Two of the leaders tell their life stories in Lyman Abbott, *Reminiscences* (Boston, 1915), and Washington Gladden, *Recollections* (Boston, 1909).

A. D. White, *A History of the Warfare of Science with Theology in Christendom* (2 vols., N. Y., 1896), is interesting as the product of a period when the issues discussed were acute and ever present. George Harris, *A Century's Change in Religion* (Boston, 1914), is valuable as a dispassionate discussion of theological reconstruction by one of the participants in the "Andover controversy." J. H. Barrows, ed., *The World's Parliament of Religions* (2 vols., Chicago, 1893), offers the best account of that notable gathering. Phillips Brooks of Trinity Church, Boston, the subject of a biography by A. V. G. Allen entitled *Life and Letters of Phillips Brooks* (N. Y., 1900), is the best example of a forceful and influential churchman who remained indifferent, though not antagonistic, to the scientific and social forces that were remaking religion.

James MacCaffrey, *History of the Catholic Church in the Nineteenth Century* (2 vols., 2d edn., Dublin, 1910), sketches briefly the history of the American Church in its international setting. Gerald Shaughnessy, *Has the Immigrant Kept the Faith?* (N. Y., 1925), is a statistical demonstration showing that the American Church assimilated and retained the vast Catholic influx from Europe. Of indispensable importance are A. S. Will, *Life of Cardinal Gibbons* (2 vols., N. Y., 1922), and F. J. Zwierlein, *The Life and Letters of Bishop McQuaid* (3 vols., Rochester, 1927). The best treatment of anti-Catholic sentiment is H. J. Desmond, *The A. P. A. Movement* (Wash., 1912). Another religion heavily indebted to immigration is dealt with historically in Joseph Leiser, *American Judaism* (N. Y., 1925).

The American history of the Salvation Army is traced in three works by its leaders: Maud Ballington Booth, *Beneath Two Flags* (N. Y., 1890); Ballington Booth, *From Ocean to Ocean* (N. Y., 1891); and F. de L. Booth-Tucker, *The Salvation Army in the United States* (N. Y., 1891). No historical account of the Christian Science movement as such has been written, but many lives of its progenitor are available. Sibyl Wilbur (O'Brien), *The Life of Mary Baker Eddy* (rev. edn., Boston, 1913), and L. P. Powell, *Mary Baker*

*Eddy* (N. Y., 1930), are biographies acceptable to Christian Scientists. Of a more critical character are Georgine Milmine, *The Life of Mary Baker G. Eddy and the History of Christian Science* (N. Y., 1909), containing valuable documents, and E. F. Dakin, *Mrs. Eddy* (rev. edn., N. Y., 1930). Mrs. Eddy's version of her life work is presented in the various editions of *Science and Health,* in *Retrospection and Introspection* (Boston, 1891) and in *Miscellaneous Writings* (Boston, 1896), the last embracing many of her contributions to the *Christian Science Journal* (Boston, from 1883), the files of which should be examined for accounts of cures claimed by healers. For Mormonism it is important to consult the *Millennial Star* (Liverpool and Salt Lake City, from 1840), which contains exegetical articles from the Mormon point of view and official resolutions and proceedings.

## THE FINE ARTS

GRAPHIC ART: Sadakichi Hartmann, *A History of American Art* (2 vols., Boston, 1901), includes, besides painting, a discussion of sculpture, while Suzanne La Follette in *Art in America* (N. Y., 1929) extends her treatment to architecture. Standard historical manuals are Eugen Neuhaus, *The History and Ideals of American Art* (Stanford, 1931); Samuel Isham, *The History of American Painting* (J. C. Van Dyke, ed., *The History of American Art,* III, rev. edn., N. Y., 1927); C. H. Caffin, *The Story of American Painting* (N. Y., 1907); Pauline King, *American Mural Painting* (Boston, 1902); and Frank Weitenkampf, *American Graphic Art* (rev. edn., N. Y., 1924), which covers the various forms of illustrative art. The monthly reviews of "The Field of Art" in *Scribner's Magazine* during the period give a "close-up" of developments. Royal Cortissoz, *American Artists* (N. Y., 1923), brilliantly characterizes a number of the painters of the eighties and nineties, while among the larger biographical studies are Alfred Trumble, *George Inness* (N. Y., 1904); W. H. Downes, *John Singer Sargent* (Boston, 1925); Cecilia Waern, *John La Farge* (*Portfolio*

*Monographs,* XXVI, N. Y., 1896); Frank Rutter, *James McNeill Whistler* (N. Y., 1911); and C. H. Abbott, *Howard Pyle* (N. Y., 1925).

A. B. Maurice and F. T. Cooper, *The History of the Nineteenth Century in Caricature* (N. Y., 1904), is perhaps the best work on the evolution of the cartoon. Contemporary collections of drawings include F. B. Opper, *The Tariff Question* (N. Y., 1888), selected from his contributions to *Puck;* C. D. Gibson, *Drawings* (N. Y., 1894), and *Sketches and Cartoons* (N. Y., 1898), taken from *Life;* Charles Nelan, *Cartoons of Our War with Spain* (N. Y., 1898), which originally appeared in the *New York Herald;* C. L. Bartholomew, *Cartoons of the Spanish-American War* (Minneapolis, 1899), drawn by "Bart" for the *Minneapolis Journal;* F. G. Attwood, *Attwood's Pictures: an Artist's History of the Last Ten Years of the Nineteenth Century* (N. Y., 1900), first contributed to *Life;* and Homer Davenport, *Cartoons* (N. Y., 1898), drawn for the *New York Journal.*

SCULPTURE AND ARCHITECTURE: The chief general discussions of plastic art are Lorado Taft, *The History of American Sculpture* (J. C. Van Dyke, ed., *The History of American Art,* I, rev. edn., N. Y., 1924); C. H. Caffin, *American Masters of Sculpture* (N. Y., 1903); and J. W. McSpadden, *Famous Sculptors of America* (rev. edn., N. Y., 1927). The greatest American sculptor tells of his life in *The Reminiscences of Augustus Saint-Gaudens* (Homer Saint-Gaudens, ed., 2 vols., N. Y., 1913).

J. W. Dow, *American Renaissance* (N. Y., 1904), is a badly jumbled history of American architecture, which has been superseded by such surveys as T. E. Tallmadge, *The Story of American Architecture* (N. Y., 1927); Fiske Kimball, *American Architecture* (Indianapolis, 1928); and G. H. Edgell, *The American Architecture of To-day* (N. Y., 1928). W. A. Starrett, *Skyscrapers and the Men Who Build Them* (N. Y., 1928), gives the best account of the origins of what the author calls "the most distinctively American thing in the world." Popular taste is mirrored in manuals

*Augustus Saint-Gaudens' statue
of "The Puritan."*

*John W. Alexander's portrait of President McCosh of Princeton.*

Art

like S. B. Reed, *House-Plans for Everybody* (N. Y., 1878),
L. H. Gibson, *Convenient Houses* (N. Y., 1889), and same
author, *Beautiful Houses* (N. Y., 1895). Outstanding architects receive biographical treatment in Mrs. Schuyler Van
Rensselaer, *Henry Hobson Richardson and His Works* (Boston, 1888); Harriet Monroe, *The Life of John Wellborn
Root* (Boston, 1896); Charles Moore, *Daniel H. Burnham*
(2 vols., N. Y., 1921); same author, *The Life and Times
of Charles Follen McKim* (Boston, 1929); and C. C. Baldwin, *Stanford White* (N. Y., 1931).

MUSIC: Four comprehensive surveys of American music
are L. C. Elson, *The History of American Music* (J. C. Van
Dyke, ed., *The History of American Art*, II, N. Y., 1904;
rev. by Arthur Elson, N. Y., 1925); W. L. Hubbard, ed.,
*History of American Music* (same ed., *The American History
and Encyclopedia of Music;* N. Y., 1910); Arthur Farwell
and W. D. Darby, eds., *Music in America* (D. G. Mason, ed.,
*The Art of Music,* 14 vols., N. Y., 1915-1917, IV); and
J. T. Howard, *Our American Music* (N. Y., 1931), the
latest and best. H. C. Lahee, *Annals of Music in America*
(Boston, 1920), supplies a chronological record of significant
musical events. Important periodicals for historical reference
are the *Musical Courier* (N. Y., from 1880); the *Musical
Year-Book of the United States* (Boston, 1886-1893); and
the *Etude* (Phila., from 1883).

For orchestral music the following works are particularly
helpful: Theodore Thomas, *A Musical Autobiography* (G.
P. Upton, ed., 2 vols., Chicago, 1905); C. E. Russell, *The
American Orchestra and Theodore Thomas* (N. Y., 1927);
M. A. DeW. Howe, *The Boston Symphony Orchestra* (rev.
edn., Boston, 1931); and Walter Damrosch, *My Musical
Life* (N. Y., 1923). The best general account of grand opera
during the period is H. C. Lahee, *Grand Opera in America*
(*Music Lovers' Series;* Boston, 1902). The lives and work
of leading composers are sympathetically appraised in Rupert
Hughes, *Contemporary American Composers* (Boston,
1900). Separate biographies and memoirs of importance include W. H. Humiston, *MacDowell* (N. Y., 1921); Vance

Thompson, *The Life of Ethelbert Nevin* (Boston, 1913); Joseph Kaye, *Victor Herbert* (N. Y., 1931); Mrs. Reginald de Koven, *A Musician and His Wife* (N. Y., 1926); and J. P. Sousa, *Marching Along* (Boston, 1928).

Julius Mattfeld, comp., *The Folk Music of the Western Hemisphere* (N. Y., 1925), lists much material on the folk music of Negroes, cowboys, lumberjacks, mountaineers, sailors, miners, etc. Two volumes by Sigmund Spaeth recall the vogue of popular songs: *Read 'Em and Weep* (Garden City, 1926); and *Weep Some More, My Lady* (Garden City, 1927). On the personal side, such books should be supplemented by C. K. Harris, *After the Ball* (N. Y., 1926), and Theodore Dreiser, *Twelve Men* (N. Y., 1919), which contains an account of the author's brother, Paul Dresser.

### SPORTS AND RECREATIONS

SPORTS: Compiled by C. M. Van Sockum, *Sport* (N. Y., 1914) is an "attempt at a bibliography of books and periodicals published during 1890-1912" on that subject in the United States and other countries. Of periodicals, *Outing* (N. Y., from 1882) is particularly useful as it deals exclusively with sports and was itself an outgrowth of the sports movement. Important reference works for baseball are A. G. Spalding, *America's National Game* (N. Y., 1911); G. L. Moreland, *Balldom* (N. Y., 1914); F. C. Richter, *Richter's History and Records of Baseball* (Phila., 1914); and E. J. Lanigan, ed., *Baseball Cyclopedia* (N. Y., 1922). The A. G. Spalding Baseball Collection, consisting of manuscripts, books and pamphlets, is in the New York Public Library. Developments in the chief college sport are traced in Walter Camp and L. F. Deland, *Football* (N. Y., 1896); P. H. Davis, *Football* (N. Y., 1911); and A. M. Weyand, *American Football* (N. Y., 1926), while the rôle of two masters of strategy is set forth in Harford Powel, jr., *Walter Camp* (Boston, 1926), and A. A. Stagg and W. W. Stout, *Touchdown!* (N. Y., 1927).

Besides the general accounts of professional boxing in

Alexander Johnston, *Ten—and Out* (N. Y., 1927), and Jeffery Farnol, *Famous Prize Fights* (Boston, 1928), the careers of three heavyweight champions are elucidated in R. F. Dibble, *John L. Sullivan* (Boston, 1925), J. J. Corbett, *The Roar of the Crowd* (N. Y., 1925), and R. H. Davis, *Bob Fitzsimmons* (N. Y., 1926). For other sports, see J. P. Paret, *Lawn Tennis* (N. Y., 1912); J. D. Travers and J. R. Crowell, *The Fifth Estate* (N. Y., 1926), dealing with golf; R. P. Elmer, *Archery* (Phila., 1926); Samuel Crowther and Arthur Ruhl, *Rowing and Track Athletics* (Caspar Whitney, ed., *The American Sportsman's Library;* N. Y., 1905); R. F. Kelley, *American Rowing* (N. Y., 1932); W. P. Stephens, *American Yachting* (N. Y., 1904); and Nigel Lindsay, *The America's Cup* (London, 1930).

THE THEATER: Varied aspects of theatrical development are treated in A. H. Quinn, *A History of American Drama from the Civil War to the Present Day* (2 vols., N. Y., 1927); Arthur Hornblow, *A History of the Theatre in America* (2 vols., Phila., 1919); Mary C. Crawford, *The Romance of the American Theatre* (rev. edn., Boston, 1925); M. J. Moses, *The American Dramatist* (rev. edn., Boston, 1926); and same author, *Famous Actor-Families in America* (N. Y., 1906). T. A. Brown, *A History of the New York Stage* (3 vols., N. Y., 1903), traces theatrical development in one city, while Eugene Tompkins and Quincy Kilby, *The History of the Boston Theatre, 1854-1901* (Boston, 1908), reviews the situation in another. Indispensable sources are the *New York Clipper* (N. Y., from 1853) and the *New York Dramatic Mirror* (N. Y., from 1879), the leading journals of the theatrical profession. Special collections of playbills, clippings and the like can be found in the Library of Congress, the public libraries of New York and Boston, and at the Harvard and University of Chicago libraries.

The intense popular interest in the theater led to the production of a number of books, usually journalistic in character but valuable as reflecting contemporary taste: F. E. McKay and C. E. L. Wingate, eds., *Famous American Actors of To-day* (N. Y., 1896); J. B. Clapp and E. F. Edgett,

*Players of the Present* (3 vols., Dunlap Soc., *Publs.*, n. s., nos. 9, 11, 13, 1899-1901) ; Norman Hapgood, *The Stage in America, 1897-1900* (N. Y., 1901) ; L. C. Strang, *Players and Plays of the Last Quarter Century* (2 vols., Boston, 1902) ; and the volumes contributed by L. C. Strang to the *Stage Lovers' Series* (Boston, 1899-1902). Leading figures in the legitimate drama are pictured at greater length in such works as Lester Wallack, *Memories of Fifty Years* (N. Y., 1889) ; J. F. Daly, *The Life of Augustin Daly* (N. Y., 1917) ; Percy MacKaye, *Epoch* (2 vols., N. Y., 1927), a biography of Steele MacKaye; and William Winter, *The Life and Art of Joseph Jefferson* (N. Y., 1914). Reminiscent writings by important dramatic critics include Henry A. Clapp, *Reminiscences of a Dramatic Critic* (Boston, 1902) ; J. R. Towse, *Sixty Years of the Theater* (N. Y., 1916) ; and William Winter, *The Wallet of Time* (2 vols., N. Y., 1913).

M. B. Leavitt, *Fifty Years in Theatrical Management* (N. Y., 1912), is valuable as a hodgepodge of information in regard to musical, burlesque, minstrel, vaudeville and circus attractions. H. B. Smith, *First Nights and First Editions* (Boston, 1931), written by a prolific librettist, and Rudolph Aronson, *Theatrical and Musical Memoirs* (N. Y., 1913), by a leading manager, throw light on the evolution of light opera, while Robert Grau, *Forty Years Observation of Music and the Drama* (N. Y., 1909), is a repository of theatrical gossip with particular reference to vaudeville. Comic-opera stars have their innings in H. C. Barnaby, *Reminiscences* (G. L. Varney, ed., Boston, 1913) ; Felix Isman, *Weber and Fields* (N. Y., 1924) ; De Wolf Hopper, *Once a Clown, Always a Clown* (Boston, 1927) ; and Francis Wilson, *Life of Himself* (Boston, 1924). The one-hundred-per-cent-American minstrel show is discussed from different angles in Carl Wittke, *Tambo and Bones* (Durham, 1930), and Dailey Paskman and Sigmund Spaeth, *"Gentlemen, Be Seated!"* (Garden City, 1928). The burlesque stage is treated in Bernard Sobel, *Burleycue* (N. Y., 1931).

# INDEX